SHMUEL ALMOG

ZIONISM AND HISTORY

ZIONISM AND HISTORY

The Rise of a New Jewish Consciousness

SHMUEL ALMOG

ST. MARTIN'S PRESS, New York

THE MAGNES PRESS, THE HEBREW UNIVERSITY, Jerusalem

Translated from the Hebrew by
INA FRIEDMAN

© The Magnes Press, The Hebrew University, Jerusalem, 1987
All rights reserved. For information, write:
Scholarly & Reference Division,
St. Martin's Press, Inc., 175 Fifth Avenue, New York, NY 10010
First Published in the United States of America in 1987
Printed in Israel
ISBN 0-312-89885-1

Library of Congress Cataloging-in-Publication Data

Almog, S.
  Zionism and History.

  Revised translation of: Tsiyonut ve-historyah.
  Bibliography: p. 311
  Includes index.
  1. Zionism – Philosophy. 2. Jewish nationalism – Philosophy. 3. Jews – History – Philos-
ophy. I. Title.
DS149.A677813   1986   956.94'001   86-6493
ISBN 0-312-89885-1

CONTENTS

PREFACE

Zionism, a movement that is in many respects unique, nonetheless comprises certain features that are universal. It has been an agent of modernization, a nation-building apparatus, and a rallying point for Jewish solidarity. Characteristically, then, Zionism has often been misunderstood; and praised or decried, it is rarely discussed without emotion. We approach it here from a somewhat unusual angle in examining its attitude – actually attitudes – toward the past. At first glance, this perspective may seem somewhat removed, as it does not touch upon any of the burning issues of the day. Yet approaching Zionism via the channel of history may prove to be the key to understanding this complex phenomenon, in regard both to its obvious success and its many shortcomings.

This book has developed from a doctoral dissertation written under the supervision of Professor Shmuel Ettinger of the Hebrew University of Jerusalem. A Hebrew version was published in 1982 by the Magnes Press and the present volume is a revised and updated version, including a new introduction for the benefit of readers who may not be familiar with the history of Zionism, and modifications in the footnotes, index, and bibliography.

I wish to take this opportunity to extend my thanks to all those who made the publication of this book possible: the Institute of Contemporary Jewry at the Hebrew University; the Alexander Silberman International Scholarship Fund; Aryeh L. Dulzin; the late Aryeh Tzimuky; special thanks to Ina Friedman, whose skill and understanding were invaluable in rendering, the book into English, as well as to Dr. Moshe Goodman, Moshe Shalvi and Pini for their part in preparing the book for publication.

Much credit is due to Shmuel Ettinger, who guided the original research; to the Zalman Shazar Center for Jewish History; to the Magnes Press; and to the many colleagues, as well as archives and libraries that have been of such great assistance.

Shmuel Almog

Jerusalem, 1987

7

INTRODUCTION

Until roughly the end of the eighteenth century, Jews regarded themselves – and were regarded by others – as members of a distinct religious and ethnic group that had preserved the vestiges of an ancient civilization. Although not a nation in the modern sense, the Jews were nevertheless distinguished as a separate people. Widely scattered and often subject to persecution, they remained closely tied to each other by a common heritage and bonds of social solidarity.

These bonds began to shred as emancipation steadily made inroads on the traditional Jewish way of life. The nineteenth century witnessed a rapid influx of individual Jews into European society and, concomitantly, a considerable weakening of age-old loyalties. Society's acceptance of Jews was even made conditional upon the relinquishment of their specificity, which barely left room for an adulterated "spiritual" Judaism.

With the advent of nationalism as a driving force in Europe, Jews strove to integrate more fully into the lives of their respective nations, inevitably – indeed, deliberately – losing some of their distinctiveness in the process. Operating in fits and starts, however, the emancipation process left behind areas where Jews were still discriminated against openly. And even where the emancipation impulse was more rigorous, the host society's acceptance of the Jews was often begrudging or at best half-hearted.

The patterns of emancipation and integration were far from uniform across the continent. While Western Jews shed their particular traits, Eastern Europe continued to foster closely knit, traditional Jewish communities. Yet even there modernization gradually set in, and Jews migrated from rural and backward regions to advanced urban areas. In the West acculturation and outright religious conversion were followed by religious reform and the development of the so-called Science of Judaism. As outdated structures gave way to modern types of Jewish organization, new forms of Jewish identity evolved and more sophisticated expressions of Jewish solidarity came to the fore.

By the second half of the nineteenth century, the harbingers of a specifically Jewish nationalism had appeared on the European stage. They made their entrance rather haltingly, proposing that emancipation need not be confined to the individual but could be applied to the Jews as a whole. Some of these early visionaries dreamed of national restoration in the Holy Land; others contemplated nothing more ambitious than a spiritual reawakening. This proto-nationalism drew on a variety of sources, such as the messianic hopes roused by the events of the day, the wounded pride that lingered after spurned attempts to enter society, and a feeling of a loss at the erosion of Jewish tradition, as well as a growing uneasiness in the face of conflicting loyalties, particularly in multi-national regions.

The general ferment came to a head in 1881, when anti-Jewish riots broke out in Russia and cast grave doubts on the very viability of Jewish emancipation. In the first instance, the pogroms generated a sudden exodus of Jews from Russia that had far-reaching repercussions. Although Western Jews clung to the vision of emancipation, they were forced to concede its limitations. And as Jewish philanthropists and organizations extended assistance to the refugees from Russia and became involved in their destiny, it became increasingly evident that, at least as far as the Russian Empire was concerned, emancipation and integration held little promise as the solution to the plight of the Jews.

Russian Jewry was thoroughly shaken and particularly disappointed by the pronounced lack of sympathy on the part of Russian society at large. In reaction, Jewish intellectuals and radicals who had pointedly identified with the Russian people now began to find their way back to the Jewish fold. Plans were afloat to settle Jews on the land in countries overseas, and agricultural colonies were indeed established in the United States, Argentina, and Palestine. At the same time, national-minded groups spoke of achieving a solution to the "Jewish Question" by means of a Jewish state in America, cultural autonomy in Eastern Europe, or a return to the Holy Land. Out of the turmoil came the loosely consolidated movement of Lovers of Zion (*Hovevei Zion*) who subsequently laid the groundwork for Zionism by founding colonies in Palestine, participating in the revival of the Hebrew language, and creating a network of support for the resettlement of the ancient homeland.

The Russian pogroms had their counterpart in an upsurge of antisemitism of a more subtle kind in other European countries. Though it reared its ugly head only in times of genuine crisis, antisemitism gradually permeated through all strata of European society and colored the prevailing attitude toward the Jews. So palpable was this Western brand of antisemitism at times that under its impact Theodor Herzl convened the First Zionist Congress in 1897 and founded the World Zionist Organization. His initiative marked the official inception of Zionism as a movement that strove, notwithstanding vacillations, to establish a Jewish state in Palestine.

Though it occupied but a marginal position in Jewish life at the time, Zionism boldly challenged the respective assumptions of both traditional and liberal Judaism. In proclaiming that the Jews constituted a separate entity that was destined to become a modern nation, with all the conventional trappings of nationhood, Zionism assailed the commonly held belief that the Jews constituted a religious community, which was acceptable, *mutatis mutandis*, to Orthodox and Reform Jews alike. The Zionist view held that Jews were linked by a primordial bond stronger by far than any other allegiance they might profess. Jewish history endowed the new nascent movement with both a pedigree and a frame of reference. It became the powerhouse for the construction of a national culture and accorded Zionists a sense of dignity – retrieved, as it were, from oblivion. Jews had, of course, always been conscious of their biblical antecedents, but Zionism now transformed them into a direct lineage, portraying modern Jewry as descendants and heirs of ancient Judea – much like the claim of modern Greeks to be the heirs of their classical ancestors or the association of the Italians with the Roman Empire.

In the absence of more tangible attributes on which to base Jewish nationalism (such as a commonly inhabited territory or a uniform and exclusive culture), history became the crucible of Zionist thinking. Yet it also proved to be the cause of some bemusement, as when the Zionists were called upon to substantiate the claim that they, rather than their detractors, offered the correct interpretation of Jewish history. For Zionists were bent upon altering the pattern of Jewish life and were thus prepared to shatter existing historical continuity, yet they also affirmed that the unity of Jewry exceeded the bounds of time and place. Some tried to solve this apparent contradiction by placing the accent on revolution, while others espoused continuity and yet a third approach predicated a historical leap from ancient Israel to modern Zionism, arguing that at any rate the Jews led only a shadow existence in the diaspora.

Three themes – historical continuity, revolutionary change, and classical restoration – informed the writing of the Zionist thinkers during the movement's formative years, and they appeared in a variety of combinations. Often they ran counter to each other, though they were not presented as clear-cut alternatives. Sometimes, however, they tended to cohere, even exerting a mitigating influence on each other. The latter was particularly true during the East Africa dispute, which erupted in 1903. Palestine was at first quite marginal to Zionist thinking, so that for the purpose of creating a Jewish national entity any suitable territory would do – or so it seemed. Yet when the British made an alternative proposal, namely, Jewish settlement in East Africa, the Zionist ranks split in two and aligned for a bitter struggle. Even those Zionists who apparently wished to wipe the slate clean – historically speaking – could not reconcile themselves to establishing a homeland in an unknown place in darkest Africa.

Furthermore, while the Zionists took the Jewish condition to be an inherent state of alienation from other nations, they hoped to alter this relationship once the Jews had themselves become a proper nation. They arrived at this conclusion from the recent upsurge of antisemitism, as well as from the long history of Jewish suffering; and on the face of it they seemed to concur with the basic tenet of antisemitism that Jews did not belong in their respective countries of residence. Ironically, by inveighing against the condition of diaspora, they conceded many of the faults that had been attributed to the Jews – though assuring that all such blemishes would vanish once the Jews became a "normal" nation again.

The fact is that the early Zionists took a rather dim view of their fellow-Jews and of their recent history and were inclined both to glorify the ancient past and project a utopian vision of the future. Between these two poles, however, there was still ample room for the interplay of conflicting notions about the time perspective. For example, while there was a strong future-oriented aspect to Zionism that accentuated the break with the past, some consideration had to be paid to the *here and now*, as well. As an overall solution to the Jewish problem tarried, Zionists inevitably became involved in formulating stopgap measures. Despite their lofty ideals, they could not divorce themselves entirely from the diaspora reality, and so at times a balance was struck between the negation of the diaspora, as a matter of principle, and a commitment to deal with the actualities of contemporary Jewish life. This balance modified the Zionist praxis somewhat but never actually overshadowed the movement's long-range view. On the contrary, the historical factor came into play, adding a far-sighted quality to Zionism's short-range plans and activities.

Unlike those Jewish nationalists who aspired to some form of cultural autonomy in Eastern Europe, the Zionists had set their sights on a mass exodus of Jews from Europe. Although they were willing to share some of the burden of improving contemporary conditions, they lacked confidence in a secure future for the Jews on European soil. Thus Zionism was not only a national movement but an agency for migration and colonization that saw its main task as nation building, well before that term had gained currency.

Paradoxically, Zionism also became an agent of modernization while seemingly drawing Jews away from modern industrial Europe. Its goal of settling Jews on the land in a backward country like Palestine appeared to run counter to the main thrust of modernization, and Zionism indeed had a flavor of rustic romanticism tinged with populist ideas. To succeed, though, the Zionist colonization enterprise had to be dynamic and oriented toward the future, so that it did not retain its back-to-nature mood for long. It goes without saying that in changing its setting, Zionism gradually modified its outlook as well. Here again it relied heavily on Jewish history to provide both an element of continuity and symbols for identification within a fluid situation. Zionism generated new ideals – such as heroism, the simple life, and physical labor – while invoking social justice as a derivative of Jewish tradition. Its ideals drew their inspiration from the Maccabees or earlier biblical sources, whereas Judaism was often portrayed as a vessel that had become tainted in the diaspora but should be tapped for its precious value. An amalgam of old symbols and new meanings was worked into the fabric of modern Hebrew culture. Zionism advocated both innovation and a return to pristine values while rejecting recent and contemporary patterns of Jewish conduct. And ultimately Zionist ideology transcended the realm of discourse to become a lifestyle, particularly in Palestine.

Zionism is just one example of the oft-cited link between nationalism and history. European historiography, having been spurred by national ideals, gave substance to many national claims. In this sense, history and nationalism were, together with romanticism and vitalism, part of a broader climate of opinion that reigned in the nineteenth century. However, Zionism expressed a far greater need for historical roots than any other national movement. The Jews were both more and less of a nation than others. They had age-old traditions yet lacked the most elementary conditions for self-determination. Thus Zionism turned to history to compensate for what was so sorely lacking in the present.

Social and Ideological Patterns

In focusing on Zionism's early years, we find ourselves dealing both with people whose perception of the past had been forged by Jewish tradition and also those who were products of modern European culture and whose view of the past was thus less affected by Judaism in its traditional form. In the language of the day, these two groups were known respectively as "Eastern Jewry" and "Western Jewry," though the dividing line usually ran between the Jews of Eastern and Central Europe. The dominant image of "Eastern Jewry" was of a traditional, populous, and destitute community living under conditions of discrimination within a relatively backward country; that of "Western Jewry" was of individuals who had undergone the process of emancipation, which was taken to mean that they had grown distant from Jewish tradition and had integrated into the economy and culture of developed and enlightened societies.

The above notwithstanding, it should be noted that many of the leading Zionists were not, in fact, natives of the countries in which they lived. This was especially true of the many Russian- and Galician-born Jews who had moved to cities in Central and Western Europe in order to pursue their studies, some of them eventually remaining there. To this channel of the Jewish population shift we must add the internal migration from small towns to cities and from the Jewish communities in outlying regions to major urban concentrations. The champions of Zionism in the West tended to be drawn from quarters that maintained a certain adhesion to the traditional Jewish community, whereas many of its activists in Eastern Europe, even when firmly rooted in Judaism, were members of the intelligentsia and possessed, to one degree or another, a European education. These broader societal trends, coupled with the difficulties that the Jewish intellectuals experienced in striking roots, endowed this particular class with a sense of transience and minimal identification with its environment. They also created a deep sense of individual identification with Zionism's promise of change and at the same time worked toward making the new movement less accessible to the Jewish public at large.

The more Zionism became established, the more it became an integral part of Jewish life in many of the various Jewish communities, but the East-West contrast prevailed. It is particularly difficult to explain the resilience of this polarity in light of the above-cited traits of the circles that were drawn to Zionism and especially because it contradicted the Zionist tenet on the shared fate of all Jews. At any rate, we should note that the division between East and West was not an accurate reflection of the social character of Zionism, and we would do better to find a more suitable tool of classification, such as the political boundaries of the three empires on the European continent: Russia, Germany, and Austria. This division, though not strictly congruent with the differences pertaining between the Jewish communities, is at least based upon more objective criteria. Before leaving this issue, it should be stressed that there was no direct relationship between one's rootedness in Judaism and one's attitude toward the Jewish past. At best it can be said that the matter of the past very much preoccupied those Zionists who had received a thorough grounding in Jewish studies.

Parallel to the influence of demographic changes was the impact that current philosophical trends had upon Zionism and its adherents. In exploring this point, a distinction must be drawn between the intellectual biography of any one thinker and the aggregate of concepts and ideas prevailing in any one society, which often has a marked but unacknowledged influence on an individual's thinking. For example, it is relatively easy to trace the effect of Nietzsche's philosophy or of Marxist doctrine on certain Zionist writers. Yet it is considerably more difficult to describe the broader intellectual climate in which Zionism emerged or single out its sources of ideological sustenance. Zionism's first decade (1896-1906) and its immediate predecessors comprise a time frame on which a number of influences converged. We must bear in mind here that the primary agent of disseminating European culture among the Jews during this period was the German language and culture. At the same time, many active Zionists were schooled in the Hebrew language and literature and identified to varying degrees with the ideas of the Jewish Enlightenment (*Haskalah*). The world of Zionism was littered with the dashed hopes that the Jews had placed on liberalism and the belief that the "Jewish Question" would be resolved through *progress*. This disillusionment soon fused with anti-rationalist attitudes that were making headway in Germany, especially those centered on the vogue known as *Lebensphilosophie*, while the organic approach to society and the ideas evolving from the school of Social Darwinism also carried weight at the time. Add to them the rise of historicism and the nationalist mood referred to above, along with radical ideologies in the form of Marxism and Russian populism, and you have a rough picture of the main influences of the day.

Despite the obvious distinctions between these various influences and the ideological gradations within Zionism itself, many of the early Zionists shared common intellectual underpinnings. Generally they perceived life as an arena of constant struggle between various contenders, so that the Jews, like all the others, had to fight for their position. This outlook challenged the rationalist world view that had informed the philosophy of the Enlightenment, but did not gainsay

its criticism of Judaism and the Jews. On the contrary, Zionism's
view of Jewish life – including its attitude toward the past – drew
heavily upon ideas associated with the Jewish Enlightenment. The
main difference between the two approaches was that the men of the
Haskalah wanted to reform Judaism so as to make it consonant with
the enlightened non-Jewish world, whereas the Zionists wished to
change it as a means of preparing the Jews to contend in the universal arena. The transition from Enlightenment thinking to the Zionist
doctrine also required a reversal in the assessment of the past. Contrary to the Haskalah's tendency to extol the biblical era, the Zionists displayed a distinct preference for the Second Temple period
(from the Return to Zion under Ezra and Nehemiah to the fall of
the Second Temple in A.D. 70). The event they repeatedly cited as
the paragon of Jewish self-esteem was the Maccabean revolt, which
they portrayed as the valiant war of a small people fighting for political and cultural independence. In this war Zionism found a symbol
that not only invited identification with the glorious past but also
implied struggle with the outside world. More than being the
emblem of an idealized past, it became the paradigm of a fight for
national self-expression.

This brings us to the organic conception of society, which was
closely bound up with Zionism's view of the past. The conception
of human society as a living organism actually goes back to antiquity
and had ramified social and philosophical implications. Simply put,
it drew an analogy between society and a living body composed of
various organs, ascribing to each organ a definitive task and implying the mutual dependence of the organs and the preponderance of
the organism as a whole over its separate parts. Moreover, it determined that every society existed in some sort of vacuum and that
interaction between societies was bound to be solely external, like
that between two different bodies. Furthermore, society was viewed
as an indivisible entity that united body and soul together. The
essential point for our purposes here was the growth process of the
organism – or the continuity between a nation's youth in the distant
past and the stages of its maturation in the present – which also
raised the question of the fate awaiting the national organism once
it grows old and the time comes for it to die.

Zionism usually did not address itself to the conservative connotations inherent in the organic approach. But it was highly attracted to the continuity of the national organism, for this notion suggested historical integrity and the essential solidarity of all the Jewish communities throughout the world. It implied far more than an integrated framework of time and place, for the very premise that the Jews had been and continued to be a single national organism bespoke a Jewish entity whose essential nature was immutable despite changes in its external form. This principle was so cogent that it was able to coexist with a selective and negative attitude toward various manifestations of Judaism in the past and present. Herein lay the great appeal of the organic conception – which at one point was also brandished as a slogan of the evolutionary approach toward the realization of Zionism.

One Decade

The book covers a period of a single decade: from 1896, the year in which Herzl's book *The Jewish State* was first published, to 1906, when the Russian Zionists convened their conference in Helsingfors. It concentrates mainly on the Herzlian period – when Zionism evolved from the pastime of small and scattered groups into an organized national movement – but spills over into the post-Herzlian era, whose hallmarks were the end of the Uganda controversy, the consolidation of a consensus favoring "present-day work" (meaning practical activities in the diaspora), and an affirmation of the settlement efforts in Palestine – in short, the triumph of the gradualist approach toward the realization of Zionism.

In the course of this decade, Zionism grew from a marginal phenomenon to a factor of consequence in Jewish life. Public opinion and sovereign governments began to pay it note. The social composition of the movement also underwent change as new ideological and political currents came to the fore. At the start of the period, Herzl was still dependent upon the involvement of the veteran Lovers of Zion and their like from the previous era; but by its conclusion a new generation of activists had arisen, swelling the ranks of the movement, leading its different factions in various countries, and assuming positions of leadership in the world movement. The term "factions" is used here in its broadest sense, ranging from formally organized groups such as Mizrahi (Orthodox Zionists), the Democratic Fraction, and Poalei Zion (Labor Zionists), to more broadly defined currents, such as "political Zionism," "spiritual Zionism," and "practical Zionism."

There were three distinct layers of organization in early Zionism built in chronological order. The first was a vestige from the era of the Lovers of Zion and comprised erstwhile members of Bnei Moshe, the Bilu, and some proto Zionist groups. Built over it was the second, consisting of Herzlian Zionism, including all the factions and currents that vied within it or existed parallel to it. Finally, the third level extended from the Uganda crisis onward, with the basis of internal organization centering on the Palestine question, so that the breakdown shifted to the Zionists of Zion (*Zionei Zion*) vs. the Ugandists, Territorialists, etc. In each era, however, traces of earlier forms of organization prevailed, so that as in an archaeological excavation, the remains of deeper strata were always to be found under the surface. One reflection of this situation was the differences that existed in Herzl's day between Menahem Ussishkin, Moses Leib Lilienblum, and Ahad Ha'am, each of whom represented a different tradition held over from an earlier era (Bilu, the Odessa Committee, and Bnei Moshe, respectively), though they might be unanimous in their stand on major issues (e.g., their support for Palestine in the Uganda controversy).

The decade was also a time of a cultural florescence that was related more or less directly to the national impetus and the Zionist movement. Writers and artists, thinkers and publicists of various leanings were all drawn to Zionism and devoted their energies to promoting it. Periodicals and other literature in Hebrew, Yiddish, and European languages began to encourage an examination of Judaism from a Zionist standpoint. The advent of Zionism was attended by the rise of an intelligentsia that conducted a public debate on Jewish affairs and, more than just legitimacy, accorded prestige to the exploration of all questions Jewish. It can be said without exaggeration that European Jewry's finest intellectual talents were devoted to Zionism during this period – though for many members of this intelligentsia, Zionism was merely a passing fancy.

Be that as it may, the nascent movement made its mark as the bearer of a new gospel – tidings that ranged beyond the promise of a future political solution to touch upon a wide spectrum of issues connected with contemporary Jewish life.

The same decade was a time of both tentative ideological probing and full-blown, mature polemics. Thus we can trace the road that Zionism traveled over this period by a dynamic application of the time factor. Zionism appeared to serve a double role both reflecting and forging the attitude toward the past. The result was that even as it was being made, its own history was being merged into the picture of the past and became the object of scrutiny and judgment by the following generation of Zionists. This continuous flow from past to present may account for the conspicuous absence of any systematic research into the Zionist attitude toward the past. Instead, it remained a live issue that continued to spark controversy. Perhaps our own generation is the first that has been able to handle this turbulent subject with the necessary academic detachment.

Although the book was not conceived as being built around any one personality or another, clearly Herzl and Ahad Ha'am assume dominant positions in the pages to come. Each represents a polar approach and each was regarded as the emblem of his doctrine by a community of supporters and explicators that extended well beyond the sphere of his direct influence. Not only do we have much of their own writings, they are also mentioned often by others, supporters and adversaries alike.

Also of interest are the changing appreciations of past figures; thus some of the presumed Titans of the age eventually sank into oblivion, while the passage of time occasionally elevated their lesser-known contemporaries to positions of renown. The personalities discussed in this book are usually described in exclusively contemporary terms, with no more than passing reference to details of their past or future. Difficult though it may be to break a personality down into its composite factors, we must be wary – as in the case of Martin Buber, for example – not to confuse the "early" personality with its "later" incarnation.

The book is divided into four main chapters, the first "Historical Consciousness" which deals with the basic trends of the period and other subjects of general import, while the other three each addresses itself to a specific issue: "The Significance of Culture" as the vehicle for a contest of ideas, "A Future-Oriented Present" on practical work in the diaspora, and "The Uganda Crisis." Both the issues of culture and present-day activities remained a bone of contention throughout the decade, whereas the controversy over the Uganda proposal raged for a more limited period – though its impact was felt for many years thereafter. The approach to the material in these pages is usually chronological, while the breakdown of the chapters is organized thematically. Consequently, it has sometimes been impossible to avoid reference to the same matter more than once – albeit from a different perspective each time. As most of the issues explored here naturally had a prior history, I have cited antecedents and occasionally drawn analogies with other periods or other movements in an effort to point out elements common to Zionism and other intellectual, social, and political currents – Jewish or otherwise – and thereby highlight what is unique to Zionism.

CHAPTER ONE

HISTORICAL CONSCIOUSNESS[1]

The Retrieval of Jewish Dignity

Leon Pinsker established as early as 1882 the point of departure for the Zionist attitude as the depletion of Jewish honor. He wrote: "Seeking to maintain our material existence, we were constrained only too often to forget our moral dignity."[2] For many years thereafter, the quest to restore the lost dignity of the Jew remained the driving force of the Jewish national movement, and many a Zionist, especially in Central Europe, wrote about it in terms of a powerful personal experience. Bertha Schalit, for example, the president of Moriah, a Zionist women's organization in Vienna, related in 1893 that, "We found the courage to present ourselves openly as young Jewish women," and she decried the "nonsense now in vogue of being ashamed of one's Jewish origins."

Another testimony on this subject, presumably by Victor Jacobson (who was later to become a Zionist leader and was then a member of the Russian-Jewish Scientific Society in Berlin), was written in the following year: "The consistent humiliation and slander of the Jews has led us to begin believing these lies." Jacobson described the Jewish mentality of treating all matters Jewish with an eye to the possible arousal of antisemitism, noting in this context the disloyalty of German Jewry to the Russian Jews. He also advanced the argument – destined to become popular among Zionists – that "the

1 The concept "historical consciousness" is used here in its empirical sense as a general and dynamic concept, as in Raymond Aron, *Dimensions de la conscience historique* (Paris, 1961), p. 113.
2 Leon Pinsker, "Autoemancipation" in Arthur Hertzberg, ed., *The Zionist Idea* (New York, 1981), p. 190.

Christians are skeptical of denials to the effect that the Jews were not a tribe," referring to the contention that Jews were citizens like all the others and Judaism merely a religious denomination. He went on to elaborate: "They are unable to grasp how anyone could be ashamed of a people with a history like that of the Jews." The one German Jew who belonged to the Russian-Jewish Scientific Society, Heinrich Loewe, took this reasoning a step further and explained antisemitism as a product of Jewish self-hatred, asking rhetorically, "How can others respect us if we show contempt for ourselves?" Loewe saw the remedy to humiliation as brandishing the "glorious past" and turning the clock back in the Land of Judah, where "the dignity of the Jewish nation will be restored as that of a nation esteemed by all men."

The most influential Zionist thinker in Central Europe at the time, Nathan Birnbaum, did not stop at reproaching those who disavowed their Jewishness but charged that "This shame also dwells in the hearts of all who haltingly declare that they are proud of their Jewishness." Birnbaum exposed the feeling of shame that lay behind the bombast of the Reform Jews in speaking of their Jewishness and was hardly less critical of the Orthodox Jews, for he believed that "only national Judaism can wipe out [the shame]."[3] At about the time that this critique was printed, Birnbaum's journal, *Selbst-Emancipation*, published the manifesto of the national Jewish students in Prague, which spoke of the ridicule and humiliation suffered by the assimilationists at the hands of non-Jews. Set down in the midst of the struggle between Czech nationalism and German culture, these Jewish students felt themselves isolated and were thus moved to establish a Jewish-national student organization, like the existing societies in Vienna, Czernowitz, Berlin, and Heidelberg. Its manifesto stressed that the Jews were a people "by virtue of their origin, history, thinking, and feelings" and concluded with the cry: "You, Jew, you are not entitled to be a slave. Yours were the Maccabees!" This was evidently a paraphrase of a poem by Ernst Moritz

3 "Chronicle of the Moriah Women's Society," *Selbst-Emancipation* (February 15, 1893), p. 5; W. Jacobsohn, "Antisemitismus und Nationalität," *Jüdische Volkszeitung* (January 16, 1894), p. 1; Heinrich Loewe, "Hierosolyma est perdita," *Jüdische Volkszeitung* (February 6, 1894), pp. 1-3; B. (Birnbaum), "Was Thun?" *Jüdische Volkszeitung* (February 2, 1894), p. 2.

Arndt, one of the fathers of German nationalism: "*Der Gott, der Eisen wachsen liess, Der wollte keine Knechte.*" Instead of iron mentioned in the original, however, the reference here is to history – the Maccabees liberating their people from subjection, which stands for both oppression and humiliation.

The theme of Jewish dignity cropped up repeatedly in writings of the period, and particularly prominent was the purported connection between the contempt of the non-Jewish environment and the Jews' loss of self-respect. This relationship was depicted as a vicious circle whereby the Jews absorbed their sense of self-deprecation from their environment and their consequent lack of self-esteem in turn made them an object of scorn in the eyes of others. Theodor Zlocisti, an early Zionist in Germany, was a student of medicine and characteristically entitled his article "What Ails Us." "Lacking self-esteem," he wrote, "we have necessarily depreciated not only in the eyes of our enemies but in the eyes of our friends as well." Max Jungmann, who was Heinrich Loewe's assistant in his Zionist work in Berlin, sharpened the focus of Jewish dignity by placing the blame for the sorry state of affairs on the assimilationists, who either supported the German Liberals or were avowed German nationalists. "Neither the Orthodox Jew nor the national Jew are despised," he pronounced, "only the snob who does not wish to make his life miserable because of his well-known birth defect, the stigma of having been born a Jew." Conversely, the rabbi of Memel, Dr. Isaac Rülf, who had been among the earliest Lovers of Zion, explained the "feeling of abjectness" into which the Jewish people had settled as a function of the oppression to which it had long been subject, and he invoked the aid of the "glorious past" to remedy the situation. In an article published in 1896 in the quarterly *Zion*, Rülf addressed his protest to the antisemites: "You are the enslavers and I am the enslaved; you commit injustice and I suffer from injustice; you are barbarians and I am the bearer of culture; you may abhor me and persecute me, but you are no longer entitled to look down your nose at me."[4]

4 "Das Vertrauensmänner-Collegium der jüdisch-nationalen Studentenschaft in Prag," *Jüdische Volkszeitung* (July 10, 1894), p. 5; Theodor Zlocisti, "Woran wir kranken," *Zion* (September 15, 1895), p. 224; Max Jungmann, "An die Arbeit," *Zion* (March 30, 1896), pp. 74-75; J. Rülf, "Der deutsche Staatsbürger jüdischen Glaubens," *Zion* (May 17, 1896), p. 110.

In a similar, though far less aggressive mood of self-assertion, *Kadimah*, the organ of the Jewish national students in Paris, which attracted mostly émigrés from Eastern Europe, advocated the study of the biblical and post-biblical "glorious past." In one article, an anonymous writer analyzed the Jewish state of mind by taking a sober view of the situation: "Since we are being held responsible for one another in shame and disgrace, let us have the courage (is that asking too much?) to reconcile ourselves to our fate and together embrace the glorious or inglorious legacy that our forefathers bequeathed us." Contrary to the usual pattern, the "glorious past" was not juxtaposed here with the undignified behavior of the assimilationists, which purportedly served as the stimulus for antisemitism. Once again the driving force behind Jewish nationalism was the need to respond to the humiliating and hostile attitude of the environment, but the form of response recommended here was to foster Jewish solidarity and adopt the Jewish heritage as a fait accompli, be it positive or otherwise. Further on we shall again have an opportunity to examine the assessment of the Jewish past in Zionist thinking. Here we shall confine ourselves to exploring the relationship between the need to overcome the Jewish inferiority complex and the tendency toward *idealizing the past* (the above-cited quote being in the nature of the exception that proves the rule).

Characteristic of this approach was David Hescheles, a Zionist from Lemberg who was concerned about counteracting the influence of Polish nationalism on Jewish youngsters and strove for a situation in which "our children will not be ashamed of their fathers; on the contrary, they should be proud of their great forefathers." He adopted a characteristic mode of recourse to the "glorious past" in citing the "martyrs and heroes" of Jewish history and pointing out that all the great peoples of antiquity had vanished from the face of the earth while "we continue to exist, and who knows after which other peoples we will go on existing." In a similar vein, Gustav Cohen, an aging banker from Hamburg, prescribed in an anonymously published Zionist pamphlet that "The name 'Jew' must again become a title of respect." In comparing the Jews to the resurgent Greeks, Italians, and Balkan peoples, on the one hand, and the extinct ancient peoples, on the other, he concluded: "The obstinate, heroic endurance of our forefathers, despite vilification and slavery, torture and death, must find its justification."

Young Jewish men and women in Breslau and Vienna flocked to lectures on Jewish history and literature in which the concepts of self-awareness and self-esteem abounded. The moral of these addresses was always that the Jews should not be ashamed of their forebears but, much to the contrary, should continue to cultivate their great heritage.[5] Not surprisingly, perhaps, the activities of the Zionist societies began to attract the attention of non-Jewish circles, and to a certain degree the national movements in the Austro-Hungarian Empire actually regarded the new phenomenon favorably. In fact, from time to time voices from these circles were heard to say that the Zionist world view was similar to their own. They especially welcomed the phenomenon of Jews who were prepared to concede that the Jews are essentially outsiders. On the face of it, this tenet was even a point of contact between the Zionists and the antisemites.

Indeed, in 1892 the newspaper of the antisemitic pan-German movement in Austria asserted that the Zionists based themselves on Karl Eugen Dühring's proposition that the Jews were a distinct ethnic group. The only difference between Dühring and the Zionists, the paper contended, was that Dühring ascribed repulsive characteristics to the Jews, while the Zionists alleged their virtues. Such claims prompted Nathan Birnbaum, for one, to train his sights on the assimilationists – who exploited pieces of this sort to charge that there was an identity of views between the Jewish nationalists and the antisemites – and to go about proving that Zionism and antisemitism were in fact diametric opposites.

In 1894 Birnbaum published in his journal, *Selbst-Emancipation*, Dr. Jacob Kohn's "Letters from Galicia" on the attitude of the Polish press toward Zionism. Kohn quoted the Polish press as saying, "We have always taken the Jews to be just what they are – Jews; it is laudatory that they have ceased to engage in an immoral farce" –

---

5   *Kadimah, Journal des Etudiants juifs nationalistes de Paris* (November 1, 1896), pp. 87-88 (in the Jewish National and University Library, Jerusalem); David Hescheles, "Jewish Politics," *Yudisher Folks-Kalender* (1896/7), p. 41 (Yiddish); Gustav G. Cohen, *Die Judenfrage und die Zukunft* (Hamburg, 1896), p. 7.

a reference to the Jewish attempts to integrate into the Polish nation. The Ruthenians (Ukrainians of Galicia) "are enthused about us," Kohn reported, as Zionism was consonant with their interests – by which he apparently meant that the Ruthenians believed the rise of a distinctly Jewish nationalism would preclude Jewish identification with their Polish rivals. It is impossible to mistake Kohn's great satisfaction with these responses, for they vindicated the Zionist position in the debate with the assimilationists. Similar expressions of satisfaction seemed to be forthcoming each time the antisemites mocked the Jewish effort to assimilate. "What are the antisemites rebelling against," asked a Zionist from Bosnia (another region of the Austro-Hungarian Empire), "assimilation or Jewish nationalism?" His conclusion was that the validity of the antisemitic argument had to be conceded, for the Jews were indeed members of a foreign nation and would therefore do better to stop humiliating themselves by imploring other nations to extend them hospitality.[6]

The national awakening of the various peoples living within the Austro-Hungarian Empire had an impact on young Jews not only because it affected the process of assimilation but also because it provided them with a model to follow. One product of this compound influence was Alfred Nossig, a tragic and complex figure who ultimately met his death at the hands of the Jewish underground in the Warsaw ghetto, accused of having collaborated with the Nazis. Nossig had been an ardent Polish patriot in his youth in Lemberg (he actually regarded the Polish struggle for independence as a sequel to none other than the Maccabean wars) until he despaired of fully assimilating into Polish society and turned to Zionism instead. Another witness to the influence of Polish nationalism on the Zionist youth in Galicia recalled much later: "We translated their national holidays, their heroes, into our own national figures, and in our longing for redemption all that was lovely and noble in Polish history assumed a Jewish form.[7]

6　"Unverfälschte Deutsche Worte," *Selbst-Emancipation* (July 2, 1892), p. 136 (apparently N. Birnbaum); Jacob Kohn, "Briefe aus Galizien," *Jüdische Volkszeitung* (January 23, 1894), p. 4; Gustav Seidemann, "Die Gründe der Assimilation," *Zion* (July 20, 1895), p. 155.

7　Shmuel Almog, "Alfred Nossig: A Reappraisal," *Studies in Zionism*, 7 (Spring 1983), pp. 1-29; Joseph Tennenbaum, *Galicia, My Old Home* (Buenos Aires, 1952), p. 133 (Yiddish).

Thus we can see that prior to Herzl's advent, there were already many expressions of the desire to restore to the Jew his tarnished dignity by means of nationalism. It is equally clear that the restoration of Jewish self-esteem – as distinct from a response to persecution or the fear of growing assimilation – was a prime motivating force in Zionism, though these other drives also existed and contributed to the movement's emergence and growth. The issue of self-esteem arose as a result of the Jews' encounter with modern society, but it was not confined to the countries of the emancipation and typified the Jewish intelligentsia as a whole. As we have been able to infer from Birnbaum's writings and the romanticism of the young Nossig, identification with the "glorious past" was a way of overcoming the degradation of the present. This theme was attended by a readiness on the part of Zionists to admit that the Jews were fundamentally aliens in their countries of residence and the hope that they would become "a nation like all the others," as Moses Leib Lilienblum put it in 1890.[8]

Herzl and Jewish Dignity

Theodor Herzl, who was moved by the "predicament of the Jews" to find political solutions, likewise set out from the need to restore Jewish dignity. The very shift in his thinking from the prospect of mass conversion (which, by his own testimony, he had contemplated somewhere about 1893) to *The Jewish State* was apparently influenced by the fear that religious conversion "would be taken as [a sign of] cowardliness and ambition." Essentially, he was implying that conversion was undesirable because it was undignified, at least on the face of it. Yet even in aspiring to a Zionist solution to the Jewish problem, Herzl remained ambivalent in his attitude toward the Jews. On the one hand, he unabashedly admitted that he "[understood] what anti-Semitism is about" because the Jews are a "foreign body among the various nations" and displayed a "number

8   M. L. Lilienblum, "What Do the Palestinians Want?" in A. Druyanow, ed., *Documents on the History of Hibbat Zion and the Settlement of Eretz Israel*, Vol. III (Tel Aviv, 1932), pp. 93, 100 (multilingual).

of anti-social qualities." Still, he regarded the corruption of the Jewish character as "an historical product," since "all these sufferings rendered us ugly and transformed our character, which had in earlier times been proud and magnificent." "After all," Herzl reasoned, "we once were men who knew how to defend the state in time of war, and we must have been a highly gifted people to have endured two thousand years of carnage without being destroyed." Following this thinking to its logical end, he concluded that pride and honor could again become Jewish traits. Perhaps, indeed, he would embody them himself. After the publication of *The Jewish State*, the Austrian-Jewish writer Richard Beer-Hofmann wrote to Herzl: "Finally, we have a man who does not bear his Judaism resignedly as a burden or a tragedy but is proud to be among the legitimate heirs of an ancient culture."[9] Here again we can see the link between Zionism and Jewish pride and between that pride and the historical legacy of the Jews.

Even after becoming the acknowledged leader of the Zionist movement, Herzl continued to accentuate the importance of Jewish self-esteem. Thus in his address to the Second Zionist Congress, following the pogroms that had broken out in Galicia in 1898, he stated: "Neither bloodshed nor devastation nor insults are the worst. These disturbances do grave damage to the soul of our people. Ever and again they undermine our sense of right and honor and they cause their victims to become enemies of a social system which permits such things." In an interview given a year later, Herzl spoke at length of the "moral pollution" that clung to the Jews as a result of persecution and isolation and contrasted it with the vision that "finally my people may no longer be the dirty Jews but the people of light that they are capable of being."

The ambivalence of Herzl's feeling about the Jews was underscored by the apologetic tone he adopted in writing to his benefactor, the archduke of Baden, after his meeting with the kaiser in Jerusalem. Herzl bemoaned the fact that "the present conditions of the Jews in Jerusalem – unfortunately elsewhere as well – could not

---

9   Theodor Herzl, *The Complete Diaries of Theodor Herzl*, Vol. I (New York-London, 1960), pp. 9-10, and Richard Beer-Hofmann's letter in Theodor Herzl, *Letters*, Vol. II (Jerusalem, 1958), p. 74, n. 55 (Hebrew).

make a good impression on His Majesty the Kaiser" and explained that it was for precisely that purpose – to change those conditions – that Zionism had come into being. He referred the archduke to the Jews living in the agricultural colonies in Palestine, who were already showing signs of a "change for the better in both the physical and moral sense," as tokens of the change that Zionism was destined to effect in the lives of the Jewish masses. This was not a diplomatic démarche but an attempt to convey something of the profound experience Herzl had undergone upon meeting the young settlers of Rehovot. Tears filled Herzl's eyes and those of his companions "when we saw those fleet, daring horsemen into whom our young trouser-salesmen can be transformed." All his reservations about small-scale settlement in Palestine vanished in the face of such unassailable proof that Jews could change for the better.[10]

In a class with the experience Herzl underwent in Palestine was his own impact on others who had become alienated from Judaism but, under his influence, found a new object of identification. Max Nordau testified to a transformation of this sort in speaking before Jewish students (who, incidentally, were his own paragon of *the new Jew*): "Thanks to my dear friend, our leader Herzl – who by dint of his personality won me over to the perfect incarnation of the Zionist idea – I have come to know another Judaism that has enabled me to come to terms with myself and my race." Just as Herzl wished to dissociate himself from the Jews of Jerusalem as they appeared to the kaiser, Nordau expressed shame at the sight of the beggars of Palestine: "For Jewry as a whole cannot be indifferent to the fact that many people of all faiths who make annual pilgrimages to Palestine come upon listless Jews dressed in tatters in the figure of beggars and *shnorrers*. Let us first of all abolish this disgrace." These words were written in criticism of the initiative undertaken by the so-called practical Zionists in Galicia to found the settlement of Mahanayim in the Galilee. Nordau was firmly opposed to the settlement and proposed instead the resettlement of the Jews already liv-

---

10 Theodor Herzl, *The Congress Addresses of Theodor Herzl* (New York, 1917), pp. 12-13; Herzl, *Diaries*, Vol. III, p. 873, Vol. II, p. 774. "Trouser-salesmen" was the German historian Heinrich von Treitschke's derogatory catchword for Jewish immigrants.

ing in Palestine, such as the beggars who brought shame on Jews the world over.

Nordau delivered himself of the most striking expression of this viewpoint years later when speaking at the opening of the Popular University in Paris. His topic then was Hebrew as the Jew's pedigree. Nordau forecast that "the laborer will see that he is actually an aristocrat who has come down in his station but had behind him a whole line of noble forebears: conquerors – we had those – martyrs, heroes of the spirit and the mind, of brotherhood and justice." The term "laborer" obviously did not refer to the proletariat as such but to the simple Jew who worked hard for his living, was almost certainly an immigrant and stranger to the big city, and attended a Jewish popular university in the evening. In his identification with the Jewish national movement, such a laborer would presumably find a way to rise above his base condition by virtue of the lineage that Nordau offered him.[11]

In examining the subject of Jewish dignity, there was special value to the comparison that the Zionists made between the condition of the Jews and that of other national movements. We have already noted the inherent connection between overcoming feelings of inferiority and the discovery of the "glorious past." Yet the past played another specific role in the argument popular among national movements. The national awakening in the nineteenth century introduced the distinction between "historical" and "non-historical" nations, on the premise that only peoples that had lost their independence, such as the Greeks or the Poles, were entitled to political autonomy. Nevertheless, the so-called non-historical peoples – the Slovaks, Serbs, and the like – cited evidence to the effect that they, too, were national entities with historical roots. The Jews often found themselves caught in the middle between the rival national movements, especially in Austria-Hungary, but this experience provided them with a lesson about national organization and the search for historical legitimization.[12]

11 M. Nordau, "A la jeunesse juive," *Le Flambeau* (February 1899), p. 25; Max Nordau, "'Practical' and 'Political' Zionism," *Yudisher Folks-Kalender* (1899/90), p. 47 (Yiddish); Max Nordau, "Discours à l'inauguration de l'Université populaire juive," *l'Echo Sioniste* (March 15, 1903), p. 54.

12 Peter G. J. Pulzer, *The Rise of Political Anti-Semitism in Germany and Austria* (New York, 1964), pp. 138 ff.

In broad strokes, then, the past was not only a source for satisfying the craving for dignity but also a basis for substantiating the claim to nationhood. Looking around them, the Jews discovered that they were certainly on a par with other peoples demanding recognition of their national status. This realization was particularly characteristic of the Zionists from Galicia, in the Austro-Hungarian setting. In the year that *The Jewish State* was published, for example, one of Herzl's earliest supporters, Saul Raphael Landau, a resident of Vienna who had come there from Cracow, pointedly asked if: "Peoples smaller than we, peoples that were semi-barbaric, uncultured and uncivilized like the Serbs and Bulgars, for example, peoples that had intermingled under foreign occupation for centuries have suddenly awakened and become *independent* – are we incapable of doing so?" A year later Josua Schauer, likewise from Galicia, published a polemical tract scoring the chief rabbi of Vienna, Dr. Moritz Güdemann, for having come out against "national Judaism." By way of explaining the rise of Zionism, Schauer wrote: "The Jews saw peoples that, culturally speaking, lagged far behind them – Greeks, Rumanians, Bulgars – awakening after centuries of subjugation to a new political life." He described the growth of the realization that the Jews were in no way inferior to these peoples and asked why their lot was better, speculating, "Is it because we lost our country?" Both these writers cited well-known examples of peoples being liberated from the yoke of the Ottoman Empire but for obvious reasons failed to mention the one example with which they were certainly familiar from close observation: the Poles and their national movement.

Ahad Ha'am reacted to Schauer's pamphlet by quoting Schauer's own autobiographical story – "How he himself floated from one people to the next until he finally returned to his own, the people of Israel" – and concluded on a somewhat ironic note: "This story, which bears the stamp of Austria, answers the question of why Zionism spread through Austria more than other Western countries . . ." This remark reflected Ahad Ha'am's own position in favor of the *uniqueness* of Jewish nationalism, another echo of which can be heard in Chaim Weizmann's complaint against the Socialists that: "They can understand Zionism only by analogy with other nationalist currents of this century. . . . They cannot see the purely Jewish side of the picture."[13]

Another native of Galicia who became a prominent Zionist was the Viennese architect (and co-founder of *Die Welt*) Oskar Marmorek. Asked by Herzl to develop ideas on how to go about building up Palestine, he wrote an article about the construction of the Temple in which he characterized the nineteenth century as "the century of the renaissance of the nations." Referring to the Germans, Italians, Rumanians, Serbs, Bulgars, and Greeks, who had already achieved national independence, and the Armenians, who were still struggling toward that end, Marmorek asked: "Are the Jews inferior to these peoples, either in number or in spirit?" Herzl, on the same theme, did not confine himself to rhetorical questions, for as far as he was concerned it was beyond all doubt that the Jews were a developed and cultured people superior to the Greeks, Rumanians, Serbs, and Bulgars, "poor shepherds and huntsmen [who] have founded communities which later became states." Yet Herzl brought the discussion back to its point of departure in saying: "Until now, however, we have lacked self-confidence. On the day that we believe in ourselves, our moral tribulations will come to an end."[14]

Such self-confidence is not acquired in a single stroke, however, and for many years to come the question of Jewish self-esteem would hover over various practical issues in Zionism. Perhaps the Zionists themselves were able to overcome the sense of shame that was associated with being Jewish – particularly in educated circles – but they were aware that their own feelings in no way changed the lowly status of the Jews in the estimation of their environment. One striking example of the resilience of the Jewish inferiority complex can be seen in a letter written by Max Bodenheimer – among the earliest German Zionists – to the Zionist Executive in Vienna demanding

13 S. R. Landau, "Reflections on the Year 1896/7," *Yudisher Folks-Kalender* (1897/8), p. 112 (Yiddish); Josua Schauer, *Briefe eines Polnischen Juden* (Prague, 1897), p. 42; Ahad Ha'am, "Little Digest," *Hashiloah*, 3 (1898), p. 177 (Hebrew); Chaim Weizmann, *The Letters and Papers of Chaim Weizmann*, Vol. I (London, 1968), p. 80 .

14 Oskar Marmorek, "Baugedanken für Palästina," *Die Welt* (June 25, 1897), p. 11; Herzl, *Diaries*, Vol. IV, p. 1347.

that the venue of the Fourth Zionist Congress be changed from Basel, where the first three congresses had met. One reason for his demand was that: "We should not remain in a city that has offered us hospitality in view of the danger that ultimately we shall be regarded as a burden that cannot be disposed of. There must be some feeling whether one is wanted, and twice as much where *we* are concerned."

The First Zionist Congress had convened in Basel after its organizers were forced to abandon their original choice of venue – Munich – due to pressure from *Jewish* opponents there. The reception the Zionists enjoyed in Basel was warm, even enthusiastic. There is no reason to believe that there was ever any objection to hosting the congress in Switzerland, whose income was based on tourism. Moreover, after the 1900 congress held in London, the Zionists returned to Basel. Yet Bodenheimer was hypersensitive to the possibility that someone might conceivably interpret this move as imposing upon Swiss hospitality. His approach seems to derive from the concept of "hospitality" as applied to the condition of the Jews in their so-called host countries of residence. For as Bodenheimer put it, "As long as we are in Exile, we must wander; we have no *right* to establish ourselves in Switzerland."[15]

Zionist ideology consistently depicted the assimilationist Jew as a tragic and pitiful figure, a rootless middleman who lacked all creativity within the non-Jewish culture and aroused the mistrust of his Christian environment. Zionism, by contrast, was meant to restore human dignity to the Jew by virtue of his glorious past in the land of Judah and Israel and by reason of the long suffering that the Jews had heroically endured in exile.[16] This contrast implied a metamor-

---

15 Max Bodenheimer, *Im Anfang der Zionistischen Bewegung* (Frankfurt on Main, 1965), pp. 176-177.
16 The typology of the assimilationist is described here following: F. S. (Fabius Schach), "Der Zionismus," *Jüdischer Volkskalender 5658* (1897-8), p. 17; Bernard Lazare, "Solidarité," *Zion* (May 31, 1897), p. 24 (French section); Jacques Bahar, "Sionisme et Patriotisme," *Le Flambeau* (February 1889), p. 13; Ben Aaron, "Sionisme occidental," *Le Flambeau* (June 1889), p. 7; S. Poliakoff, "Deux Conférences," *l'Echo Sioniste* (May 15, 1903), p. 94; Franz Oppenheimer, "Referat über Ansiedlung," *Die Welt* (August 27, 1903), p. 11; Fabius Schach, *Über die Zukunft Israels* (Berlin, 1904), p. 13.

phosis that would engender a radical change in spirit and behavior while the Jews were still in the diaspora, even before Zionism had realized its goals as a political movement. In essence, all shades of opinion within Zionism subscribed to this expectation, as we shall see in the chapter entitled "A Future-Oriented Present." Let us merely note here in passing the disappointment that descended upon the Zionists when they encountered a reality far more complex than the picture they had drawn for themselves, and especially when they realized that their new conception of honor remained quite alien to the Jewish public at large.

In the course of discussing a proposal to establish a Jewish university in Europe, for example, Shmarya Levin, another member of the Russian-Jewish Scientific Society who was to become a life-long Zionist, complained that the great majority of Jewish students from Russia studying in universities in the West "not only relates to all the spiritual assets of the Jewish people with complete disdain but regards [nationalism] with utter contempt." Here, too, the subject was essentially pride, but in this case the students' contempt was directed not toward their Jewish origins but toward the Zionists and their national ambitions. Perhaps it was a sense of inferiority that elicited this response to the Zionist demand for heightened Jewish identification. However, it is reasonable to assume that Jewish students, who were generally inclined toward universal values, looked down upon the Zionists for their presumed nationalist narrow-mindedness, without necessarily being ashamed of their own Jewishness.

One way or the other, the Zionist attitude toward Jewish dignity was filled with scorn for the allegedly self-abasing Jews and sought to rebuild Jewish pride on the foundations of the distant past. As the Zionist movement developed, it repeatedly came into confrontation with the realities of the Jewish condition, and that only seemed to reinforce its criticism of the Jewish traits of character. Paradoxically, then, while Zionism aspired to restore Jewish self-esteem, it actually contributed to the criticism that was so damaging to it – sometimes to the point of outbursts of what could well be described as "Jewish self-hatred" in Zionist dress.[17]

17 S. Halevy, "Overview – A Hebrew University," *Hashiloah*, 10 (1902), p. 554 (Hebrew); Theodor Lessing, *Der jüdische Selbsthass* (Berlin, 1930).

In January 1904, for instance, after a young Zionist tried to assassinate Max Nordau in Paris for advocating Uganda, the organ of the Zionist movement in France, *l'Echo Sioniste*, published a piece on the incident by one of its regular contributors, the Syrian-born poet Albert Rokéach. Entitled "An Act of Madness," the article depicted the attempt on Nordau's life in terms of the complex relationship between fellow-Jews, on the one hand, and between Jews and gentiles, on the other. "The Jew abjectly capitulated to every outsider," he wrote. "Anyone who was not a member of his race has every right to persecute him, beat him, humiliate him, reduce him to naught. . . . All he would find is a false, ingratiating smile, deferential words of surrender." In sharp contrast, Rokéach depicted the relations between Jews as follows: "Ah, when it comes to a Jew, all deference dissolves. Every mark of excellence, any personal merit attesting to the moral virtue of its bearer is considered as naught." Note that the criticism is not longer related to an actual event but is expressed as a generalization about traits ostensibly characteristic of the Jews – in short, a Jewish stereotype. Rokéach's analysis was similar to the judgment passed on the Jews, at about the same time, by the most infamous purveyor of "Jewish self-hatred," Otto Weininger, in writing: "*Unwittingly*, every Jew esteems the Aryan [*Arier*] as superior to himself."[18] Rokéach and Weininger set out from very different premises, for Weininger regarded the Jew's self-abasement in the face of the "Aryan" as a justified expression of inferiority, whereas Rokéach discountenanced it and would certainly have wished to foster Jewish pride. What is more, one should not judge such casual remarks too harshly, and the bitter criticism leveled by one Zionist should not be taken as fully representative of prevailing thought. Nevertheless, Rokéach's utterances could be viewed as quite indicative of a more general frame of mind.

In terms of the approach to rehabilitating Jewish dignity, generally speaking there was some continuity between the period prior to the founding of the Zionist Organization and that immediately following it. From Herzl onward, however, a gradual change can be discerned on this issue. During the earlier period, Zionism meant the

18 A. Rokéach, "Acte de folie," *l'Echo Sioniste* (January 15, 1904), p. 2; Otto Weininger, *Geschlecht und Charakter* (Vienna, 1921), p. 414.

individual's decision on whether or not to accept his Jewish identity, whereas later on the Zionists as a group had to grapple with the problem of identifying with the reality of Jewish life. Phrased somewhat differently, one could say that the early Zionists were saved from the Jewish inferiority complex by identifying with the "glorious past" and it was sufficient for them to shun the ambition to assimilate. However, the Zionist movement as such had to provide solutions applicable to the entire Jewish people, so that its members were dogged by frustration over the enduring patterns of Jewish behavior that clashed with their concept of dignity. In a sense, the more the Jews continued to remain what they were, despite the innovative means offered by Zionism to raise their self-esteem, the more the Zionists construed their behavior as proof of the fundamentally negative character of the Jewish stereotype. Here was an issue on which the Zionists kept stubbing their toes, as it were. They wondered about the true nature of the Jewish entity that was the object of their activities. The issue embraced many questions, from the formal definition of the group – as a religion, people, race, or what have you – to more intricate matters, such as whether the Jews were indeed capable of becoming a nation, what changes must they undergo in the process of their consolidation, or even whether they were *worthy* of a national renaissance.

We shall now address ourselves to a number of these in the order of their historical development. The Zionist assessment of the Jewish character and the changes that the Jews would have to undergo will be discussed mainly in the chapter "The Significance of Culture."

Nation and Race

The emancipation brought with it the principle that the bond between the Jews was solely one of religion. Even Pinsker, in his call for "Autoemancipation," protested that "*we do not constitute a nation, that we are merely Jews.*" And when Herzl tried to win Max Nordau over to the Zionist idea, the two men asked themselves whether the Jews were "still anthropologically fit for nationhood" – all of which implies that the Jews were not considered a nation.

Shortly thereafter, in *The Jewish State*, Herzl made his famous pronouncement, "We are a people, *one* people"; but it was a programmatic declaration, not a statement of fact. That he deemed it necessary to make such a pronouncement – its definitive tone notwithstanding – suggests that he felt obliged to persuade his readers of something that was not readily evident at the time.

When Herzl made approaches to the Baron de Rothschild in Paris and Jewish notables in London, he was told in no uncertain terms that "our masses are not made to be organized." Unlike Herzl and Nordau, these dignitaries were not expressing some vague anthropological notion about the nature of the Jews but a basic lack of confidence in their ability to act in concert.[19] Or, as Kalman Marmor (then a Zionist student in Switzerland) subsequently related in his memoirs, while visiting his family in the vicinity of Vilna he met with ridicule from a local Jewish intellectual who jeered that "Jews will never be able to maintain a state of their own." Even Herzl had his doubts. A few years after becoming head of the Zionist movement, he wrote bitterly (in response to criticism from his opponents within the movement) that perhaps future historians would properly appreciate his achievement in having made "a people out of a decadent rabble." Such vituperation can be explained as the resentment of a leader over his treatment at the hands of an ungrateful public. What is important for our purpose is that Herzl took it for granted that a leader could create his nation. Moreover, the issue was a persistent one. Even after the outbreak of the Uganda crisis, Nahum Sokolow would raise it again in crying out, "Don't you realize that we don't even have a people yet?"[20]

All these utterances reflect a lack of confidence in the ability of the amorphous group known as the Jews to reconstitute itself as a nation. They were also closely bound up with the concept of Jewish dignity, considering that the speakers were less concerned with finding a new, formal definition of the existing situation – i.e., whether

19 Pinsker, "Autoemancipation," p. 189; Herzl, *Diaries*, Vol. I, p. 276; Theodor Herzl, *The Jewish State* (New York, 1970), p. 33; Herzl, *Letters*, p. 131.
20 Kalman Marmor, *My Autobiography*, Vol. II (New York 1959), p. 461 (Yiddish); Herzl, *Diaries*, Vol. III, p. 1151; N. S. (Nahum Sokolow), "The Foundations of the Renaissance (3): Where Did the Many Go Wrong?" *Hatzfirah* (December 7, 1903), p. 1 (Hebrew).

the Jews were a nation or a religious community – than with assessing the potential inherent in the Jews for the future. There was a definite connection between Pinsker's pronouncement "We do not constitute a nation" and the shame that he wished to strip off the Jews. The penetration of the national idea throughout Europe made human dignity dependent upon the individual's affiliation with a national group, so that for a long time Zionism was haunted by the fear the Jews would not have enough self-respect to become a nation.

This was, of course, a dynamic criterion based on subjective assessments and on the presumed potential of Zionism itself. As long as the existing situation did not provide a definitive answer as a result of the Jews engaging in national activities, it was unclear whether the Zionists were right in claiming that the Jews were indeed a nation. Thus attempts were made to suggest objective criteria for defining the Jews as a nation. They derived from two sources:

* Historical material attesting to the continuity between contemporary Jewish life and the history of the Jews throughout the ages in various countries of their dispersion.
* Characteristics that – in the absence of such obvious attributes as a common territory and language – were generally employed to establish the identity of national groups (e.g., ethnic origin).

From the outset, the Zionists had been hard pressed to find semantic tools for conveying the innovation of their approach, in contrast to the terminology in vogue among Western Jews. Rather than treat Judaism as a religious phenomenon, they sought concepts that would stress its national aspect and often used the terms people, nation, tribe, and race interchangeably. They even reverted to using the adjective "Jewish," rather than *Israélite* or *mosaisch*, which were preferred by Western Jews during the era of the emancipation.[21] Invoking the concept of "race" was prevalent in European thinking at this time, especially in Germany and France, and did not necessary imply a definite racial outlook. However, defining the Jews as

21 E.g. George Wormser, *Français Israélites* (Paris, 1963), p. 170.

a race had a particularly strong appeal to the Zionists, as it validated their contention about the objective existence of a Jewish entity. As far back as 1885, when the first issue of Nathan Birnbaum's *Selbst-Emancipation* was published, it was argued that the assimilationists had failed to obliterate their typically Jewish character, because "nature, which has accorded different tribes different spiritual proclivities, different ways of thinking, different inclinations, laughs at such efforts." Over a decade later, Birnbaum again spoke admiringly of the racial doctrine's "scientific criteria" that proved the cogency of the Zionist credo.[22]

One of the early Zionists in Lemberg, Aaron Trieber, described the discord between the Polish national movement and the assimilationist Jews. He quoted a speech by Dr. Nathan Lowenstein – one of the leading assimilationists in Galicia – commending the Polish patriotism of the Jews and decrying their exclusion as they did not belong to the Slavic race and the Catholic religion. Lowenstein espoused the individual joining the nation *"on the basis of his subjective feeling."* Trieber, the Zionist, countered that if the subjective feeling determined one's nationality, then "what tie keeps you attached to the Jews?"[23]

Here we see how the complex weave of relations among the various ethnic groups in Galicia served as a fitting background to the emergence of Zionism's ethnic or racial approach, parallel to the racial motifs found in Polish nationalism. Trieber naturally focused on the weak point in the argument of the Polish-Jewish patriots. For in insisting upon their right to be considered Poles in every way – despite the antagonism of the Polish Christians – it was difficult for them to clarify their continued attachment to the Jews. It was easier, however, to explain the factual or existential connection between these Polish patriots and the Jewish collective as an ethnic-biological link.

On a number of occasions, Herzl applied the racial concept to the

22 "Erlöschung – Erlösung," *Selbst-Emancipation* (February 1, 1885); Matthias Acher (pseud. for N. Birnbaum), *Die jüdische Moderne* (Leipzig, 1896), p. 22; and see Jacques Barzun, *Race, A Study in Superstition* (New York, 1965), pp. 133 ff.

23 A. Trieber, "Briefe aus Galizien," *Jüdische Volkszeitung* (June 12, 1894), p. 5; and cf. Moritz Lazarus, *Was heisst national?* (Berlin, 1880), p. 12. .

Jews in the sense of a group of people with common hereditary traits. One such instance was his remark that "The decline of our once-vigorous race is revealed most clearly in our political lethargy." Another came in the wake of Herzl's talks with Nordau on the Jewish question, when he reported in his diary: "He even said that there was no such thing as Jewish dogma. But we are of one race." Herzl was encouraged by his conversation with Nordau and did not demur his conclusion. A few months later he visited the writer Israel Zangwill in London and tried to persuade him to join his movement. In this talk, however, one can discern a change in Herzl's approach to the racial ingredient in the making of a Jewish entity. "However, his point of view is a racial one – which I cannot accept if I so much as look at him and at myself," Herzl wrote in his diary. "All I am saying is: We are an historical unit, a nation with anthropological diversities. This also suffices for the Jewish State. No nation has uniformity of race."[24]

This is a seemingly unequivocal statement. Yet the influence of the racial doctrine on Herzl had not run its course. At the end of 1901, he wrote to Martin Buber – then editor of the Zionist weekly, *Die Welt* – praising one of his articles that was suffused with racial symbolism, in the style characteristic of the young Buber (about which more will be said later). Buber had described the ideal of the Jewish people as: "To create new values, new works of art, from the depths of its ancient uniqueness, out of the singular, matchless potency of its blood." A year later *Die Welt* published selections from the polemic that Heinrich Driesmans, a non-Jewish anthropologist, was carrying on with official Jewish circles in Germany. Driesmans, who espoused the racial doctrine, contrasted the "Jewish race," as the epitome of "racial pride," with the Germans, "who have been endowed with so weak a racial feeling." Herzl, it seems, heartily concurred with this view and even sent the article to Walter Rathenau (later to become foreign minister of the Weimar Republic), with whom he maintained a correspondence.[25]

24 Herzl, *Diaries*, Vol. I, pp. 194, 196, 276.
25 Martin Buber, "Wege zum Zionismus," *Die Welt* (December 20, 1901), p. 6; Martin Buber, *Briefwechsel aus sieben Jahrzehnten*, Vol. I (Heidelberg, 1972), p. 170; Heinrich Driesmans, "Zur jüdischen Rassenfrage," *Die Welt* (December 12, 1902), p. 5.

This is the place to note the quandary over the question later to be known under the rubric "Who is a Jew?" Theoretical discussions about the essential nature of Judaism inevitably gave way to more practical considerations when it came to determining the basis on which an individual was to be considered a Jew: rabbinical law or some other criterion. Thus Simon Bernfeld, an historian, publicist, and erstwhile rabbi, assailed the First Zionist Congress for failing to acknowledge the religious basis of Jewish nationalism. In an article published in *Hatzfirah* following the Congress, he reported that: "Almost all the 'nationalists' – according to the new way of putting it – with whom I spoke after the return from Basel . . . told me in no uncertain terms: The entire Torah may be sacrificed for the sake of the rebirth of our people." Bernfeld even told of a Zionist who had converted to Christianity in order to marry a Christian woman but claimed that this act in no way detracted from his being a national Jew.

A few days later, a piece was published in the same paper (evidently penned by its editor, Nahum Sokolow) refuting Bernfeld's charge. Dismissing the conversion story as irrelevant, Sokolow nevertheless broached the basic question of the relative weight of religion and race as components of Judaism. Speaking of himself, he said: "For the past fifteen years, the writer of these columns has seen it as his obligation to combat those who would deny the pertinence of the Torah and spiritual Judaism and base everything upon race and homeland." He ascribed the racial thinking within Zionism to the influence of the American poet Emma Lazarus (who avowed her Jewish identity in the poems collected in *Songs of a Semite*). However, the conception of race was not drawn very clearly in Sokolow's writings. He did not deny the existence of a "racial force" but opposed those of his fellow-Zionists who wished to "*base everything upon race.*" Thus his approach can be interpreted as a commendation of the Jewish cultural heritage as much as a challenge to basing Jewish nationalism exclusively on the principle of race."[26]

In light of this equivocation, it is interesting to return to

---

26 Simon Bernfeld, "A Clarification," *Hatzfirah* (October 15, 1898), p. 1095 (Hebrew); *Hatzfirah* (October 17, 1898), p. 1102 (Hebrew; probably by Sokolow).

Bernfeld's story of the faithful Zionist who had allegedly converted. Sokolow regarded this as a trivial matter because such behavior was certainly not representative of the norm in Zionist circles. Even the political Zionists viewed religious conversion with a jaundiced eye, if only because it smacked of a lack of dignity and implied desertion in a time of distress (Herzl had opposed conversion even in his pre-Zionist period for these very reasons). Even when it came to the parallel issue of intermarriage, the Zionists were opposed (although it did not entail conversion), sometimes invoking such racial notions as the need to preserve the racial purity of the Jews. That is apparently how we are to interpret the piece published on this subject in 1897 in the periodical *Zion* (evidently by Heinrich Loewe). "It is precisely the Zionists, who no longer view religion as the means binding our people," Loewe wrote, "who should be particularly vigilant that the element that does unify all of us Jews – the tribal affiliation – is kept as immaculate as possible." The reason for this stricture is to ensure that "the talented race" will not squander any of its vitality on the "less talented Indo-Germanic race." Admittedly, this approach may have been an expression of the fear that intermarriage would result in defections from Jewry and thereby weaken the national entity. Still, one should not ignore the new racial terminology in which the long-standing opposition to intermarriage was clothed.

Perhaps it is more appropriate to present the pragmatic argument against intermarriage, which was doubtless more attuned to the mood of the Jewish public. Let us quote from the letter written to Herzl by the Zionist deputy from Kishinev, Dr. Jacob Bernstein-Cohen, who reported in 1898 that he was in a state of "overt war" with the "benighted band of the Orthodox." Yet even he was disturbed by the rumor that Max Nordau had married a non-Jewish woman. "My own attitude toward the event is certainly total indifference," Bernstein-Cohen wrote, "but our adversaries exploit this trivial fact to disparage the entire movement and its leaders. If he really did so, then his deed is both impolitic and impolite."[27]

---

27 Saxo Judaeus (probably Heinrich Loewe), "Mischehe und Blutmischung," *Zion* (May 31, 1897), p. 140; J. Bernstein-Cohen, *The Bernstein-Cohen Book* (Tel Aviv, 1946), p. 225 (Hebrew).

Like religious conversion, intermarriage was a pet peeve of the Jewish public to which Zionism addressed itself. The objections to it on racial grounds were merely a matter of vogue, considering that such reasoning could equally well condone conversion without disqualifying the convert as a Jew. At any rate, the importance of the racial argument was negligible, just as the opposing reasoning – that conversion was essentially a personal affair – carried little weight. The public at large presumably wanted Zionism to act in the interests of Jewish survival and fight against any countervailing tendencies; the finer points of ideology were of little interest to it. Still, we can take the issues of conversion and intermarriage as a touchstone of the acceptance or rejection of the racial criterion as a basis for defining the Jewish collective.

Although there was undoubtedly a need to establish an objective definition that would embrace all Jews and clearly distinguish them from non-Jews, the racial doctrine did not provide it. The main problem was not the inability to accept the premise of a Jewish race (which was a fairly common notion) but rather the difficulty in reducing the heterogeneous nature of the Jewish collective to a racial definition. Judaism was more complex than the monistic framework of the racial doctrines. It comprised elements such as history and religion that deserved inclusion and required expression in the Zionist view. Thus the racial approach could play a supportive role, and in certain instances it even bore emotional weight; but it could not serve as the standard norm for Jewishness.[28]

The Integrity of Jewish History

The question of whether there actually was a Jewish nation that could be defined by objective criteria brings us back to Jewish history. In presenting its case Zionism set much store by historical rationale, as did other national movements. Nevertheless, a vital link was missing in the chain of evidence cited for Zionism, namely,

---

28 On the monism of race see: Ernst Cassirer, *The Myth of the State* (Garden City, N.Y., 1955), p. 291.

proof that there was a real bond between contemporary Jews and the "glorious past."

This was no simple matter, for Christianity had tried to negate the association of the Jews with the ancient Israelites. Modern European culture had inherited this outlook as part of its Christian heritage, and even the so-called Science of Judaism subscribed to it by dissociating the biblical period – dubbed "Hebraic" history – from the subsequent centuries of "Jewish" history. Here again Zionism coined a concept and bridged the gulf by declaring that there was but one, integral Jewish history.[29] The prominent Israeli historian Benzion Dinur regarded this "new perception of Israel's past" as one of the prime ingredients of Zionist ideology, for it signalled a desire to "utilize the legacy of the past as a whole." This development was, moreover, in stark contrast to the Jewish liberal historiography, which, as Dinur saw it, had tried "to excise the Land of Israel from the heritage of the Jewish past." It is hardly surprising that the integrity of Jewish history became a salient issue for the Zionists of Western Europe, especially as it defied the assumptions of their cultural environment. Yet even in Russia there was evidence as far back as the 1880s of a Zionist attempt to speak on behalf of the "entire nation of Israel throughout the continuum of history."[30]

Theodor Herzl was intuitively aware of this problem even as his Zionist outlook was just beginning to take shape. While contemplating the type of regime that should be established in the future Jewish state, he referred approvingly to monarchy as a force for stability, though he doubted the feasibility of reviving the ancient monarchic format, because "our history has been interrupted too long for us to attempt to resume this institution." Essentially he held that the political history of the Jews had come to a halt with the destruction of the Temple and would be resumed only with the constitution of his "*Judenstaat*." This reading implied that a gaping void stretched between the ancient era and sometime in the future, wholly ignoring

29 Jacques-Bénigne Bossuet, *Discours sur l'Histoire Universelle* (Paris, 1966), p. 249; Ismar Schorsch, "From Wolfenbüttel to Wissenschaft," *Leo Baeck Yearbook*, XXII, 1977. pp. 117-118.

30 Benzion Dinaburg-Dinur, ed., *The Book of Zionism*, Vol. I, Part I (Tel Aviv, 1939), p. 13 (Hebrew); Bernstein-Cohen, *The Bernstein-Cohen Book*, p. 88.

the need to account for and define Jewish existence in between. (It was Max Bodenheimer who clearly addressed this need in his speech before the First Zionist Congress by stating that: "Through a conscientious study of our history, we must foster the awareness that although we have been scattered among the nations, we have always presented ourselves as a national entity." His conclusion was that Zionists in the West should acquire and foster a knowledge of Jewish history).

After the First Zionist Congress, Herzl again touched upon this issue in referring to those who denied that the Jews were a people because they believed a people to be "an accumulated mass of humanity living together in territorial unity." Seeking a more accommodating definition of the nation, he proffered the formula of "a historic group of human beings of evident kinship held together by their common enemy." This definition appeared to him to be universally valid and therefore proved the cogency of the Zionist approach to Jewish nationalism. His reasoning was that "the Jews had endured eighteen centuries of unexampled suffering. But they had outlived it all and preserved intact the consciousness of the state and the sense of territorial possession." Consequently, a people was to be defined not by its concentration in a given territory but by historical continuity, for as Herzl postulated: "Let a nation only be there and it will create for itself the plot of ground which it requires."[31]

Occasionally the historical explanation for the endurance of the Jewish nation was woven together with the motif of Jewish pride, as in a 1902 article about the impact of Zionism on the Jewish students in France: "Zionism appeared and suddenly everything changed. We too have become men. We are beginning to scrutinize our consciousness, to study our past, and we find nothing to justify the accusations being hurled at us . . . We must proclaim that Jewish university youth are beginning to appreciate the integrity of their past, the uniformity of their aspirations regardless of their country of residence." Here the accent in articulating Zionism's conception of history was

31 M. J. Bodenheimer in *Protokoll des 1ten Zionistenkongresses in Basel, 1897* (Prague, 1911), p. 142; Theodor Herzl, "The Zionist Congress," *The Contemporary Review*, LXXII (October 1897), pp. 589, 596-597.

on sentiment, whereas the young Martin Buber expressed it in characteristically mystical terms by calling for the creation of a bond between the life of the individual Jew and the martyrdom of a hundred generations gone by. He also attempted to foster an affinity between "the individual's corporal history and the history of the countless cadavers who had once suffered" (and similar images reminiscent of the "integral nationalism" of the French writer Maurice Barrès).[32]

During the few years that elapsed between the First Zionist Congress and Buber's publication of this article, Zionist thinking began to branch out in a number of directions, and we shall have occasion to return to them. Here, however, let us focus on the critical attitude of Zionist intellectuals toward the long history of Jewish dispersion – which, as noted earlier, contravened the image of the past as depicted by emancipated Jews. In its own way, Zionist criticism called even the continuity of Jewish history into question – prompting Ahad Ha'am (the leading Zionist intellectual of his day) to respond by asserting the integrity of Jewish history even more emphatically. Speaking to the Russian Zionist Conference in Minsk in 1902, Ahad Ha'am explained that "the difficult conditions in which we have lived since being exiled from our land have inevitably left their mark on our creative spirit. But the fundamental nature of that spirit has not changed and has not ceased to fulfill its function, even in the diaspora."

That same year Shmarya Levin, a disciple of Ahad Ha'am's, took issue with views that were attributed to Leo Motzkin, one of the leaders of the Democratic Fraction. (Then at the height of its power, the Democratic Fraction was a radical opposition within the Zionist movement from 1901 to 1904 and called for the democratization of Zionist institutions.) Levin accused Motzkin of claiming that "the Zionist movement is an entirely *new* phenomenon." Thus Motzkin was presumed to have carried the innovation of Zionism even beyond the point that Ahad Ha'am had refuted ("that the Bible

32 Dr. Filderman, "La jeunesse universitaire et le sionisme," *l'Echo Sioniste* (October 15, 1902), p. 203; Martin Buber, "Die Schaffenden, das Volk and die Bewegung" in Berthold Feiwel, ed., *Jüdischer Almanach, 5663* (Berlin, 1902), p. 22; Maurice Barrès, *Barrès par lui-même* (Paris, 1954), pp. 30, 33.

alone is the true Hebrew culture"), advocating a complete break with the past, as it were. Levin struck back with the well-worn analogy that: "Just as the bearded patriarch is none other than the child grown old, so the people with its long history is the very same as it was in its youth."[33]

Two years later, *Hashiloah,* the monthly in which Levin and Ahad Ha'am had published their articles, carried a piece entitled "On the Question of Jewish Existence" that raised a storm of controversy among many of the journal's readers. Its author, Samuel Joseph Ish-Horowitz, an eminent Hebrew writer associated with the Lovers of Zion, was profoundly pessimistic about the future of the Jewish people. "Do we indeed have a constant, immutable national idea?" he challenged. "Our ancient ideal – the majesty of government and national honor, power and glory – was trampled underfoot back in the Middle Ages; strict observance of the commandments, requited by the Leviathan and the Legendary Bull [rewards that, according to Jewish lore, were reserved for the righteous in the Next World], which caused the elders *then* to go through fire and water, is held up to ridicule now." In other words, Judaism's hour had passed, both as a national-territorial manifestation (destroyed in the ancient past) and as a spiritual-religious one (rejected in modern times). This sharp assault on the notion of historical continuity and Ish-Horowitz's profound pessimism about the Jewish future led him to the question: "What, then, can Zionism add? How can it avail us?" We should bear in mind that these words were written just after the Uganda Affair, a critical time for Zionism, which undoubtedly heightened criticism of the movement's claim to express the vital forces in Jewry.

One of Ish-Horowitz's many disputants, M. L. Lilienblum, the veteran leader of the Lovers of Zion in Russia, took the opportunity of the present polemic to settle accounts with Jewish intellectuals from the time of Heinrich Heine and Ludwig Börne onward. Lilienblum ascribed the integrity of Jewish history to the "natural national feeling, that eternal feeling" and concluded that "the fate of an entire historic people, a people that can point to more than three thousand

---

33 Ahad Ha'am, "The Revival of the Spirit," *Hashiloah,* 10 (1902), p. 389 (Hebrew); S. Halevy, "Overview," *Hashiloah,* 9 (1902), p. 274 (Hebrew).

years of existence, cannot be dependent upon some philosophical inquiry, regardless of its quality." Joseph Klausner, the editor of *Hashiloah*, availed himself of the anthropomorphic simile in writing: "The young man and the old are a single person because they possess an awareness of their personal unity." Klausner went on to contrast the nationalism of the Jews and that of other nations as follows: "A deep chasm separates the ancient Romans from the Italians, the ancient Hellenes from today's Greeks: religious beliefs and even the names of the nations have changed. But the same has not happened where the Jews are concerned." And after noting certain changes that had nonetheless occurred in the beliefs professed by the Jews since the days of the First Temple, he concluded: "All of this notwithstanding, they never lost their awareness of the integrity of the national personality."[34]

Thus the road led backward from Herzl's "historic group of human beings of evident kinship" to Lilienblum's "natural national feeling" and Klausner's "awareness of the integrity of the national personality." It proceeded from the objective approach, which could be acknowledged by the world at large, to a purely subjective consciousness – perceptions and emotions – and essentially implied a return to subjective criteria for defining a nation – as proposed for instance by the German-Jewish philosopher Moritz Lazarus. Years of Zionist activity and scholarly inquiry had not resulted in the establishment of a recognized historical basis for Zionism. For the Zionists sought incontrovertible proof that they were proposing not an arbitrary hypothesis but the one and only correct interpretation of the Jewish condition. They wanted to prove that Zionism expressed the purpose and direction of Jewish history and was fully consonant with the natural course of Jewish life – in a word, that it was an historical inevitability.

These speculations were joined by a line of thinking that, at first glance, appeared to run in exactly the opposite direction and was epitomized by the attempt to portray Zionism as a movement that

34 S. J. Ish-Horowitz, "The Question of the Existence of Judaism," *Hashiloah*, 13 (1904), p. 300 (Hebrew); M. L. Lilienblum, "Aimlessness and the Right to Exist," *Hashiloah*, 13 (1904), pp. 490-491 (Hebrew); Joseph Klausner, "Between Necessity and Will," *Hashiloah*, 14 (1904), pp. 393, 396 (Hebrew).

makes history. Apparently polar opposites, these two trends can be schematized as follows:

* The deterministic orientation, which tended to emphasize historical continuity.
* The voluntary trend, based on the principle of renewal.

In tracing the development of these ideas, we shall note the extent to which, though locked in conflict, they nevertheless went hand in hand throughout the period under review.

Historical Action

When Leon Pinsker concluded his pamphlet *Autoemancipation* with the words, "Help yourselves and God will help you," his point was to contrast this adage with the belief in the messiah, which, he claimed, contravened all concern for Jewish national liberation. But it is Leo Motzkin, a young man who accented the innovative aspects of Zionism, who merits attention here as a proponent of Jewish activism. One of the outstanding personalities of his day, Motzkin was mentioned above in connection with the debates centering on the Democratic Fraction. Yet prior to that period, even before the advent of Herzl, he was already speaking in terms of the Jews taking action to shape the nation's future. In 1891, when the Russian-Jewish Scientific Society of Berlin celebrated the Festival of the Maccabees (deliberately using this name rather than Hanukkah), the gathering was attended by many German Jews, which was quite unusual. In addressing that audience, Motzkin, a Russian Jew educated in Germany, chose to focus on issues that were of import to Zionist circles: the glorious Jewish past and the lessons to be learned from the Greek and Italian national revivals. Moreover, he appealed to his listeners in terms such as: "Let us forge our own destiny, let us arise to a normal, independent life" – slogans typical of Zionism's striving for innovation, with the emphasis placed on an activist approach.

Vasily Bermann took a similar tack. One of the earliest Lovers of Zion in Russia, Bermann was a lawyer who came from an assimilated family and who met an untimely death prior to Herzl's appearance. His recollections of a visit to Palestine, published in 1894, gave succinct expression to motifs that would later preoccupy Zionism. "Our people is on the brink of a new history in Palestine," he wrote. "It rests entirely on us to mold it in the form we wish it to take." Further on in the same piece he spoke of "Israel returning from Europe" to be the "sire of the future nation," and he expressed the fear that "unless you match him with *Bat Zion*, the perennially young daughter of this land," the nation would remain sterile. Turning more prosaic, Bermann explained that in coming to live in Palestine, Russian Jews would have to change, and he contrasted "the creative Jewry of Palestine" with the "moribund Jewry of the diaspora." Later on we shall elaborate upon the sources and substance of Zionism's criticism of diaspora Jewry; for the moment let us simply note the connection between such criticism and the self-reliance required to reshape the future course of Jewish history.

Though Isidor Schalit spoke in more practical terms than Bermann, his words likewise reflected the Zionist impulse to spur Jews to action as the prime factor in determining their fate. Schalit, also born in Eastern Europe, became active in Kadimah, the Zionist Student Association in Vienna. In 1895 he addressed a Jewish gathering in Bohemia on the idea of organizing a Jewish national party, if only because the Jews' prospects would improve "if they do something for themselves," rather than sit back and "wait for the Golden Age." The allusion here, as in Pinsker's writing, was to the passive nature of the messianic faith; however, Schalit drew his imagery from Greek mythology and did not challenge the Jewish tradition directly.[35]

The First Zionist Congress went a long way toward buoying the hopes of the activists that Zionism would indeed make history. On the eve of the gathering, Nathan Birnbaum, who had been critical of the Lovers of Zion and had been advocating political action for years, wrote that "The people does not shy away from the great goals

---

35 Pinsker, "Autoemancipation," p. 198 (Pinsker's adage is attributed to multiple sources, such as La Fontaine and Benjamin Franklin); *Selbst- Emancipation* (February 1, 1892), p. 31. W. Bermann, "In Judäa," *Jüdische Volkszeitung* (August 21, 1894), p. 2; "Nationale Bewegung," *Zion* (June 17, 1895), p. 148.

of the future." Speaking of the Jewish people's latent capacity for eminence and its heroic spirit, he argued that "the great deeds of human history" – such as the Exodus from Egypt, the Greek victory over the Persians, the spread of Christianity and Islam, and the Crusades – were accomplished by dint of "implacable" will. His romantic thinking connected Zionism with major events in the history of mankind by virtue of the same power of human determination and effective action that propelled them all. In addressing the First Zionist Congress, Birnbaum spoke of the generation that had "learned from the vigorous nations of Western civilization how to exercise willpower." Like Vasily Bermann before him, he described the encounter between the Jewish people and its land in erotic terms, likening European Jewry to the daughter of Israel and the land to the groom who would rouse her to a new, fruitful life. And once again we can see the connection between Zionism as a procreator of history and the process of inner renewal that could be expected to ensue once the Jews were reunited with their land.[36]

Heinrich Loewe viewed the First Congress from an historical perspective, going back as far as the destruction of the ancient state of Judea. "Since that time," he wrote, "the Jewish people has played only a passive role in world history," but he implied that Zionism could make amends even in regard to the historic role of the Jews. This theme was discussed more explicitly by the noted Hebrew writer Micha Josef Berdyczewski when he wrote of the First Zionist Congress: "Three hundred people have come from the four corners of the diaspora to lay the cornerstone of the nation's fallen Tabernacle. They wish to pick up the thread of history that spanned more than eight hundred years. They wish to be a people, to be what they were long ago – a nation standing on its own feet." Berdyczewski joined together the First and Second Temple periods, as if the rest of Jewish history were of no consequence, and wanted to "pick up

---

36   Matthias Acher, "Zum Münchner Kongresse," *Zion*, Berlin (May 31, 1897), p. 158 (Birnbaum published the article before the venue of the congress was changed to Basel); Nathan Birnbaum, "Das jüdische Nationalleben" in *Protokoll des 1ten Zionistenkongresses in Basel, 1897* (Prague, 1911), p. 103.

the thread of history" where it had been dropped, as it were, in the distant past.[37]

Like Pinsker, Theodor Herzl availed himself of the maxim "Help yourself and God will help you" when he wrote to the British Zionist Herbert Bentwich, who was about to lead a group of people on a "Maccabean pilgrimage" to the Holy Land in 1897. "We do not believe that it is sufficient to turn to Zion in prayer," he unwittingly reiterated Pinsker's message, "we wish to do so in deeds, as well." A few months later, while preparing for the First Zionist Congress, Herzl sent organizational directives to the Rumanian Zionists and took the occasion to declare: "You and we together, we are the nation, and we will help ourselves." He regarded the convening of the congress as the first step in the process of Jewish self-help and accordingly wrote: "Above all, you have been granted an auspicious opportunity to determine your fate by yourselves." Five years later Herzl described the process of realizing the Zionist vision in his book *Altneuland* ("Old-New Land"). Citing manifestations of growing self-awareness on the part of other peoples, he went on to speak of the awakening of Jewish consciousness: "Only then did our own people, the pariah among the nations, realize that they could expect nothing from fantastic miracle workers, but everything from their own strength . . . '*Gesta Dei per Francos*,' the French once said – and 'God's deeds through the Jews' say the truly pious today, those who do not let the partisan Rabbis incite them."[38]

The new approach that called for an end to Jewish passivity clashed head-on with the long tradition that prescribed waiting for redemption from Providence. This conflict was more than a theological debate. In fact, it became a full-blown struggle for influence over the Jewish public and was therefore marked by sharp polemical exchanges. As we have seen, Herzl himself took a stand in this controversy, but the Zionist position found sharper expression in the

37 Heinrich Loewe, "Der Zionisten Kongress in Basel," *Zion* (October 1897), p. 266; Micha Josef Berdyczewski, *On the Agenda* (Warsaw, 1900), p. 70 (Hebrew).

38 Herzl, *Letters*, pp. 190, 266; Theodor Herzl, *Old-New Land* (Haifa, 1960), p. 83. *Gesta Dei per Francos* is the title of a famous medieval work on the Crusaders. The saying crops up from time to time in the writings of modern national movements.

arguments wielded by Max Nordau, who was a trenchant polemicist. Cogent and positive though its style appeared to be, one of Nordau's articles (published in Hebrew in 1898) elicited a vehemently negative response from Orthodox circles. "Every single one of our brethren," Nordau wrote, "must be fully cognizant of the fact that he is now living through a highly significant period in his history, that the world is waiting for evidence that his powers are enhanced, his spirit uplifted." He posited his irreligious outlook by adding: "Each of us should know that we owe reckoning to future generations" (not to God, as his antagonists would have it).[39] Nordau was even more explicit in a lecture delivered in Vienna on the subject of "Currents in Judaism": "We have abandoned the traditional pathetic stance of our tribe," he said, "and have decided to forge our own destiny on this earth by exercising all our forces." However, Nordau was sometimes known to exceed the norms befitting a broad-based movement and to express his doubts in the form of clever aphorisms. In speaking to the Fifth Zionist Congress, for example, he suggested the startling idea that self-awareness might be overvalued, as it could cause weakness, even impotence: "Who knows whether our forefathers would have kept their faith and upheld their folk traditions with that zealous loyalty that left its indelible mark on history, had they been granted an overview of their people's condition." Nordau depicted earlier generations as being nurtured by a "great past" and believing in "a glorious future of redemption," while paying no mind whatever to the reality of the present. "Unfortunately, " he exhorted his listeners, "we can no longer cloak ourselves in the benign ignorance of our forefathers."

In this case the attitude toward the past was one of complete dissociation. Yet it was a break caused not by choice but arising almost as a *fait accompli*. One could long for the "benign ignorance" of one's forebears or one could deride it (Nordau seems to do both); but there was no denying that the present generation had been inflicted with a sober, clear-eyed view of reality that ran contrary to the ways of the past. It is worthwhile noting that the past is mentioned twice in this passage: once as the "great past" that sustained

---

39 Max Nordau, "The Aim of Zionism," *Ahiasaf Calendar* (1898/9), p. 169 (Hebrew).

earlier generations, a source of consolation and encouragement; then as the more recent past of ignorance and naiveté that constituted real life for them. Since the lives of these generations were intertwined with history, there was apparently absolute continuity between the two phases of the past. Thus unlike Berdyczewski, whose injunction to "pick up the thread of history" essentially meant to return to the point where it had once been torn, Nordau focused his attention only on the present.

To better understand Nordau's approach, we must refer to his book *The Interpretation of History*, where he denied the impact of the "historical sense" on the actions of those who actually make history. "In forming a resolution," he wrote, "the determining factor is the necessity of the present, not the experience of the past." To substantiate this point he further ventured that "the great conquerors, rulers and lawgivers have never possessed what is called the historical: that they had it not was a condition of their success." It was not that Nordau ignored the existence of a Jewish historical heritage, he merely tried to play down its importance. After Herzl had told him of the incipient Uganda program, for example, Nordau remarked at a public lecture that, "Zionism embraces the Jewish historical heritage in its very name," but then immediately qualified the statement by adding, "Do not place the accent on the word 'Zion.' Accentuate the idea that one must take into one's own hands the preparation of one's proper destiny." And to illustrate what he meant, he added, "The Zionists are determined to leave that passive track of the martyr's glory and embark on the high road of vigorous action."[40]

Nordau deserves a special place among those who viewed Zionism as a force capable of creating history for having carried his revolutionary thinking further than anyone else. Not only was he an astute writer with a flair for the unexpected, he was also a more systematic thinker than most of his colleagues. At the close of the nineteenth century, Nordau was known among European intellectuals – and particularly those conversant with German culture – as an incisive

40 Max Nordau, "Strömungen im Judenthum," *Die Welt* (February 3, 1899), p. 2; Max Nordau, *The Interpretation of History* (New York, 1910), p. 23; M. Nordau, "Discours sur l'éducation du peuple juif," *l'Echo Sioniste* (July 15, 1903), p. 128.

critic and brilliant thinker. He was erudite in both the arts and the sciences, a physician and psychiatrist as well as a renowned author and journalist, and he commanded a wide audience within the Zionist fold, not least because of his reputation far beyond it. Nordau was at the pinnacle of his success when he came to Zionism and was well aware of his impact upon the movement. Yet more than any other Western Zionist, he found it difficult to reconcile his *Weltanschauung* with his being a Zionist.

This is of course not the place to examine all of Nordau's views in detail, so that we shall confine ourselves to the more relevant issues. An unabashed atheist, rationalist, and individualist, Nordau had been profoundly influenced by the advances of the natural sciences in his day. As suggested above, he had a very jaundiced view of the "historical sense," regarding it as no more than an "artificial product of the ruling classes who use it as a means for investing the existing order, which is advantageous to themselves alone, with a mystic and poetic charm. . . . Its practical purpose, in a word, is to oppress and deceive the present with the assistance of the past." Nordau also analyzed the ability of a few men of determination and strong character – who were rooted in reality, rather than abstractions – to rule the masses, either by recourse to violence or by forging the symbols of power. Juxtaposed to these rulers was another kind of elite, men of genius and scholarship whose ties extended over many generations; and as Nordau aphorized the nature of this second elite: "Humanity lives by its men of genius but they do not live by it."[41]

How could Nordau's views be reconciled with Zionism? It was reasonable that a man who had been remote from Jews and Judaism for years and then found his way to Zionism would identify mainly with the forward-looking, anti-historical current therein. One may also surmise that Nordau's personal experience as a Hungarian Jew who had lived as a German writer in Paris had predisposed him to adopt an individualistic approach and belittle the value of an historical heritage. When he became a Zionist, rather than joining in the effort to endow the movement with an historic dimension, Nordau

41 Nordau, *The Interpretation of History*, pp. 45, 359; and cf. Karl Mannheim, *Ideology and Utopia* (New York, no date), pp. 134 ff.

threw all his weight behind what he called "the high road of vigorous action."

In concluding this aspect of our discussion, we should note that the advocacy of independent endeavor or self-generated action on the part of the Jews should not be construed as in any way detracting from the international importance that the Zionists ascribed to the Jewish question. Nor did it diminish their expectation of receiving outside help in solving the problem. Pinsker confirmed this principle in writing, "Of course the establishment of a Jewish refuge cannot come about without the support of the governments," and Herzl concurred in his well-known pronouncement, "The Jewish State is something the world needs, and consequently it will come into being." Even a revolutionary Socialist like Ber Borochov, who was skeptical of the motives of the Great Powers, echoed Herzl's words, adding, "*International guarantees* – that is the essence of political Zionism." Clearly, then, while the idea of independent Jewish action negated the prescription to passively await messianic redemption, or to rely on political emancipation and universal progress, it did not preclude seeking and accepting help from outside forces.[42]

Zionism and Messianism

Zionism's attitude toward the messianic idea was highly problematic. For on the one hand it took up arms against reliance on the traditional faith in the coming of the messiah (and thereby sparked an intense conflict with ultra-Orthodox Jewry), while at the same time embracing an Orthodox constituency that had to take a stand on the role that Zionism should play in the process of redemption. Other constituencies within the Zionist movement were also sensitive to the historic associations evoked by the messianic idea. Unsettling encounters with messianism throughout the ages – from the deep, unremitting crisis caused by the advent of Christ through the

---

42 Leon Pinsker, *Road to Freedom: Writings and Addresses* (New York, 1944), p. 105; Herzl, *The Jewish State*, p. 29; Ber Borochov, "On the Question of Zion and Territory" in *Selected Works*, Vol. I. (Tel Aviv, 1944), p. 97 (Hebrew).

more recent experiences with Shabbetai Zvi and Jacob Frank – had left a lasting sense of disappointment in their wake. Nevertheless, there was a certain affinity between the desire to revive Jewish political independence and the traditional messianic hopes.[43] And being conscious of this parallel, the Zionists had to consider the possibility that their movement would be construed as having a definitively messianic bent.

The distinction between messianism and practical Zionism was elucidated as far back as 1881 by Perez Smolenskin, the veteran Hebrew writer and promoter of the Love of Zion movement. When the young Eliezer Ben-Yehuda (later famed for his efforts to revive Hebrew as a vernacular) argued the cause of vigorous Zionist activity, Smolenskin admonished that, "If you are trying to establish colonies in Palestine, more power to you, for in this way you will save many poor souls and offer a haven, etc. . . . But if you claim that through these activities you are paving the way for the messiah, both the believers and the enlightened will rise up against you."[44] On the eve of the establishment of the Zionist Organization, some intellectuals in the West were attracted to the messianic idea because they associated it with the "glorious past," to which they now related with new-found pride. In lecturing to a young audience in Berlin on the occasion of the Ninth of Av, for example, Heinrich Loewe reviewed the events traditionally commemorated on that date (the destruction of both Temples, the fall of Bar-Kokhba's bastion at Betar, and the expulsion from Spain) and declared that the day should stand as a reminder to the Jews that they must "solve the Jewish problem once and for all." Loewe concluded with the pronouncement that the Ninth of Av would then become the day on which the messiah was born (as foretold by ancient Jewish lore).[45] Thus he drew an historical connection between modern Zionism and traditional belief and made no attempt to resolve the clash between the two kinds of redemption, the miraculous and the self-achieved.

43 Jacob Katz, "The Jewish National Movement" in H. H. Ben Sasson and S. Ettinger, eds., *Jewish Society Through the Ages* (New York, 1969), p. 277.

44 Eliezer Ben-Yehuda, *Israel to Its Land and Its Language*, Vol. I, (Jerusalem, 1929), p. 221 (Hebrew).

45 "Nationale Bewegung," *Zion* (August 15, 1895), p. 212.

Another approach proposed a solution that harmoniously embraced both kinds of redemption. Osias Thon, one of several young men from Galicia studying in Berlin who were closely associated with Ahad Ha'am, wrote an article at the end of 1896 propounding a basis for Zionism that was derived from the philosophy of history. Thon claimed that Zionism was not a reaction to antisemitism but a response to an immanent need in Jewish history. This was one of the differences in outlook that divided Ahad Ha'am's followers from the political Zionists. Thon's contribution was in forging a link between modern Zionism and traditional messianism by determining that "messianism was the way in which Jewish nationalism expressed itself in the past." His argument was that messianism had assumed many forms, ranging from "silent hope, prayer and longings" to "eruptive outbreaks of the messianic revolution," and he considered Zionism to be "an extension of messianism." What distinguished it from these earlier manifestations, however, was the shift from "the anticipation of a miracle" and "a redeemer from without" to what Thon characterized as "redemption from within."[46] This view traced the various manifestations of Jewish messianism – including Zionism – to a common denominator: Jewish nationalism. Moreover, it would seem to have resolved the contradiction between the passive messianic expectations of the ultra-Orthodox and Zionism's advocacy of self-assertion, and it even endowed Zionism with something of an historical lineage.

With the rise of political Zionism, the messianic association became even more pronounced because of the movement's contention that it could solve the Jewish problem at a single stroke, on a large scale, and with panache. Herzl was even depicted by his admirers – and mocked by his detractors – as a latter-day biblical hero, the king of the Jews, even as the messiah incarnate and hence the very epitome of the messianic motif.[47]

---

46 O. Thon, "Zur geschichtsphilosophischen Begründung des Zionismus," *Zion* (December 1, 1896), pp. 320, 322.

47 Israel Zangwill compared Herzl to Tiglath-pileser, king of Assyria; see Maurice Wohlgelernter, *Israel Zangwill: A Study* (New York and London, 1964), p. 155.

It must be said that Herzl was not oblivious to the messianic image that he and his movement projected; nor was he loath to play upon it for his own ends. For he not only spoke of having had messianic dreams as a child, he even contrasted himself with Shabbetai Zvi, the seventeenth century "false Messiah", in noting that: The difference between myself and Shabbetai Zvi (the way I imagine him), apart from the difference in the technical means inherent in the times, is that Shabbetai Zvi made himself great so as to be the equal of the great of the earth. I, however, find the great small, as small as myself." Yet clearly Herzl was taken by Shabbetai Zvi's character. In *Altneuland,* his novel projecting into the future, Herzl had Shabbetai Zvi appear at a performance of the opera attended by the book's main characters. As they discussed the matter of the "false Messiah", Herzl had one of them remark that Shabbetai Zvi was ahead of his time and that "the longing brings forth the Messiah."[48] Thus his attitude toward Shabbetai Zvi was romantic and essentially positive (whereas the assessment of Ahad Ha'am, who disparaged the political Zionists as the "kind of people who once followed Shabbetai Zvi," was wholly negative[49]).

Herzl was also compared to an Assyrian prince by Emma Gottheil, a Zionist from the United States, see Tulo Nussenblatt, ed., *Theodor Herzl Jahrbuch* (Vienna, 1937), p. 225. Marcus Ehrenpreis called him "a king from head to toe," see L. Yaffe, ed., *The Congress Book* (Jerusalem 1950) p. 235 (Hebrew). The writer Mordecai Ben-Ammi referred to him as "the messiah, son of David" (*ibid.*, p. 125). Shmarya Levin compared Herzl to Gideon, Samson, and most of all to Moses; see Shmarya Levin, *Memoirs*, Vol. III (Tel Aviv, 1939), p. 121 (Hebrew). Repeated references to him as "king" and "messiah" during his visit to Palestine can be found in Aaron Vardi, *My King in Zion* (Tel Aviv, 1931), pp. 36, 56, 76, 78, 84, 113, 152-153 (Hebrew). He was referred to ironically as "king of Zion" in Karl Kraus, *Eine Krone für Zion* (Vienna, 1898), p. 20, and Rabbi Sigmund Maybaum spoke of Herzl's delusions of grandeur in regarding himself as a second Bar-Kokhba (letter dated July 21, 1897, preserved in the Central Archives for the History of the Jewish People, Jerusalem, marked Gesammtarchiv M 4/1).

48 Alex Bein, *Theodore Herzl* (Philadelphia, 1962), pp. 202, 306; Herzl, *Diaries*, Vol. III, p. 960, Vol. IV, p. 1544; Herzl, *Old-New Land*, p. 83.
49 Ahad Ha'am, "The Weepers," *Hashiloah*, 12 (1903), p. 145 (Hebrew).

Yet characteristically, perhaps, to the world at large Herzl insisted that Zionism bore no relationship to messianism. At an audience with the king of Italy in 1904, when asked "if there were still Jews who expected a Messiah," Herzl replied unequivocally, "Naturally, Your Majesty, in the religious circles. In our own, the academically trained and enlightened circles, no such thought exists, of course." He stressed that the Zionist movement was a "purely national" one (as opposed to a religious-messianic movement) and even amused his royal host by describing the pains he took in Palestine to avoid riding a white horse or donkey "so that no one would embarrass me by thinking I was the Messiah." Thus it was sound political sense as much as secular rationalism that prompted Herzl and his colleagues to distance themselves from any hint of messianism. Nordau too made a point of stressing that the Zionist leaders had never pretended they could "perform miracles for their people," adding that "The leaders of the Zionist movement do not entertain the heretical thought, Heaven forbid, that they are messiahs to their people, not even petty messiahs." And elsewhere he wrote, "None of us makes himself out to be a messiah or an instrument of the messiah."

J. C. Ravnitski, an associate of Ahad Ha'am's, wrote in an almost identical vein: "None of the great Zionists refers to himself, Heaven forbid, as anything of a messiah."[50] But Ahad Ha'am ascribed messianic pretensions to political Zionism, both in the sense that it magnified illusions (in contrast to the pathetically poor prospects) and that it invested unwarranted faith in the power of the movement's leader. Immediately after the First Zionist Congress, he deplored the imprudence of the Zionist leadership in not having stated "clearly that the Messiah was not yet in sight" and by this omission having "kindled the false fire" in peoples' hearts. In analyzing the relationship between the Zionist movement and its leader, albeit after Herzl's death, he concluded that political Zionism was "essentially the 'old messianic' belief." Thus he had no doubt that Herzl's passing would bring about a fundamental change in the character of Zionism and

50 Herzl, *Diaries*, Vol. IV, p. 1599; Max Nordau, "The Aim of Zionism," *Ahiasaf Calendar* (1898/9), p. 166 (Hebrew); Max Nordau, "On Zionism's Message," *Hashiloah*, 4 (1898), p. 554 (Hebrew); R. (J. C. Ravnitski), "Who Is a Jew?" *Der Yud*, 9 (1899), p. 2 (Yiddish).

that it would cease to be a "big mass movement." In a private letter Ahad Ha'am expressed himself rather more caustically in writing, "I do not believe in the prospect of keeping 'messianism' alive now that the 'messiah' is dead," and forecast hopefully that Zionism could return to being a "movement of *historic national rebirth.*"[51]

This dim view of the messianic tenor of political Zionism was not very different, as it turned out, from the reproof of Ahad Ha'am's own Orthodox critics. Rabbi Elijah Akiva Rabinowitz, who broke with the Zionist movement after the Second Congress because of his opposition to the "*kultura*" advocated by Ahad Ha'am's disciples, reminded his readers of the divine proscription: "*Do not force the issue*" (of the coming of the messiah). His depiction of the perils lurking in political Zionism is reminiscent of the traditional admonitions against messianic movements in the past: "It may distract the people from the constant task of providing for their families and from their obligations to their countries of residence." Rabinowitz expressed fears, much like those of Ahad Ha'am, that political Zionism was "no more than a vain illusion" that would end in utter despair.

But Orthodox Jews who championed the Zionist cause maintained precisely the opposite view. At about the same time, another rabbi who also happened to be named Rabinowitz, came out in support of Zionism on religious grounds. Rabbi Samuel Jacob Rabinowitz, one of the Lovers of Zion, drew support for his stand from the dictum charging Jews to "dwell in the Land of Israel." Like Herzl, however, he focused attention on the "contemporary conditions in which we live," for they enabled the Jews, "with the help of the Almighty, blessed be He, to put the idea of settling the land into practice." Rabinowitz distinguished between Zionism and the "pure, unadulterated faith, the messianic faith," and like Heinrich Loewe before him referred to the legend that the messiah had been born on the day that the Temple was destroyed. He proclaimed that "Zionism does not force that issue" and declared emphatically that "Zionism

---

51 Achad Haam, *Ten Essays on Zionism and Judaism* (London, 1922), pp. 27-28; Ahad Ha'am, *Collected Works* (Tel Aviv-Jerusalem, 1961), pp. 250-251 (Hebrew); Ahad Ha'am, *Letters*, Vol. III, (Tel Aviv, 1957), p. 354 (Hebrew).

bears no relation, connection, or resemblance to the false messianic movement."[52]

Religious Zionism's clear-cut distinction between messianic faith and the injunction to dwell in the Land of Israel was not adequately understood by its secular opponents. Take, for example, Jacob Bernstein-Cohen's complaint that at the Second Zionist Congress, Herzl had opportunistically favored the Orthodox delegates so as to "disseminate throughout the world the fiction that the Zionists pay homage to the ancient spiritual tradition." He fairly jeered in his memoirs that Herzl had used a delegation of rabbis headed by Elijah Akiva Rabinowitz to "adorn the congress hall," adding no less derisively that "the rabbis demonstratively kissed the hand of the new messiah." Apparently the connotation of the term "new messiah" was different for Bernstein-Cohen than it was for Ahad Ha'am. The latter spoke mockingly of Herzl as the "messiah" but expressed his fears in the traditional vein regarding false messiahs, whereas Bernstein-Cohen saw the "new messiah" as the epitome of the clericalist ambitions so abhorrent to him. Bernstein-Cohen mentioned this in his memoirs and thus had sufficient time to develop the perspective necessary to grasp the difference between religious Zionism and the anti-Zionism of the ultra-Orthodox; yet he continued to perceive all religious groups, including modern Western rabbis, as cut from the same cloth. At any rate, he completely misjudged the attitude of the religious Jews; none of them – including the supporters of Zionism – ever regarded Herzl as the messiah.

This misapprehension is even more apparent in the words (penned at about the same time) of a Zionist in Paris who was in sympathy with the Democratic Fraction. Early in 1902 Albert Rokéach expressed in *l'Echo Sioniste* his apprehension that people might consider Zionism "a religious, messianic movement," particularly when they saw men in long caftans with sidelocks and skullcaps dominating the rostrum of the Zionist Congress as if they were in "a conquered land." Rokéach required no further proof of the connection between religious Zionism and messianism, and he favored the

---

52 Elijah Akiva Rabinowitz, *Justice Shall Redeem Zion* (Warsaw, 1899), p. 10 (Hebrew); Samuel Jacob Rabinowitz, *Religion and Nationalism* (Warsaw, 1900), p. 127-129 (Hebrew).

establishment of the Democratic Fraction in order to keep Zionism from being identified with this trend.[53]

In contradistinction to the anti-clericalism that associated messianism with religion and thus repudiated it, a secular-messianic current reemerged in Zionism after Herzl's death and synthesized certain ideas that had been circulating for some time. It inverted the wide-spread criticism of Jewish passivity in waiting for the messiah and tried to reimbue messianism with the earthy, militant quality that it had apparently originally possessed. Micha Josef Berdyczewski, cited here for his call to "pick up the thread of history," was representative of this mood. In an article published in 1905, he wrote that: "Zionism has had the courage to negate the period of history since the Jews entered the lives of the nations, simply to leap over it and link up again at the point where the Jewish people still harbored hopes for itself and raised the banner of redemption. Zionism is the continuation of messianism." Israel Zangwill, the Territorialist leader, approximated Berdyczewski's outlook when he spoke of renouncing the belief in a messiah "who is perpetually coming tomorrow." Offering his own alternative to the savior who never arrives, he proposed that the messiah had already come in the form of Zionism. Zangwill's approach to messianism was also similar to Berdyczewski's in substance. He spoke of the Zionist flag that would soon fly over a chunk of land where "Marrano Judaism" would be superseded by "Maccabean Judaism"[54] – thus inadvertently warping the image of the Marranos from martyrs desperately trying to maintain their Jewish identity into renegades eager to deny it.

One cannot ignore the recurrent contradiction between the invitation to leap over an entire era of history and the desire to establish historical integrity of both time and place. Yet the leap can be viewed as a dialectic process, following Gershom Scholem's proposition that "The ideal content of the past at the same time delivers

---

53 Bernstein-Cohen, *The Bernstein-Cohen Book*, p. 122; A. Rokéach, "Le Congrès de la Jeunesse," *l'Echo Sioniste*, Paris (February 15, 1902), p. 44.

54 M. J. Berdyczewski, "Zur Klärung" in Lazar Schön, ed., *Die Stimme der Wahrheit* (Würzburg, 1905), p. 282; Israel Zangwill, *Speeches, Articles and Letters* (London, 1937), p. 226.

the basis for the vision of the future."[55] Against that leap stands Thon's conception of messianism, which integrated historical continuity and various messianic currents with modern Zionism.

In summary, we can divide the views about Zionism and messianism into three categories:

* Zionism is a messianic movement and is therefore deplorable.
* Zionism is essentially a messianic movement, but that is to its credit.
* Zionism is not a messianic movement, which is as it should be.

Logic dictates that we add a fourth category, namely: Zionism is not a messianic movement, which is to its detriment. But no one held that position – and understandably so, since at the time there was hardly justification for arguing that Zionism was not messianic enough. Much to the contrary, those who looked favorably upon messianism had every reason to be pleased with the general disposition of the Zionist movement. Thus Zionism had surpassed traditional messianism, whose most outstanding feature was passivity, and was moving toward a new kind of messianism symbolized by the striving for self-generated salvation. Moreover, both the advocates and the opponents of Zionist messianism seemed to have concurred in their assessment of Zionism as a modern messianic movement.

We have also looked into another kind of opposition to messianism, one that charged Zionism with having absorbed its messianic tenor from religious sources. In their desire to purge Zionism of clericalism, these critics of messianism demonstrated a fundamental misunderstanding of the forces at work in religious circles. At the time, religious Zionism was not yet imbued with the perception of Zionism as "the onset of the redemption." The fact is that Zionist messianism during the period under discussion was fundamentally secular, despite its exploitation of historical themes and symbols borrowed from the religious tradition.[56]

55. Gershom Scholem, *The Messianic Idea in Judaism* (New York, 1971), p. 4.
56 On Zionism as messianism, see Simon Dubnow, *Nationalism and History* (New York, 1970), p. 157; for a contrary assessment, see Scholem, *The Messianic Idea in Judaism*, pp. 35-36.

Historical Necessity

The search for historical evidence to prove the Zionist contention, which we have already viewed from a number of vantage points, was not the only endeavor that involved an inquiry into Jewish history. From the outset, the past played a basic role in the personal search for Jewish identity, especially on the part of those Jews who came to Zionism from an assimilated background. The Jewish community and the religious rite as practiced in the West did not attract the national-minded Jew, because they signified a negation of Jewish nationhood,[57] while the incipient Zionist movement could not as yet be an object of identification. Hence the early Zionists coming from an assimilated environment looked to history as the link connecting them with Judaism. For example, Heinrich Loewe, who can well symbolize the awakening of Jewish national consciousness among German Jews, regarded Zionism as a means of falling in with the trend of historical development. In two articles published on this subject in 1895, he explained the relationship between nationalism and history as follows: "If the nation is indeed a result of historical evolution, a product of its history, then the link with consistent national thinking lies in the acknowledgment of one's own past." Further on in the piece he stated: "In settling in the land of our fore-fathers, we are drawing a conclusion from our history." And else-where Loewe spoke of the need to establish a Jewish museum in Jerusalem and to collect building stones for the sake of "reconstructing the past," explaining that "historians are the earliest harbingers and noblest bearers of national ideas and truly popular aspirations."[58]

His brand of nationalism was heavily influenced by German His-toricism, which held that "the value of anything can be accounted for through the discovery of its origins."[59] It also reflected a desire

---

57 Sammy Gronemann, *The Memoirs of a Jekke*, Vol. I (Tel Aviv, 1946), pp. 27-31 (Hebrew).
58 Heinrich Loewe, "Der Nationalismus," *Zion* (March 15, 1895), p. 41; Heinrich Loewe, "Ein jüdisches Museum," *Zion* (June 17, 1895), p. 124.
59 Dagobert D. Runes et al., *Dictionary of Philosophy* (Ames, Iowa, 1955), p. 127.

to draw conclusions from history – in this case to place the Zionist endeavor within an historical process, or, put differently, to ascribe to history certain immutable laws that must be recognized in order for human activity to take place therein. Armed with this historical approach, young Zionists were determined to challenge the ethos that had reigned in German-Jewish life since the days of Moses Mendelssohn. They regarded the rationalist philosophy of the eighteenth century as a force that encouraged assimilation and conversion because it lacked an understanding of history and its implications. Thus Theodor Zlocisti, a doctor, Zionist writer, and poet, accused Mendelssohn and his associates of suffering from a lack of "historical *sense* that regards history as *more* than a series of arbitrary, consecutive events devoid of all coherence." Zlocisti was not obliged to produce any better proof of his claim than Mendelssohn's well-known saying, "I constantly yawn when I read anything historical." And from there he led his readers directly to the fact that Mendelssohn's offspring had converted, as if conversion were the direct corollary of – or retribution for – Mendelssohn's indifference to history. Zlocisti also inquired at length into the writings of Moses Hess, and it was probably there that he found his inspiration for a heightened faith in history's power to accord meaning to Jewish life.[60]

Evidently, this great faith in the power of history had long been a feature of the Zionist critique and of nationalist expectations. Even Pinsker invoked history when he wrote that "the *general* history of the present day seems called to be *our* ally." He characterized the recurrent phenomenon of Jewish refugees as "the fugitives whom our historic and predestined fate will always create for us." Similarly, Gustav Cohen, a native of Germany who had spent many years in South Africa and England, drew a lesson from the great wave of emigration from Eastern Europe to the West and concluded fatalistically: "No, I have become increasingly aware that sooner or later the old game will start here all over again."[61]

60 Theodor Zlocisti, "Woran wir kranken," *Zion* (August 15, 1895), pp. 190-191; Arthur Hertzberg, ed., *The Zionist Idea* (New York, 1981), pp. 36-37.
61 Pinsker, "Autoemancipation," p. 196; Cohen, *Die Judenfrage und die Zukunft*, p. 37.

The Zionist and Socialist Saul Raphael Landau spoke of history in theological terms that were evocative of Hegel's philosophy: "Let us open the pages of our history, and throughout it we shall find the stamp of a more Divine Providence, the manifestation of that great verse: 'World history is the world's judgment'" (Friedrich Schiller). Another little-known figure from the early days of Zionism was the American lawyer Adam Rosenberg, an Orthodox Lover of Zion who had emigrated from Germany. In 1895, while in Paris on a mission for a Zionist society in New York, Rosenberg called for the establishment of a world Zionist organization that would make the Zionists into a force of consequence among the Jews "as they must surely become, sooner or later, by virtue of historical necessity."[62]

Two Zionists who were interested in the philosophy of history, Nathan Birnbaum and Osias Thon, both developed the theme of Zionism's role as an intermediary between European culture and the Orient, and both spoke of it in terms of "the will of history." In 1896 Thon wrote that the Jews were being deposed from their positions as middlemen in the economy and were being driven toward Zionism "whether we wish it or not." On the other hand, he regarded the constructive side of carrying European culture to the Orient as a voluntary mission. Birnbaum, in contrast, spoke of the return of the Jews to their homeland, symbolizing a fusion between East and West, as a matter of predestination. All of Jewish history was his evidence that it was no mere coincidence that the Jews had remained "one people, imperishable and indivisible," and that "Zionism fathomed the will of history and interpreted it correctly." Elsewhere Birnbaum again articulated the notion of "the imperative of the Jewish state" in the process of integration between East and West.[63] This article was written after the publication of Herzl's *The Jewish State* and therefore brings us into the focal period of our discussion: the

62 Saul Raphael Landau, *Sturm und Drang im Zionismus* (Vienna, 1937), p. 270; Adam Rosenberg, "Der Zionismus in Amerika," *Zion*, Berlin (August 15, 1895), p. 202.

63 Osias Thon, *Essays zur Zionistischen Ideologie* (Berlin, 1930), p. 22; B. (Birnbaum), "Die Antwort der Zionisten an das Freie Blatt," *Selbst-Emancipation* (March 20, 1893), p. 2; Matthias Acher, "Die jüdische Moderne," *Zion*, Berlin (November 1, 1896), p. 298.

era of political Zionism and the establishment of the World Zionist Organization.

As we saw in the discussion on historical action, Herzl occupied the middle ground between those who subscribed to historical determinism and the anti-historical innovators. As a visionary he was suffused with a sense of historical mission, but as a Zionist statesman he had to pay heed to the realistic prospects of the day and feared that he would miss the "historic moment." Herzl did not take an interest in the philosophy of history, but he often spoke of history in a sense that provided emotional depth to immediate objectives. If we arrange certain of his pronouncements in chronological order, we can see that he perceived matters dynamically, rather than being bound by a rigid system of thought or set of principles.

In *The Jewish State* Herzl made the famous pronouncement that "the Jewish State is something the world needs, and consequently it will come into being." The implication here was almost deterministic. In any event, it was heavily dependent upon objective processes that Herzl believed were working in the direction desired by Zionism. His main objective at that point was to prove that his vision was not utopian. In the course of 1896, as he took his first steps toward political negotiations, he occasionally expressed the fear that he would fail to act at the opportune moment, though he expected that luck would smile upon him and effect a decisive turnabout in favor of his cause. Herzl was troubled because, in his words, "if today I simply dropped the project, it would surely remain undone." Shortly afterward he wrote, "It's now or never that we shall obtain Palestine" and "I believe we are at a great turning point in our history," but then he fretted that "the historical moment in which the solution of the Jewish Question is possible may be missed." Such sentiments punctuated his letters, conversations, and diary. In 1897 Herzl was already complaining that if only the proposal he had made the previous year had been heeded, "we would already have (Palestine) today." It is as if he believed that man has the power to accomplish almost anything, if only he acts at the right moment. Hence the theme dominating Herzl's writings is the "historic moment," not the general course of history.

In summing up the first two Zionist congresses, Herzl combined the theme of will, which was so pronounced during his first year of

70

public activity, with the historical perspective (of which he spoke in his Foreword to *The Jewish State*). On September 9, 1897, he wrote in his diary that "our movement has entered the stream of history," immediately adding the pronouncement, "At Basel I founded the Jewish State." What we have here is not a flight of rapture over the establishment of the Zionist Organization but the endowment of that act with an historical dimension. At the same time, it is portrayed not only as an act of human will but, indeed, as the accomplishment of a single man. One could say that Herzl regarded himself as a man who had made history by channeling human action into the course of objective processes. To illustrate that he had not created history in a vacuum, we have his qualification in *Altneuland* (which was styled as a retrospective upon the already established Jewish state): "It could not have been different – and it could not have been earlier. The technical age had first to arrive." And subsequently he enumerated the prerequisites for the realization of the Zionist program: modern technology, colonialism, and the regeneration of the Jews themselves.[64]

His dual role as ideologue and political leader evidently led Herzl to effect a synthesis between the two orientations – the volitional and the determinist – without being disturbed by the internal contradictions that occasionally resulted from this approach. It is interesting to compare this phenomenon with the synthesis forged by a young East-European Zionist student in Heidelberg by the name of Joseph Klausner. In 1897 Klausner published a long theoretical article in the periodical *Hashiloah* – edited by his mentor, Ahad Ha'am – in which he juxtaposed the development of Zionism and the new Hebrew culture with the prevailing intellectual currents in Europe. The point of this article was essentially to refute the doctrine of determinism – and especially the Hegelian analogy between nations and living organisms that pass through the stages of youth, maturity, and old age. Klausner disputed the very existence of historical laws. He defined himself as a champion of "personal initiative" but nevertheless recommended a sophisticated dialectical approach "to the

---

64 Herzl, *The Jewish State*, p. 29; Herzl, *Diaries*, Vol. II, pp. 439, 459, 467, 497, 533, 581; Herzl, *Old-New Land*, p. 144.

forces of history" with the intention "to exploit them in order to defeat them."

The implications of this formula can be seen in Klausner's treatment of the Maccabean war. As if reiterating Nordau's judgment about the myopia of earlier generations, Klausner wrote: "If the Hasmoneans in antiquity had measured their forces against those of the Syrians, if they had weighed through cold logic how superior were the forces of Greek culture . . . compared to the meager and isolated forces of Jewry, our heroes would unquestionably have come to the conclusion that there was no hope for Israel." However, in contrast to Nordau, who regarded such behavior as outmoded "benign ignorance," at best, Klausner spoke of the same phenomenon in unequivocally positive terms: "The Hasmoneans were filled with a sense of courage and were not concerned with calculating the odds." He transformed their irrational conduct into a qualitative factor in the balance of forces with the Seleucids. As a disciple of Ahad Ha'am, Klausner accorded moral and spiritual import to the Hasmoneans' subjective faith. Thus his description of what at first appeared to be a pointless struggle by a group of fanatics against a superior culture, culminated with the writer betraying his deep emotional identification: "They believed that the spirit would prevail over matter – and the great *psychological force* actually did achieve a massive and wondrous victory over the awesome *physical force*." Klausner, who was to become a renowned historian of the age of Jesus, discovered a universal key in the Maccabean revolt, namely, the "psychological force." Even though he seemed to accentuate the singular, individual, and volitional in history, he maintained that the key was not limited to the Hasmonean period alone but was valid for all times. In the last analysis, this was an attempt to create a theory of history based on spiritual nationalism, which in the course of time becomes in turn one of the "forces of history."[65]

Just as Klausner found that faith can motivate action and become a "force of history," so it was possible to note a parallel phenomenon, namely, that the Zionists drew encouragement from the belief

---

65 J. Klausner, "The Establishment of a New Jewish Movement," *Hashiloah*, 2 (1897), pp. 541, 543, 544 (Hebrew); on Hegel's approach see G.F.W. Hegel, *The Philosophy of History* (New York, 1956), p. 75.

that their endeavor was consonant with the laws of history. This motif recurred in the writings of various personalities within different Zionist factions. Sometimes it was a spontaneous expression of faith; at others it derived from the writer's world view. One example of this sense of congruity with the forces of history can be found in the address delivered at the First Zionist Congress by Max Bodenheimer, one of the most prominent leaders of the German Zionists. Bodenheimer lambasted the opponents of Zionism, comparing them to the Hellenists of the Hasmonean era and to Josephus Flavius in Roman times. "History will march on," he declaimed, "condemning the derision of these gentlemen just as it condemned the traitors of antiquity – the Hellenistic High Priest Menelaus and the pseudo-Roman Josephus Flavius – to everlasting infamy."[66]

Just as there was an implied historical or typological connection between the traitors of antiquity and the assimilationists of Bodenheimer's time, so too there was a parallel connection between the faithful throughout the ages and the modern Zionists. Of course it was difficult to single out the paragons as categorically as the villains. Still, we are able to point to military heroes such as Judah the Maccabee and Bar-Kokhba as figures popular among Zionists. The criterion for history's judgment seemed to be national fidelity, an unequivocal yardstick equally applicable to all generations. Yet such thinking assumed that history was on the side of the faithful and against the traitors – which inevitably led to the need to account for the common disparity between lofty ideals and actual success. This was a very real issue because a political movement uses history as an ideological weapon to assert itself. Hence Bodenheimer's and Klausner's historical analogies could be taken as evidence that Zionism was inclined toward reckless adventurism and preferred the heroic ideal over sober political considerations. Herzl also faced this problem in measuring himself up against the figure of Shabbetai Zvi and seeking to prove that because conditions had changed, he and his movement were immune to the failure that had defeated his predecessors. These pitfalls explain the inherent need to appeal time and again to the "Tribunal of History" for assurance that Zionism

---

66   Max Bodenheimer, "Rede am 1ten Zionistenkongress," *Die Welt* (September 10, 1897), p. 9.

was likely to succeed. For the heroic motif and the heritage of national fidelity were dwarfed by – and perhaps even at odds with – the supreme need to support the Zionist claim to success – or, to put it another way, the dynamic reading of history superseded the immutable historical ideal.

In the rather indignant words of Fabius Schach, an East-European Jew who became a Zionist writer in Germany: "We Zionists are idealists, but we are no dreamers." After appraising the actual value of Zionism for East-European Jewry and examining the obstacles to reaching its objectives, Schach concluded emphatically: "*But this is the only way dictated to us by history and reason.*" And Lilienblum concurred: "The death of a people, like its birth, is an *historic pageant*, and history is not made by intention. All one can do is clear the way before its inexorable course." The well-known ophthalmologist from Kiev, Dr. Mandelstamm, explained his commitment to Zionism on the grounds of both historical feasibility and historical necessity. At first he chided that "solving the Jewish question or leaving it unsolved depends solely on the will of the Jews themselves," but in the end he proclaimed that "the Zionist movement is a marvelous force that we should not, *could* not oppose, even if we wanted to." And to leave no doubt about the significance of this sentence, he added: "It is the voice of the times, a reflection of nature as seen among other nations . . . This movement has been sired by neither arrogance nor malice but by *natural necessity.*"

Nahum Sokolow approached the same point from a somewhat different angle. "Zionism," he stated, "is not a human creation; it arises as an inevitable outcome of the situation."[67] Sololow was not a dogmatic man, and although this statement was couched in absolute terms he was not arguing the case of historical determinism but reinforcing the image of Zionism as a genuine popular movement. This is apparently how we are to interpret the many spontaneous statements of a similar order. Though usually not anchored in a specific

---

67 F. S. (Fabius Schach), "Der Zionismus," *Jüdischer Volkskalender* (1897-1898), p. 20; M. L. Lilienblum, "Aimlessness and the Right to Exist," *Hashiloah*, 13 (1904), pp. 490 (Hebrew); Max Mandelstamm, "Why I Am a Zionist," *Hashiloah*, 6 (1899), pp. 557, 559-560 (Hebrew); Nahum Sokolow, *To Masters and Mentors* (Warsaw, 1901), p. 107 (Hebrew).

world view, they try to prove the Zionist case by associating the movement with great historical forces. Even Max Nordau, whose denigration of "the historical sense" was quoted at length earlier in this chapter, sometimes slipped into lapses of this sort. Ironically, it was in his rebuttal of Ahad Ha'am's critique of Herzl's *Altneuland* that Nordau resorted to arguments characteristic of his adversaries. In his desire to establish the legitimacy of political Zionism, he insisted that it was not a whim or the arbitrary product of an individual effort. Much to the contrary, he argued, it "arose organically, as a natural necessity, out of the Jewish condition in Exile."[68] As we have said, however, this contention was not characteristic of Nordau's thinking.

A definite inclination toward historical determinism began to emerge among the young disciples of Ahad Ha'am, members of the Democratic Fraction. One of these young men, Martin Buber, made a highly impressive speech about Jewish art at the Fifth Zionist Congress, proclaiming the renewal of Jewish life in its entirety. In speaking of the literary awakening as one aspect of the Jewish national movement, Buber said that it should be regarded not as a "chance episode but as a necessity." True to his system of thought, he spoke of the new movement, replete with its spiritual manifestations, as a "living organism." In the Introduction to the *Jüdischer Almanach* of 1903, his friend Berthold Feiwel wrote of the "liberated powers of the race" and of the birth of "the new spirit" through "the marriage of the people with Mother Earth" (a paraphrase of the erotic motif previously favored by Vasily Bermann and Nathan Birnbaum). Further on he elucidated the connection between the heritage of the "magnificent past" and modern national culture. Yet he concluded in a tone tinged with some intellectual skepticism: "One would think that history had aimed toward these days to come."

Reviewing the above-mentioned *Jüdischer Almanach* in *Hashiloah* for the benefit of Hebrew readers, Marcus Ehrenpreis spoke of the need for liberation from both tradition and the Enlightenment, whose spokesmen "had brought the great forces of history down low." He believed that the rationalist Enlightenment was guilty of

68 Max Nordau. "Achad Haam über *Altneuland*," *Die Welt* (March 13, 1903), p. 4.

spreading "the beautiful dreams about the future victory of some *humanity* that never existed" and were an obstacle to "the natural and necessary process of our 'resurrection.'" Even the most down-to-earth member of the Democratic Fraction, Chaim Weizmann, wrote in a personal letter: "We are Jews, our destiny is different from that of any other people, we are a chosen nation, chosen in suffering, in torment." However, further on in the letter he admitted parenthetically: "I feel that some sort of an ascetic attitude to life has begun developing in me, and I am afraid of it."[69]

During the Uganda crisis Ahad Ha'am, the spiritual mentor so revered by this group, spoke derisively of the "weepers" from the ranks of the opposition to Herzl, for not fighting him forcefully enough. In proclaiming his own resolute attitude toward Palestine, he used familiar terminology: "We raise our eyes to Zion, and to Zion alone, not out of free choice but out of natural necessity." And lest it be said that Ahad Ha'am had adopted the deterministic approach solely in regard to the Palestine question, using it to reinforce his already emphatic opposition to the least deviation from principle, let us quote from a letter he wrote a few years later describing the migration from Russia to America in terms of historical determinism, somewhat similar to his friend Simon Dubnow's "law of survival of the Jewish people": " 'And the sun rises and the sun goes down': that is the law of development of the Jews in the diaspora till the end of days, when its sun will again rise in the place toward which it strives and will roam no more."[70]

To understand the disposition of Ahad Ha'am and his disciples toward historical determinism, we must examine their common point of departure. The relationship between Ahad Ha'am and the Democratic Fraction was not organizationally binding, and neither could they be regarded as an entity in the ideological sense. Even the Fraction itself was not all of a piece and certainly should not be

---

69 M. Buber, "Jüdische Kunst" in *Protokoll V Zionistencongress, Basel 1901* (Vienna, 1901), p. 166; Feiwel, ed., *Jüdischer Almanach*, p. 11; M. Ehrenpreis, "A Literary View," *Hashiloah*, 11 (1903), p. 187 (Hebrew); Weizmann, *Letters*, Vol. III, p. 271.

70 Ahad Ha'am, "The Weepers," *Hashiloah*, 12 (1903), p. 149 (Hebrew); Ahad Ha'am, *Letters*, edited by the author, Vol. III (Jerusalem-Berlin, 1924), p. 255 (Hebrew); cf. Dubnow, *Nationalism and History*, pp. 325-335.

credited with a consummate philosophy. However, some ideas were characteristic of this group, as was a mood shared by many of its members, and together they determined the Fraction's approach to current affairs and its *modus operandi* within Zionism. On a number of issues, the Fraction did not follow the lead of its mentor – the most prominent of these being its participation in the Zionist Organization, while Ahad Ha'am remained outside of (indeed, reserved toward) that framework. Nevertheless, Ahad Ha'am and the Democratic Fraction similarly regarded Judaism as an historical organism. Both were opposed to Herzl's political Zionism – which was based upon the Jews responding to pressure from without – and this was the platform of their common cause against the policies of the Zionist leadership in many spheres. Since Ahad Ha'am and the Democratic Fraction both viewed the Jewish people as an organic entity with historical roots, they likewise shared a desire to make Zionism into a movement for immanent revival.[71]

The organic-historical approach did not attempt to create something *ab ovo* but sought rather to release forces latent within the people. To this school of thought, political Zionism seemed extraneous and artificial, whereas it strove to identify with a phenomenon that had existed for centuries and sought to give new direction to internal processes. Ahad Ha'am, Buber, Feiwel, and others of their ilk had an intellectual need to resort to concepts such as the "law of development" or "the natural and necessary process." It is not by chance that those who preached the doctrine of the historical organism came by these terms, for such concepts reflected a certain intellectual climate. In this context it is interesting to note Joseph Klausner's misgivings about historical determinism for fear that it might pronounce the Jews an organism whose time had come to die.

Members of the Democratic Fraction had many tenets in common, but certainly not an entire world view or systematic philosophy. However, two other groups within the Zionist movement professed a full-fledged doctrine: the religious Zionists and the Marxists. During the period under consideration, there was scant theoretical discussion among religious Zionists, and very few

---

71 See the program of the Democratic Fraction in Y. Klausner, *Opposition to Herzl* (Jerusalem, 1960), pp. 179, 182 (Hebrew).

expressed a penchant for theological determinism. One argument of this kind can be found in a book published with the consent of the leader of Mizrahi, Rabbi Reines, though it sounds inordinately simplistic: "And we Israelites who truly believe that man does not so much as lift a finger on earth unless it is ordained from above, can we believe that so great a movement as the Zionist movement is a matter of chance? And can we believe it natural that a single Jew would be so bold as to initiate a great movement such as this?" In other words, Herzl's advent was not a matter of a personal initiative; it was not even a natural phenomenon but rather the work of Divine Providence. Also of interest is the concluding part of this argument: "For we know that the nature of the diaspora Jew is to be as timid and terrified and as cowardly as a rabbit." Here was presumably proof that Providence was responsible for the appearance of Herzl, the emergence of Zionism, and the transformation of cowardly Jews into heroes. It is reasonable to assume that religious Zionists did not usually adopt the deterministic stance, considering that their ultra-Orthodox opponents could use it more easily to justify the status quo and stave off any changes. Faced with the ultra-Orthodox masses that would not admit Zionism while clinging firmly to a rigid deterministic tradition, the religious Zionists apparently wished to bring tidings of change more than predestination.[72]

Without question, historical determinism left its clearest stamp on Zionist Socialism, which tried to base its thinking on the tenets of the Marxist doctrine. In his Foreword to a collection of Ber Borochov's writings, Zalman Shazar-Rubashov, a future president of the State of Israel, explained that "Zionist reasoning was the reasoning of a volitional movement" and as such it could not vie with the "compelling, wide-ranging Marxist system that inquires into processes of social and economic development and builds its faith and vision on the objective forces entailed within the changing social life." To penetrate the thinking of the Zionist Socialists at the beginning of the century, it is worthwhile looking at a program authored by Benzion Dinaburg-Dinur in 1904. Then a young Zionist Socialist, Dinur characterized the objective of Zionism as "the very epitome

72 Meshullam Nathan Brozer, *The Righteousness of Zion* (Berdichev, 1903), p. 70 (Hebrew).

of Jewish history, and all the processes of our lives lead toward it, whether we wish it or not." Those familiar with the writings of Dinur the historian may be able to discern here signs of his future thinking about the focal role of the Zionist ideal throughout Jewish history. At the same time we get a taste of the terminology typical of the leftist Zionist circles in Russia when we read, in the same text, of the need "to take control of all the stychic processes in our lives."[73]

The major theoretician of Marxist Zionism was Ber Borochov, and it was he who determined the incidence of historical determinism in Zionism – in his 1905 piece "On the Question of Zion and Territory." According to Borochov, *The prospect of achieving the exodus from the diaspora is ensured by historical necessity.*" The deterministic inquiry focused primarily on the issue of territory – must it be specifically Palestine – with the Marxists divided between the so-called Ugandists and the Zionists of Zion. The Marxists could not rest content with the reasoning that Palestine was woven into the historical memory of the people, or even with utilitarian arguments, namely, that the country was attractive for Jewish settlement due to its climate, resources, or political status; they sought indisputable proof that objective processes were leading the Jews to Palestine by virtue of historical necessity.

Nahum Nir-Rafalkes, one of the leaders of Poalei Zion in Warsaw and an associate of Borochov's, related in his memoirs that he derived scant satisfaction from Borochov's article, even though it "cited seventeen reasons supporting the premise that Palestine is the best place to concentrate the Jewish people." Nir conceded that Borochov had successfully analyzed the conditions of Jewish life, but complained that he had solved the territorial question "metaphysically rather than dialectically." And that, of course, was reason for reproach in the eyes of a young and enthusiastic Marxist. Nir knew no rest until he heard from his friend Yitzhak Tabenkin (who was to become one of the leaders of the labor movement in Palestine)

---

73 Z. Rubashov-Shazar, "B. Borochov and His Legacy" in Borochov, *Selected Works*, Vol. I, p. 25; Benzion Dinur, *A World in Decline* (Jerusalem, 1958), p. 211 (Hebrew) and cf. Benzion Dinur, *Historical Writings, Vol I.* (Jerusalem, 1955), p. 73 (Hebrew).

about a Russian article that dealt with the issue of historical necessity, where he found what he was looking for. Later on he noted with satisfaction: "This theory was the very foundation for establishing the Palestinian idea in the life of the Jewish people. Palestine follows from the internal development of the people over two thousand years."[74]

Hence Nir arrived at a formula similar to that of Benzion Dinur, though their respective brands of Labor Zionism were not at all alike. In these formulas the Marxist Zionists took historical determinism to its furthest limits, with the forces of history filling the role that Divine Providence played in the parallel system of religious thought. Yet we cannot ignore the idea that these radical Zionists had opted for Palestine even before they had created the theoretical structure to stamp their choice with the Marxist seal of approval. Thus radical determinism was essentially an *ex post facto* justification, arrived at "dialectically" after a decision had already been reached "metaphysically," as Nir put it. Needless to say, this parlance was part of the everyday language of the Left and does not stand up under more rigorous scrutiny, for determinism itself can well be taken as a classically metaphysical motif. What concerns us here, however, is not a conceptual critique of the prevailing jargon, but an attempt to understand these schools of thought and their relation to the social movements and events of the day. Thus we can clearly discern the impact of determinism upon many Zionists in the early years of the twentieth century, at first within the ranks of the Democratic Fraction and thereafter, as the influence of the labor movement grew within Zionism, in its Marxist version.[75]

Conclusions

We have proposed as the point of departure for the Zionist credo – meaning its constant motivation both prior to the establishment of the Zionist movement and for years thereafter – the desire to

74 Borochov, *Selected Works*, pp. 41-42; Nahum Nir, *Chapters of a Life* (Tel Aviv, 1958), p. 97 (Hebrew).

75 On Marxist determinism see K. R. Popper, *The Open Society and Its Enemies*, Vol. II (London, 1966), p. 202.

restore Jewish dignity. A focal element in the rehabilitation of trampled Jewish pride was the discovery of the "glorious past" and its use as an object of Jewish identification. It appears that the importance of this motivation declined among organized Zionists as the individual's identification with the movement increased, and this trend became even more pronounced as new constituencies – especially Jews from Eastern Europe who had not experienced the rigors of a full-blown Jewish identity crisis – joined the movement's ranks.

One strong impetus toward the rehabilitation of Jewish dignity emerged from a comparison of Jewish latent nationalism with the achievements of other national movements. Contact with these other national groups brought to the fore the singularity of Jewish nationhood and inspired a search for its roots. It also raised the question, whether Zionism was a response to outside pressures and stimuli, or was a unique phenomenon that drew its force from internal processes in Jewish history. We have touched upon these questions but not examined them in depth, and they will come up again later in these pages. However, we have pointed out the fundamental differences on these issues between the political Zionists and the followers of Ahad Ha'am, while religious Zionism (which leaned toward the outlook espousing uniqueness) did not participate in the theoretical debate.

In its endeavor to rehabilitate Jewish dignity through nationalism, Zionism met with strong opposition from Jewish circles of a different bent. As a result of this friction, the Zionists were led to subscribe to the negative stereotype of the Jew. The antagonism and indifference that many Jews exhibited toward the nascent movement generated a certain degree of alienation on the part of the Zionists toward the existent Jewish community. This predicament will likewise be discussed at greater length in the coming chapters. Here, however, it is worthwhile recalling the extreme critical tendency of Micha Josef Berdyczewski, who wanted to skip over the period of diaspora history altogether. This leap was the counterpart of the historiography spawned by emancipation and the Haskalah, which had shattered the integrity of Jewish history by subjecting it to the norms of the Christian outlook.

This chapter also discussed the integrity of history in the context of Zionism's search for criteria to establish objectively that the Jews were a people (after the concept of race failed to meet this need). The proposition that the same Jewish entity had existed in the past and continued to exist in the present led back to the criterion of subjective self-awareness and opened up a welter of issues, related to the means of expressing historical consciousness and whether or not history is governed by immutable laws. We have touched upon two opposing currents: the volitional trend, which strove to create history; and the determinist trend, which sought validation in the presumed judgment of history. These currents clashed and merged with each other, both in theory and in practice, throughout the period under consideration. Both were essentially reflections of opposing currents in European thought. However, the uniqueness of Jewish nationalism did come out in a feature that derived from and was particular to it, namely, the attitude toward messianism.

Zionism touched upon messianism at a number of points of contact, both in deploring the passive tradition of waiting for the messiah and in defending itself against the charge of false messianism leveled by its opponents. It was particularly undecided about how to view its own messianic role and thus reached a point where Zionism was considered a link in the chain that joined all manifestations of messianism throughout history. This was characteristic of the school of thought referred to here as "historical organism," which expected the national renaissance to come about through the release of innate forces (as opposed to the intervention from without, purportedly advocated by political Zionism). Ahad Ha'am and most of the members of the Democratic Fraction obviously belonged to this school.

Special attention should be drawn to the recurrent argument that Jewish history throughout the centuries was essentially national and that religion was external to the national essence. The Mizrahi movement of religious Zionism had yet to develop its original theory, so that it refrained, as we have said, from engaging in general ideological debates. Although we cited an example of religious determinism, which explained Zionism as divinely inspired, determinism was generally associated with the school of historical organism and thereafter with the Marxist Zionists, whose influence grew appreciably during the first decade of the twentieth century.

Finally, we should mention in passing the importance of the heroic motif that cropped up repeatedly in appraisals of the past and focused primarily on the Hasmonean revolt as a source for historical analogies and for the creation of new symbols to signify Zionist innovation.

CHAPTER TWO

THE SIGNIFICANCE OF CULTURE

The Roots of the Controversy

The topic most hotly debated within the Zionist Organization from the time of its foundation in 1897 until the Uganda crisis of 1903 was unquestionably the issue of culture. Even after six years of unremitting controversy, the matter was not put to rest; it was merely shelved when attention shifted dramatically to the East African issue, and subsequently a certain linkage arose in the minds of Zionists between one's position on the culture issue and the so-called Uganda Affair. It is difficult to comprehend why so seemingly innocent a matter as the desire to foster Jewish culture within the Zionist Organization should have met with such emphatic dissent. Even after examining the positions taken by the various sides, certain questions remain to be scrutinized at greater length.

For all intents and purposes, there were three distinct positions on the culture issue:

* That of the spiritual Zionists and the Democratic Fraction in favor of "cultural work".
* That of the religious Zionists against incorporating cultural activities within the Zionist program, for fear that secular Jews would undermine tradition and religious observance.
* The neutral stance adopted by Herzl, who was interested merely in the political aspect of Zionism and feared that internal disputes would shatter the movement's unity.[1]

---

1   See David Vital, *Zionism, The Formative Years* (Oxford, 1982), pp. 207-208; Klausner, *Opposition to Herzl*, pp. 146-148.

The truth of the matter is that these positions reflected more profound differences regarding both the aim of Zionism and the nature of Jewish culture. Hence we cannot confine ourselves only to a discussion of what was termed "cultural work" but we must inquire into the background and development of the ideas it entailed as well.

The three positions on cultural work – which began to take shape at the First Zionist Congress and were expressed with increasing stridency from the Second Congress onward – were merely the most recent manifestation of a debate that started in the days of the Lovers of Zion, back in the 1880s. The resemblance between the old controversy and the latest one was noted by the veteran leader Moses Leib Lilienblum, in an article published on the eve of the Second Zionist Congress. Lilienblum actually saw nothing new or different in the culture debate. Much to the contrary, he regarded it as a rehash of well-worn and outdated issues. "Sixteen years ago," he wrote, "writers began to raise the question of settling [Palestine] and the rebirth of the nation, and the late poet Judah Leib Gordon was stricken by a terror of the *Shulhan Arukh*." This was an allusion to the code of Jewish law compiled in the sixteenth century, which the Enlightenment poet Gordon took as a symbol of the domination of religion over Jewish life. Gordon also regarded the shattering of the "broad wall" (meaning the Talmud) as a means of exit from the "spiritual diaspora," which he deemed a prerequisite to the actual departure from the diaspora. He had wanted to use the stones of this breached wall selectively to "build the new House of Israel." Lilienblum, however, professed himself to be neutral on religious issues – or at least qualified that "We must not mix religious questions with the issue of settling the country." Nevertheless, he related, "One rabbi was incensed by that statement of mine and countered that even in returning to the land of our forefathers [and here he quoted the words of the outraged rabbi, Saul Halevy Levitan], not a single one of the things covered in the *Shulhan Arukh* will be relinquished in Palestine, not so much as a single strand of hair."[2]

2   Moses Leib Lilienblum, "Thoughts of Peace," *Hamelitz* (August 19, 1898), p. 1 (Hebrew); Saul Halevy Levitan, "Letter of Protest to So-called Religious Reformers in General and Mr. M. L. Lilienblum in Particular," *Hamelitz* (July 11, 1882), p. 494 (Hebrew).

Here, then, is Lilienblum's rendition of the three positions in the ongoing debate:

* That of Judah Leib Gordon as the spiritual father of those advocating "cultural work" within the Zionist movement.
* That of the Orthodox Jews, who wished to return to Zion only on condition of the rule of religion there.
* That of the Zionist leadership, which drew a distinction between Zionism and matters of culture and religion.

Lilienblum identified with Herzl's neutral stance so strongly that he tended to obscure the differences between the present time and the period of the Lovers of Zion. The position he ascribed to Rabbi Levitan as being typical of the Orthodox Jews was in fact representative of neither the religious anti-Zionists nor the religious Zionists, who actually collaborated with their secular comrades. At best it was reminiscent of that section of the Orthodox community that had begun to move in the direction of Zionism but quickly recoiled from it because of the culture problem. Even greater was the difference between Gordon's position sixteen years earlier and that of the promoters of cultural work now. For in contrast to Gordon's pronouncement that "our redemption can only come *after the deliverance of our soul*," cultural work was currently envisioned as augmenting, not vying with, Zionism; it was meant to be a complement, not an alternative. Even Ahad Ha'am, who was more radical than other champions of cultural work, rejected Gordon's formula and affirmed Zionism as an expression of the fusion between the "spiritual center" and the "*genuine and natural life*.[3]

Furthermore, the supporters of cultural work in the Zionist Organization, though mostly disciples of Ahad Ha'am, were Zionists in the fullest sense. Marcus Ehrenpreis, with whom Lilienblum took issue in his above-cited article, is an excellent example. In the pamphlet he published on the eve of the Second Zionist Congress, Ehrenpreis distinguished between his own views and those of his mentor, Ahad Ha'am, metaphorizing that: "He insists that we keep

---

3   J. L. Gordon (printed anonymously), "Our Redemption and the Deliverance of Our Souls," *Hamelitz* (April 3, 1882), p. 215 (Hebrew); on Ahad Ha'am's attitude toward Gordon see Ahad Ha'am, *Collected Works*, p. 2.

the wine in a broken barrel." While Ahad Ha'am saw Zionism as a solution for Judaism and Herzl's aim was to alleviate the "predicament of the Jews," Ehrenpreis confronted Zionism with a double task: "To deliver Judaism and the Jews from their distress."[4] Nevertheless, there were definitely grounds for Lilienblum's assessment of cultural work and its proponents. For in a certain sense they carried on the tradition of the Haskalah and approximated the approach of Judah Leib Gordon, both in their criticism of the Jews' "spiritual exile" and in their desire to use the old stones "to build the new House of Israel." Moreover, many Zionists – and not only those who actively supported cultural work – associated Zionism with a desire to change the Jewish way of life in the spirit of the Haskalah.

We have two attestations of this mood from the 1880s, prior to Herzl's advent. One is by the banker Gustav Cohen of Hamburg, whose pamphlet first appeared in Herzl's time but had been written under the impact of the wave of emigration from Russia in the 1880s. Cohen suggested that a group should be organized to build Jewish settlements in Cyprus as a stage toward the establishment of a Jewish state in Palestine, and in the spirit of the times he spoke of educating the younger generation to carry out this mission as well as honor "tradition, though not sanctify every custom that has become hollow." He drew a distinction between "all the positive traits of the race, which should be preserved" and the "bad [traits], which should be fought relentlessly." On one side of the balance he listed intolerance, arrogance, avarice, and ostentation – "weeds that have grown through extended neglect" – and on the other the commendable traits of decency, simplicity, and modesty.

Such thinking was born of the prevailing mood in Germany, England, and South Africa – with which Cohen was familiar – and it is interesting to compare it with the criticism of Jewish traits voiced by Ahad Ha'am. In 1891 the latter wrote that the role of literature is not "to extol Israel and its nationhood" and pointed to a number of rather disagreeable traits among the Jews. First he cited harmful social traits, "the lack of unity and order," "the lack of a

<hr>

4   Marcus Ehrenpreis, *Thoughts on the Second Zionist Congress* (Berlin, 1898), pp. 5, 12 (Hebrew).

general sense and of social cohesion," and even "rebelliousness and resistance to their great men and leaders." Then he spoke of the negative traits of the individual Jew as "the narcissism that holds such terrible sway over the prominent members of the people . . . the thrill of showing off and the arrogance that belies an innate baseness . . . the tendency always to be too clever, which bespeaks ignorance and lack of common sense." The piece ends by repeating a number of the negative traits that Gustav Cohen had ascribed to the Jews, leading us to conclude that more than a denunciation of traits characteristic of certain individuals under specific conditions, this is essentially a litany of more-or-less standard stereotypes.[5]

Another example dating to the 1880s comes from the memoirs of Dr. Jacob Bernstein-Cohen, who described his impression of the Lovers of Zion and members of the Bilu he met in Odessa. "I found nationalists," the future Zionist leader related, "but most of them sang the same tune to me, and their words smacked of the balm and incense of the Russian churches. They spoke to me of the Torah, of the Bible, of the 613 commandments – all this was not to my taste, incomprehensible and, I confess, left me feeling resentful." Seeking an answer of another kind, Bernstein-Cohen broached the question that did seem of importance to him: "Where are the likes of the Jewish heroes from the days of the Spanish Inquisition?" While clinging to the act of martyrdom in the name of national heroism, the young writer denied the religious content of the act.

A later example of a similar approach can be found in an article that was printed in 1894 in Nathan Birnbaum's paper, *Selbst-Emancipation*. The piece was signed by one Abnon, known to be the pen name of Armand Kaminka, who was then a Reform rabbi. It called for a "return to Hebrew education" as a condition for winning "the bitter war for the existence of our tribe," by which he evidently meant prevailing within an assimilating environment. To reveal the "capacity for development and historical rejuvenation," Judaism would have to become the "*common property of the people*," and this could only be achieved by breaking free of "the arbitrary rule of the rabbis and preachers." Unlike Bernstein-Cohen, Kaminka took a

5 Cohen, *Die Judenfrage und die Zukunft*, p. 21; Ahad Ha'am, *Collected Works*, p. 51.

positive view of Judaism's spiritual heritage, though he believed it would have to be purged of clerical influences if it was to serve as a weapon in the Jewish struggle for survival.[6]

Clearly, then, the transition from emancipation and assimilation to Jewish nationalism required the Zionists to take a new position on the Jewish religion. In an article by a young literary critic, Samuel Lublinski, published in 1896 in the periodical *Zion* in Berlin, we find an attempt to meet this challenge. Writing of "Moses Mendelssohn and Modern Zionism," the author readily admitted that, "Indeed, a number of sincere and committed Zionists tell me that it is precisely to establish the state that we must associate with tradition, with the popular sentiment. Thus a national Jew must be sincerely Orthodox. That sounds highly reasonable, most historical. There may even be a grain of truth here, but only a single grain. Other than that, I regard this approach as fundamentally misguided, a Jewish version of the early-century European national romanticism." Lublinski's article opened with a reassessment of Mendelssohn and the philosophy he bequeathed to modern Judaism and concluded with the need to destroy the temporary bridge built out of "*the traditions of exilic Judaism.*" It described the "wall around the Torah" that sometimes blocked the penetration of "the light and air of Heaven." According to this view, Mendelssohn had erred in perpetuating the diaspora tradition, albeit in his own fashion. In the end, Lublinski concluded, Zionism would have to dissociate itself from both the influence of Reform Judaism and the romantic approach to Orthodox Judaism.[7] This was a juncture at which Zionism began searching for its identity as a unique alternative, not only in the political and practical sense but also in terms of its spiritual character.

A characteristic expression of this quest can be found in the writings of Heinrich Loewe, who was a leading figure of the nascent Zionist movement in the West at the close of the nineteenth century.

---

6   Abnon (Armand Kaminka), "Die Rückkehr zur hebräischen Erziehung," *Jüdische Volkszeitung* (September 11, 1894), p. 1; Bernstein-Cohen, *The Bernstein-Cohen Book*, pp. 75, 76.

7   Salomon Liebhardt (a pen name of Samuel Lublinski), "Moses Mendelssohn und die modernen Zionisten," *Zion* (November 1, 1896), pp. 291-292.

Two years before the first Zionist Congress, he had written an article entitled "Our *Kulturkampf*" positing that, "For us today, the guiding ideal is above all the period of ancient Israel" and going on to explain that the source of inspiration was both Hellenism and "classical Judaism." "Even though we realize it is impossible to revive a time gone by," he wrote, "the same is not necessarily true of its *ideals*." Loewe enthused about the creation of a "new Jewish culture" that would evolve from "the nature of our people" and "the eternal ancient truths" so that "moral progress" would be attained – which was somehow consonant with the demands of science and the arts. Since the theories on the new Jewish culture often coincided with the criticism of existing Jewish traits, this is also the place to quote an article in which Loewe attacked Jewish skepticism for denying the prospect of a better future: "Since the great national tragedy inflicted on our people by the Romans' brutal fist, it has been infected by such an idiosyncratic form of skepticism that hairsplitting and censoriousness are believed by Jews and non-Jews alike to be an inborn national trait." Yet Loewe did not despair, for such traits were not in fact congenital; they resulted, rather, from the loss of Jewish sovereignty and from dispersion and exile, enabling him to hope for a renewal of "classical Judaism" in the future.[8]

A similar spirit was evinced in the writings of Loewe's contemporary, Vasily Bermann, who was among the earliest Lovers of Zion in Russia and had given particularly cogent expression to the innovative aspect of the national movement. On the one hand Bermann wrote: "Be faithful to the old Judaism and the new true culture because these two concepts are one and the same." Yet he rebelled against diaspora Jewry in asking bitingly: "Can it be that the Jew has nothing better to show the world than the distorted face of a slave and at best of a martyr? Have we taught the world nothing but the art of being oppressed, of dying at the stake?" Once again, as in Loewe's writings, we can see the juxtaposition of the old Judaism (referred to by Loewe as "classical") and the new, "true," Judaism, while caught between them was a subjugated and martyred Jewishness that was to be dissolved.

8 Heinrich Loewe, "Unser Kulturkampf," *Zion* (October 15, 1895), p. 263; Heinrich Loewe, "Eine jüdische Palästina Ausstellung," *Zion* (July 15, 1896), p. 161.

The writer J. C. Ravnitski, a moderate and serious-minded man, was actually interested in restoring the link between Zionism and the Haskalah, the Jewish Enlightenment movement. He too focused on the often-suggested connection between two objects of criticism: religion and the diaspora way of life. In 1896 Ravnitski wrote about the backlash against Enlightenment values that had swept through the Lovers of Zion after the 1880s and warned against going to extremes: "The 'People of the Book' must beware not to preach calumnious sermons against general culture and the learning of the enlightened nations, not to spread stale and moldy ideas – namely that the Jewish people must not extend outward but must draw inward with all its might, like a snail in its shell, and be a people that dwells alone with an antiquated 'culture' and peculiar ways, different and separate from every other people and every other language in every possible way."

Up to here Ravnitski was attacking the Jewish proclivity toward insularity – an approach that bore the hallmarks of the Haskalah's attack on the sway of religion over Jewish life. But Ravnitski was not interested in perpetuating the ideals of the Haskalah as they stood. As a self-styled spokesman of "the enlightened Lovers of Zion," he envisioned the coveted future in Palestine as the diametric opposite of life as it was in the Pale of Settlement: "Not the life of the ghetto in its despicable and harrowing form, leaving its inimitable stamp on body and soul, but a healthy and natural life, a life of normal people with healthy bodies and healthy minds, a life of study and civility, of tillage and industry."[9] Hence Ravnitski both restored to Zionism its link to the ideas of the Haskalah – which had been summarily rebuffed during the backlash of the 1880s in Russia – and revitalized these ideas by combining them with the ideal of a new Jewish society in Palestine. This was yet another aspect of the attempt to accord Zionism the status of an autonomous spiritual current. We should likewise note the motif of "a healthy and natural life," which would play a growing part in the future.

One connecting link between the pre-Herzlian era and the age of

---

9   W. Bermann, "In Judäa," *Jüdische Volkszeitung* (August 21, 1894), p. 2; Editor (J. C. Ravnitski), "To the Divisions of the House of Israel" in *Pardess*, Vol. III (Odessa, 1896), pp. 7, 19 (Hebrew).

political Zionism was a lecture given by Leon Kellner in Vienna that was attended by Herzl himself. Kellner had been friendly with the late Hebrew writer Perez Smolenskin but did not accept Smolenskin's national doctrine; later, however, he grew close to Herzl and became an active Zionist. His words not only echoed the motif of the "natural life" but offered a taste of things to come in projecting the anti-rational intensification of this element. "We have been out of touch with mother earth for two thousand years now!" Kellner told his audience. "As far as I am concerned, the land a people calls its own is the primary source, the basic condition, the critical moment of its culture." A scholar of language and literature, Professor Kellner believed it was impossible for earth-bound man to break free of the soil without incurring some form of retribution, and of the Jews he said: "We have not developed among ourselves any science," for "every science has it origin in nature, in the earth, and must return its finest products to the earth." Another theme in Kellner's lecture touched upon the historical dimension and the conviction that "the Strength of Israel will not lie" (I Samuel 15:29), of which he said: "We are proud of our eternal youth, of our immortality; but it is of little consolation to one who never lives that he shall never die." His challenge to the passive faith in the future of the Jews, tinged with criticism of their lifeless existence, is an appropriate prelude to coming back into touch with mother earth.[10]

In summing up this survey of the pre-Herzl period, we can speak of a number of ideas associated with the Haskalah that were passed on to the Jewish national movement and of the attempts to develop a Zionist-Enlightenment philosophy as a spiritual alternative to both liberal and Orthodox Judaism. The factor common to most of the sources we have cited is a wish to create a modern Jewish culture in Palestine based upon ancient Judaism while selecting only the most desirable features thereof. Particularly striking in these writings is the negative attitude toward the way of life being pursued in the diaspora and to the powerful influence of religion, especially in Eastern Europe. On the other hand, the dissatisfaction with liberal Juda-

---

10 Leon Kellner, "Juden und Puritaner," *Zion* (February 1, 1897), p. 60, and cf. George L. Mosse, *The Crisis of German Ideology* (New York, 1964), p. 15.

ism in the West and its cosmopolitan aspirations were far less pronounced. The quotes cited here come from a number of different countries and extend over a period of almost two decades. Involved was a broad spectrum of Lovers of Zion and Zionists, not all of whom identified with the school of Ahad Ha'am or were sworn believers in cultural work. Hence the ideas surveyed in this section were not necessarily the stock in trade of any one current in Zionism or the product of conditions peculiar to one Jewish community or another. They arose out of a mood that was typical of the Jewish national movement prior to the official constitution of the Zionist Organization.

A Return to Judaism

The more removed a person was from Judaism, the more the association with Zionism required him to redefine his attitude toward it. Herzl is a fine example of a man whose association with the Jewish world as such was slight (though most of his personal ties were with Jews) and who, as a result of having arrived at the Zionist solution, was suddenly confronted by the need to reexamine his attitude toward Judaism. As a man who had borne his Judaism with difficulty and doubt, Herzl betrayed fundamentally negative feelings about it. As a young man of twenty-two, he expressed these feelings in his diary after having read a historical novel about the Jews:

> Were it not for this wicked ghetto of modern times and those preceding it, this ring finger of humanity called Jewry would not have developed as it has, or shall we say been deformed as it has. If only one would allow the tortured limb at last to move freely, without coercion or constraint, just like the rest, then it would quickly lose the dim memory of the pressure; the unnatural depression deeply incised by the painful ring would straighten out, and it would move energetically, unrecognizably free and alert, for the benefit of humanity.
> At first the Jews were most proud of being this chosen ring finger; but the ring gradually pressed deeper into the flesh, and

then they were glad it was removed. Now they must make up for their retarded growth.[11]

For the young Herzl, the metaphorical ring had become an onerous shackle to be removed by conversion and intermarriage – to the point of wholly obliterating the difference between Jews and all others. In contrast to this renunciatory attitude, which Herzl confined to the pages of his diary, his speech before the First Zionist Congress was tinged with a flavor of repentance. "Zionism is a return to Judaism even before a return to the land of the Jews," he told the delegates and went on to explain: "We are the prodigal sons who return home to find some things in our father's house that require urgent repair; that we have brothers in the throes of profound distress. Yet they welcome us back in the old house for they know that we do not contemplate the impudent notion of upsetting what is deserving of respect."

Further on, Herzl characterized the harmony between the various parts of Jewry that Zionism achieved through the common national framework as "a close union between the ultra-modern and the ultra-conservative elements of Jewry," all without "undignified concessions" from any party.[12] What we have here is a combination of the two meanings of the German word *Judentum*: the Jews as a collective (Jewry) and their religious and historical heritage (Judaism). Herzl was so eager to win support for the Zionist idea that he was prepared to concede somewhat on the issue of Judaism as a religion. Yet he also stood by the proposition that the national aspect of Judaism was the element common to all Jews, regardless of the profound differences between them on all other issues. What's more, he tried to reinforce this point by claiming that the national criterion was already accepted by all circles of the Zionist fold and would certainly manifest itself throughout the future. He chose to ignore the flagrant contradiction between his partial concession on the validity of Judaism as a religion and the prospect of reaching a national consensus without any side having to concede on its principles. As far as he

11 Nussenblatt, ed., *Theodor Herzl Jahrbuch*, p. 32. The ring metaphor had first appeared in a medieval legend and was later adopted by the German dramatist Gotthold Lessing to distinguish between the true and false in religion.

12 Herzl, *The Congress Addresses of Theodor Herzl*, p. 6.

was concerned, religion was merely a long-standing tradition that should be honored out of courtesy, and he could easily sail past the contradiction.

Indicative of Herzl's attitude toward religion was his reaction to Max Nordau's attack on the anti-Zionist tract of Vienna's chief rabbi, Moritz Güdemann. "Zionism has nothing to do with theology," Nordau wrote. "If the Jews are touched by a desire to establish a new kingdom of Zion, their inspiration comes from neither the Torah nor the Mishnah, but from the hardships of the times." Nordau also pronounced – and this is particularly worthy of attention – that: "A people has no other purpose than to live and fully develop all its inherent talents" (this being the antithesis of the thinking behind cultural work and Ahad Ha'am's missionary outlook.) After reading the manuscript of this article, Herzl admonished Nordau, "We must not drive off the *Zionist* rabbis." He believed that it would not be difficult to negotiate the gap between this tactical necessity and his essentially condescending attitude toward religion and warned that "We must not dampen their spirits, even if we are far from placing power in their hands."[13]

This exchange between Herzl and Nordau took place at about the time of the First Zionist Congress. And since the addresses delivered on that festive occasion were taken as programmatic declarations about the course that the new movement should take, we shall dwell here on the speech given by Nathan Birnbaum, which provoked reactions from all sides. Birnbaum was then the chief secretary of the Zionist office in Vienna, and anyone not familiar with the movement's internal affairs would undoubtedly have regarded him as one of the pillars of the Zionist leadership. His address on "Jewish National Life" expressed the mood characteristic of the Jewish intelligentsia of the day. Birnbaum spoke of the "scent of the soil" that the Jews of the East [meaning Eastern Europe] need "to transform the culture of the ghetto into a progressive national culture," while submitting that the Jews of the West need "to overcome their abstract Europeanism." According to his scheme of things, the East

13 Max Nordau, "Ein Tempelstreit," *Die Welt* (June 11, 1897), pp. 2-3; Moritz Güdemann, *Nationaljudenthum* (Leipzig, 1897); Herzl, *Letters*, Vol. II, p. 294.

European Jews would pass through *two* phases in their "process of recuperation," while it would be sufficient for the Jews of the West to come into direct contact with the Zionist solution. The first stage – which the Jews of Western Europe had already put behind them – was "putting their Jewish ghetto culture to death through Europeanism." This was the phase of overcoming the static posture in which "the past is rendered immutable." In short, the role of Zionism was first of all to revolutionize East European Jewry's traditional way of life.

Birnbaum's words were received with alarm by the Orthodox Jews in the audience and with pronounced dissatisfaction by other critics. Lilienblum, for example, who regarded cultural work as inimical to the prime objective of Zionism, feared that the movement would be split along lines of religious observance. In something of a pique, he characterized Birnbaum's address as one of those "nonsensical sermons that come out of darkness and will pass back into darkness" and said of the speaker, "I doubt whether he knows how to read Hebrew properly and even more so whether he has ever read a single Hebrew book in the original." Ahad Ha'am bracketed Birnbaum's address with Herzl's in regarding them both as typical expressions of Western Zionism. "Dr. Herzl, it is true, said . . . that 'Zionism' demands the return to Judaism before the return to the Jewish State," he wrote. "But these nice sounding words are so much at variance with his deeds that we are forced to the unpleasant conclusion that they are nothing but a well-turned phrase." He treated Birnbaum's piece as an official statement of policy, noting that Herzl himself had perused the text and approved it. Yet Ahad Ha'am, and Lilienblum after him, were imprecise in their interpretations of Birnbaum's terminology and accused him of wanting to "destroy the past." Ahad Ha'am even apologized for this error at a later point. Still, as he saw it, Birnbaum's speech had revealed political Zionism's true colors – which Herzl had managed to camouflage with a clever turn of phrase about returning to Judaism.[14]

14 Nathan Birnbaum, "Das jüdische Nationalleben" in *Protokoll des 1ten Zionistenkongresses in Basel*, p. 105; Moses Leib Lilienblum, "Warning Against a Dangerous Animal," *Hamelitz* (June 22, 1899), p. 1 (Hebrew); Achad Haam, *Ten Essays on Zionism and Judaism*, p. 48.

Actually, the entire affair was a series of paradoxical misunderstandings. Birnbaum was presented to Herzl as a veteran and distinguished Zionist, and the two took a dislike to each other from the start. Ahad Ha'am and Lilienblum, old rivals from the Love of Zion era, both did Birnbaum an injustice: the first (a champion of cultural work) by identifying him with Herzl; the latter (who opposed it) by dissociating him from Herzl. Before long, Birnbaum did indeed part ways with Herzl, and Zionism as a whole – to the point where he ultimately joined the ultra-Orthodox camp. We must keep in mind that the conflict over cultural work was principally between Ahad Ha'am's followers and the religious Zionists, with both of the warring camps presuming to speak on behalf of the Jewish past and historical continuity. Herzl – who took the past to be a marginal issue, at best – and Lilienblum – a veteran reformer who remained antagonistic to strict Orthodoxy all his life – both wanted to play down the differences between the religious Zionists and the rest. The crux of the problem lay in the complex attitude toward the past taken by most of the parties to the controversy. Ahad Ha'am, who attacked Birnbaum in the name of the "thread connecting [us] with the past," extolled Rabbi Yohanan Ben-Zakkai and his spiritual retreat in Jabneh and decried Herod's rule of ancient Judea. His point was to portray Judaism's spiritual heritage as the antithesis of political might, yet by this distinction he also showed that he himself approached the past selectively.

On the face of it, there was a point of convergence between Ahad Ha'am's criticism of political Zionism and that of the Orthodox circles. For example, an 1898 tract by Dr. Mendel Hirsch, of the neo-Orthodox school in Germany, related to political Zionism almost patronizingly because it had grown out of "the situation created by the antisemitic movement" and came in response to "social discrimination," while Hirsch represented those who stood on "the ground of historical Judaism." When religious Jews tried to translate the abstract concept of "historical Judaism" into the mode of everyday life, all they could do was hold fast to the Torah and the commandments as the sole expression of their Judaism. Hence the Zionists who founded the religious Mizrahi in 1902 stressed their opposition to the "culture seekers" as a function of their fidelity to "the spirit of our Torah." This would imply that Ahad Ha'am's "historical

Judaism" was fundamentally different from that of the religious Zionists: Ahad Ha'am saw history as the variable in Judaism, whereas the religious Jews believed that Judaism was beyond the vicissitudes of history.[15]

It was these two outlooks that clashed in the controversy over cultural work, with the Zionist leadership being equally distant from them both. We have already cited Ahad Ha'am's skeptical view of Herzl's call to return to Judaism. It must be said that his assessment is not unfounded, especially if we view it in light of one of Herzl's later statements on the same subject. At the beginning of 1899, an interesting debate developed between Herzl and Nordau over Zionism's attitude toward the Jewish Socialists. Nordau felt a certain degree of sympathy toward them and concluded that it was no coincidence that men like Marx and Lasalle had rocked the cradle of Socialism, for they had imbibed from Judaism – even unwittingly – "an enthusiasm for social justice." Herzl, on the other hand, espoused pure Zionism based on the elementary need to help the Jews cure what ailed them. Quoting a famous poem by Heine on Judaism as the worst of maladies, he commented: "Zionism is the new Jewish method of treatment, and it addresses itself to the most difficult of the three ailments, the thousand-year-old hereditary disease." He then explained that Zionism would cure the patient of all his physical and moral ills by the natural approach: "It will return him to the soil . . . bring him back to a natural way of life."[16] The debate between Herzl and Nordau was therefore not so much about different attitudes toward the socialists or even disparate appreciations of Zionism; it was essentially a difference of opinion on the nature of Judaism. Nordau, who at one point declared that national existence is an end in itself, nevertheless found in Judaism "latent folk traditions" of great universal value. Herzl commended a return to Judaism but at the same time regarded it as an illness and Zionism as its remedy, so that the aim of Zionism was essentially to cure the Jew of his Judaism!

15　Mendel Hirsch, *Der Zionismus* (Mainz, 1898), p. 28; "Cast ye up!" *Hamelitz* (April 13, 1902), p. 3 (Hebrew; the founding manifesto of Mizrahi).
16　Max Nordau, "Strömungen im Judenthum," *Die Welt* (February 3, 1899), p. 5; T. Herzl, "Der Nordau Commers," *Die Welt* (February 3, 1899), p. 7.

To appreciate Herzl's attitude toward Judaism from a contemporary perspective, let us quote two contradictory assessments of it. After Herzl's death, Buber wrote an article entitled "Herzl and History" in which he spoke of Herzl's inability "to experience the Jewish renaissance in his heart" and disparaged political Zionism on the grounds that "a movement does not draw historical justification from helping people unless it enriches them with new values." This was Buber's way of saying that Herzl's Zionist solution was mechanistic and out of touch with living Judaism. The article was challenged by Samuel Lublinski, who had in the meanwhile broken ranks with Zionism. Lublinski conceded that Buber had his facts right but he himself took issue with Herzl from a diametrically opposed standpoint, namely, that "for opportunistic reasons he believed it necessary to make concessions to the historical-romantic so-called national Judaism."[17]

Thus even at the height of his Zionist career, Theodor Herzl was perceived as being an assimilationist in spirit. "Historical Judaism" – both in its religious version and according to Ahad Ha'am's interpretation – remained fundamentally alien to Herzl, and it is doubtful whether he fully understood the advocates of "cultural work." He hoped to provide a cure for all of Jewry's ills at a single stroke and lacked patience for any presumed trifle that might stand in his way. We shall not go into Herzl's position on specific cultural questions, such as the future language of the Jewish state. But we shall deal later on with Palestine's role in the Zionist scheme of things, and there was of course a certain connection between the attitude toward Hebrew and the stand on Palestine, which were hallmarks of the rival camps within the Zionist movement. Suffice it to note Herzl's absolute indifference to the Hebrew language as an indication of his overall attitude toward Jewish culture.[18]

To conclude our discussion on Herzl's relationship to Judaism, we will quote two testimonies taken from the memoirs of early Zionists. Dr. Abraham Jacob Freidenberg, a Russian Zionist who had

17 Martin Buber, *Der Jude und sein Judentum* (Cologne, 1963), pp. 789, 790; Samuel Lublinski, "Die Organisation der Juden" in Schön, ed., *Die Stimme der Wahrheit*, p. 181.
18 Herzl, *Diaries*, Vol. I, p. 170; Herzl, *The Jewish State*, pp. 99-100.

belonged to Ahad Ha'am's Bnei Moshe Society prior to the emergence of Zionism proper, regarded Herzl's attitude toward cultural work as essentially negative, explaining it as follows: "The emancipated West European Jews considered the demand [for] Jewish culture as reactionary, a surrender, and forfeiting the gains of the emancipation era." Maximilian Apolinary Hartglas, one of the leaders of Polish Zionism, described two kinds of Zionists: "As a rule," he wrote, "I have observed that initially *The Jewish State* spoke mainly to the assimilationist type." After listing various personalities who had been attracted to Zionism for a time and soon parted ways with it, Hartglas analyzed their motives: "Apparently the assimilationists, who made up the educated and more European class of Polish Jewry, understood that a state is the basic condition for the healthy existence of a people, and Herzl presented them with a colorful picture of the people's return to its historical homeland, depicting the idea as a direct and imminent outcome of diplomatic agreements." But when it turned out that the realization of the idea was not imminent, that in fact it faced major obstacles, and that "they sensed it was necessary both to embrace the tradition of the ancient Jewish culture and to accept and develop the folklore of the Jewish masses – 'the riffraff in long black coats' – their enthusiasm cooled and they returned to the bosom of assimilation." As to the other type of Zionist, Hartglas wrote: "Among the non-assimilationists, Herzl's idea sank in more slowly but more deeply."[19]

If these fundamentally identical assessments are correct, then the culture controversy was more than an ideological debate between factions within Zionism; it was a socio-cultural clash between various Jewish groups based on the degree to which they had distanced themselves from the traditional way of life and integrated into non-Jewish society. This is a complex sociological issue, for the concept of assimilation expresses not only an objective, measurable situation, but also a subjective matter of choice. Moreover, there are varying degrees of outright assimilation and varying degrees of

---

19 Abraham Jacob Freidenberg, *The Memoirs of a Zionist Soldier* (Brussels, 1938), p. 89 (Yiddish); M. A. Hartglas, "Between Two Worlds" in M. Mishkinsky, ed., *Gal-Ed – An Anthology on the History of Polish Jewry*, Vol. II (Tel Aviv, 1975), p. 365 (Hebrew).

desire to assimilate, and the two are not always consonant. The problem expressed itself all the more sharply within the Jewish national movement because of its basically ambivalent attitude toward Judaism. Zionism, for instance, was dedicated to the principle of identification with Judaism, yet the movement was awash with criticism of it. Hence it is difficult to establish a formula for behavior patterns in a broader societal sense.[20] Instead, we shall trace the development of the culture issue while noting the socio-cultural background of those involved in the controversy, without assuming any definitive connection between rootedness in Jewishness and the espousal of this particular cause.

The Heart of the Matter

The debate over cultural work first broke out at the Second Zionist Congress in 1898. After the congress had appointed a Cultural, Educational, and Literary Committee, the religious delegates tried to counter its effect by establishing a Rabbinical Board to oversee the cultural activities within the movement. Consequently, negotiations began behind the scenes to strike the kind of compromise that would make the continuation of joint Zionist work possible. Herzl touched upon the cultural issue in his opening address, but it was clear from what he said that he did not acknowledge a distinctly Jewish culture. To him culture meant European civilization. As far as he could see, the ethos that the Jews would bring with them to their state would be an amalgam of the mores and cultures of the peoples among whom they had lived. In speaking of the assets that the Jews had acquired from the cultures of their surroundings, Herzl mused: "Perhaps the efficiency of the Germanic peoples, the versatility of the Latin peoples, the great patience of the Slavs, have not passed us over without leaving an impression." He regarded the congress delegates as an example of the demographic character of the future Jewish state, "an assemblage of men of all cultures," and he depicted his ideal as "Jewish artists, philosophers, and scholars from all coun-

---

20 Cf. Simon N. Herman, "Zionism and Pro-Israelism, A Social-Psychological Analysis," *Forum*, Jerusalem, 2:25 (1976), p. 18.

tries, united on the basis of work, into a *tolerant* society."[21] The choice of tolerance as Zionism's cultural acme was undoubtedly affected by the increasingly bitter struggle between the proponents of cultural work and their religious adversaries. As we have noted, Herzl was determined not to allow supposedly marginal issues to impede the course of Zionism.

The spokesman of the Cultural Committee at the Second Congress was Dr. Moses Gaster, a native of Rumania who had been raised in a German cultural milieu and had subsequently served as the chief rabbi of the Sephardi community in London. In his address, Gaster reflected the outlook shared by many of the proponents of cultural work. On the one hand he acknowledged the link with "the historical tradition" while objecting to the practice of immersing oneself in the past, on the grounds that it was an "Aryan" custom: "We do not summon up the dead because we do not believe only in the past. We believe much more in progress and in the future." The erudite Gaster explained that the Jews had never longed for a "Golden Age" gone by, because they had always looked to the future. That is why the Jews were capable of identifying with the cultures of the peoples among whom they lived. And Gaster was unwilling to relinquish a single asset drawn from that broader culture, providing, he said to the applause of his listeners, "that this culture has become part of our flesh and blood, that we have assimilated it completely into Judaism, that we have adapted it to the Jewish spirit."[22]

In his memoirs, Bernstein-Cohen called Gaster's speech "a masterpiece, a sermon designed to delude both the Orthodox and the non-believers." He even likened Gaster's address to Herzl's speech which he saw as making "overtures to both sides." The radical writer Berdyczewski likewise commented on the debate over culture at the Second Zionist Congress, but rather than be drawn into the struggle between the Orthodox and their opponents, he pounced furiously on the ideological assumptions behind Gaster's stand. For Berdyczewski saw no need to create a synthesis between the future and the traditions of the past, and he wished to dissociate Zionism from attempts

21 Herzl, *The Congress Addresses of Theodor Herzl*, pp. 15, 16.
22 M. Gaster, "Rede am 2ten Zionisten-Congress," *Die Welt* (September 9, 1898).

to falsify its true nature, which to him was just "earthly matters, temporal affairs." Paradoxically, it was the secular camp that he tried to endow with an aura of holiness in speaking of "their sacred will and the loftiness of the goals to which their souls aspire." Unlike Herzl, Berdyczewski was no stranger to Jewish culture, yet he yearned to be free of it: "Here we thought that *now* the Jewish people had finally realized that it took preference over the Torah, that [the people itself] is the heart of the matter and the one and only cause in the war for existence." Finally he exclaimed in rage: "Had I enough saliva, I would spit in the face of all these culturists!"[23]

Rather than enter into the details of the struggle over culture, we shall limit ourselves to citing a few typical examples. At the beginning of the chapter, reference was made to Lilienblum's call for Zionism to remain neutral on the question of culture. As the debate proceeded to intensify, he also expressed the fear that "Zionist unity will be shattered over this rather dubious issue." He also spoke as one well versed in dealing with Orthodox Jewry: "I am quite familiar with the mood of the rabbis and the pious," he wrote, "their fear of anything that bears the least relation to the Enlightenment, and their habit of suspecting anyone outside their fold of all manner of corruption." He concluded by calling for tolerance and consideration for the sensitivities of the Orthodox camp.

Lilienblum's main reason for maintaining neutrality on the culture issue was set forth in 1900 in an article that drew a sharp distinction between Zionism and cultural work. He regarded the "culturists" not only as threatening the peace within the Zionist movement but also as forcing an extraneous issue – mixing "one thing with another," as he put it. Noting that the Haskalah had already espoused ideas similar to those of the "culturists" ("fostering a knowledge of the Hebrew language, [European] languages, Jewish history, fondness for the people, physical fitness, the proper outlook on life, etc."), he argued that these principles were not pertinent to Zionism for another reason: "Who is even now deeply immersed in the history of our people if not many of our learned brethren abroad who are neither Zionists nor nationalists but Germans of mosaic

23 Bernstein-Cohen, *The Bernstein-Cohen Book*, p. 122; Berdyczewski, *On the Agenda*, p. 70.

persuasion?" Lilienblum, the ex-reformer, wanted to sever Zionism completely from its roots in the Enlightenment so as to make it acceptable to all and thereby accord it national legitimacy. On the face of it, he abetted the Berdyczewskian impulse toward rebellion against Judaism. But in essence his criticism of the "Science of Judaism" (*Wissenschaft des Judentums*) – a modern, critical approach to Jewish scholarship that was the hallmark of the Jewish Enlightenment in the West – was no different from the standard complaint of the "culturists" headed by Ahad Ha'am. In his essay "The Rebirth of the Spirit," Ahad Ha'am wrote: "It was not an inner need to *continue developing* the national spirit *in the future* that led those engaged in the Science of Judaism to turn to the *past*." He went even further in deploring this approach by claiming that it tended "to deny the national connection not only between the past and the future but also between various parts of the nation dispersed in the present."[24]

Here is the appropriate place to quote Albert Rokéach, the Zionist poet residing in France who advocated "national education" based on the fostering of the Hebrew language. He proposed to the leaders of the Democratic Fraction – who were tireless evangelists of cultural work – that they concentrate on passing on the language, for the experience with the scientific approach to Jewish studies showed that "the countless scholars and learned men of Germany, France, and England publish the results of their historical research in more- or less-widely read journals, but nevertheless remain enthusiastic advocates of assimilation." In contrast to Ahad Ha'am, who found fault with these scholars for treating the past in a manner alien to "the national spirit," Rokéach seemed to harbor an antipathy toward the past itself. He attacked the Jewish scholars in the West because "they regard the Jewish people as an ancient monument" and deplored those who would preserve the past "in dusty museums" with the aim of "turning our present and our future back into the

---

24 M. L. Lilienblum, "The Symbol of Zeal and Enmity," *Hamelitz* (April 11, 1899), pp. 1, 2 (Hebrew); M. L. Lilienblum, "To the Libel Hunters," *Hamelitz* (March 9, 1900), p. 1 (Hebrew); Ahad Ha'am, *Collected Works*, p. 178.

night of the past."[25] Though his critical tone is unmistakable, it is difficult to grasp the particular point of Rokéach's assault on the Science of Judaism. Perhaps he believed that there was an inherent connection between estrangement from Jewish life and the academic pastime of picking over the past – and between both of these and sinking "back into the night of the past." At any rate, this complaint appears to be a somewhat tempered version of Berdyczewski's approach, including his opposition to spiritualism and his rejection of the past, though these themes are only alluded to and Rokéach himself may not have been fully aware of them.

We have already heard from Lilienblum about the Orthodox Jews' mistrust of anything coming from outside their closed society. Nahum Sokolow, another product of the Haskalah who found his way to Zionism, did not agree with this analysis and tended to minimize the importance of the conflict. In his book *To Masters and Mentors*, written in a mock-rabbinical style, he asked in feigned innocence: "What is this great fear of culture about? Reformed *heders?*" (a reference to the new primary schools in which Hebrew was taught as a living tongue, not just the language of prayer). In essence, Sokolow had a simplistic explanation for the Orthodox opposition to cultural work, a demonological explanation, if you will: "The truth is that all the calumny, all the denunciations, and all the vitriolic sermons against culture in the Zionist movement can be traced to a few rabbinical literati who have swept many naive and pious savants up in their wake." Thus in Sokolow's assessment, the "men of true genius" were trapped in the net of a few intriguers because they themselves were cut off from real life. "They are told that people are creating culture under the guise of Zionism; they are informed that culture will be the nemesis of religion; they are called upon to rise up and forbid it – and some of them do."

Clearly Sokolow underestimated the intensity of the religious opposition to cultural work, for a profound fear of secular culture was exacerbating an already extant hostility to Zionism in Orthodox circles. Even the moderate leaders of the religious Zionists adamantly rejected cultural work and all it implied. Following the Third

25 A. Rokéach, "Pour la langue hebraïque," *l'Echo Sioniste* (March 15, 1902), p. 63.

Zionist Congress, Rabbi Isaac Jacob Reines, who was subsequently to become the leader of the Mizrahi movement, expressed his satisfaction over the fact that "the kosher restaurants [in Basel] were filled with congress delegates – doctors, professors, lawyers, and the like." But he was particularly pleased about the *"spiritual benefit"* derived from the congress in that *"culture has been totally abolished."* Three years later, one of the more moderate rabbis in the Mizrahi movement, Samuel Jacob Rabinowitz, reassured the Orthodox public that the Fifth Zionist Congress had in no way altered the status quo on culture. Admittedly, it had elected a "Cultural Commission," this time without rabbis; yet "the Orthodox people who feel anxious about culture can feel confident that just as the cultural accomplishments were *naught* with the rabbis involved, so the accomplishments of the commission will be naught without the rabbis involved."[26]

At this point the cultural issue appeared to be the Zionist movement's chief preoccupation. Not only was it the factor behind the formation of the Democratic Fraction and the Mizrahi Party, an open clash between the "culturists" and the Zionist leadership dominated the proceedings of the Fifth Zionist Congress. Hence the leading political Zionists were forced to concede the importance of the subject, though they cautioned against allowing it to become the main issue on the agenda and distract attention from Zionism's true aims. Prior to the Sixth Zionist Congress, in writing about the tasks facing the forthcoming conclave, Max Bodenheimer placed the words "Jewish culture" in quotes to indicate his misgivings about the very use of this concept. He facetiously admired the boundless energy and enthusiasm of the "tempestuous scribes in their youth," but he decried their pretensions to make "the so-called *question of culture*" into the cardinal issue of Zionism. Bodenheimer wondered why so many of the younger set believed "the creation of a new Jewish culture to be more important than obtaining a charter for the Jewish country." He scoffed at all the vagueness and confusion over

---

26 Sokolow, *To Masters and Mentors*, pp. 19, 28 (Hebrew); Isaac Jacob Reines, Letter to the Bnei Zion in Plonsk (according to Micha Josef Berdyczewski, *Epigones* [Warsaw, 1900], p. 50 [Hebrew]); Samuel Jacob Rabinowitz, "Letters on Zionism," *Hamelitz* (February 12, 1902), p. 1 (Hebrew).

the form and content of the culture for which they were so eager to obtain the congress' approval. In essence, Bodenheimer echoed Herzl's sentiment that the very concept of "Jewish culture" was open to question and was certainly unworthy of commanding so much of the delegates' time, especially as it caused dissension in the ranks. At the same time, however, he implied that since the Second Zionist Congress, involvement with the issue had become so intense that it might actually overshadow the real matter at hand: the effort to obtain a charter.[27]

One may well wonder about the widely disparate assessments that the respective factions held of their own and their adversaries' strengths. Ahad Ha'am, probably the leading "culturist," tended to agree with the Mizrahi spokesman, Rabinowitz, that nothing had changed in the status quo he was so desirous of changing. Yet sometime later, one of the leaders of the political Zionists complained that the subject had assumed massive proportions, though he personally regarded it as trivial. We must distinguish, of course, between a private assessment and one meant for publication. Rabbi Rabinowitz hoped to assuage the fears of the religious public by assuring it that the sponsors of cultural work had achieved nothing, while the skeptic Ahad Ha'am expressed his pessimism in a private letter – and at any rate tended to view most everything about the Zionist Organization with a jaundiced eye. Bodenheimer seemed to have no vested interest in magnifying the import of the phenomenon, but he may have been drawn into exaggeration in the course of his polemic with the young literati. Still, there is good reason to accept his implication that the cultural question sometimes eclipsed the real – political – point of Zionism. On the other hand, it can be argued that Zionism's weakness as a political force and the lack of any headway in the diplomatic negotiations permitted an internal issue of presumably moot importance to assume pride of place in the movement's deliberations.

The dispute over cultural work was not exacerbated at the Sixth Zionist Congress because in the midst of its sessions, quite unexpectedly, attention was diverted to the Uganda Scheme, bringing the cen-

---

27 Max Bodenheimer, "Die Aufgaben des 6 Kongresses," *Jüdische Rundschau* (July 17, 1903), p. 291.

ter of gravity back to the political arena. Before entering into the Uganda issue, however, we should first examine the ideological underpinnings of the clash over culture, for that may well be the best way to approach our inquiry into the Uganda Affair.

"Muscular Jewry"

At the beginning of the chapter we spoke about the impact of the Haskalah upon the Lovers of Zion and early Zionism. It remains to elucidate the combined influence of national thinking and Enlightenment ideas on the period under scrutiny here. A point of departure common to both the Haskalah and Zionism was their rejection of the traditional Jewish way of life. The Zionists, it must be said, were likewise critical of the way in which the Jews conducted themselves in the countries of emancipation, but they continued to direct the cutting edge of their criticism at the quality of Jewish life in Eastern Europe. The Zionist ideal, like that of the Haskalah, was the creation of a new kind of Jew. Admittedly, the Zionists were not unanimous about the features of this prototype; nevertheless, it is possible to cite some characteristic traits. The new Jew would be proud, brave, and militant, a fighter who had traded his excessive spirituality for a love of nature and the cultivation of the body – or, to use the phrase coined by Max Nordau, he would be the epitome of the "muscular Jewry." It is interesting to note that this ideal was shared by political Zionists and "culturists," Zionists from Eastern Europe as much as from the West.

The physical ideal was influenced not only by the Haskalah outlook but by the Zionists' immediate environment, as well. We know, for example, that the duel as a convention for defending one's honor, so widespread among the aristocracy, preoccupied the Jewish student organizations at the end of the last century. It is therefore pertinent to cite Fabius Schach, one of the earliest Zionists in Germany, who in 1893 advocated the fostering of physical fitness among the Jews. His position reflected the tradition of physical fitness that had lingered on in Germany from the days of Friedrich Ludwig Jahn, one of the fathers of German nationalism at the beginning of the nineteenth century. Here is what Schach had to say to the Young

Israel Society in Berlin: "We national Jews must never be bookish people. Instead we must be men who relish life, who are worldly and armed to struggle for survival, to fight for their honor and for their aims." Further on he spoke of developing "the manly virtues of courage and loyalty, of might, endurance, and daring." After listing all the benefits that physical exercise would have for the Jews, he intimated that it could triumph over the "ways of the ghetto" so that it would be possible to "look the world in the eye, in a forthright and courageous manner, and demand rights rather than sufferance."[28]

The physical ideal was entailed by the national ideal to the point where it was impossible to separate the two, and all their components seemed to merge into a single element: physical qualities with the desired mental qualities; the rejection of intellectualism and the spirit of the ghetto; and a new approach to national activism. Ravnitski, for instance, associated his physical ideal with "working the soil, which will heal the fractured bodies of the sons." In describing the results of the healing process, he compared the future "sons of Zion" with the figure of the average Jew: "And rather than small and puny, thin and frail Jews born of the ghetto who have no bodyhood, it will raise big, strong, hearty and lively people." Here, too, the rehabilitation of the body was linked with the healing of the soul and the idea of productivization with the desire to go to Palestine, all this woven into a fabric of Jewish and human renewal: "The soul too will shed its ghetto lineaments – which arouse pity and sometimes contempt, as well – and assume a form befitting a man as such and a Jew as such."[29]

Another statement of the physical ideal was presented a while later in Nordau's lecture symbolically entitled "On the Jewish Soldier." Marked by an apologetic tone, the purpose of this address was to hearten his audience by demolishing the negative image of the Jew. "The Jews were never deserving of the charge of cowardice. Much to the contrary, on many occasions they displayed unparalleled cour-

---

28 Fabius Schach, "Von der Theorie zur Praxis," *Selbst-Emancipation* (October 15, 1893), p. 6.
29 Editor (J. C. Ravnitski), "To the Divisions of the House of Israel" in *Pardess*, Vol. III, p. 19 (Hebrew).

age." He cited David as a paragon of Jewish valor in his confrontation with Goliath, prompting one of his listeners to write: "All of Jewish history was there before our eyes, this history of a small, proud, and determined people." Continuing in this vein, Nordau quickly arrived at the above-quoted formulation of Zionism's physical ideal: to recreate the "lost muscular Jewry." "Zionism has awakened Jewry to new life," he told the Second Zionist Congress, "morally through the National ideal, materially through physical rearing." He bemoaned "the fearful devastation which eighteen centuries of captivity have wrought in our midst" and lauded Bar-Kokhba's desperate war as an even loftier paragon than the victories of the Hasmoneans. There can be no doubt that the catch phrase "muscular Jewry" connoted not only a physical ideal but national heroism that was the antithesis of diaspora submission and an integral part of Jewish renewal through Zionism.

In his address to the Fifth Zionist Congress, Nordau compared "these stately horsemen, these first-rate fighters, these stylish dancers, these prize-winning gymnasts and swimmers" descended from wealthy Jewish families with "the emaciated and cough-racked frames of the Eastern Ghettos." But then he abandoned pathos to present his listeners with a more prosaic vision of raising the masses in Eastern Europe to the level of physical fitness that had been attained by the wealthy class of Western Jewry over three generations.[30]

The years that elapsed between these two speeches had given rise to a more sober style. Yet although the 1901 speech was anchored already in a much firmer sense of reality, Nordau's main points remained the same:

* The Jews of Eastern Europe were the epitome of physical degeneracy.
* The Jews had the potential to change.
* The task of Zionism was to bring about that change.

---

30 Judaeus, "Conférence de M. Max Nordau sur le soldat juif," *Zion* (French section), (May 31, 1897), p. 29; Max Nordau, *Max Nordau to His People* (New York, 1941), pp. 88, 137.

The Second Zionist Congress, where Nordau delivered his address on "muscular Jewry," also heard a report on the Jews in Palestine from Leo Motzkin, who had been sent there to study the situation at first hand. Motzkin stressed that there was "an enormous difference between the Jews of the colonies and the Jewish masses in Eastern Europe. Most of the farmers are only too well aware that they alone must protect themselves and defend their lives." Yet it was clear from his speech that self-defense in the colonies was more than just a function of the poor security situation under Ottoman rule. The difference between the lifestyle in the colonies and in the settlers' countries of origin was that the settlers had broken the behavior patterns generally associated with the Jews. As Motzkin explained: "And if the stamp of the diaspora is still noticeable on the old generation, the new generation is wholly free of the stigma of exile. Village life far from the ghetto has had an ameliorating effect, which is clearly attested by the difference in the character of the two generations."[31]

Thus Zionism's physical ideal was the junction at which products of the East European Haskalah met on common ground with the Zionists of the West who had absorbed an appreciation of the body from German culture. If we continue to quote Zionists on this subject, in purely chronological order, we will get an impression of consistency despite differences of background and circumstances. In 1900 the Hebrew writer Israel Chaim Tawiow published an article in *Hamelitz* memorable for its bitter attack on the "ghetto spirit." He lambasted the ghetto's social conventions and religious life, the livelihoods of the Jews, and the "stooped backs and warped minds, the abnormality and the indignity." Later in the article he pronounced, "And Zionism calls for utterly sweeping out all this filth and rubbish," whereupon he listed the ideals that should come in their place, from the adoption of Hebrew through the fostering of genuine culture and, of course, "a healthy mind in a healthy body." The specifically Zionist motif hardly played any role here, and there was little difference between the change that stood to evolve in Palestine and the revolution that the Zionists would have to effect immediately.

31 Leo Motzkin, *The Motzkin Book* (Jerusalem, 1939), p. 46 (Hebrew).

In contrast, Nahum Sokolow described the preliminary stages that the Jews would have to go through in order to "*sustain themselves and stand on their own feet.*" Sokolow was far more indulgent toward the Jews' failings than Tawiow. Even though he remarked that "their culture is the culture of the ghetto and not a natural culture," he saw this aberration as merely temporary "because this is not the natural state of the people of Israel of old." The problem, as Sokolow saw it, was that the Jews "have not learned and are not accustomed to conquer the forces of nature; they are all rather weak and spoiled. There are no tillers of the soil, laborers, or artisans *of various kinds* among them." Sokolow used the terms "nature" and "natural" in a variety of senses. One was in the context of "natural culture," which was "alive, vital, broad," whereas its opposite, Jewish culture – "the culture of the ghetto" – was presumably dead or dying and at any rate confining. Then there was the "natural state," meaning the original condition of the Jews before they were deformed by "exile and dispersion, pressure and poverty and the abnormal conditions." Finally Sokolow referred to overcoming the "forces of nature" as a way to achieve productivization and penetrate all branches of the economy, which was a prerequisite for independence. Nature was therefore Sokolow's key word for transforming the Jews from their presumably abnormal state into a future way of life that would approximate their original condition in the distant past.[32]

What follows here are a series of statements by members of the same circle within the Democratic Fraction, all of whom were disciples of Ahad Ha'am. Most of them came from Galicia and had studied in Germany, so that they had been nurtured on a combination of the Haskalah tradition and that of emancipated Jewry. In 1901 Osias Thon wrote an article about Samuel Lublinski, who had briefly belonged to the Zionist movement but preferred his attachment to German culture over his Jewish commitment. Delving into this phenomenon, Thon portrayed Lublinski as typical of certain Jewish intellectuals. "The Jews are doubtless to be counted among the most highly cultured people," he wrote, "but only in the sense of abstract, elite Europeanism. The earthy scent of the autochthons

32 I. C. Tawiow, "An Augury of Wealth," *Hamelitz* (March 11, 1900), p. 2 (Hebrew); Sokolow, *To Masters and Mentors*, p. 85.

is wholly missing in the substance of their culture." Later on Thon again distinguished between education and culture and noted that the Jews suffered from the absence of cultural roots. His explanation for this lack was that "Here the sole determinants are race, blood, and other 'dark forces.' "

It would appear that we have leaped here from the motif of physical fitness – or, in a broader sense, the theme of a return to nature – to an entirely new subject: blood and race. But for all intents and purposes, this is merely an extrapolation of the same motif. We can see this quite clearly in Leon Kellner's 1896 statement about mother earth or Bernard Lazare's 1897 pronouncement that: "The truth of the matter is that the Jew in Christian societies cannot help being an assimilationist. He will not restore his creativity until he goes back to drawing upon Jewish sources." Yet Thon's express reference to race and blood and the "dark forces" nevertheless begs comment.

Thon lived in Berlin in the 1890s, and we can safely assume that his statement reflected trends that were widespread during that period among the German intelligentsia. The intellectual climate of the day was awash with anti-rationalist attitudes like those which found expression in Julius Langbehn's book on Rembrandt as an educator. Langbehn advocated physical fitness and a folk wisdom rooted in the soil of the homeland, as opposed to book learning; the sway of German blood, as opposed to the decadence of the assimilationist Jew. Thon, the Zionist, regarded Lublinski, the scholar of German literature, as a prime example of the assimilationist Jew: talented but rootless, cerebral and abstract, a man who dissociated himself from his race but who, as an outsider, could never penetrate down to the heart of the culture "that grows organically from within." In statements of this kind, it is difficult to determine where Jewish nationalism ends and German ideology begins. Yet it is certainly interesting to note how the Zionist approach laid the ground for the absorption of these influences and accorded them positive weight.[33]

33 Osias Thon, "Ein Abgefallener," *Die Welt* (December 15, 1901), p. 4; Bernard Lazare, "Solidarité," *Zion* (French section), (May 31, 1897), p. 24. On Langbehn and his influence, see Fritz Stern, *The Politics of Cultural Despair* (New York, 1961), pp. 167, 179, 183, 200.

Martin Buber persistently developed the same outlook, though he expressed it less categorically than Thon. In an article entitled "The Jewish Renaissance," an appellation of which he was so fond, Buber wrote in 1901 of the need to revive a "sense of life," as opposed to "pure intellectualism." The man who would one day sing the praises of the Hasidic spirit was at this point still speaking of "impudence and Hasidism" in the same breath as "sick phenomena." On the other hand, Buber called upon the Jews "to feel as though they are an organism and to aspire to harmonize their powers, to invest as much soul in walking, singing, and working as in solving intellectual problems, and to derive pleasure out of pride and love for a healthy and perfect body." This is not yet an outright rejection of all things intellectual, but the stress is laid on things that had been neglected because of an excessive preference for the workings of the mind. Further on Buber spoke of the national movement as a harbinger of "the new culture of beauty for our people" and of the modern Hebrew language "which alone would be able to find the appropriate words for the passion and pain of our soul."[34]

Buber's subsequent biography and the fame he won the world over must not be allowed to distort the assessment of his role during the period under scrutiny. Even then he had an inimitable style, though he could not yet be said to be the original thinker of later years. He belonged to an intellectual circle that shared a similar approach to questions of culture and nationalism – to the point of comprising a consistent outlook that influenced the Democratic Fraction. Berthold Feiwel, Osias Thon, Marcus Ehrenpreis and others spoke in much the same spirit. Ehrenpreis, for example, wrote two articles in 1903, one in the *Jüdischer Almanach* (which Feiwel edited) about the renascent Hebrew literature, the other in *Hashiloah*, where he reported to the Hebrew reader about Feiwel's Almanac. In the German article he spoke of the renascent culture of "our race," saying, "We wish once again to redeem the plenitude of beauty, the beauty of the self, that has been repressed for thousands of years and develop it to its ultimate." In the Hebrew article he spoke of the need to forge a new life based "not only on the brain but on feeling; not only

34 Martin Buber, "Jüdische Renaissance," *Ost und West*, 1 (1901), pp. 9-10; cf. George L. Mosse, *Germans and Jews* (New York, 1970), pp. 85-90.

on the utilitarian but on the aesthetic; not only on morality but on power; not only on the spiritual but on the material." The juxtaposition of morality and power suggests a Nietzschean influence, which will be discussed further on in these pages.[35]

In 1903 Max Bodenheimer, who certainly was not associated with this circle, likewise reflected similar influences – and added a flourish of his own. This was at the time of the Sixth Zionist Congress in a celebratory speech on the establishment of an organization dedicated to physical fitness. "The oppression of centuries has rendered our people faint-hearted. Living in foul, horribly overcrowded neighborhoods has weakened it physically. The mind has been nurtured at the expense of physical prowess and health. This lopsidedness has caused damage from which even our young national movement suffers." Bodenheimer went on to complain of the poor understanding of hierarchy so necessary for a movement that had ambitions of leading the masses; of the overdeveloped critical faculty; and of the prominence of the "ego." He disparaged the intellectual and hypercritical types that peopled the Zionist organization and commended "strong, robust, and courageous men with a sense of discipline and fealty." One may recall that a similar decrial of Jewish skepticism had been expressed earlier by Heinrich Loewe. Blaming the diaspora condition was a recurrent theme in Zionist writings, and so was the notion of restoring the body to its proper stature in place of the emphasis on intellectual pursuits. However, in Bodenheimer's writings, the cultivation of the body was completely devoid of Buber's "sense of life" or Ehrenpreis's longing for "the plenitude of beauty," and of course they bore no resemblance to Ravnitski's ideal of tilling the soil or Sokolow's ideas about nature. Even Motzkin, who spoke in glowing terms of the colonists' will to defend themselves, did not subscribe to Bodenheimer's hierarchical ideal. The one writer who did bear a certain resemblance to Bodenheimer is Fabius Schach, then a close associate of his who accentuated "the manly virtues of courage and loyalty" and the like.

Bodenheimer's words were essentially an expression of dissatisfac-

---

35 M. Ehrenpreis, "Junghebraeische Dichtung" in Feiwel, ed., *Jüdischer Almanach*, p. 43; M. Ehrenpreis, "A Literary View," *Hashiloah*, 11 (1903), p. 188 (Hebrew).

tion with petty busybodies, for he had little patience with the short-comings of a voluntary movement like Zionism. Yet they clearly bespoke an identification with the ideals of Wilhelmine Germany favoring "strong, robust, and courageous men" over the "thinkers, philosophers, and critics" who tended to resist authority. Boden-heimer's outlook also came out quite clearly in a memorandum he submitted to Herzl a few months later setting forth his reservations about the approach bequeathed to Zionism by the Lovers of Zion. He lamented that Zionism had inherited a preference for agricul-tural settlement and argued that Zionist colonization should be based upon "military occupation" so that the colonists would not fall "victim to the fanaticism" of the local majority population. In fact, Bodenheimer proposed that the nucleus of a military force be established immediately.[36]

This was not the first time that Herzl had been approached with proposals of this kind. Just as he was becoming involved with Zion-ism, two students from the Kadimah Society broached the sugges-tion of establishing a battalion of 1,000-2,000 volunteers that would attempt to drop anchor at Jaffa. "I advised them against this fine Garibaldean idea," Herzl wrote in his diary. Still, he did not disre-gard the military side of the Jewish revival, and in his early days as a Zionist he wrote, "After all, we once were men who knew how to defend the state in time of war." Thereafter, in appearing before the Lovers of Zion in London, Herzl explained that he wanted "only the kind of colonization that we could protect with our own Jewish army." And in 1901, after a few years of fruitless diplomatic activity, he actually contemplated the possibility of a military conquest. In the wake of a rumor that rule over Cyprus would be transferred into German hands, he wondered whether it would be possible to "rally" on the island, move on to Palestine, and "take it by force, as it was taken from us long ago." The "lurid idea" – Herzl's self-judgment – was a fleeting one, and the Zionist leader never even answered Bodenheimer's memo. Although he promised Bodenheimer to dis-cuss the points it covered, this conversation never took place. The

---

36 Bodenheimer, *Im Anfang der zionistischen Bewegung*, pp. 294, 339; cf. Barbara W. Tuchman, *The Proud Tower* (New York, 1967), pp. 358-360.

memorandum was sent on February 28, 1904, and Herzl died on July 30.[37]

At best it can be said that the same strivings which filled the hearts of so many Zionists assumed different forms, so that one man's "Jewry of brawn" was not necessarily another's. Actually, striking ideological and political differences lay behind this term. Despite the frequent convergence of Haskalah ideas and general intellectual trends, we must point out the varying degrees of congruence between these two influences. For this purpose the Zionists can be divided into three groupings:

* The Polish-Russian group, which aspired to create a new type of Jew in the spirit of the Haskalah.
* The German group, which wanted to model the new Jew along the Wilhelmine pattern.
* The Galician group, which interpreted the tradition of the Haskalah in the spirit of the German intelligentsia.

There was much talk then – and much exaggeration – about the differences between the Western Zionists (meaning essentially Zionists in Germany and Austria-Hungary) and their East European comrades. The dividing line between East and West in the Zionist movement was not as definitive as one might gather from these internal debates. Many of the Western Zionists were in fact natives of Eastern Europe, adding to the difficulty of establishing exactly where the border ran between "East" and "West." Far clearer were the frontiers dividing the three European empires – Russia, Germany, and Austria-Hungary – especially as these borders also delineated the main Jewish centers of population (notwithstanding the considerable differences between various regions) and accounted for certain differences within the Zionist movement as well. The Zionists generally labeled as Westerners were brought up in the German culture and susceptible to its influence, almost to the exclusion of all others, even though they subscribed to Jewish nationalism. In contrast, the Zionists of both Russia and Galicia were exposed to many currents, through both Hebrew culture (in which many of them were schooled) and the cultures of their environment, which

37 Herzl, *Diaries*, Vol. I, pp. 355, 9, 420, Vol. III, p. 1023.

were open to influences from the West. As the middle ground between Polish-Russian Zionism and its German counterpart, the Zionist intelligentsia from Galicia strongly reflected the impact of various trends and perhaps, too, the consequent cultural cross-fertilization. Certainly it would appear that way from our inquiry into the theme of the "muscular Jewry," but we should nevertheless keep these distinctions in mind when examining other subjects.

A Revaluation of All Values

Nietzsche's call for the revaluation of all values became the battle cry of his Zionist disciples, headed by Micha Josef Berdyczewski. Berdyczewski had spent many years in Germany and even wrote in German, but the controversy over the "revaluation of values" was confined mainly to the Hebrew-writing intelligentsia and did not spread to other Zionist circles. Berdyczewski's writings were aimed primarily at spiritual Zionists and elicited strong responses – positive and negative – mostly among Ahad Ha'am's followers. One may well wonder why the ideas of a philosopher like Nietzsche, who was already renowned by that time, found their way into Zionist thinking via the interpretation of a Hebrew writer, of all people. In Berdyczewski's hands Nietzsche's doctrine was reconstituted and adapted to the spiritual needs of the new Hebrew intellectual. In a sense, Berdyczewski's reading of Nietzsche was the crucible in which ideas popular among the young intellectuals of the day were blended, sorted out again, and ultimately used to leaven Zionist thinking. If there were other avenues through which Nietzsche's doctrine influenced Zionist thinking, they are not readily apparent.[38]

We shall begin our survey of the controversy over the "revaluation of values" with Berdyczewski's reaction to Ahad Ha'am's programmatic article in the first issue of *Hashiloah*. Ahad Ha'am insisted that only pieces having a direct bearing on Jewish affairs were to be published in his journal and even banned "poesie" from its pages. It was a policy opposed by both Thon and Ehrenpreis and most adamantly by Berdyczewski, who assailed Ahad Ha'am's decision as a

38 See Walter Kaufmann, *Nietzsche* (Cleveland, 1962), pp. 15-16.

whole. "The moment we limit our compass in the name of 'Judaism,'" Berdyczewski admonished, "it follows that there is a non-Jewish life to which we have no access." Further on in the same piece he stated: "By dividing life into two spheres, ours and theirs, we are exacerbating the rift in the hearts of our young people, who are at any rate in the throes of a relentless struggle between the lure of Japhet [the gentiles] and the tents of Shem [the Jews]." Berdyczewski maintained that "we want to be Hebrew human beings at one and the same time."[39]

This was an expression of the desire to eradicate the distinction between the Jew and the human being, as prescribed in Judah Leib Gordon's aphorism (which was already classic by then), "Be a man outside and a Jew at home." The ambition to dispose of this dichotomy was not peculiar to Berdyczewski; neither was it at all exceptional in the generation after Gordon's. Even Ahad Ha'am availed himself of Gordon's formulation – albeit in reverse – in commenting that since the rise of nationalism the prescription to "*be a Jew outside*" had been in full force, but what remained to be achieved was the part about being "*a man at home.*" Presumably this reverse construction was an attempt to provide the Jew with a sense of self-esteem in his contacts with the world, while simultaneously enriching the humanist content of Jewish culture. Such word play was undoubtedly pleasing to the ear of those familiar with Gordon's dichotomy, but actually Ahad Ha'am himself did not accept the distinction. He believed that the two roles had to be amalgamated or, as he put it, "In vain shall we labor to give our national life a new, improved shape; the deformed *man* lurks within" – by which he meant that nationalism could not content itself with outward appearances; it would have to be judged by its inner nature, and if it did not stand up to the "human" test, it would be meaningless.

J. C. Ravnitski, one of Ahad Ha'am's associates, phrased things in a similar spirit in the article referred to above when he pro-

---

39. Ahad Ha'am, "The Mission of *Hashiloah*," *Hashiloah*, 1 (1896), p. 1 (Hebrew); M. J. Berdyczewski, "At a Crossroads" (An Open Letter to Ahad Ha'am), *Hashiloah*, 1 (1896), pp. 154-159 (Hebrew).

nounced that: "The Jew must be a man both at home and outside."[40]
Though Ahad Ha'am, Berdyczewski, and Ravnitski all wanted to
bridge Gordon's dichotomy between the Jewish being and the
human being, there were substantive differences between the meaning that each of them ascribed to the concept of man. Ahad Ha'am
regarded man as basically a moral category; Ravnitski used the term
to connote the need for a general culture; and Berdyczewski's man
symbolized the affirmation of life, which was also the key to his
whole outlook and the new thrust associated with his "revaluation
of values." This impulse was not toward creating a new aesthetic or
establishing a literary-philosophic school, but toward resolving the
crisis that had overtaken the Jews and might, he feared, result in
their total obliteration. Berdyczewski did not articulate the symptoms of this crisis – as either the weakening of Jewish identity or a
threat from without – but he definitely did convey the sense of crisis
in speaking of the choice coming down to "being or extinction."

In the course of indicating a way out of this crisis, Berdyczewski
proffered a series of presumed antipodes: Jews vs. Judaism, "the law
of the heart" vs. false spirituality, a national renaissance vs. a rejection of the past. In an article entitled "Destruction and Construction," submitted to Ahad Ha'am in 1897 for publication in
Hashiloah, he framed a dichotomy that suggested a fundamental
change in the view of history and of Jewish identity. Speaking of the
choice between being "the last Jews or the first Hebrews,"
Berdyczewski implied that a cure was not enough, radical though it
might be. The Jews, he believed, were at the end of the Jewish phase
of their history, and the time had come to embark upon a new phase
that would revitalize forgotten symbols from the distant past. It is
possible, of course, that the difference between the "last Jews" and
the "first Hebrews" was a slip of Berdyczewski's pen incidentally,
and that he himself did not realize the far-reaching implications of
the statement. In fact, the explanation that followed seemed to miti-
gate the impact of the original aphorism: "In concentrating on the

40 Judah Leib Gordon, "My People Has Awakened" (1863) in *Poems* (Jerusalem-
    Tel Aviv, 1952), p. 5 (Hebrew); Ahad Ha'am, *Collected Works*, pp. 50-51;
    Editor (J. C. Ravnitski), "To the Divisions of the House of Israel" in *Pardess*,
    Vol. III, p. 7.

heart of the matter, the renaissance of the people, we are unable to address ourselves to the people's traditions as well." This led him to explain the opposition between renaissance and tradition: "Admittedly, it is by virtue of our past that we have the historic right to go on existing in the future and to manifest the right to exist; and at a time when we are on the march and are waging a battle for our existence, we turn back to the days of Jewish glory, to our heroes and warriors, to our great men and the kindlers of our spirit. But neither can we conceal that the heritage of our forefathers has caused us a great loss." Thus Berdyczewski was able to appreciate the past not only as a source of heroic inspiration but also as embracing "the kindlers of our spirit" and most of all as the basis for claiming the right of national existence. The close of the Jewish chapter in history was not entirely volitional; it was more of an apocalyptic vision of the "last Jews" whose approaching end was inexorable. To Berdyczewski, alienation from Judaism and the Jewish past sometimes appeared to be a fate that he foretold with mixed feelings.[41].

Ahad Ha'am wrote to Berdyczewski expressing his regrets that he could not print a piece "that publicly impugns historical Judaism" and was not even supported by "strong topical and historical evidence." He also admitted that he chose not to publish the article so as to protect *Hashiloah* against charges that it was "against the Jewish religion." About a year later Ahad Ha'am addressed himself to Berdyczewski's doctrine (without mentioning him by name) in an article he would later entitle "A Change in Values." "The entire course of our people's history," he wrote, "from the age of the prophets to the present, is taken by these wordsmiths to be one long mistake that requires immediate, complete rectification." He also touched upon this doctrine in his sarcastic reference to the new values that "would remove the fetters from the soul that thirsts for life."

Paradoxically, perhaps, Ahad Ha'am regarded Nietzsche himself with great admiration and even tried "to show that the doctrine of 'a revaluation of values' is capable of being grafted on to that of Judaism." Thus true to his system, Ahad Ha'am attempted to adapt even this philosophy to Judaism "in a way that is beneficial and con-

41 Micha Josef Berdyczewski, "Destruction and Construction" in *Complete Works*, Articles Volume (Tel Aviv, 1960), p. 29 (Hebrew).

sonant with its spirit," and he lashed into "our young writers" who chose to accept Nietzsche at face value. For his part, Ahad Ha'am was confident that it was quite impossible to "overthrow mercilessly and at a single blow the edifice which our ancestors have left us." He then likened the "national character" to:

> a fruit which ripens little by little through the ages under the influence of innumerable causes, some permanent, some transient, not in accordance with a system laid down and defined at the outset. Hence it results that in both cases, logical contradictions abound, the norm and the exceptions live side by side. No man has the power to pull them down and build them up according to his desire and taste: they change constantly of their own accord, reflecting the changes in the nation's circumstances, character and needs.[42]

I have quoted from Ahad Ha'am at length to elucidate the methodological difference between his approach and that of Berdyczewski, who followed Nietzsche in rejecting history. If, in speaking of "our young writers," Ahad Ha'am meant not only Berdyczewski but also his associate Ehrenpreis and other members of their circle, then he failed to appreciate the shades of difference between them. All, it is true, subscribed to the principle of affirming life, but Ehrenpreis was actually closer to Ahad Ha'am himself in his perception of the historical organism. Ahad Ha'am also overlooked the tragic aspect of Berdyczewski's rejection of the past and failed to see that this rejection was selective rather than absolute – dialectic, if you wish.

There were many facets to Berdyczewski's rejection of the past, though his abstruse style does nothing to enhance access to them. We have already described the incongruity between a positive assessment of the past as a source of the national rationale and the sense of Judaism's inexorable doom, implying the loss of all the accumulated assets of the past. The contrariety he established between *Jews* and *Hebrews* bespoke his propensity to hark back to ancient history

---

42 Ahad Ha'am *Letters*, edited by the author, Vol. I (Jerusalem-Berlin, 1923), p. 98 (Hebrew); Ahad Ha'am, *Nationalism and the Jewish Ethic* (New York, 1962), pp. 183-184.

and divorce it completely from the annals of the Jews in the diaspora – this, too, more as a rescue effort than a desideratum. In an article written in 1897 he placed Jewish history in the dock, judged it by modern national criteria, and found it wanting. He censured the Jews exiled from their land centuries earlier because, unlike other defeated peoples, "We alone did not sacrifice our existence for our country, and we chose to flee it even before it cast us out; we chose to traffic among the nations without leaving so much as a trace of ourselves in our land." He argued that despite "all the historical and compelling reasons for our dispersion," it would have been possible to avoid exile had the Jews been possessed of "a strong national will." This indictment reached its height in his decrial of Judaism's spiritual heritage:

> The people and its finest knew the virtue of their soil and fought for it to the last drop of blood; they had a vibrant spirit, a sense of themselves and of their duty. But the people's leaders perverted the natural instinct with their false spirituality and led it to choose Jabneh and her dependent villages over the fortress of Jerusalem – the bastion of the nation's being.

Obviously this historical example was not a matter for academic inquiry but the symbol of a world view that far exceeded the bounds of the ancient era. It is as if Berdyczewski took it for granted that there was an obvious continuity or analogy between Rabbi Yohanan Ben-Zakkai – the founder of the Pharisaic spiritual center – and the present champions of "false" spirituality, on the one hand, and between the fighters of antiquity and the present bearers of a "strong national will," on the other. However, Berdyczewski was not the only one to choose Jabneh as a symbol of both historical and contemporary significance; his opponent Ahad Ha'am did likewise in denouncing political Zionism for failing to comprehend the Love of Zion movement "just as the demand of [Rabbi Yohanan Ben-Zakkai for Jabneh] was strange and unintelligible to the corresponding people of that time."[43]

---

43 Berdyczewski, *Epigones*, p. 33; Ahad Ha'am, *Nationalism and the Jewish Ethic*, p. 79.

Jabneh, which embedded itself in Zionist thought as a symbol of excessive spirituality and national defeatism, became almost a synonym for Ahad Ha'am's spiritual Zionism. In 1905, for example, an unidentified "member of the editorial board" of the newspaper *Hazman* restated Berdyczewski's thesis and warned that Zionism was being eroded by "rot" – by which he meant Ahad Ha'am's school of thought. "We must not crave real life," he complained, "we must not yearn for real earth, to develop naturally." In attacking the historical approach of the spiritual school, he asked: "What is this natural development of Jewish history that our spiritual Zionists refer to with such awe?" The writer believed that Jewish history up to the destruction of the First Temple was essentially a "natural development," but only relatively short intervals of the Second Temple period deserved to be labeled "natural." He then extended his polemic by inveighing against the historical approach construed by the religious tradition: "Hanukkah commemorates only the miracle of the cruse of oil . . . and the Jewish war against the Romans was the work of 'desperados.' Were it not for what Ben-Zakkai did, there would be no point in discussing the matter at all, for in any event the only important thing was the destruction of the *Temple*." Ben-Zakkai's preference for a center of learning over political independence is the high point in this diatribe against the historiography that had extolled the Pharisees over the militant Zealots. Finally, we can see the leitmotif of Zionism's historical approach in the portrayal of the Hasmonean revolt as the antithesis of the miracle of Hanukkah.[44]

The quarrel here centered on the meaning of "natural development," for which two different interpretations were in evidence. One had to do with a kind of theodicy, as implied to some extent in Ahad Ha'am's organic system; the other ascribed a normative value to the concept and therefore opted for a conventional development of history. Thus the author singled out "natural" or normal periods in the Jewish history – such as the First and, to a lesser degree, the Second Temple periods – which stand in contrast to the examples he

44 Editor, "One Thing and Another," *Hazman* (February 10, 1905), p.1 (Hebrew); cf. Jacob Neusner, *Development of a Legend* (Leiden, 1970), p. 298.

deplores. Like Berdyczewski, he lodged his complaint not just against the unfolding of history – what actually took place – but against the framing of historical consciousness. In this scheme of things, "what Ben-Zakkai did" is quite unimportant in itself; what counts is the reigning outlook in Judaism, which made light of the Hasmonean war and much of the Temple and the cruse of oil. The point is unmistakable: history has supplied us with various models of Jewish behavior, and there are two opposing examples from the end of the Second Temple period – the war of the Zealots against the Romans, and Yohanan Ben-Zakkai's flight from beleaguered Jerusalem to Jabneh by the grace of the Romans. And yet it is Jabneh that has remained the standard in Jewish tradition! Even an event of such major political consequence as the Hasmonean victory has been reduced in the historical consciousness to the mere backdrop to a miracle. All this apparently resulted from the self-serving view of the Pharisees, later bequeathed to traditional Jewish history.

Hence the brunt of the blame was placed on those who had fashioned the Jewish tradition, just as Berdyczewski reviled the leaders for impressing their "false spirituality" on the unsuspecting people. Yet Berdyczewski went even further and did not absolve history itself. He denounced the people, too – the Jews who had abandoned their land unnecessarily – not just their leaders and the religious tradition. As we have said, Berdyczewski's attitude toward the past was fraught with contradictions and surprises. In an article published in the *Jüdischer Almanach* in 1902, he spoke ruefully of the Hebrew literature that had turned its back on the past: "The stalk was severed from the roots in order to move about freely; but the past weighed like a debt, which only heightened the soul's torment."

Here Berdyczewski sounded as though he were trying, unsuccessfully, to forge a synthesis between the old and the new by treating the past as an ongoing process. His dictum that "Historicity demands its right" is consistent with his subsequent talk of "the life of the people that stands on its own," whereas the genuine poets were caught "in the ban of this great negation" – apparently dissatisfied with the detachment of the writers, who remained outside the historical process of nationalism by sustaining the themes of the Haskalah. Thus in place of the wholesale rejection of the past that we have come to expect of Berdyczewski, we find here an expression of another characteristic motif: his deep-seated pessimism. Ahad Ha'am, for all his skepticism and faultfinding, espoused a world view that held out hope for the survival of the national organism. But Berdyczewski's revolt against history offered no ideological assurance of a better future. Even in viewing the historical process as an opportunity for renewing national life, he was unable to overcome a sense of despair. Pessimism and a "tragic bent," as Berdyczewski himself characterized his posture, remained the dominant tone of his essays.[45]

Our discussion takes on an interesting slant when we discover that the unnamed "member of the editorial board" who assailed spiritual Zionism from a position similar to Berdyczewski's was none other than the feature writer Israel Chaim Tawiow – the same Tawiow who in 1900 had written a series of articles entitled "The Obligations of Spiritual Zionism" in praise of Hebrew culture. Back in 1900 Tawiow was already writing in a mode that approximated his later style, though his sights were trained on different targets. Then he warned against the insinuation of the "ghetto spirit" into Zionism; now he was crying out against those responsible for introducing the "rot" of spiritual Zionism into the national movement. When Berdyczewski derided the proponents of cultural work, Tawiow was still commending it and calling for "a complete revaluation of diaspora values." His target then was religious Judaism and its allies within the Zionist movement, and he shared the same vantage as the "culturists" – Ahad Ha'am and the Democratic Fraction. But now he reproached spiritual Zionism for not going far enough in its assault on the traditional content of Jewish culture.[46]

Nietzschean rhetoric ("a complete revaluation of diaspora values") did not make Tawiow stand out among the advocates of cultural work, for in fact it was quite common in these circles – either because the "culturists" accepted Berdyczewski's reading of Nie-

45 M. J. Berdyczewski, "Das Neuhebraeische" in Feiwel, ed., *Jüdischer Almanach* (1902), pp. 31-32.
46 I. C. Tawiow, "The Duties of Spiritual Zionism," *Hamelitz* (June 8, 1900), p. 1 (Hebrew); I. C. Tawiow, "An Augury of Wealth," *Hamelitz* (March 11, 1900), p. 2 (Hebrew).

tzsche, or because they were at any rate influenced by his philo-
sophic mood. Berdyczewski's friend Ehrenpreis joined issue with
Nietzsche in proclaiming, "Not Jerusalem *vs.* Rome – as Nietzsche
said – but Jerusalem *with* Rome." Chaim Dov Hurewitz, a member
of the Democratic Fraction, wrote: "Preparing our people for a great
and enlightened future demands a negative attitude toward the mental results that our *strange life* in the diaspora have brought to bear,
toward the 'slave morality' that was appropriate in its day but has
now become an absolute evil."[47] Hurewitz did not take Nietzsche at
face value. He did not deem the "slave morality" as implicitly negative, but borrowed a concept from Nietzsche to distinguish between
the Jews' "natural qualities" and the "negative effect of ghetto conditions." Both Hurewitz and Ehrenpreis availed themselves of concepts that were widespread among the intelligentsia to do precisely
the opposite of what Berdyczewski had done: not adapt Nietzsche's
doctrine, but utilize it to prove their own theses. After all, whoever
tried to fuse Rome and Jerusalem or to equate the "slave morality"
with the negative qualities that had adhered to the Jews in the diaspora was repudiating Nietzsche's philosophy. The German philosopher regarded Jewry not as an evolving historical entity but as a spiritual one whose hallmarks had been impressed upon it in antiquity.
Hence it was no coincidence that Berdyczewski's criticism – and
Tawiow's in its wake – was directed at a specific Jewish tradition
that traced back to before the destruction of the Temple and was not
a result of the condition of exile.

Thus we can either take Berdyczewski's and Tawiow's approach as
the antithesis of the culturist school or we can categorize these two
writers along with the rest and view them as an extreme wing of the
same ideological camp. Berdyczewski's qualms about his rejection
of the past and Tawiow's original appreciation of spiritual Zionism,
added to Berdyczewski's close friendship with Ehrenpreis and the
devotion of this entire circle to Ahad Ha'am and his doctrine – all
point to the existence of a common ground. To define the limits of

---

47 M. Ehrenpreis, "A Literary View," *Hashiloah*, 11 (1903), p. 188 (Hebrew);
    C. D. Hurewitz, "Theory and Action," *Ahiasaf Calendar* (1903), p. 121
    (Hebrew).

this partnership, it is enough to cite a figure who falls squarely outside this camp.

Moses Leib Lilienblum also responded to Berdyczewski's call for "a revaluation of values," but his reaction attested to a substantial difference in outlook. "We don't need a change in values," Lilienblum scoffed, "merely a change in our lives, a change of the diaspora – and that is dependent primarily upon others. Any new values introduced into the circumstances of our old life will do us no good." He did not debate the question on its own merits for it was irrelevant to him; everything depended upon the change of external circumstances. Compare this with Berdyczewski's statement that "The renaissance will surely come only from *within*." It is true that both Berdyczewski and Lilienblum held cultural work in low esteem, but their objections stemmed from different reasons. Berdyczewski opposed it because he wanted to change the *content* of Jewish culture, while Lilienblum was against any undertaking that did not lead to "a change of the diaspora."[48]

From Lilienblum's vantage, the dispute over a "revaluation of values" was a family spat, rather than a full-fledged ideological fray. Zionists of Lilienblum's bent were not concerned with Nietzsche and the philosophy of life, for their main interest was in an external change that was "dependent primarily upon others." This may also explain why the Nietzschean doctrine had such a meager impact upon the political Zionists. All the others – from Berdyczewski to Ahad Ha'am – were primarily interested in engendering a change in Jewish life and therefore needed the instrument of theoretical debate to elucidate the form that change would take. This is an observation that encompasses the whole range of Zionist life during that period but affected the cultural issue in particular. The disparity between the basic outlooks of the political Zionists and their rivals was so great that their differences often seemed to eclipse their common properties. What emerges, moreover, is a picture of no understanding whatever for the motives of the rival camp. Despite the rancor that occasionally marked the exchanges between Berdyczewski and Ahad Ha'am, they shared a common cultural frame of reference; and

48 M. L. Lilienblum, "On Upheavals," *Ahiasaf Calendar* (1901), p. 201 (Hebrew); Berdyczewski, *Epigones*, p. 74.

although they may have disagreed, they certainly understood each other – which could not necessarily be said of the political Zionists and their opponents. In the latter case, ideological debate would not clarify or resolve the differences between the two sides, and only figures like Lilienblum – who was not really identified with either group – were capable of fully appreciating these differences and defining the issues at stake.

The Jewish Renaissance

Having placed Berdyczewski at one extreme of spiritual Zionism, we should devote some attention to this school. Spiritual Zionism was not a party or a faction, and association with it was solely a matter of ideological rapport. Yet even in matters ideological, it had no formal framework – no official platform, no symposia, not even a permanent circle of activists. The characteristic common to most of the members of this rather amorphous camp was their status as East European intellectuals, who had been exposed to Western culture but remained attached to Judaism in a cultural sense. The spiritual Zionists included writers, journalists, modern rabbis, and the like, and all were associated to one degree or another with Ahad Ha'am and the journal *Hashiloah*. This circle also produced the nucleus of the Democratic Fraction, an organized wing of the Zionist movement that was loosely associated with, but not identical to spiritual Zionism.

The absence of a common framework of activity, the difference in age between Ahad Ha'am and most of his disciples, and their geographical dispersion, all had an effect upon the views and leanings of this school. If we examine the writings of its adherents over the span of a decade, we will be able to discern differences wrought by time as well. Nevertheless, there were many similarities to their assessments of the Jewish past and its value as an instrument to forge a modern Jewish culture. On the whole, spiritual Zionism seemed to place an unequivocal emphasis on the historical, in contrast to the pragmatic line pursued by Herzl, who was consequently perceived as being "a stranger to Judaism" (as Aaron Kaminka put it in 1898) and oblivious to its "historical ideals."

The approach to the past taken by Ahad Ha'am, the father of spiritual Zionism, was essentially dialectic. He viewed modern Jewish nationalism as a revival of the classical past, but he did not hold that it was imperative to embrace the heritage of the past *in toto*. Here, for example, is what he had to say about the nationalists who "feel obliged to say 'amen' – be it merely as lip service – to everything about our ancestral heritage that has become sacrosanct to the people." Here Ahad Ha'am appeared to be subjecting this heritage to scrutiny by the criteria of historical criticism, but in fact his approach was far more complex. Further on in the same paragraph he argued that the nationalists who sanctified tradition believed "in the erroneous assertion that it is impossible to regard the past objectively and to see what is out of place by our contemporary standards, without implicitly passing a negative judgment on the *intrinsic value* of the ancients." Apparently Ahad Ha'am was confident that even if we approach the past critically, the relevance of tradition would not be undermined at all. His ideal was historical research along the lines of the natural sciences – "whose purpose is not to *pass judgment*" – and here is how he envisioned the realization of his ideal: "It is as if every educated man who delves into the past in this way is entered by the soul of every generation, sees and understands the thinking of his ancestors and feels their spiritual needs, and therefore no longer attaches any stigma to their spiritual mien because their views and mores were not consonant in every detail with our concepts and needs today."

Hence understanding history requires an empathetic more than a critical approach. After penetrating through the layers of the past, we must deal with each period on its own terms. This realization leads one to ask: Other than becoming acquainted with the life of generations past, what broader significance does the study of history have for modern man? Much ink has been spent on Ahad Ha'am's doctrines, and he can be criticized for the internal contradictions in his writings or his mixture of a positivist approach with historical determinism and certainly for his attempt to impose upon an entire society his ideal of "the educated man who delves into the past."[49]

49 A. Kaminka, "The Preliminary Conference and the Next Congress," *Jewish Chronicle*, London (May 6, 1898), p. 12; Ahad Ha'am, "Little Digest – Ancestral Portion," *Hashiloah*, 2 (1897), p. 381 (Hebrew).

But we are not concerned here with philosophical criticism; our interest is in understanding Ahad Ha'am's role in the development of Zionist thinking during the period under consideration. Hence we shall juxtapose the above quote with a statement that reveals another side of his attitude toward the past – this one written against the background of the dispute over cultural work.

While the above-quoted complaint was against the sanctification of the past, about a year later Ahad Ha'am redressed the balance by stressing the imperative of maintaining a link with the past. In an article written at about the time of the Second Zionist Congress, he tried to establish a common ground between the spiritual and religious Zionists, as distinct from the "new Jews" who were devoted to political Zionism. In doing so he distinguished between two concepts – "rebirth, not creation" – and posited that a spiritual Zionist and a religious Jew shared "a feeling of love and respect for the people's spiritual assets and a desire for a national renaissance based on the historical bond between God, the Torah, and the Jews." Further on he added: "They both hold fast to the long thread of the historical past and are merely trying to extend it under more auspicious circumstances." This article was ostensibly written in response to a letter from a man who defined himself as a "Jew who loves his people and its literature but is nonetheless a free thinker," and Ahad Ha'am made him into the prototype of the spiritual Zionist.[50] The article's portrayal of the secular Jew's relationship to history was essentially anchored in Ahad Ha'am's determinism. It was as if he were trying to say that the way things are is the way things should be; so that if Jewish history had assumed a religious coloration – that too was part of the legacy binding upon the modern Jew.

We have seen that even when Ahad Ha'am claimed to take a critical approach toward the Jewish heritage, he limited the scope of his criticism by invoking the "intrinsic value" of earlier generations, which should not be measured against the concepts of the modern critic. He was not trying to restore the secular Jew's lost faith; nor was he trying to conceal that he himself preferred the "national free thinker" to the religious Jew. What he did was endow the secular

50 Ahad Ha'am, "Little Digest – Rebirth and Creation," *Hashiloah*, 4 (1898), p. 192 (Hebrew).

nationalist with a sense of respect for religion because it was integral to Jewish history. In its most concise formulation, Ahad Ha'am's attitude toward history was an attempt to incorporate two major elements into a single system: (1) history as a *sine qua non* that modern man must perpetuate; and (2) history as the foil through which modern man characterizes himself ("rebirth, not creation"). It is in this context that the spiritual Zionist outlook on the Jewish renaissance developed.

We will be able to get a closer look at this mode of thinking if we follow its development by one of Ahad Ha'am's associates, the scholar and publicist Simon Bernfeld. In 1899 Bernfeld published an article in *Die Welt*, the official organ of the Zionist Organization, on the differences between political Zionism and spiritual Zionism. The weekly's editorial board saw fit to append the caveat that it was publishing the work of a "non-Zionist writer," and Ahad Ha'am expressed both his pleasure over the article and his surprise that *Die Welt* had agreed to print it. In the piece Bernfeld reiterated the well-known distinction – drawn by Ahad Ha'am and Berdyczewski – between *Judaism* and *Jewry*, with the Zionists portrayed as champions of the existential sense of the concept and the author professing an interest in the "spiritual renaissance of Judaism." On reconsideration, however, Bernfeld confessed that "you can't have one, from an historical standpoint, without the other." Thereafter, in an article written on Ahad Ha'am in 1900, he again leveled his criticism at the "Western Zionists" in saying, "It is impossible to ensure the future of a nation by destroying its past" – a reference to the conduct of the political Zionists in failing to pay sufficient attention to the past. But that was not the author's main point. Bernfeld's article on Ahad Ha'am remained unpublished until five years after its composition. It comprised two different sections: the original part, which treated Ahad Ha'am and his philosophy with admiration and benign criticism; and the coda – written shortly before its publication – which was a sharp attack on Ahad Ha'am's "romantic" outlook.

As it happened, Bernfeld's *volte-face* on Ahad Ha'am was concurrent with Tawiow's dissociation from spiritual Zionism. By 1905 Bernfeld was complaining that in recent years Ahad Ha'am's thinking had changed for the worse and that he was trying to construct a more "positive doctrine" as a result of pressure from opponents of his highly critical approach. One gets the impression that the original adherents of spiritual Zionism were disappointed by the stress that Ahad Ha'am had begun to place on idealistic philosophy, rather than the biological nationalism that had once been the central motif of his thinking. Evidently they felt the need to reexamine his doctrine in order to clarify how far they were still prepared to follow him and how much emphasis it placed on rebirth and the new, rather than on history and the old. Bernfeld now charged Ahad Ha'am with being too willing to accept the Jewish tradition as is, "even though he concedes its ability to develop naturally." He defined the relationship between the old and the new in Judaism in a way that redoubled his dissatisfaction with Ahad Ha'am's stance: "I do not want to revive one of the standard forms of our historical development but to invent a form that never existed before. Only a development of that sort is natural and viable; anything else is essentially *reaction and restoration*. Ahad Ha'am's outlook strives for restoration; it is romantic without the poetic essence of romanticism."[51] Even then, however, Bernfeld did not demolish the theoretical framework of spiritual Zionism. He, too, propounded the integration of its two key elements: a devotion to the past and a thirst for innovation. Yet his preference for invention seems to be so far-reaching that it exceeded beyond Berdyczewski's ken, for while calling for an historical leap, Berdyczewski also recommended a return to the distant past. Bernfeld, on the other hand, had no specific historical paradigm. He accentuated invention, but it can be safely assumed that he did not wish to rule out utilizing particulars from the past, for he also admonished that "it is impossible to ensure the future of a nation by destroying its past."

This rejection of Ahad Ha'am's interpretation of the Jewish renaissance, together with recourse to such presumably negative terms as reaction, restoration, and romanticism and the failure to credit Ahad Ha'am with anything positive, was also a function of the poor personal relations between the two men. Yet that has little bearing on the actual issue at hand. Bernfeld believed that in integrating the

---

51 S. Bernfeld, "Max Nordau in Berlin," *Die Welt* (February 3, 1899), p. 10; S. Bernfeld, "Asher Ginzberg" (literary portrait), *Ha'eshkol*, 5 (1905), pp. 68, 76 (Hebrew).

two key factors cited above, preference should be given to the "natural and viable" development, and this was apparently the dominant tendency among the spiritual Zionists – Ahad Ha'am's drift notwithstanding. The result was neither historical continuity nor an historical leap but the selective use of history.

Martin Buber provides us with another interesting example of how thinking was developing in this direction. In 1899 Buber wrote his grandmother in Galicia of the great admiration he had encountered in Zionist circles for his grandfather, Salomon Buber, a renowned rabbinical scholar. He concluded the letter by saying: "You can therefore see how faithful the Zionists are to their Jewish cultural treasures and the degree to which they readily honor men whose works have raised Judaism's star and whose lives are ample testimony that the vitality of our people has not been destroyed." This view of Judaism's spiritual legacy as the source of present Jewish vitality was not fortuitous for the young Buber. Two years later he would address the Fifth Zionist Congress in a similar vein, saying: "Although we stand wholly within [the bounds] of modern civilization, we cannot forfeit even the least of the things by which the soul of our people has expressed itself." And what were those things? "Language, customs, the innocent folk art of poems and melodies, of candlesticks and costumes." Here Buber stretched the conception of Judaism, shifting from its written culture to the symbols that expressed the emotional richness of Jewish life. For Buber, the collective soul apparently retained all the strata of the past and all the variegated manifestations of Jewish creativity and folklore. And at that point he arrived at a conclusion with direct bearing on our subject here: "Yet we needn't regard all these things with diffident awe as something holy, for they are rather the materials from which we must fashion a new beauty."

That same year Buber wrote an article entitled "Juedische Renaissance," in which he set forth his ideas on the selective approach to the past. Writing of the concept of renaissance, Buber stated: "It has been customary to view it as a return to the old sentimental traditions rooted in folkways and their expression in language, ethics, and thought." But Buber wanted to reject that approach and was determined to wage war against the destructive forces of the ghetto – "the subjugated spirituality and the imposition of a tradition that has been drained of its meaning" – and against the destructive forces of the exile – "the slavery of an unproductive money market and the dulling lack of a homeland that destroys all coherent will." Buber believed that this struggle would release dormant energies and revive in modern life "the features of our tribe that came to the fore during its history of independence, to be stifled by the hardships of the diaspora." He interpreted the etymology of the term renaissance as "rebirth," rather than a return to the classics, and applied the same interpretation to the Jewish renaissance: "Once again, not a reversion but a recreation, using age-old materials." It appears that Buber was reviving the metaphor of using the old building stones, and he dressed the stones according to the pattern of the Jews' independence in antiquity.

Buber was not advocating an historical leap, however. Much to the contrary, his organic-historical approach was not consonant with the notion of an arbitrary leap, and in the final analysis even the selective approach to the heritage of the past was supposed to accord, in one way or another, with the course of history. This point came out clearly in the piece that Buber wrote in 1904 in memory of Herzl, an article in which he called for taking an "*historical* view." Toward that end he strung together a number of contemporary phenomena in Jewish life that were seemingly unrelated: Zionism and the *Bund*, the emergence of a Jewish proletariat in the diaspora and settlement in Palestine, religious reform and the revival of Hebrew, Ahad Ha'am and Herzl. All these served as Buber's proof of a ramified and multi-faceted but common Jewish movement, notwithstanding the differences between the various phenomena he cited. Here is how Buber described it: "This Jewish movement was not born yesterday and is not the work of individuals but is a deeply rooted phenomenon of the life of the Jewish nation, a stirring of the initially convoluted and distorted but increasingly normal and organized response of a shackled and tortured folk organism."[52]

As a Zionist Buber placed the accent on the national renaissance in Palestine but nevertheless displayed a readiness – rare among the

---

52 Buber, *Briefwechsel*, p. 152; M. Buber, "Jüdische Kunst" in *Protokoll V Zionistencongress*, p. 154; Martin Buber, "Juedische Renaissance," *Ost und West*, 1 (1901), pp. 8-9; Buber, *Der Jude und sein Judentum*, p. 783.

Zionists of the day – to adopt a broad Jewish perspective and take a positive attitude toward rival movements. Such broad-mindedness stemmed not from tolerance per se but from the idea of historical organicism, which attempted to identify Zionism with the objective course of change in Jewish life. We should stress that Buber's approach was not based on the affirmation of Jewish existence as is, but on a revolutionary orientation that was well disposed toward all the forces struggling for change. Moreover, he was not particular about the nature of the change and was prepared to approve of opposing trends, as long as they admitted to some order of attachment to Judaism. Buber's system is a good example of the combination of two currents – the selective attitude toward the past and the desire to identify with the historical process.

The notion that it was possible to choose from the past whatever elements appeared to deserve a place in the future opened the way for every individual to pick and choose whatever struck him as being most appropriate.[53] From here the views of those who affirmed the principle of selection branched out into various and often contradictory directions, to the point where any cohesion between them all but disappeared. We can take as an example the Ehrenpreis-Zitron controversy over historical continuity in Hebrew literature. In 1897, at a time when he was planning to found a new publishing house with his friend Berdyczewski, Marcus Ehrenpreis wrote an article on the young Hebrew literature, that fairly bristled with hostility toward "those who have set the tone of our literature till now" and voiced the pretensions of the young writers "who are destined to begin the literary enterprise anew." Given his stridency, it is hardly surprising that a disciple of the East European Haskalah and Lover of Zion like Samuel Leib Zitron came forward to rebuff Ehrenpreis's attack. The interesting point here is that Zitron, who was only nine years older than Ehrenpreis, took a conservative stand on the past – and thereby obscured the militant nature of the Enlightenment movement.

"Only a people without a future must dissolve into its past," wrote Ehrenpreis. "But we can take from yesterday only what may serve as the basis for tomorrow. For us there is no dogmatic Judaism gaz-

---

53 Cf. Roland H. Bainton, *The Reformation of the Sixteenth Century* (Boston, 1952), pp. 5, 211.

ing frozen-faced at the present, out of lifeless parchments like an historical abstraction. For us there are only Jews – living, feeling, human beings in-the-making, who create values and destroy values. For us there is no petrified culture that we had to perpetuate and bear like a burden. The culture we need must be continually fresh and vibrant and developing." One can discern a number of familiar themes here: the contrast between Judaism and Jewry, the "revaluation of values," and an attack on the abstract "Science of Judaism" for being divorced from living Jews. This quote leaves an impression of arrogance, perhaps even excessive zeal. But its tone may be misleading. In any case, Ehrenpreis was speaking not about a complete break with the past but of discarding the ingredients that failed the test of relevance to modern man – which essentially meant a selective approach to the past.

Zitron, on the other hand, failed to take in the broad historical canvas that Ehrenpreis had spread out before his readers and interpreted his words in the narrowest sense, as a desire to denigrate the literature of the Haskalah. He accused Ehrenpreis of trying "to uproot the literature of the past and plant in its stead a new literature that will not touch upon anything that preceded it." For his part, Zitron assured his readers that "we ourselves cannot imagine a future literature that does not secure itself in the literature of the past." Zitron had evidently missed Ehrenpreis's point in writing that, "The Jews of the *Galuth* are able to do only brain work; the free national Jews will let the soul speak," for the contrast between intellectuality and the liberated soul was something of a novelty conceived by Ehrenpreis's generation. It represented a rejection of the rationalistic demeanor typical of the Enlightenment movement, though its basic position toward the Enlightenment remained positive. Within a few months, for example, Ehrenpreis was to write: "The Haskalah has still not gone bankrupt."

Zitron, meanwhile, was energetically defending the past and historical continuity, though he too had not forgotten the basic tenets of the Enlightenment. Even in pursuing the attack, he reminded his readers that "our public life is abnormal; disarray and darkness reign in all its institutions; and therefore the writing that the young people call the literature of the past has much work to do, throwing open windows in gloom-filled houses, spreading light in filthy alleyways, and cleaning up all the dust and dirt – leftovers from the Middle Ages that have stuck to the nation's back like lichens and are destroying it body and soul." Hence Zitron, no less than Ehrenpreis, objected to what had become the Jewish way of life, and both shared a desire for change from within. A half-hearted defender of the past, Zitron actually spoke of only one very specific portion thereof: the Haskalah literature of the previous generation. It is significant that he even grumbled over the term "the literature of the past." While defending the Haskalah in the name of history, he failed to understand that the revolt of the younger generation was against the past as an "historical abstraction," rather than history itself.[54]

This review of the debates within the scope of spiritual Zionism must not be allowed to obscure the fact that its basic outlook on the relationship between the past and the present was shared by a large constituency, including the disciples of Ahad Ha'am, the Democratic Fraction, and the proponents of cultural work in general. To illustrate this point, we shall quote from the writings of various figures (all of East European origin) published at the start of the new century, for they attest to a common point of departure, namely, history as a treasury from which to select whatever elements were desirable for modern culture and the national renaissance.

Reuben Brainin, a radical Hebrew and Yiddish writer, published a survey entitled "On the Threshold of the Twentieth Century" in which he looked forward to the new century with optimism, because it would "compromise and reconcile between the heart and the mind, the past and the future." Still, Brainin held that "of all the peoples on the earth today, we are the one special people whose past is greater and richer [than all the rest]." This pronouncement elevated the past to a place of honor in the heart of the Jew, and Brainin confirmed that "our past is infinitely loved by and dear to us." At the same time, however, he warned against subjugation to the past, in writing, "Nevertheless, our past must not become a burden to us, and it must not destroy our bent toward and aspirations

---

54 Marcus Ehrenpreis, "Die junghebräische Literatur," *Die Welt* (July 16, 1897), p. 15; Samuel Leib Zitron, "The Writers' Precinct: The Old Build and the Young Tear Down," *Hamelitz* (October 22, 1897), p. 3 (Hebrew); M. Erez-Ehrenpreis, "An Overview," *Hashiloah*, 3 (1898), p. 170 (Hebrew).

for the future." Brainin was sensitive to the seeming contradiction between an attachment to the heritage of the past and the trend toward innovation. He hoped to extricate himself from it by the selective use of the past and prescribed "taking from its treasury only what is good, necessary, and beneficial." Rather than dispose of the burden of history, he chose instead to exploit it for his own purposes: "Our entire glorious past will become a device and instrument for rising up to a higher plane in the future." The process of transforming the past from a burden into a "device and instrument" is not adequately clear, but the implication was obvious and it was embodied in the great hopes that Brainin placed on the approaching twentieth century. The resolution of the inimical opposites lay not in ideological formulas but in action, and indeed, Brainin called for "inaugurating fruitful national work."[55]

With a single stroke of his pen, Nahum Sokolow resolved the contradictions that roused qualms in more skeptical or tempestuous souls. Writing of Zionism as a renaissance movement in his book *To Masters and Mentors*, published in 1901 and already quoted above, Sokolow stated: "The cult of Zion, the memories and reflections, the songs and celebrations, the signs and the symbols that bear the seal of Zion restore Judaism to its *old glory*; they are what the Renaissance was to the Middle Ages . . . to peoples that had been submerged for generations in the slimy depths of ignorance and then returned to the ideals of beauty, grace, and glory through classical education." Sokolow had no difficulty in identifying Zionism with the Enlightenment, just as he drew a close parallel between the revival of the classics in the European Renaissance and the effect of Zionist ideals: "Zionism does not return the Jews to the Pale and the darkness of Judaism but to Zion and to the light in Judaism. The spirit of Zion is the spirit of a Hebrew renaissance." More than some deeper thinkers, perhaps, Sokolow succeeded in expressing the feelings of a broad segment of the Zionist public – especially members of the East European intelligentsia – that was trying to induce a general enlightenment grounded in Judaism. Zionism, these circles believed, more than the Haskalah before it, would be able to effect

---

55 R. Brainin, "On the Threshold of the Twentieth Century – A Look Forward and Back," *Hador* (December 20, 1900), p. 10 (Hebrew).

a renaissance in Judaism. By its very nature it would be better equipped to counter the negative legacy of the diaspora and reveal "the light in Judaism," as well as revive the Hebrew classics through a renewal of contact with Palestine.

Leo Motzkin essentially shared these expectations, though his attachment to Jewish tradition was weaker and he tended to highlight the differential qualities, while Sokolow was better at expressing the cohesive ones. Motzkin was one of the leading speakers at the founding convention of the Democratic Fraction in 1901, and his address provoked a spate of exchanges and misunderstandings. He called for "ridding ourselves of the idea that Zionism is a direct continuation of the ancient culture," but he nevertheless wished to take from that source "whatever appears to be required by our contemporary culture." This was another instance of the critical approach to the past that we have seen in the writings of so many Zionist activists, even well beyond the compass of the Democratic Fraction. However, Motzkin was considered more radical than the rest. Indeed, we have already seen how Shmarya Levin attacked him over the issue of rejecting the past – though in retrospect Levin confessed that he had leaned too heavily toward conservatism at the time: "I bound myself too firmly to the heritage of previous generations, to the old, to the original, and I even regarded the building of my people as a revival, as a return to its former greatness."[56]

Clear evidence to the effect that programmatic formulas were unable to strike the necessary balance between the old and the new was provided by Salomon Schiller, who was counted among the young Zionist intellectuals in Lemberg, but he was less known outside Galicia than was Ehrenpreis or Thon. In 1902 Schiller asked: "How can one use the diaspora culture to fashion Judaism in the future? How can one make the hardened material malleable? For after all, a people cannot start over again . . ." He went on to elaborate upon the complexity of the problem: "Because of its petrified and sealed content, the ghetto culture, which has endowed us with a formal-functional ability to absorb modern ideas and currents of

---

56 Sokolow, *To Masters and Mentors*, p. 132; L. Motzkin, "Speech at the Convention of Educated Zionist Youth in Basel" in Klausner, *Opposition to Herzl*, p. 119; Levin, *Memoirs*, Vol. III, p. 172.

thought – we have inherited from it sharp-wittedness and mystic longings – bears no relation to modernity. It is not surprising that the unsatisfied individual has nothing to fall back on. To restore equilibrium (albeit by modern means) is one of Zionism's most difficult but noblest tasks." Schiller's pronouncement that "a people cannot start over again" was not merely a reiteration of the well-known contention that it was advisable to choose among historical elements. His point of departure was, rather, a concession of the absolute certainty that it was *impossible* to start over again, even if that were the more desirable course. And it was this certitude, more than longings for the "glorious past" or a striving toward the "light in Judaism," that made one's attitude toward the past and the adaptation of the historical heritage to modern life so important. It removed the question of one's approach to the past from the limited context of reforming Jewish life and placed it on the agenda of the Zionist movement, which aimed for a radical change in the very existence of the diaspora. In other words, the conviction that one could not dispose of the past inexorably led to a national solution of the Jewish problem while also dictating the *content* of Jewish nationalism.

We shall conclude our examination of this issue with Chaim Weizmann's poignant remark, made in 1901, about the heritage of the past: "Our fate, the fate of people who live in a time of transition, is to be given activities of a purely negative character. To understand and ponder over old Jewish values, to understand only to discard them perhaps, or to reappraise them at a later stage."[57]

European Culture

The Zionist literature of this period generally depicted European culture as a counterweight to the Jewish heritage. All the Zionist circles (with the exception perhaps of the Orthodox Jews from Eastern Europe) felt deep admiration for European culture, yet they were dogged by the fear that Zionism would be interpreted as a reaction

---

57 Salomon Schiller, "Zu den Fragen unserer Kulturarbeit" in Feiwel, ed., *Jüdischer Almanach*, pp. 157-158; Weizmann, *Letters*, Vol. I, pp. 122-123.

against it. This anxiety traced back to the misconception that the vision of a Jewish renaissance implied a retreat or withdrawal into traditional Judaism. The Western Jews, who had undergone the process of emancipation, seemed to have difficulty apprehending the modern nature of Jewish nationalism. Interesting testimony to this effect can be found in a letter written to Martin Buber by Paula Winckler-Buber in 1899 about a conversation on this subject with an unidentified woman: "I was astounded most of all by her impression that the Zionists wish to divorce themselves from all their acquired culture and revert to some kind of utterly primitive state. The herding tribes of the Old Testament may be what she had in mind."[58]

It must be said, however, that the attitude toward European civilization was not altogether unequivocal. On the one hand, European culture was perceived as a boon that the Jews had acquired from outsiders but must not relinquish anymore; on the other, there was a sense that the Jews, too, had played a role in the creation of European culture, making it a legitimate part of their own heritage. Yet there was also a third leitmotif, an undercurrent of disappointment in Europe and its culture and a desire to renew contact with the Orient through the instrument of Zionism. In 1892, during his Zionist period, Nathan Birnbaum examined the various sides of the Zionist attitude toward European culture in a lecture on "The Recuperation of the Jewish People":

> For civilization does not mean discoveries and inventions (though the Jews have played an outstanding role in these too); civilization is the ethical ingraining of the soul of man and nation. And this civilization – at one with the ideals of liberty, equality, and fraternity – was given to the world by the Jewish spirit. In essence it should have been called the Oriental civilization or, more precisely, *Hebrew civilization*.

The equation of Judaism with the motto of the French Revolution was an approach that would later develop into the identification of Judaism with progress and Socialism, and both paralleled the attempt to associate Judaism with conservatism and fidelity to the

58 Buber, *Briefwechsel*, p. 148.

ancien régime, in the broadest sense of the term. We shall return to this phenomenon later in these pages. For now, suffice it to say that up to that point, Birnbaum was addressing himself to the debt that European culture owed to the Jews. Thereafter, however, he forecast the regeneration of European culture thanks to Zionism: "The Jews need not fear that they will lose European civilization in the Orient. Quite to the contrary, there, on its native ground, its purer forms will be regenerated through a complete return to Orientalism."

That same year Birnbaum's journal published an article calling for "lively and constant contact between the Jewish-national idea and the rich and wonderful world of thought of the civilized nations," to which Birnbaum appended the comment that the European spirit was at any rate the spirit of Israel![59] Strictly speaking, the national version of the Jewish contribution to European culture was but a variation on a familiar theme in modern apologetics. We can take as an example Disraeli's 1851 statement in praise of the conservatism and "natural aristocracy" of the Jews: "The Jews represent the semitic principle, all that is spiritual in our nature." Or Joseph Salvador's work, which antedated Disraeli by thirty years, in which he asserted that: "The role that the Hebrew people has played in the history of mankind . . . is enormous."[60]

Further on we shall survey attempts to play up the Jewish contribution to Western civilization in response to the challenge from the socialist movement. At first Socialism appeared as a cosmopolitan movement, and the competition between Zionism and the Bund – the General Jewish Labor Union in Lithuania, Poland and Russia – for influence over Jewish workers was bound up with the issue of identifying with Judaism or repudiating it. The opposite of this cosmopolitan current was not political Zionism as such, but a national trend that embraced the Jewish contribution to world culture, including Socialism. One such approach found expression as early

59 "Die Heilung des jüdischen Volkes," Vortrag von N. Birnbaum in Lemberg, *Selbst-Emancipation* (November 15, 1892), p. 202; S. M., "Zur Klärung," *Selbst-Emancipation* (February 23, 1892), p. 42; cf. Bernard Lewis, *History – Remembered, Recovered, Invented* (Princeton, N.J., 1975), p. 76.

60 Benjamin Disraeli, *Lord George Bentinck* (London, 1851), pp. 496-497; Joseph Salvador, *Histoire des Institutions de Moïse et du Peuple Hébreu* (Paris, 1892), p. 2.

as 1896 in *Kadimah*, the Jewish student newspaper in Paris, most of whose readers were Russian émigrés. In its pages, one writer disputed the socialist claims against Jewish nationalism, by enumerating the historical achievements of the Jews as "the nation that, after losing its autonomy, was able to pass on the scientific legacy of ancient civilization to the Middle Ages; that, in exchange for the Inquisition, gave the world the philosopher Spinoza, and in return for the German *Hep-Hep* gave it Marx and Lasalle, Heine and Börne." In short, the Jews requite good for bad, with special emphasis on Judaism's cultural and spiritual contribution to progress and social justice.

In a similar vein, Jacques Bahar, a Zionist socialist from Bernard Lazare's coterie who published his own journal in Paris at the end of the century, offered a prize to the reader "who can show me anywhere in Christian civilization a single precept of generosity, fraternity, love, liberty, or equality – in short, of the familial-social virtues – of compassion that extends even to animals, that did not originate in biblical or talmudic Judaism." Bahar also developed a historiosophic theory about the social mission of the Jewish religion. In March 1899 he wrote that Judaism had spread throughout the ancient world because it "was so superior, from a purely social standpoint, compared with the absurdity of paganism." The rulers of the time reacted by prohibiting conversion to Judaism, and in order to defend themselves the Jews established a protective fence for the Torah – "the allegories and the artifices of the Talmud and the commentators." Bahar's conclusion was that the only right path was to return to "the true Judaism," whose social content had been disregarded over the years.[61]

At the end of the same year, Bernard Lazare published a letter he had sent to Ludovic Trarieux – one of Alfred Dreyfus's supporters and a one-time French minister of justice – a few days after Dreyfus had won his appeal. Speaking of the importance of the Dreyfus trial for the Jewish people, Lazare commented: "I belong to the race of

---

61 S. Ginsburg, "Les Juifs et le socialisme," *Kadimah, Journal des Etudiants Juifs de Paris* (July 12, 1896) (in the Central Zionist Archives); *Le Flambeau* (February 1899), p. 34; Jacques Bahar, "La jeunesse juive et le Judaïsme, *Le Flambeau* (March 1899), p. 7.

people who, in Renan's words, were the first to introduce the idea of justice to the world." Further on he traced his spiritual genealogy from the Prophets through the "poor poets who sang the psalms" up through Marx and Lasalle, and "the humble martyrs of the revolution who have atoned in the Russian Hell for their faith in the ideal of equity."[62] In so doing, Lazare tended to blur the dividing line between Judaism and revolution. One can assume that in alluding to those struggling against the czar's regime, he meant the Jews, though he certainly could not claim that Jews were the only ones fighting for the revolution.

A similar problem bedeviled Dr. Bernstein-Cohen, who regularly sent ideological circulars to the Zionist societies in Russia in his capacity as the head of the Zionist center in Kishinev. His "Third Theoretical Letter" stated: "And the life current that brought the Torah of Israel, Jewish ethics, to the pagan world – the same doctrine that informs Zionism now in our own day – has had an indirect influence upon the cultures of all the peoples surrounding us." There, however, Bernstein-Cohen came to an abrupt halt on the border between nationalism and universalism by bemoaning the Jew's inability to affect the world. "But his influence," he wrote, "was lost among the many other influences and cultural encounters and the many different forms of social order." By the same token, there was no point to the Sisyphean labors of those who spoke of the mission of Judaism in the modern era, "because the meager portion of our culture that we contribute to European life is insignificant, compared with countless more powerful factors."

Thus Bernstein-Cohen and Lazare both regarded the Jews as a revolutionary factor and chose to ignore the existence of another, more conservative sector of Jewry. However, while Lazare highlighted the role that Jews played in the revolution, Bernstein-Cohen insisted that they were lost in the crowd. How, then, would it be possible to strengthen their revolutionary influence upon humanity? Bernstein-Cohen's answer was: through the realization of Zionism. "In settling in his land, [the Jew] will quickly enact the necessary reforms in the

---

62 Bernard Lazare, "Lettre à Trarieux sur la portée du procès Dreyfus pour le peuple Juif," *l'Echo Sioniste* (October 20, 1899), p. 57; Ernest Renan, *Histoire d'Israël*, Vol. III (Paris, 1891), p. vi.

social order," he concluded, and then the Jewish people would fulfill its universalist role "and take part in the general war not as a foundling and a bastard who has no stake in the country, or a good-for-nothing among the proletariat, but as a warrior who has a right to be counted among all the other fighters!" Of course the question remains whether the Jewish influence upon world culture was profound, as Bernstein-Cohen proclaimed at the opening of the piece, or merely fleeting, as he contended later on. In any event, he posited a definite connection between "Jewish ethics" and social progress, as well as between the social content and the national movement. Here the thinking of the radical Bernstein-Cohen converged upon the outlook of the conservative Ahad Ha'am, who spoke of Jewish nationalism "as *one entire society*" wielding "the power of justice, as opposed to all the other powers ruling the world."[63] Ahad Ha'am's deep devotion to Jewish culture, in contrast to Bernstein-Cohen's token reference to it, in no way detracts from the element common to spiritual Zionism and the radical leanings of the Democratic Fraction. Both required the addition of substance to the national movement – be it ethical-spiritual or ethical-social – to accord it its universal significance.

Nachman Syrkin is deserving of special attention in the context of this discussion, for he not only symbolized the fusion of Zionism and Socialism but also provided its ideological justification, as a construct of Jewish history. Syrkin attempted to uncover Judaism's inherent social substance and credited the Jewish people with "prodigious creative powers," despite "the horrid disfiguration of its life." From the outset of his career, Syrkin had rejected Hegel's famous dictum "Thus perish peoples by a natural death" and cited the Jews as evidence disproving this theory. In contrast, Syrkin developed his own theory of destiny, positing that "universal values and the progressive and timeless qualities are initially the property of a special people, its unique character, its primacy in history." As might be expected, this law applied above all to the Jews.

Syrkin's system attempted to synthesize ostensibly antithetical concepts. Thus he called for rejecting the contrariety of nationalism

---

63 Bernstein-Cohen, *The Bernstein-Cohen Book*, p. 218; Ahad Ha'am, *Collected Works*, p. 92.

and universalism – "world culture" and "Israel's national assets"; of the negation of "diaspora Judaism" and the desire for "a Jewish awakening"; and of "obliterating religious Judaism" and "aspiring toward the development of Judaism's eternal ethical and metaphysical qualities in real life." The dualism so characteristic of Syrkin – despite his constant striving for synthesis – was essentially between positive "prophetic Judaism" and negative "talmudic Judaism." Obviously, the future "socialist Jewish State" would inherit the Judaism of the prophetic variety and manifest the qualities that had characterized it in the past.[64]

The competition between Zionism and Socialism for the support of the Jewish public was especially prominent on the left wing of the Zionist movement, that is, within the Democratic Fraction and among the Zionist Socialists. The Bund was, as we have said, merely cosmopolitan at first. But a few years after its establishment, it changed its approach to the point of acknowledging the validity of a Jewish entity. Thus the debate between the Bund and Zionism was no longer over the legitimacy of Jewish nationalism as such. Still, the two movements disagreed over a wide spectrum of issues, and for both propaganda and political reasons it was deemed advisable to bring the difference between the Bund's perfunctory nationalism and Zionist Socialism into sharper focus. The most obvious difference was the Bund's internationalism, in contrast to Zionism's national version of socialism, enabling the Zionist Socialists – and especially those who were not strict adherents of Marxist doctrine – to draw upon Judaism's historical legacy. As an example of this approach, one can cite a speech delivered by Dr. Daniel Pasmanik in 1905, when he was one of the leading spokesmen of the Poalei Zion party. "Jewish romanticism will endure," he said, "not the romanticism of the oppressed and persecuted *Galuth* Jew, but the proud romanticism of the free and self-aware Jew that has always been among the loftiest and most precious values admired by mankind, like the democratic social legislation of the Bible and the highest ethical ideals of the Prophets."[65]

64 Nahman Syrkin, *Works* (Tel Aviv, 1935), pp. 68, 169, 171, 172 (Hebrew); Friedrich Hegel, *The Philosophy of History*, p. 75.
65 D. Pasmanik, "Zeit und Streitfragen im Zionismus," *Die Welt* (March 24, 1905), p. 6.

We have assembled a number of statements that essentially reiterate the theme of Judaism's contribution to human culture. While extolling this contribution, however, their authors are often forced to admit that it was not accepted gladly or that its effect was not of major consequence. The very need to single out the Jewish contribution to civilization and stress its value underscored the apologetic strain in many of these writers. Added to this leaning was their selective attitude toward the Jewish heritage, often preferring its universal elements to the point of gauging its worth by its consonance with general culture. Yet none of this mitigated the grim acknowledgment of the tension that had always existed between "Christian civilization" (Jacques Bahar) and "Jewish ethics" (Bernstein-Cohen). If we delve into the literature dealing with the Jewish contribution to mankind, we will reach the conclusion that certain values evolved within the framework of Jewish history and became part of civilization at large, through the message of Judaism or flesh-and-blood Jews. The Christian view on the transference of Israel's legacy to the Church comes into play here, for it had colored all of European culture – in positing an implicit connection between the appropriation of the Judaic heritage by the "new Israel" and the consequent rejection of the Jews as an empty vessel fallen from grace. This was the background to much soul-searching among modern Zionists.

While lauding the Jewish contribution to civilization, the Zionists pointed out that the Jews must not rest on their laurels and had to engage in an on-going involvement. A more vexing problem, from the Zionist viewpoint, had to do with the culture-heroes of Jewish origin, for although they symbolized a continuous Jewish contribution, they usually approximated the assimilationist type that Zionism deplored.[66] Such difficulties highlighted the disparity between the Jewish contribution and the unfriendly world that failed to appreciate it – and nurtured the hope that Zionism would bridge the gap. As if paralleling Christianity's eschatological belief in the ultimate redemption of the Jews, the Zionist thinkers held that the Jewish contribution to civilization was incomplete, that the world was still in need of Judaism's message, and that it would be revealed when the Jews were able to act in unison.

66 Walter Laqueur, *A History of Zionism* (New York, 1972), pp. 390-391.

This analysis may give us a better handle on the inherent contradictions in Nathan Birnbaum's approach, with which we opened this
discussion. Some two years after predicting that European culture
would flourish among the Jews returning to Palestine, Birnbaum
described this process in 1894, by availing himself of racial and ecological imagery. "The center of gravity of Jewish life would shift
from the Occident to the Orient," he wrote, "from the foreign-Aryan
world to the familiar-Semitic one." Not only did he reiterate the
popular dichotomy between the Aryan and Semitic races, he alluded
to a natural connection between race and habitat, aiming at trans-
planting the Jews in their primordial setting. The ecological motif
seems particularly strong here, as Birnbaum was not talking about
a return to Palestine per se but of settlement throughout the Ottoman Empire – thereby implying that it was not the religious and cultural tie between a people and its homeland that would be of decisive
consequence, but the association of a race to the region with which
it has presumably been bonded from antiquity.[67] After Herzl's
advent, Birnbaum continued to develop his vision of the Jews' role
in the worldwide process of forging a modern culture: "All the contemporary forces of the Jewish people will be released, and it will
act both on the classical cultural soil of Europe and especially toward
the attachment of the ancient Near Eastern nations, the Semites, to
the family of European peoples."

For all that, however, in his speech before the First Zionist Congress, Birnbaum contended that: "We do not wish to be missionaries
of culture or civilization anywhere, neither in the West nor in the
East." That was not the mission that Zionism had taken upon itself
– though on second thought, the return of the Jews to Palestine inevitably implied a civilizing role: "A Jewish state-people settling in Palestine will therefore be not just a mediator between the intrinsic
socio-ethical and political-aesthetic components of Europeanism,
but also a long-needed extrinsic intermediary between the Occident
and the Orient. For if any people is capable of this, it is the Jewish

---

67 B. (N. Birnbaum), "So Lange es Zeit ist!" *Jüdische Volkszeitung* (April 3,
    1894), p. 2; cf. George L. Mosse, *Towards the Final Solution* (London, 1978),
    p. 28.

[people], with its innate Oriental character and its European education."

In contrast to the explicitness of Birnbaum's ethnic axiom, the implications of the cultural imperialism suggested in his address were far less clear. In speaking of the attachment of the nations of the Near East to the family of European nations, was he alluding to political annexation? And what European Power had long been seeking a mediator with the Orient and would find it in Zionism? In considering these questions, one should bear in mind that this was the age of the decline of the Ottoman Empire and the florescence of imperialism, which identified itself with the civilizing mission of Europe.[68] It was not due to a specific political orientation that Birnbaum superimposed imperialistic thinking upon Zionism. For him, the crucial point was the cultural synthesis between the Oriental character of the Jews and their European education, together with the ensuing effect of this synthesis upon the entire environment. Sensitive to the mood of the period, Birnbaum highlighted all the nuances of the Zionist attitude toward European culture, from criticism of its materialism – as being contrary to the "Jewish spirit" – to the vision of Zionism as the vanguard of European culture in the East. On the face of it, he depicted European culture and the Jewish spirit as being antithetical, but in essence he strove to achieve a synthesis between them.

A similar synthesis, free of the internal contradictions found in Birnbaum's reading, was conceived by Osias Thon. In 1896 he published a work on the philosophical-historical foundations of Zionism, in which he characterized the movement as the post-emancipatory phase of Jewish history and as a consequence of the shortcomings of assimilation. "It was necessary that there be an emancipated, European, Jewry before the need for an autochthonous cultural center would arise among the Jews," he explained and went on to reject the idea of a Jewish mission – as it was conceived in the

---

68 Matthias Acher (pseud. for N. Birnbaum), "Die jüdische Moderne," *Zion* (November 1, 1896), p. 298; Nathan Birnbaum, "Das jüdische National-leben" in *Protokoll des 1ten Zionistenkongresses in Basel*, p. 108; cf. Michael D. Biddis, *The Age of the Masses* (Harmondsworth, Middlesex, 1977), pp. 43-44.

diaspora – but proposed his own theory of destiny regarding the Jews' return to Palestine. "It cannot be denied that we once led – or at least helped to lead – the culture of the Orient to the West through a thousand channels. Should it not to some extent be our role to lead European culture back *to* the Orient?"[69] Thon was definitive in his preference for European culture and displayed none of the ambivalence present in Birnbaum's attitude to Europe. Nor was he concerned with the issue of an original Jewish contribution to European culture. Instead, his interest lay in the role of mediation that the Jews fulfilled between cultures. In contrast to Birnbaum's great expectations, Thon envisioned the Jews only as a debtor vis-à-vis the Orient. Yet he, too, was unable to conceive the realization of Zionism without attributing it a more universal function and significance.

In this context it is worthwhile quoting a non-Jewish supporter of Zionism, Baron von Suttner, who in 1897 expressed the hope that the Jews would establish "a model state that would not suffer within its borders the miserable and decadent conditions of Old Europe." In a similar vein, Dr. Moses Gaster told the Third Zionist Congress: "We wish to show the world that there is still a *Weltanschauung* that is fundamentally different from the one that presently ails humanity in Europe." But whereas Baron von Suttner was speaking about a progressive society and social experimentation in the spirit of Fourier, Dr. Gaster proffered "God's kingdom on earth" as the alternative to Europe – earning himself applause in the congress hall and a derisive remark in Herzl's diary.[70]

In voicing his criticism of European culture from a Zionist-Socialist viewpoint in 1903, Kalman Marmor, a young radical leader, integrated the motifs of the Jewish contribution to society and the Zionist mission in the East: "The Jewish people has long fought for its ancient prophetic ideal, but has yet to attain it. Even today, the modern civilized world is still not prepared to fulfill it. If we wish

69 Osias Thon, *Essays zur zionistischen Ideologie*, pp. 15, 27.
70 A. Gundaccar v. Suttner, "Gedanken zur Zionistenbewegung," *Die Welt* (July 23, 1897), p. 2; "Rede des Vicepräsidenten Dr. M. Gaster am III Zionisten-Congress," *Die Welt* (August 25, 1899), pp. 10-11; Herzl, *Diaries*, Vol. III, p. 862.

to perpetuate this ideal, we 'Asians' will not be regressing but, on the contrary, will be leaving Europe far behind us." When Marmor ridiculed the disdainful attitude toward the Asians, he apparently did so as a Jew of the so-called Semitic stock, whose natural place was supposedly in Asia – though his remark may also have been a response to the negative attitude toward non-Europeans in general. In any event, Marmor was trying to do what others had done before him: transform humiliation into a source of pride. In this sense there was a great difference between Marmor, a destitute Jewish student from Eastern Europe, and Baron von Suttner, who also called for building a new and progressive society in Palestine and scorned the "Old Europe," though he himself was counted among its social elite.[71]

Having cited these repudiations of Europe and its culture, we must stress that they were definitely exceptions to the rule. There may have been salient internal contradictions in Birnbaum's thinking, as we have seen, but even they did not obscure his essentially positive attitude toward European culture. Going even further, a sense of unequivocal admiration for European culture as the epitome of beauty and goodness emerged from Vasily Bermann's impressions of his journey to Palestine, published in Birnbaum's *Selbst-Emancipation* in 1893: "Order and cleanliness signify culture, Europe; filth and disorder – Asia, barbarism."[72] Marcus Ehrenpreis expressed a similar sentiment less bluntly four years later, in the context of discussing the new Hebrew literature: "Aspiring to a national renaissance in our historical homeland does not mean that we wish to be Asians again." He regarded European culture as the acme of human achievement – or perhaps it is more correct to say that he could not imagine any other culture: "We are Jews, but European Jews; hence our culture, which is an extension of our selves, must be both national and European."[73]

In speaking of "European Jews," Ehrenpreis was referring not to

71 Marmor, *My Autobiography*, Vol. II, p. 655.
72 W. Bermann, "In Judäa, Eine Reiseschilderung," *Selbst-Emancipation* (November 15, 1893), p. 3.
73 Marcus Ehrenpreis, "Die junghebräische Literatur," *Die Welt* (July 16, 1897), p. 15.

their place of residence but to the culture they had internalized. His identification of Europe with universal culture was so strong that he essentially equated its importance to nationalism itself. This reading was reminiscent of the Marxist-style formula on national form and socialist substance or the well-known saying that France is every man's second homeland, meaning that nationalism alone was not enough to answer man's needs and had to be supplemented by another element that was universal in nature. Viewed from a different perspective, Ehrenpreis's approach could be said to be a new rendering of the prescription to "Be a man outside and a Jew at home."

Martin Buber's conclusion was not very different but bore a different emphasis. For while Ehrenpreis expressed a degree of anxiety about losing European culture, Buber regarded that culture as essential to modern Jewish nationalism. In his address before the Fifth Zionist Congress in 1901, he deplored the tendency (which he charged was growing among Zionist circles) to sentimentalize the ghetto, by drawing a picture of "the delicate and bizarre beauty of the insular communal life we pursued in Europe until the eighteenth century." Buber cited two conditions for the Jewish national awakening. One was emancipation (or, as he put it, "our marriage to Western civilization"), which made it possible "to express our age-old impulse toward national vitality – that for centuries has been expressed either in grief-laden longings or in wild messianic ecstasy – in the modern form we call Zionism." The other condition was European nationalism, which Buber believed had superseded the cosmopolitan Enlightenment: "Instead of a bloodless vision of humanity, a healthy national self-awareness has emerged." Buber drew no distinction between the Jewish and the European elements, for he believed in an organic development of all the components and an immanent connection between them.

Another member of the Democratic Fraction, Joseph Klausner, discussed this same subject in his first article as the new editor of *Hashiloah* in 1903. In explaining the changes he intended to make upon Ahad Ha'am's retirement from the journal, Klausner wrote: "There are so many keen minds among our yeshiva students; there are so many great talents among the authors of works of casuistry and exegesis. They lack only one thing: a European education. And so *they* remain idlers, and their writings are devoid of all value."[74] Viewing this statement in light of the editorial changeover at *Hashiloah*, it is evident that Klausner had reservations about his predecessor's editorial policy, and thus particularly emphasized the superiority of European culture. This is also the most pertinent place to discuss the *Altneuland* affair, since it revived support for Ahad Ha'am among many of his followers, who had criticized his growing conservatism.

At the close of 1902 Herzl published the novel *Altneuland*, which projected the realization of his Zionist plan twenty years hence. In reviewing the novel, Ahad Ha'am scoffed at the notion of organizing the emigration and settlement of hoards of people within a few months and the naive vision of attracting international capital for the development of industry in a backward country. But his main thrust was directed at Herzl's handling of the spiritual and cultural sides of the Zionist implementation. His pen dripping with irony, Ahad Ha'am attacked Herzl's proclivity to imitate the other peoples of the world:

> The Jews did not invent anything here or add anything of their own; they merely imitated and assembled together what they had seen scattered among the enlightened nations of Europe and America. Not because they are wiser than the other peoples. That is not why they managed to assemble all this together. But because it was easier for them than for other peoples, since those had been "forced to bear the burden shouldered by their ancestors," and everything that was *new* to them would clash with the *old*, which prevented it from developing and taking its proper place. But the Jews here, even though they were also "*forced* to link the present with the past," nevertheless established their new society without "the burden of the legacy" and were able to accept without inhibition all the good things they had seen among others.

In *Altneuland* Ahad Ha'am found a wealth of evidence vindicating his long-standing complaints against political Zionism, the most

74 M. Buber in *Protokoll V Zionistencongress*, pp. 152-154; Joseph Klausner, "Our Objective," *Hashiloah*, 11 (1903), p. 5 (Hebrew).

prominent of which was undoubtedly that Herzl supported the Jews' "cosmopolitanism." Herzl held that the Jews' ability to adapt themselves to modern technology stood in inverse proportion to their devotion to outmoded traditions, and herein lay the essence of the conflict between the two men. The controversy that evolved after the publication of Ahad Ha'am's review centered on the clash between deep-rooted Judaism and the influence of European civilization.

Herzl asked Nordau to reply to Ahad Ha'am's criticism, and in complying he resorted to such strident language that he set off a wave of protest from many of Ahad Ha'am's sympathizers. As the debate grew increasingly heated, the sides edged further toward frenzy, to the point where Nordau accused Ahad Ha'am of bigotry and animosity toward European culture, while pledging for his part that "we shall never allow the return of the Jews to the land of their forefathers to be a retreat to barbarism, as our enemies claim in their slander. The Jewish people will develop its distinctiveness within the general Western culture, like every other civilized people, and not beyond it in wild, culture-hating Asianism, as Ahad Ha'am would apparently have it."

Of the long list of articles that fuelled this polemic, we shall quote only one, famous for its acerbity but quite typical in essence. It was printed anonymously but was probably written by Benjamin Segel, who had once been among the young Zionists of Lemberg. Entitled "The Jews of Yesterday," the piece lashed into Herzl and Nordau, much as Nordau had done to Ahad Ha'am. "Two principles confront each other here," Segel wrote. "On the one hand the nuclear, rooted, solid Jewry that has always existed, that did not have to be shocked and attacked from without to be reminded of itself, the *Jewish* Jewry that has always been at one with itself and with the people, tirelessly flowing from the pristine well, never losing its bond with the past, and always striving forward in a constant current of development." Its diametric opposite was political Zionism, "the Jewry of yesterday, the Jewry of 1897, that had its revelation at the Basel Congress, the Jewry-by-the-grace-of-antisemitism that would long ago have been lost in the sands of indifference and apostasy had it not been thoroughly rattled and badly bruised from without."[75] The epithet "yesterday" symbolized something both outdated and ephemeral, and that is precisely what Segel must have intended by choosing the title "The Jews of Yesterday."

The truth of the matter is that Herzl's *Altneuland* contained passages reflecting a respectful attitude toward the past and Jewish tradition, just as it is clear that Ahad Ha'am did not call upon the Jews to break with European culture. In vain Ahad Ha'am insisted that he advocated "genuine national liberation and a genuine national life based on *general human foundations.*" Herzl believed the time was ripe to challenge Ahad Ha'am's influence, and he admitted as much during his visit to Russia. Asked by the leading Russian Zionists about the *Altneuland* affair, Herzl explained that "you cannot be both a Zionist and an Ahad Ha'amist," and he did his best to drive a wedge between Ahad Ha'am and his supporters. If we examine the two men's outlooks, we will indeed find differences in their positions on European culture and Jewish sources, but not to the point of diametric opposition. Hence we must understand this affair as a corollary of the cutting criticism that Ahad Ha'am had been voicing for years against the leadership of the movement he himself never joined but nonetheless deeply influenced.

It is rather ironic that the polemic over Herzl's bright vision of the future coincided with the negotiations with Britain over Jewish settlement in Sinai and in El Arish, whose failure was a great disappointment to Herzl. The *Altneuland* controversy raged on until the time of the Kishinev pogroms, which left Ahad Ha'am thoroughly shaken and further highlighted the yawning gap between Herzl, who was now more impatient than ever for a political solution, and Ahad Ha'am, who complained despairingly of Jewish impotence "as if Zionism could really have put an end to events like Kishinev."[76]

---

75 Ahad Ha'am, "Altneuland, Roman von Th. Herzl," *Hashiloah*, 10 (1902), p. 572 (Hebrew); Max Nordau, "Ahad Ha-Am über Altneuland," *Die Welt* (March 13, 1903), p. 2; "Die Juden von Gestern," *Ost und West* (April 1903), p. 223.

76 Ahad Ha'am, *Collected Works*, p. 322; "Herzl in St. Petersburg," *Hazman* (August 23, 1903), p. 2 (Hebrew); Ahad Ha'am, *Letters*, Vol. III (1924), p. 124.

Uniqueness and Normalization

The polemic over *Altneuland* sharpened the focus on the differences in approach between the Herzl-Nordau camp – which conceived of Zionism as a "purely national movement" – and the disciples of Ahad Ha'am – who held that "the salvation of Israel will be achieved by *prophets*, not by *diplomats*."[77] Yet as we have already seen, the categorical opposition of outlooks personified by Herzl and Ahad Ha'am was an oversimplification. For while disputing one another, each of these approaches influenced and mitigated the opposing thrust – one a striving for the normalization of the Jews within a national framework, the other an impetus to use Zionism as a buttress of Judaism's singularity.

One instance of that uniqueness was well put by Birnbaum in 1893 in speaking of a people "without a real friend, abandoned in times of distress by the most fervent preachers of human kindness and champions of equality." For Birnbaum, Jewish history held the key to understanding the fate of the people that had been "pursued throughout history by the fiend of antisemitism." Such an outlook going beyond the particulars of time and place to accord Jew-hatred and its demonological imagery a focal role in the history of the Jews necessarily heightened the sense of Jewish distinctiveness. Hence Birnbaum was speaking not only of the response to contemporary antisemitism, but of an approach that epitomized Jewish existence over the centuries.[78]

Of course one could also view Jewish uniqueness in more positive terms, as did Simon Bernfeld for example, in discussing the Hebrew language. In a study published in 1899, Bernfeld wrote: "Just as our people is a national collective whose character can be understood only on its own terms, for it has no parallel in the history of other nations, so is our Hebrew language a creature unto itself." Unlike his predecessors, Bernfeld was not interested in accentuating the antipathy between the Jews and the non-Jews, and we shall have more to say on this point later on.

77 Achad Haam, *Ten Essays on Zionism and Judaism*, p. 31; Herzl, *Diaries*, Vol. IV, p. 1599.
78 B., "Zum Makkabäerfeste," *Selbst-Emancipation* (December 1, 1893), p. 1; cf. Joshua Trachtenberg, *The Devil and the Jews* (New York, 1943), p. 6.

When the Democratic Fraction coalesced at the beginning of the century, one of its leaders, Leo Motzkin, wished to liberate Zionist propaganda from chauvinism and was particularly opposed to exploiting the concept of the "chosen people." Conversely, his comrade Chaim Weizmann wrote him (in the context of scoring the "stewards of Socialism"): "They would like to free the Jews in accordance with a plan, to confine Zionism to the little frames which fit into their little heads, and being materialists they can never understand the prophetic aspect of Zionism." Four years later Weizmann was to come out with a penetrating expression of the sense of Jewish uniqueness in writing: "We are Jews, our destiny is different from that of any other people, we are a chosen nation, chosen in suffering, in torment . . . in feelings, and in our momentary but deep joys."[79] Thus although Weizmann spoke of being a "chosen people," he did not mean it in the biblical sense of being singled out by divine election (Deuteronomy 7:6) but rather in the sense of being marked by a distinctive fate. These sentences were written at a troubling time – a few days after Herzl's death – and reflected the depressed mood that had settled over the Zionist movement. Yet they also appear to be an attempt to hearten the Jews by alluding to the powers latent in their national character that would enable them to overcome their distress.

As can be seen from these quotations, non-religious Zionists tended to interpret the tradition of Israel's election in a modern way, stressing at times the tragic moment of Jewish destiny: to differ from others; to be hated, despised, and misunderstood. Even though their proclaimed goal was to help the Jews overcome their distress by creating the conditions for normalization, some of the Zionists affirmed the Jews' uniqueness and found solace within adversity. Herein lay the crux of the controversy over uniqueness vs. normalization. In reacting to the convening of the First Zionist Congress, for example, Ahad Ha'am wrote:

> The Jewish people cannot possibly be content with attaining at last to a position of a small and insignificant nation, with a

79 Simon Bernfeld, *An Account of Our Literature* (Warsaw, 1899), p. 4 (Hebrew); Klausner, *Opposition to Herzl*, p. 119; Weizmann, *Letters*, Vol. I, p. 80, Vol. III, p. 271.

State tossed about like a ball between its powerful neighbors.
. . . An ancient people, which was once a beacon to the world,
cannot possibly accept, as a satisfactory reward for all it has
endured, a thing so trifling, which many other peoples unre-
nowned and uncultured have won in a short time without
going through a hundredth part of the suffering.

The foregoing clearly implied that, in Ahad Ha'am's estimation, the
goal of political Zionism was simultaneously too ambitious (he
mocked Herzl's *haute politique*) and too modest, for it did not
befit the people of Israel to aspire to no more than a national state
like any other.

Writing in strikingly similar terms, the radical Zionist leader of
Kishinev, Bernstein-Cohen, protested to Ahad Ha'am that, "Not for
a moment did I get so carried away that I wished for a 'Jewish State'
in the Herzlian spirit. As I see it, Herzl's 'Jewish State' is a country
of Jews, but I doubt very much whether that is quite what the Jews
are fighting and suffering for." He went on to complain that the Jewish national framework envisioned by Herzl "will not be a Jewish
State following the Torah and Moses and the living part of the Talmud." Even the progressive Bernstein-Cohen, who repeatedly
flaunted his critical stance on religion, distinguished between a
country populated by Jews and a state that embodied what was
unique to them. He, too, made reference to Jewish suffering, but bal-
anced this by citing Jewish fighting, and he asked Ahad Ha'am's
guidance in helping the Zionist societies foster "historical self-
awareness."[80]

Nahum Sokolow also touched upon this subject in his characteristically moderating fashion, that passed over differences rather than
illuminating them. He expressed his satisfaction that the Zionist
ideal was linked to a country that was neither too remote nor too
central, "that our past is not tied to some highly prized locale [or]
some wretched backwater." He believed that "if we pined for some
China, [some] Patagonia, it would be to our shame," and that the
opposite was equally true: "If we longed to establish a center for ourselves in Germany, France, or such a country, it would be to our

---

80 Achad Haam, *Ten Essays on Zionism and Judaism*, p. 26; Bernstein-Cohen,
The Bernstein-Cohen Book, p. 233.   .

detriment." One could view this argument as an assault on the propositions of the autonomists and the territorialists, since there was no real prospect of creating a Jewish national center in Europe and it was equally pointless to search for a territory at the ends of the earth, because Jewish nationalism was integrally bound up with "the spirit of Zion." Nevertheless, Sokolow's relief that the Jewish past was not tied to "some wretched backwater" is somewhat odd. If the Jews had actually originated in China or where have you, would they really feel shamed by the notion of returning there? Sokolow's contemptuous tone cannot be explained solely by the low regard in which China was held by Europeans at the turn of the century. A more penetrating explanation is in order, and it is reasonable to assume that like Ahad Ha'am, Sokolow was incapable of imagining that a Jewish state would resemble "some China, some Patagonia," meaning just one more ordinary country like all the rest.[81]

A spark was tossed into the rather lethargic theoretical discussion in 1904, with the publication of an article by the writer Samuel Joseph Ish-Horowitz entitled "On the Question of Jewish Existence." Ish-Horowitz superseded Ahad Ha'am's criticism and cast aspersions not only on political Zionism but on the very prospect of a Jewish national revival. What Ahad Ha'am called a "small and insignificant nation" was rendered as a "lowly kingdom" in his argument that:

> Even if after all the centuries of countless inhibitions and obstacles and barriers, we reached the coveted shore, even then we will have only a "lowly kingdom" that is totally incapable of elevating the spirit; because, like every lowly kingdom, its eyes will always be raised to a greater kingdom that serves as the paragon for its cultural life. Is this the bliss for which we have longed thousands of years and are sacrificing so much?

Ish-Horowitz did not stop where Ahad Ha'am had, for he lacked the latter's faith in the spiritual vitality of the Jews. Instead he argued that "even if we once had a dash of originality," great changes had set in over the generations "and we no longer bear our original countenance."

81 Sokolow, *To Masters and Mentors*, p. 132.

When the editor of *Hashiloah*, Joseph Klausner, tried to elicit Ahad Ha'am's reaction to the piece, the latter conceded that the article "had impressed many readers," but other than that he would not rise to challenge.[82] However, many responses from other writers were published in the journal, the most interesting of them coming from Lilienblum. The elderly Lilienblum was the perfect contender for Ish-Horowitz's skepticism because he was immune to the pretension of uniqueness. In effect, he set out from the very opposite perspective and was thus not loath to compare the future Jewish state to "a humble kingdom like Serbia or Montenegro." Echoing Herzl, who had spoken of Zionism as a cure, Lilienblum stated: "It is enough that the patient recuperate; we needn't aim for him to grow mighty and match the valor of a Samson." The crux of Zionism, as Lilienblum saw it, was in the question of "whether we shall live normal and orderly lives like all other nations"; everything else was optional. If the vision of the prophets (that Ahad Ha'am cherished and Ish-Horowitz had already despaired of) was ultimately realized, "all well and good," Lilienblum commented in a tone of dismissal, "there is no tax on hopes, and we have the right to hope without end."

In addition to the confrontation between normalization and uniqueness, this debate expressed a complex attitude toward other national movements. As we saw in the previous chapter, the Zionists had borne an ambivalent attitude of both imitation and scorn toward other national movements, as if to say: If peoples inferior to the Jews are deserving of independence, how much more so are we! This contemptuousness was now joined by a deprecation of the new nation-states and a fear that Zionism, too, would lead to retardation and cultural decline. The issue was essentially an instance of the struggle within all national movements between the impetus toward modernization and the fostering of native culture. But since Zionism attempted to extract the Jews from their integration into Europe and resettle them in a backward country, Palestine, it had to prove its

---

82 S. J. Ish-Horowitz, "The Question of the Existence of Judaism," *Hashiloah*, 13 (1904), p. 300 (Hebrew); Ahad Ha'am, *Letters*, Vol. III (1924), p. 185.

ability to both foster Jewish culture and engender modernization.[83]

In the final analysis, both Lilienblum and Ahad Ha'am had to face the challenge posed by Ish-Horowitz in arguing that the Jewish state, when and if it were established, would be both pathetic and void of Jewish content. Yet here we come to another important point. Ahad Ha'am, who believed in the uniqueness of the Jews, was concerned by the prospect of limited and narrow-minded nationalism – and on the face of it this appears to be something of a contradiction. Accentuating the unique seemingly placed Jewish nationalism at odds with the national movements of other peoples, and that was not so. Those of the spiritual Zionists who emphasized the element of uniqueness believed in it as a complement to the universalist outlook. In the same article in which he decried the "small and insignificant nation," Ahad Ha'am spoke of the prophets' eschatological vision, explaining that "this ideal for humanity has always been and will always be inevitably an essential part of the national ideal of the Jewish people." In so writing, he was following a long tradition that was developed particularly during the era of the emancipation by a wide spectrum of Jewish thinkers and reformers.[84]

This approach to universality, which regarded the uniqueness of Judaism as residing in precisely its general human content, coexisted with universality of a different sort that acknowledged the uniqueness of Judaism but placed it in a pluralistic framework, that attributed to every people its very own distinctiveness. It was a pluralism traced to Herder's influence on national thinking. The universalism that embraced it differed from Ehrenpreis's philosophy – which clearly distinguished between two elements, the European and the national – in being expressed through the uniqueness of every nation and language. Here, for example, is how Bernfeld expressed this approach to universality in a piece written in 1899: "The poetic literature of a cultured people marked by a high level of education is

---

83 M. L. Lilienblum, "Aimlessness and the Right to Exist," *Hashiloah*, 13 (1904), p. 488 (Hebrew); and cf. John Plamenatz, "Two Types of Nationalism" in Eugene Kamenka, ed., *Nationalism, The Nature and Evolution of an Idea* (London, 1976), p. 34.

84 Achad Haam, *Ten Essays on Zionism and Judaism*, p. 27, and see Jacob Katz, *Out of the Ghetto* (New York, 1978), pp. 206-209.

both national and human. It attaches a sense of humanity to the national feeling and makes it into a national asset." This outlook draws its full meaning from Bernfeld's focal axiom that the nature of the Jewish people can be understood "only on its own terms" and not through a comparison with any other nation.[85]

Martin Buber, who was a leading proponent of national uniqueness within a pluralistic framework, did wonders with this subject in explicating the connection "between the renaissance of the Jewish people" and "the progressive national-international culture movement" in his 1901 article on the Jewish renaissance. Buber's guiding principle was that "only when every nation expresses its own nature does it replenish the common repository," and he stressed that "national self-awareness" rather than the "acquisitive impulse and drive for territorial expansion," was the motive behind nationalism. He also viewed the national outlook as being anchored in a broader movement of revival and believed that "the renaissance of the Jewish people" was essentially a part of this movement.[86] That same year, in addressing the Zionist Congress on the subject of Jewish art, Buber expressed his hope that instead of "a bloodless vision of humanity," a "healthy national self-awareness" would take hold in European life. The gist of this outlook was that "like every man, every nation serves the common good in the best way when it devotes its talents to fruitful creativity."

In an article written in 1903 but not published until two years later, Buber reiterated this basic philosophy while attempting to accord the "Jewish movement" new depth. He objected to using the popular term "national movement" in characterizing Zionism, for he contended that the Jewish movement was "broader and deeper than most national movements, more original and more tragic." Here Buber resorted to a distinction – which he had avoided until then – between form and content: "Its content is national, aspiring to national liberty and independence, but its form is super-national. Its value system belongs to mankind's way of thinking and the liberation it propounds touches upon the great symbol of redemption." Here the idea of redemption – albeit in the sense of a universal myth

85 Bernfeld, *An Account of Our Literature*, pp. 4, 15.
86 Martin Buber, "Juedische Renaissance," *Ost und West*, 1 (1901), pp. 7, 10.

rather than its usual religious connotation – joined the store of concepts Buber used to characterize Jewish nationalism. The distinction between form and content notwithstanding, it is beyond doubt that Buber regarded redemption as a goal both specifically Jewish and applicable to all mankind.[87]

An extreme version of Jewish universalism emerged from the speech made by Franz Kobler of Prague at the founding convention of the Democratic Fraction. Klausner, who reported on the convention in *Hashiloah*, was highly impressed by Kobler's case and placed it in the same class as the group including Buber, Feiwel, and the artist Lilien. Klausner reported Kobler as having said that "we aspire to a renaissance because we have religious and moral 'values' that can be a boon to all mankind" – implying that the Jewish renaissance was predicated on the benefit it would bring to humanity as a whole. Neither Ahad Ha'am nor Buber portrayed the issue in quite such radical terms. Kobler spoke of culture "in the sense of the spiritual assets of the Jews" and claimed that it alone "is the rationale for Zionism." It appears that the idea of mission developed by Western Jewry has been combined here with the theme of national destiny, which had made inroads during the national struggles in the Austro-Hungarian Empire. Of course, it is always possible that Kobler, a student from Prague, failed to express himself precisely, or that his ideas had been misconstrued. It cannot be denied, however, that the gist of his message strayed far from the Zionist mean.[88] Klausner confined himself to reiterating the widely accepted position that Jewish nationalism must take its place in a pluralistic framework. In the programmatic article he published upon taking over the editorship of *Hashiloah*, Klausner proclaimed: "We are nationalists, not chauvinists, and our nationalism is based on the noble idea that all peoples must accept *all* the truth, good, and beauty from each other and pass on to each other *all* the truth, good, and beauty that they themselves have created."

87 M. Buber in *Protokoll V Zionistencongress*, p. 153; Buber, *Der Jude und sein Judentum*, p. 277.
88 J. Klausner, "The Fifth Zionist Congress," *Hashiloah*, 9 (1902), p. 67 (Hebrew); and see Oscar Jászi, *The Dissolution of the Habsburg Monarchy* (Chicago, 1964), p. 259.

Considering Buber's and Ahad Ha'am's qualms on this subject, Klausner's words sound rather simplistic. They also lack the same respect for the subject's complexity present in Bernfeld's analysis of four years earlier. But as we have noted, neither the profundity nor the originality of the thinking can serve as criteria for our inquiry into ideas and trends. Perhaps the simpler and clearer the idea, the more likely it is to win broad popular support. In any event, complex issues must undergo some process of adaptation, whether it be deliberate popularization or the inevitable effect of a social movement's inner dynamic.[89] Thus we are entitled to assume that Klausner's categorical distinction between chauvinism and nationalism was an authentic expression of a widespread sentiment. There is likewise no doubt that Zionism strove to achieve a certain balance between the qualities that distinguished the Jews and the qualities that bound them to other peoples. The desire for normalization notwithstanding, by its very nature the national idea was predicated upon the assumption of uniqueness – though during the period under review there was not a single force or faction within Zionism that did not strive to establish normal relations between the Jewish people and other nations.

Nationalism and Religion

At the beginning of this chapter we depicted the national idea as one that Herzl believed was common to all Jews, regardless of their religious orientation. Actually, this was a cardinal principle of the Zionist philosophy, which defined the Jews as a nation and presumed to speak in its name even if, in purely numerical terms, it represented only a minority of the people.

We should note, however, that it was not enough for this Zionist world view to apply the national definition to the Jews in the present; the Zionists wanted to accord this status retroactive validity as well. Ahad Ha'am, who regarded himself as something of a "national pantheist" for identifying nationalism as the prime mover through-

89 J. Klausner, "Our Objective," *Hashiloah*, 11 (1903), p. 6 (Hebrew); and see Biddis, *The Age of the Masses*, pp. 19-21.

out the centuries, stated in a letter to the Italian Rabbi Luli in 1898 that: "Even if we deny our nationhood, we are convinced that we are a special *people*." He went on to speak of "Jews who are so removed from the Torah that it is hard to believe they are Jews, but they will nevertheless sacrifice their lives for their nation without even knowing what it is that compels them to do so." So much for the objective power of nationalism, which seemed to have imposed itself almost mysteriously on the members of his generation. That same year Ahad Ha'am published his article "Renaissance and Creation," which summed up the approach of spiritual Zionism and traced nationalism to its historical roots. In comparing his outlook to the traditional one, Ahad Ha'am noted: "The more one discovers the moral light found in the Torah and the Prophets, the ethical ideal embodied in the epithets "the Giver of the Torah" and the "Lord of the Prophets," and the moral force that has preserved all these in sanctity and purity through all the tribulations and the wanderings, the more one appreciates the inherent value of *the national spirit, which possesses these things*." The implication here is that Ahad Ha'am believed the "national spirit" was embodied in the history of the Jews, which the "believing Jew" regarded as an expression of God's will. Judaism had therefore been national in character not only since the inception of the Jewish national movement but since Creation, if you will.[90]

The Zionists who aligned themselves with Ahad Ha'am wrote variations on this theme. Simon Bernfeld, who had once been a rabbi and was concerned with "refining our religious concepts," looked for a way "to furnish Judaism with a creative form instead of the present one, which has lost its value." At first glance this appears to be a way of solving the religious crisis in Jewish life, but further on Bernfeld pronounced that "that new, positive – *national* – form [was] actually Judaism's first and original form." This quote comes from an article published in 1901, but in an article on Ahad Ha'am published four years later, Bernfeld continued to grapple with the same question. Like Ahad Ha'am, he wanted to reveal the real reason for the modern Jew's attachment to the Jewish religion – namely, the

---

90 Ahad Ha'am, *Letters*, Vol. I (1923), p. 207; Ahad Ha'am, *Collected Works*, p. 292; and cf. Elie Kedouri, *Nationalism* (London, 1978), p. 73.

need to belong to the Jewish community – and he mused that, "Perhaps there is a national feeling here of which they themselves are unaware." Unlike Ahad Ha'am, whom he accused of being too intent on restoring the old Judaism, Bernfeld professed: "In my opinion the most important thing is the existence of the Jewish nation. [For] as long as our people exists, Judaism will not be lost." Essentially there was little difference between Bernfeld and Ahad Ha'am. Both tried to bridge the gap between the spiritual quality of Judaism and Jewish nationalism through some sort of "national pantheism," which explained all manifestations of Jewish life, past and future, as expressions of the national impulse. They parted ways, as we have seen, over the matter of the Jewish renaissance, with Ahad Ha'am preferring the spiritual moment to the existential one and Bernfeld accenting the opposite.[91]

True to his mentor's spiritual philosophy, in taking up the cudgels against Motzkin's secular approach, Joseph Klausner distinguished between "the Israelite faith," which he regarded as the essence, and "the religious customs," which were merely "an external manifestation of an inner force." He followed the pan-national principle in saying that "the nationalists and the Zionists regard the Israelite faith as the product of the national spirit of the Jewish people." After analyzing the customs and faith, which he found to be fundamentally national, Klausner arrived at a certain affirmation of religion, in saying, "We can no longer think of our religion as a trifling matter, whose 'self-destruction' is reason for rejoicing." Another rendering of this approach comes from Osias Thon, who was both a modern rabbi and an active Zionist. Thon tried to apprehend the motivation behind the martyrdom of masses of Jews in the Middle Ages and questioned whether they had gone to their deaths for their religious faith. Since faith is an abstract that does not involve the masses, he tried to delve "ever deeper into the psyche of this multitude" and found "a strong, inchoate feeling – the national feeling." Whereupon he determined that "they were nationalists, not consciously but unwittingly" – much as Bernfeld and Ahad Ha'am had concluded.

91 S. Bernfeld, "A Positive Moral Action," *Hador* (June 13, 1901), p. 1 (Hebrew); S. Bernfeld, "Asher Ginzberg" (Literary Portrait), *Ha'eshkol* (1905), pp. 61, 76 (Hebrew).

Thon had arrived at the same pan-national principle in his own way, positing "that in those days faith was the sole expression of nationalism." His piece was published in 1903, but if we compare it with his approach to messianism, as formulated back in 1896, we will see that he had systematically espoused this outlook. His emphasis on the unconscious in the 1903 piece may point, though, to the influence of Freud, whose work was already known by then.[92]

The conclusion that follows from these quotes is that the spiritual Zionists developed the pan-national approach, and this was not by chance. Their outlook was unquestionably well disposed toward Jewish tradition, and to a certain degree they were sympathetic toward religion; yet more than any of the other Zionists they clashed head-on with religious Jewry. For Ahad Ha'am and his disciples did not draw the line at seeking a pragmatic basis for cooperation between religious and non-religious Jews but espoused an entirely new interpretation of Jewish tradition. Even though they were closer to traditional Judaism than the political Zionists, for example, they wished to place it on a new – national – footing and change it from within. From this point of view, there was no difference between the early and the later Ahad Ha'am or between Bernfeld, Klausner, and Thon. They all excised the hand of Divine Providence from Judaism and replaced it with the "national spirit" and "national feeling" – and herein lay the crux of the controversy over cultural work. Ahad Ha'am might be bitter about the Zionist leadership for ignoring the Hebrew calendar in almost scheduling the opening of the Zionist Congress for a Saturday. That is a mere trifle in comparison to his own attitude. He and his colleagues faced a more important test that year when the Love of Zion Society instituted negotiations on granting guardianship over its settlement of Mahanayim, in Palestine, to the Hassidic Rabbi of Chortkov. Ahad Ha'am called the move a "spiritual inquisition"; Thon dubbed it "slavery"; and Ehrenpreis warned that, "The rabbis will rule us in our colonies"; and

---

92 J. Klausner, "The Fifth Zionist Congress," *Hashiloah*, 9 (1902), p. 65 (Hebrew); Osias Thon, "Historical Laws," *Hashiloah*, 11 (1903), p. 336 (Hebrew); see e.g. Paul Roazen, *Freud and His Followers* (Harmondsworth, Middlesex, 1979), p. 187.

Berdyczewski admonished, "The things you are forfeiting as mere means are in fact our ends."[93]

To scrutinize more closely their real attitude toward religion, we shall refer to two matters dating to 1902. The first was a letter Buber wrote to Herzl relating how he and a friend, the artist E. M. Lilien, went about converting the renowned artist Max Liebermann to the Zionist cause. Buber related on Lilien's behalf: "When I told him that I was a sworn Zionist but not religious, *he could hardly believe it*, [and] he saw only beautiful and idealistic sides to Zionism." Further on the letter related that Liebermann had expressed a readiness to aid the Zionist cause, also dispelling the misconception that "*every Zionist must be an observant Jew.*" Liebermann spoke of his acquaintanceship with the artist Hermann Struck (among the leaders of Mizrahi in Germany), "who ate only kosher and wore [the fringed undergarment called] *tzitzit*," and of his own reluctance to identify with "conscious Jewry" (in Buber's words) for fear that he too would be forced to eat kosher and wear *tzitzit*. The letter clearly indicated Buber's assumption that Herzl fully shared the view that the identification of Zionism with religion was an amusing curiosity and a single conversation was enough to clear up this misconception and transform a figure like Liebermann into a Zionist.[94]

A more serious incident occurred in that year, when a rumor made the rounds that Zionist students in Bern had feasted in public on the Day of Atonement and their disgraceful behavior was laid at the feet of the Democratic Fraction. Dr. Josef Seliger, who was to become one of the Mizrahi leaders in Galicia but was living in Switzerland at the time, wrote a scathing article on the affair in *Der Israelit*, the organ of Orthodox Jewry published in Mainz. He accused the Democratic Fraction of aiming to wipe out religion and expressed the fear that the Orthodox anti-Zionists would take the incident as proof that Zionism encouraged defection from "the old Judaism."

93 Ahad Ha'am, *Letters*, Vol. I (1923), p. 191; Ahad Ha'am, *Collected Works*, p. 295; Osias Thon, "Nationalism and Zionism," *Ha'eshkol*, 1 (1898), p. 14 (Hebrew); M. Erez-Ehrenpreis, "An Overview," *Hashiloah*, 3 (1898), p. 170 (Hebrew); Berdyczewski, *On the Agenda*, p. 64.
94 Buber, *Briefwechsel*, p. 174.

In the same issue, *Der Israelit* published a rejoinder written by Dr. Rudolf Schauer, the chairman of the Zionist Society of Mainz, who was aligned with Herzl. Schauer dissociated himself from the Bern students and the Democratic Fraction alike and asserted that: "The great majority of the Zionists is religious, its Zionism stemming from its religious feeling. The minority, to the degree that it is not religious anymore, regards our religion as the Palladium of the people of Israel that has held national unity together for the 1900 years in which a territorial integrity no longer existed." The flap sparked a wave of anger in the ranks of the Democratic Fraction, which believed it had been indirectly slandered by the Zionist leadership and even sent off a letter of protest signed by dozens of members, including Weizmann, Buber, and Feiwel. One may view this affair as a microcosm of the struggle over culture within Zionism. Seliger warned against differentiating between the national and religious components of Judaism and feared that the Zionists would lose their influence among the religious public. In the course of the polemic, Seliger, a modern religious Zionist – who was anathema to the old school of Orthodoxy – was actually portrayed as an enemy of Zionism. Schauer assailed the Democratic Fraction and depicted Ahad Ha'am's disciples as deliberately provocative renegades. Ironically, then, the Zionist establishment presumed to speak in the name of religion, but its argument was identical with the pan-national approach of spiritual Zionism.[95]

Beyond the tactical posturing and misunderstandings, however, all the sides to this debate shared a common basis inasmuch as they acknowledged a certain connection between nationalism and religion in Judaism. Dining in public on the Day of Atonement, like the earlier-cited story of the Zionist who converted to Christianity, was a marginal phenomenon that no Zionist defended. Of course one must bear in mind that the discovery of common ground was an *ex post facto* one and in no way diminished the vehemence of the debate. Moreover, if we compare the antagonists' positions on various issues, we can see that in actual fact there was no difference between Buber's and Herzl's attitude, for example, toward the obser-

95 Josef Seliger, "Sonderbare Auswüchse," *Der Israelit* (December 3, 1902), pp. 1823-1824; see also the rebuttal by Rudolf Schauer there.

vance of the commandments; public life required both Ahad Ha'am and Schauer to display a respectful attitude toward certain religious traditions.

Another aspect of the spiritual Zionists' attitude toward religion derived from the fact that this circle included a relatively large number of people associated with Reform or modern Judaism. Ehrenpreis, Thon, and Marcus Braude officiated as modern rabbis; Bernfeld and Kaminka had left the rabbinate for other occupations; and Moses Gaster, Zvi Malter, and David Neumark also fell into a similar category. Some of these men were closely associated with Ahad Ha'am and *Hashiloah*; others were active in the Zionist movement. They maintained contact with like-minded people, such as the leading figures in the Democratic Fraction – Weizmann, Motzkin, and Bernstein-Cohen – and particularly with the Feiwel-Buber-Lilien group. The point here is to pay note to the anti-Orthodox climate in this circle that came out in its stand on the cultural issue.

For example, in a 1903 article published in Feiwel's *Jüdischer Almanach*, Ehrenpreis wrote: "We have freed ourselves of the *rabbinical culture* that had shut us up in a narrow cage of laws and walls and decrees; that has been a barrier separating us from all that is majestic and mighty and lofty in life and in the world; that has weakened our body and deformed our shape." He also held the rabbis responsible for the passivity of the Jews – as a result of having resigned themselves to the situation – and inveighed against the despair that came in its wake, "the despair that lacks the strength or wherewithal even to want or hope." Thus the anti-Orthodox mood was in keeping with the currents we have described up to now – the call for a renewal of values and the striving for a self-redeeming endeavor by the Jews.

After Herzl's death, in assessing the condition of the Zionist movement, Osias Thon dwelled upon the role of religious Zionism: "Mizrahi as the *ecclesia militans* is today an unhidden fact. And perhaps we had better wake up in time: '*Le cléricalisme – voilà l'ennemi!*' After all, we do not wish to return to Asia as Asians but as good Europeans." Such warnings were a more pointed expression of the struggle against Orthodoxy within the Zionist movement, but they also signified a negation of Jewish isolationism and a sense of belonging to European culture. Moreover, in his article on Ahad

Ha'am, Simon Bernfeld explicitly stated that "Orthodox Judaism is inimical to the desire for a national renaissance," and further on he proclaimed that he refused to recognize the rabbis' authority to speak on behalf of Judaism, even though he avowed himself to be "quite religious." Bernfeld explained his thinking on this subject, which was wholly theological, by saying: "I do not accept the religious customs that have been imposed upon us in recent ages as the religion of Moses and Israel. They are, rather, a form of idolatry that is far from genuine Judaism." The Reform motif took pride of place here, rather than the Zionist moment, which was the main theme of the article.[96]

In closing this chapter we shall quote from an interesting piece that goes to the heart of the controversy over culture and demonstrates the innovative impulse of Zionism, compared with the traditional outlook of Orthodox Judaism. In 1899 Rabbi Elijah Akiva Rabinowitz, who had broken ranks with Zionism over the issue of culture, published a book entitled *Justice Shall Redeem Zion* (subtitled "A Rabbinical View of Zionism"). At one point, when he was lampooning the Jewish practices of his adversaries, his writing reads like a mirror image of some of the well-known attacks on the ultra-Orthodox:

> They move heaven and earth to offer people a sugar plum of worldwide renown, for it is most necessary to attract the people to its age-old virtues, its hallowed possessions and spiritual heritage – like celebrating the "Festival of the Maccabees" with the youth and maidens of Zion dancing, with pancakes, Carmel wine, and with the lighting of candles one day in a jubilant throng; the Fifteenth of Shevat with fruits and almonds and the honey of Palestine; the Thirty-third day of the Omer with bows and arrows and eggs painted the colors of the banner of Judah; by wrapping one's hat and decking one's house in black on the Ninth of Av as a sign of mourning; and celebrating Shabbat Nahamu [the Sabbath immediately following the

---

96 M. Ehrenpreis, "A Literary View," *Hashiloah*, 11 (1903), p. 187; Thon, *Essays zur zionistischen Ideologie*, p. 86; S. Bernfeld, "Asher Ginzberg," *Ha'eshkol* (1905), p. 67 (Hebrew).

Ninth of Av] with festive dances; and similar major and minor rites performed by the Children of Israel.

Beyond the sarcasm and hyperbole, what comes through here is a picture of the Zionists giving the Jewish holidays a national slant, selecting the festivals that were consistent with their world view and replacing traditional modes of celebration with ceremonies borrowed from their non-Jewish environment. More than all the ideological and political debates, this short quote conveys a sense of the chasm that existed between the spiritual world and way of life pursued by the Zionists, even East European Zionists, and the old Orthodoxy. Further on Rabinowitz satirized the Zionist-Haskalah ideology with such fidelity that if one did not know who the author was, one might well take him literally. Here, for instance, is a quote that speaks of the Zionists' objectives and attainments: "To try to clear away the dirt and the mire of the long exile that has clung to our people for eighteen hundred years and to uncover its gems, the sparkling sapphires, its moral powers and powerful feelings that aspire to life and to *freedom*." The key concept is undoubtedly the accentuated word "freedom," which had a positive connotation for the innovative Zionists but smacked of licentiousness to the Orthodox community.[97]

Conclusions

We have tried to explicate the ideological trends that clashed in the struggle over the culture issue, which raged within the Zionist movement from the Second to the Sixth Zionist Congress. The advocates of cultural work have occupied a focal position in these pages, since they placed the cause of culture at the head of their priorities, while both the Zionist establishment and the religious Zionists tried to belittle its importance. Behind this controversy lay profound differences over the proper approach to a variety of issues touching upon culture, religion, history, and nationalism. The proponents of cultural work, though not a formally organized group, were marked by

---

97 Rabinowitz, *Justice Shall Redeem Zion*, pp. 65-66.

their distinct set of ideas and were influenced, to one degree or another, by Ahad Ha'am's spiritual leadership. Yet their doctrine was not at all cohesive, and they often expressed notions that extended beyond their camp, as well. Moreover, the ongoing controversy over culture notwithstanding, *all* the currents within Zionism subscribed to a common platform whose basic tenet was the innate bond between nationalism and religion within Judaism.

Other than this basic principle, however, there was more that divided the Zionists than united them – to the point where it sometimes seemed that the Zionist Organization was composed of a medley of factions pursuing totally different objectives. The political Zionists were bent upon changing the objective circumstances in which the Jews lived while the champions of cultural work strove first and foremost to refashion the basic character of Jewish life. The connection between Ahad Ha'am's disciples and the heritage of the Haskalah was particularly salient. Although Ahad Ha'am drew a distinction between concern for Judaism – which he took to be of prime importance – and concern for the Jews – the crux of Herzlian Zionism – his associates and disciples threw themselves into Zionist activities with the aim of integrating both these principles in their endeavor.

The ideas that have been reviewed in this chapter crystallized in the course of Zionist activity and public debate, especially among East European intellectuals who were versed in German culture. The most outstanding was the Galician group (e.g. Buber, Thon, Ehrenpreis *et al.*), which served as a bridge between Russian-Polish Zionism and its German counterpart and constituted an influential element in the Democratic Fraction (many of whose members were students from Eastern Europe studying in the West). The supporters of cultural work were modern intellectuals rooted in Judaism and Hebrew culture and included many writers, journalists, and particularly a group of progressive rabbis. If we set aside the changes wrought by time and the many nuances that distinguished the various people cited here, we can sum up the general posture of the "culturists" in a number of characteristic clauses:

* Severe criticism of the diaspora way of life for having warped the character of Judaism.

* The promotion of physical fitness and aesthetics (including the myths of the dead, blood and race, and mother earth), as opposed to the rationalism and excessive intellectualism of the past (the so-called *Lebensphilosophie* had many followers, and it is worth paying particular note to the influence of Nietzsche as interpreted by Berdyczewski).

* Aspiring to a national renaissance based on the selective use of the Jewish historical heritage.

* The aim of creating a new culture in Palestine that would be a combination of Jewish and European culture.

* Affirming the uniqueness of Jewish nationalism along with a commitment to general human values.

* The rejection of religious Orthodoxy and a commitment to the pan-national approach to Judaism, past and future.

All these themes coalesced into a Zionist ideology that tried to compete with the dominant Jewish philosophies of the day – Reform Judaism no less than its Orthodox counterpart. Here was also where the missionary element came in, turning Zionism from a purely political movement into a spiritual message to the Jews and even to mankind as a whole. The universal mission ascribed to Zionism, which was conceived as having the power to create a constructive channel for the Jewish contribution to civilization, was of particular importance.

In contrast to this vision of Zionism, the movement's official (political) leadership was by and large unversed in Jewish culture and wished Zionism to be merely a realistic vehicle for solving the problems facing the Jews. Even though some of the elements we have explored in this chapter were shared by political Zionists, too, one must bear in mind Nordau's staunch opposition to the notion of a national mission and Herzl's highly pragmatic approach to the Jewish religion and those who practiced it. In this context we should draw special attention to Lilienblum, who had made the journey from the Haskalah to the Lovers of Zion and supported the position of the Zionist establishment against cultural work because he considered it immaterial to the Zionist purpose and yet liable to drive Orthodox Jews out of the movement. The Orthodox Jews, for their part, approached cultural work with an even more instrumental attitude than the Zionist establishment. Though uninterested in the ideological debates on the question, they did try as much as possible to avert the danger that the Zionist Organization would become engaged in cultural activities. On the other hand, we have found striking statements by those Orthodox Jews who had rejected Zionism, once they grasped the spiritual message implicit in cultural work. From this standpoint, they also attempted to grapple with the new ideas entailed by Zionism, going well beyond a rejection of the movement on the solely extrinsic level, to contend with its essential message.

CHAPTER THREE

A FUTURE-ORIENTED PRESENT

What is "Present-Day Work"?

The term "present-day work" (*Gegenwartsarbeit*)[1] connoted a variety of things, from day-to-day activities in the local Zionist societies to improving the economic, social, and cultural condition of the Jews; the "conquest of the communities" (a slogan for gaining control over the Jewish communal institutions in the diaspora); and taking an active part in general political life, both by putting up candidates for election and utilizing Zionist influence to score political gains for the Jews.

The adoption of present-day work as a clause in the Zionist platform raised a number of basic questions:

* How did the Zionists predict the rate of exit from the diaspora?
* What fate presumably awaited the Jews who would not leave their countries of residence?
* How would the relationship between the Zionists and the rest of the Jews operate as long as they continued to live under the same circumstances of diaspora?
* Considering the principle of pan-Jewish solidarity implicit in the Zionist idea, how would the Zionists relate to life in their countries of residence until their presumed resettlement in Palestine?

Further on we shall explore in detail the answers provided by the various factions of the Zionist movement to the questions implied

1   The term was coined by Feiwel, "Das Jahr 1900," *Die Welt* (January 18, 1901), p. 1.

by present-day work, including the ways in which they revised their thinking in response to the changes that occurred between 1896 and 1906. As the World Zionist Organization's first decade drew to an end, Zionism was heavily involved in Jewish life in the diaspora and even bore a sense of responsibility for the contemporary Jewish condition. Nevertheless, practical work in the diaspora had not evolved solely in response to a passing need. It was, rather, one of the original, historical, ingredients of Zionism that had always obtained alongside its ideological opposite – "the rebellion against the diaspora"[2] – sometimes in conflict, sometimes through compromise or mutual adaptation.

Prior to Herzl's advent, the Lovers of Zion were not a radical movement with a defined plan to quit the diaspora. Their movement was best described as a collection of autonomous cells scattered over a number of countries; only their common support for Jewish settlement in Palestine united them in the broadest sense, and they remained firmly rooted in Jewish life in their respective countries of residence. Ideological influences leading toward practical work or Jewish autonomy in the diaspora had begun to spread through the teeming Jewish communities of the Hapsburg Empire and the czarist Pale of Settlement at the close of the nineteenth century. One prominent model was the approach popular among the Austrian Socialists as reflected in Karl Renner's book *State and Nation* (1899), which served as the basis for the party's platform. It called for recognizing the various nationalities incorporated within the empire on the basis not of territory but of personal association, which was established by cultural criteria. Similar ideas circulating among Russian Jewry ultimately crystallized into a full-fledged theory in Simon Dubnow's work *Letters on Old and New Judaism* (1897-1907), in which he gratefully acknowledged the similarity between his own thinking on Jewish nationalism and the approach to nationalism in Renner's work.[3]

---

2   J. Klausner, "The Approaching Peril," *Hashiloah* 15 (1905), p. 425 (Hebrew).

3   Jászi, *The Dissolution of the Habsburg Monarchy*, pp. 179-180; Dubnow, *Nationalism and History*, p. 368, n. 16.

Members of the Jewish intelligentsia remained susceptible to socialist influences well after they had thrown in their lot with Zionism. This was true not only of their stand on nationalism but also on other issues that preoccupied the socialist camp. The contradiction between participation in parliamentary life and the complete rejection of the bourgeois lifestyle was a matter of great concern to the socialist movement. This was particularly evident in the 1900 struggle between the Marxist and moderate wings of the French Socialist Party, in the later dispute surrounding the emergence of a revisionist wing within the German Social-Democratic Party (1902-1903), and especially in the deliberations of the 1904 Socialist International Congress in Amsterdam. Echoes of the debate going on within the socialist movement over the attainment of the ultimate goal, versus the improvement of the worker's lot in the present, could often be discerned in the development of Zionist thinking on practical work in the diaspora.

Like the Socialists, there were Zionists who considered present-day work an unavoidable necessity that did not contradict the ultimate goal but did not contribute much toward achieving it, either. Others regarded it in a more positive light as a beneficial or even crucial transitory stage, to be used for building mass support and the like. Finally, it could also be depicted – either positively or negatively – as an alternative to the movement's ultimate goal. The discussion of practical work took place in a political context that had been created by two primary factors:

* The rise and fall of hopes for achieving a charter to bring Herzl's "Jewish state" to fruition.
* The democratization of the countries containing Europe's larger Jewish communities.

On the face of it, these were two independent factors, for the vicissitudes of Zionist diplomacy were played out on a completely different plane from the political developments within the Russian and Austro-Hungarian empires. Nevertheless, there was a point of contact between the two. The Zionist movement was initially borne along on the crests of Herzl's diplomatic activities and subsequently suffered grave disappointment as a result of his repeated failures, climaxing in the Uganda crisis of 1903-1904. Yet it also found an outlet in the prospects opening up before the Jewish communities in the two empires, especially as a result of the ferment that culminated in the 1905 Revolution in Russia and the institution of universal suffrage in Austria in 1906.[4] Due to the internal processes that had long been carrying it in the direction of present-day work, the Zionist movement met this new situation fully primed to take an active role in local affairs.

An Incipient Jewish Policy

In 1894 Marcus Ehrenpreis, a young Zionist from Lemberg who was to become the secretary of the Preparatory Committee for the Zionist Congress, wrote an article entitled "The Zionist Movement in Galicia" describing the movement in light of the mixture of nationalities living in that district of the Hapsburg Empire. Ehrenpreis spoke of life in Galicia much as the prophet Jeremiah had spoken of the exile in Babylon (Jeremiah 29:5-7), writing that: "We are no strangers in Galicia; we are not leaving for Palestine either today or tomorrow, and we shall be living here for many years to come. We shall yet build houses and plant vineyards until the great trumpet shall be blown for our freedom." Highlighting the difference between the Zionists of Galicia and the Lovers of Zion in Russia, Ehrenpreis described the "Jewish politics" in Galicia, whose purpose was to achieve equal rights for the Jews and enable them to participate in the country's political life. This aspect of the Galician Zionists' program was in turn augmented by cultural activities for the Jewish masses and efforts to further "Palestinian colonization."[5] The Jewish national awakening in Galicia found comfortable conditions for immediate action in the relatively tolerant Hapsburg policy, and when elections were held in Galicia the weight of the Jewish vote

4   Nora Levin, *While Messiah Tarried* (New York, 1977), p. 335; A. L. Schossheim, "Jewish Politics and Jewish Parties in Galicia" in Nehemiah Zucker, ed. *The Galician Register* (Buenos Aires, 1945), pp. 64-67 (Yiddish).

5   Marcus Ehrenpreis, "The Zionist Movement in Galicia," *Hamagid Leyisrael* (serialized from November 15–December 27, 1894; Hebrew); see also M. Ehrenpreis, "Our Aim," *Yudisher Folks-Kalender* (1895), p. 3 (Yiddish).

seemed to be an asset. A contest had been going on between the older generation, which was assimilating into German culture, and the younger one, which was attracted by Polish nationalism. The Polish orientation won out, but it soon proved a great disappointment to the Jews; for while the Polish national movement sought the support of the Jews, social integration was always quite difficult between the predominantly Catholic Poles and the Jewish assimilationists. This setback for the assimilationists prompted the Jewish national circles to believe that they might well succeed in organizing Galician Jewry as an independent factor of distinct cultural character that would exercise a certain degree of political influence in the competition between the various national groups.[6]

As far back as 1892 Nathan Birnbaum, the leading Zionist theoretician in Austria, had warned against the illusion that "Jewish politics" of this sort were capable of providing a full, long-range solution to the problems of Galician Jewry. Although he backed the decision of the Zion Society of Lemberg to create a Jewish-national political party, he argued that Zionism must nonetheless be the movement's guiding theme; for any improvements in the lot of the Jews, imperative and beneficial though they might be, would necessarily prove inadequate and temporary as long as the Jewish people lacked a territorial center. Birnbaum continued to fight against the lure of diaspora solutions in his address on "Jewish Modernism," published in the same year as Herzl's *The Jewish State*, explaining that the Jews were unable to stand together and feel at home anywhere in the diaspora because of compelling influences coming from the majority peoples.[7]

The Jewish question within the Austro-Hungarian Empire was bound up with the struggle of the various national movements in other regions besides Galicia, especially Bohemia and Moravia,

6   N. M. Gelber, *A History of the Zionist Movement in Galicia*, Vol. I (Jerusalem, 1958), p. 15 (Hebrew); Ezra Mendelsohn, "From Assimilation to Zionism in Lvov: The Case of Alfred Nossig," *Slavonic and East European Review*, 49 (1971), pp. 521-534.
7   B., "Parteiprogramme," *Selbst-Emancipation* (June 21, 1892), p. 116; Matthias Acher (pseud. for N. Birnbaum), "Die jüdische Moderne," *Zion* (October 1, 1896), p. 265 (some time thereafter Birnbaum became an advocate of Jewish autonomy in the diaspora).

where the Jews found themselves in a similar situation vis-à-vis the Czech national movement and German culture. In 1895, when Isidor Schalit, a member of the Kadimah student society in Vienna, spoke at a meeting in a small Bohemian town on the Jews' approach toward the political parties, his audience promptly decided to establish an organization "to represent the economic, social, and political interests of the Jews."[8] The period just prior to Herzl's appearance was one of upheaval in Jewish life within the Hapsburg Empire, particularly for the Jews of the capital. In 1897, the antisemites succeeded in gaining a majority in the Vienna Municipal Council, and the other parties proved rather willing to accommodate themselves to this new trend. Thus events forced the Zionists to be more attentive to immediate concerns. In addressing the Kadimah Society at the opening of the school year, Dr. Jacob Wassermann, a veteran member, observed that this group had always stood for taking a bold position, for defending the rights of the Jews, and for "independent Jewish politics." He expanded upon the idea that if only the Jews were organized around a unified platform, it would be possible to send "genuine Jewish representatives" to the country's various elective bodies and establish a party that would pursue its own policy, within a coalition arrangement, to the benefit of its Jewish constituents.[9] The increasingly hostile atmosphere in the empire also had its effect on Birnbaum, who began to seek out new partners for the Jews to replace the traditional but unreliable allies from the liberal camp. While voicing the usual admonition not to forget Zion in the process, he proposed a new approach to collaboration between Jewish nationalists and other oppressed forces and called for cooperation with the Social Democrats.[10]

Thus we have seen that the Zionists in the Hapsburg Empire deliberated highly topical questions, placing emphasis on the political plane and the prospect of activating the Jewish voter in the multinational and multi-party arena. Yet it is worthwhile exploring another theme that was destined to be of importance in Zionist prac-

8   "Nationale Bewegung," *Zion* (June 17, 1895), pp. 147-148.
9   "Nationale Bewegung," *Zion* (November 25, 1895), p. 308; cf. Pulzer, *The Rise of Political Anti-Semitism in Germany and Austria*, Chapter 15.
10 B., "Eine jüdische Volkspartei," *Jüdische Volkszeitung* (July 10, 1894), p. 4.

tical work in the diaspora. In his piece on Zionism in Galicia, Marcus Ehrenpreis wrote about the beneficial effects of Zionist activity on Jewish life. He mentioned the *rapprochement* between the Hassidim and university youth, as well as the affect this had on the non-Jewish press; all this against the background of Jewish servility in the past towards the authorities. He summed up the piece with the exultant declaration: "The Zionist movement has brought new life to our dry bones by awakening the masses to public affairs and activities related to the commonweal and because these initial signs and impressions, though not yet dominant, signal the start of a new period in our internal and political development in our country."[11]

The situation in czarist Russia differed substantially in that there was still no place for Jewish representation in the political framework there. Yet it is interesting to note that as far back as the end of the 1880s, we find testimony to the clash between the Zionist outlook and Jewish diaspora nationalism. Dr. Jacob Bernstein-Cohen, one of the future spokesmen of the Russian Zionists, told in his memoirs of the split in the Jewish Student Society: the Lovers of Zion comprising the minority and the non-Zionist Jewish nationalists the majority. Speaking of the society's interest in Jewish history, Bernstein-Cohen (who classified himself as one of the Lovers of Zion) wrote: "We have always ascribed greater importance to elucidating the Jews' present condition than to the period of their political independence in their homeland" – which was in sharp contrast to the historical approach that was taking hold among the Zionists in general.[12]

A rather different approach prevailed among the Lovers of Zion further to the West. In 1882 the rabbi Dr. Rülf, who had lived for many years in the Baltic city of Memel, was involved in aiding Jewish refugees from Russia and under the impact of this experience wrote a Zionist book entitled *Aruchas Bas-Ami, Israel's Recovery.* Two weeks after the appearance of *The Jewish State*, Rülf published an article on the Jew as a citizen of the state, stressing that only Palestine could serve as a satisfactory refuge for the oppressed Jews.

---

11 Yisrael Cohen and Dov Sadan, eds., *Chapters from Galicia* (Tel Aviv, 1957), p. 73 (Hebrew).
12 Bernstein-Cohen, *The Bernstein-Cohen Book*, p. 88.

"Despite all that," he declared, "I am a German patriot . . . Here I am and here I shall remain, as long as God so wills it, in the homeland that has been assigned to me."[13]

In the pre-Herzlian period, therefore, the Zionists posited three distinct approaches to Jewish life in the diaspora:

* Attempts to combine Jewish national activity with settlement in Palestine.
* A clash between Jewish nationalism in the diaspora and the Love of Zion movement.
* Zion for the oppressed, alongside local patriotism for the emancipated Jews.

As we shall see, these trends carried over into the official Zionist Organization and left their mark on both its debates with outside elements and its internal struggles.

Herzl vs. Ahad Ha'am

The focal issues in the debate over practical work was how long it would take to bring Zionism to fruition and how quickly the exodus from the diaspora would transpire. Herzl and his supporters perceived Zionism as a dynamic movement, whose purpose was to effect a tangible change in the Jewish condition within a brief span. In his novel *Altneuland*, Herzl projected the realization of Zionism within twenty years of the book's publication.[14] Clearly, however, he did not imagine that all the Jews would choose to reside in the Jewish state thereafter, and his prognosis for those who remained behind was based on his characteristic approach to Jewry and Judaism. Writing to the well-known literary scholar Georg Brandes in Denmark, in the hope of interesting him in Zionism, Herzl explained: "I definitely do not require all the Jews to go to Palestine . . . Those who wish to and must go will do so . . . But I assume that the Jewish State will

---

13 J. Rülf, "Der Jude als Staatsbürger," *Zion* (February 29, 1896), pp. 45-46.
14 See Herzl, *Old-New Land*. At first he believed that the process of realization would take much longer; see T. Herzl, "A 'Solution of the Jewish Question,'" *The Jewish Chronicle* (January 17, 1896), p. 12.

arise . . . together with the continued existence of the diaspora to some extent." Similarly, after a talk with his benefactor, the archduke of Baden, Herzl wrote in his diary: "An exodus of all Jews was not intended anyway. Assimilation would start in earnest then. And just as the Huguenot families, who are still flourishing in Germany today, have been well assimilated, it would then be the same way with the Jews." And in addressing the kaiser some six months later, he stated: "The way to complete assimilation can probably lead only through the established church. Zionism would be embraced only by those who were unable or unwilling to assimilate in their present places of residence; the rest would become ever better citizens of their respective countries."[15]

Along similar lines, one of Herzl's followers in Germany, Dr. Max Bodenheimer, regarded the Zionist solution as relevant primarily for the Jews of Eastern Europe. In a diary entry penned in 1898, he spoke of his attempt to convince a senior official of the German Foreign Ministry of the benefit that Germany stood to derive from Zionism, by portraying the Jews of Russia and Rumania as the bearers of German culture, while explaining that Zionism would "free the German Jews of their obligation to take in the Russian-Jewish influx." In 1902, with Herzl's approval, Bodenheimer sent a memorandum to the Foreign Ministry further justifying the claim he had made four years earlier. Among the factors impeding the full assimilation of German Jewry, Bodenheimer cited the constant flow of "the elements from the East," bemoaning it as "an annoyance to the German Jews, just as it is to the government." His conclusion was predictable: "Paradoxical as it may seem, the attainment of the Zionist objective is a prerequisite for the genuine and complete assimilation of the Jews among the host peoples, while Zionism itself is obligated to fight the present trend toward assimilation in order to achieve its objective."[16] There was, of course, a certain contradiction in portraying East European Jewry as the bearers of German culture (by virtue of the Yiddish language) while expressing dismay over the unassimilated immigration from the East, as he did in his memorandum.

15 Herzl, *Letters*, p. 181; Herzl, *Diaries*, Vol. II, pp. 658, 794.
16 Bodenheimer, *Im Anfang der zionistischen Bewegung*, pp. 118, 220-222.

Some of these pronouncements may be ascribed to the etiquette of diplomatic contacts, but we can hardly ignore the consistency of the argument in favor of assimilation. One must likewise bear in mind the prejudices of German and Austrian Jewry, which had been internalized by Herzl and Bodenheimer despite their Zionist radicalism. It is perhaps strange that the Zionists failed to perceive the incongruity between the rapid exodus of Jews from Europe and the successful assimilation of the rest. Assimilation entails gradual adjustment, and even if we accept Herzl's prognosis that the conditions for it would have been ideal after the establishment of the Jewish state, the Jewish problem in Europe could not have vanished in a single generation. Yet in the meantime, Zionists felt obliged to work *against* assimilation, so as to retard the process as much as possible. We find almost no other evidence that the Zionist's were conscious of this, for at that stage they still did not engage in serious thought about the future of the Jews in the diaspora. In the course of time, however, as the realization of Zionism tarried, they began to confront practical questions that forced them to take a stand on the matter.

The more extreme of Herzl's critics on the matter of prescribing quick solutions were Ahad Ha'am and his followers. On the eve of the First Zionist Congress, for example, Ahad Ha'am wrote to Menahem Ussishkin that diplomatic activity was pointless "as long as there are fewer than 100,000 Jewish farmers in Palestine," so that the time for such activity would be sometime in the future, "whether in the twentieth century or the twenty-first."[17] Joseph Klausner envisioned the Palestinian Jewish community growing by "a few hundred a year" and consoled himself that the time it would take to realize the Zionist idea at that rate "is not very long for a people that has been roaming for two thousand years."[18]

Ahad Ha'am repeatedly wrote that Palestine was not the solution to the problem of the Jews but rather to the problem of Judaism, and he drew a substantive distinction between these two concepts.

17 Ahad Ha'am, *Letters*, Vol. I (1923), p. 101.
18 Joseph Klausner, "The Political Zionists Opposing Diplomacy," *Hatzfirah* (July 3, 1901), p. 554 (Hebrew); see also Shmarya Levin, "Partial Reply," *Hazman* (April 18, 1903), p. 4 (Hebrew).

Not only was he skeptical of grand political designs, he regarded the establishment of a political entity in Palestine as the climax of a slow process of settlement, so that as far as he could see the national center would not offer a solution to the Jewish Question even in the distant future. For the meanwhile, he placed his hopes in America, "where both the Jews and Judaism will soon have a large center," or – in even more definitive terms – which "will be the future center of Judaism." Hence the clear differentiation between Jews and Judaism did not appear to hold where America was concerned – even though prior to pronouncing this conclusion Ahad Ha'am had distinguished between the "economic aspect of the Jewish problem," which would be solved in the United States, and its "ideal aspect," whose solution lay in Palestine, through the establishment of a "permanent center by the settlement of a great mass of our brethren."[19] In principle, Ahad Ha'am had no use for the "program of the present" because "diaspora life, even at its best, will always remain the life of exile, the antithesis of the life of national freedom, which is the goal of the Zionist movement, and two opposites cannot be the object of the same movement." Yet he not only supported cultural work in the diaspora but regarded it as "essentially Zionist work." This is not the place to go into Ahad Ha'am's inconsistency in rejecting practical work in the diaspora while affirming its cultural counterpart. One can say, however, that he placed emphasis on creating conditions for the development of Hebrew culture as a way of helping to sustain Jewish existence throughout.[20]

In comparing the political Zionists to Ahad Ha'am's coterie, we find that the two camps were divided over both the rate of exodus from the diaspora and the future awaiting the Jews who would not emigrate. Herzl forecast a rapid emigration by those Jews who would not or could not assimilate and the complete assimilation of the rest; Ahad Ha'am foresaw the creation of a national center in Palestine as a slow process accompanied by the reinforcement of Judaism in the diaspora. Paradoxically, it appears that both camps shared a neg-

19 Ahad Ha'am, *Letters*, Vol. II (1924), pp. 146, 149; Vol. III (1924), pp. 128, 134, 255; Ahad Ha'am, *Collected Works*, p. 23.
20 Ahad Ha'am, "The Revival of the Spirit," *Hashiloah*, 10 (1902), p. 483 (Hebrew).

ative attitude toward present-day work beyond the issue of culture
(which was, incidentally, one of the objects of dispute between
them). On the face of it, there was no place for such work in either
system, as both posited that the present condition of the Jews had
no intrinsic value. However, the pragmatic character of present-day
work led to its gradual acceptance, despite ideological opposition
from various sides.

"The Conquest of the Communities"

The slogan that Herzl introduced at the Second Zionist Congress in
1898 – namely, the need to "conquer the communities" – was all but
axiomatic by then and certainly did not spark off the kind of debate
prompted by other issues related to present-day work. The Zionists
had long believed that the existing Jewish leadership comprised
wealthy assimilationists and did not faithfully reflect the aspirations
of the Jewish people.[21] It had never been Herzl's dream to become
a leader of the masses; much to the contrary, he initially proposed
his plan to such affluent and influential Jews as the Baron Hirsch,
the Baron de Rothschild, and Chief Rabbi Güdemann. At one point
he even approached Bismarck![22] For two years he dallied, meeting
with other personalities, students, and simple Jews from Eastern
Europe, before arriving at the idea of a Zionist Congress.[23] Yet from
then on it was clear to him that Zionism meant not only the revival
of an ancient idea to solve the Jewish problem, as he wrote at the
beginning of *The Jewish State*; it was borne along by a new social
group that was at odds with the existing Jewish establishment.

In summing up the achievements of the First Zionist Congress,
Herzl found to his surprise that the East European Jew had made a
positive impression on him, whereas he had found the leaders of
organized Jewry in the West rather distasteful and wrote disparag-

---

21 B., "Die zionistische Partei," *Selbst-Emancipation* (February 23, 1892), p.
    41; and see Levin, *Memoirs*, Vol. III, p. 96.
22 Herzl, *Diaries*, Vol. I, p. 419; David Vital, *The Origins of Zionism* (Oxford,
    1975), pp. 248 ff.
23 Herzl, *Diaries*, Vol. I, p. 431; Vol. II, pp. 481, 506, 530, 532.

ingly of "the rôle of the rich in the lives of the communities, the moral pliancy of many priests [i.e. rabbis], the efforts of the amphibious-minded men to combine ancient tradition with an exaggerated imitation of national customs, the audacious mendacity of the economically weak." He concluded this condemnation with the somewhat obscure pronouncement that "Zionism has in view another kind of community for Judaism, a new and greater one, a single one. And also another system of representation."[24] His disappointment with the Jewish leadership and his conviction that at the congress he had established a genuinely popular movement encouraged Herzl to move in the direction of changing the traditional Jewish leadership in the diaspora, or, in his words, "Today the idea occurred to me to have the Jewish communities captured everywhere by the Zionists after the Congress." At first he dwelled solely on the tactical advantages of enabling Zionism to accord its supporters positions of influence and other benefits. But by the Second Zionist Congress he had developed a complete strategy for gaining control of the communities:

* The "large masses," which keep the communities going, support Zionism almost to a man.
* The authority of the communal bodies and the funds at their disposal must not be used against "the people's idea".
* The "conquest of the communities" would express the Zionist "will of the people" in daily life, in all Jewish centers at the same time.
* The "conquest of the communities" would demonstrate the power of Zionism and prove that the Zionists are not an isolated handful of people.[25]

The determination that the "large masses" supported Zionism, in contrast to the wealthy but alienated Jewish leadership, was a motif characteristic to many of the Zionists, including Herzl's adversary Ahad Ha'am. In any case, Ahad Ha'am shared Herzl's indignation

---

24 T. Herzl, "The First Zionist Congress," *The Contemporary Review,* 72 (October 1897), p. 594.
25 Herzl, *Diaries,* Vol. II, p. 620; Herzl, *The Congress Addresses of Theodor Herzl,* pp. 11-12.

over the sway of the wealthy in public life and expressed his ire quite strongly after having participated in a delegation that approached the Baron Edmond de Rothschild on behalf of the colonies in Palestine: "For as long as I can remember, I have never felt so degraded and my people has never seemed so small and poor to me as it did at that historic moment . . . for indeed we were witness to an historic moment that evening. The 'national movement' was put to the test and called up to show that it was steadfast not only when *begging for charity* on the doorstep of the rich but also of *rejecting charity.*" At that opportunity, Ahad Ha'am also decried the policy being pursued by Herzl in trying to hitch his wagon to all the "wealthy Jews, together with Rothschild and ICA [Jewish Colonization Association], and have them open their coffers to the Zionist cause." In following that course, Herzl, he warned, was both "deluded and deluding others."[26]

In *Hashiloah* Ahad Ha'am also published a piece by Abraham Elijah Lubarsky, a member of the defunct Bnei Moshe (a secret society along Masonic lines organized in 1889). Lubarsky attacked the leading figure among the Lovers of Zion, Moses Leib Lilienblum, for having included wealthy and well-connected Jews in the Odessa Committee, "even though they have had nothing to do with the Love of Zion to this very day" and they eventually left both the committee and the Love of Zion movement. Ahad Ha'am also printed a letter from Abraham Ludwipol, who was then living in France, describing the anti-Zionist mood of institutions such as the *Alliance Israélite Universelle* and the Jewish Colonization Association – both of them controlled (like the *Consistoire Central des Israélites* in Paris) by "our *haute bourgeoisie*, which has introduced rot and a spirit of corruption into the life of the Paris community and the Jewish religious leadership throughout France." It is not surprising that the early Zionist Socialists were given to such thinking. Similar statements were made in that same year by David Farbstein and Ezekiel Wortsmann, both of East European origin but then living in Switzerland and apparently subject to the influence of the radical émigrés from Russia. Farbstein divided the Jews into two classes: the desti-

26 Ahad Ha'am, "Little Digest – The Emissaries of a Poor People," *Hashiloah,* 7 (1901), p. 560 (Hebrew); Ahad Ha'am, *Letters,* Vol. II (1924), p. 230.

tute masses in Eastern Europe and the wealthy bourgeoisie in the West. Because he believed that the poverty of the Jewish masses was a function of economic conditions unique to the Jews, he pronounced that "there is no contradiction between Zionism and Socialism." Wortsmann, for his part, responded to an anti-Zionist pamphlet by the well-known socialist thinker Chaim Zhitlovsky, saying that it was a mistake to believe "that the rich need our help. Thank God there is nothing in the world that a wealthy Jew cannot obtain for money. Only the great impoverished Jewish masses suffer from the bitter exile, and it is these masses that Zionism wants to help."[27] These words were clearly meant to reflect the popular nature of the Zionist movement, while the old Jewish leadership supposedly represented only the selfish interests of the assimilated bourgeoisie.

Even though Herzl promoted the "conquest of the communities" in its own right, it eventually became associated with the broader issue of practical work in the diaspora. In June 1900 Léon Paperin, then one of the editors of *l'Echo Sioniste*, the Zionist organ in Paris, published an article entitled "La Conquête des Communautés" in which he came out against the doctrinaires who looked with disdain upon the mundane affairs, not touching directly upon "the national cause," that preoccupied ordinary Jews. He regarded their singlemindedness as a puerile error that afflicted all political parties in their early years due to their fixation on the ultimate objective and scorn for partial remedies and the needs of the hour. Similarly, Shmarya Levin confessed that at the time he had regarded Herzl's "conquest of the communities" as a variation on Ahad Ha'am's ideas about "preparing the hearts" – in the sense of "a new stage of Zionism, meant to destroy the barrier between the ultimate goal and the overall demands and objectives of the present."

Ahad Ha'am was unable to accept that assessment, both because of his negative attitude toward practical work in the diaspora and

---

27 A. Lubarsky, "Letter to the Editor," *Hashiloah*, 6 (1899), p. 476 (Hebrew); A. Ludwipol, "Letters from France," *Hashiloah*, 8 (1901), p. 82 (Hebrew); D. Farbstein, "Die Wirtschaftlichen Fragen des 4 Zionisten-Congress," *Die Welt* (October 11, 1901), p. 3; Ch. Wortsmann, "The Worker and Zionism," *Yudisher Folks-Kalender* (1901/2), p. 97 (Yiddish).

his animosity toward Herzl. In an article entitled "The Revival of the Spirit," he openly mocked the Zionist leader in writing:

> At one of the first Congresses, a clamor was heard: 'Conquer the Communal House!' And no sooner was it proclaimed than Zionists everywhere rushed to obey this commandment and have already spent much time and energy warring with the community leaders and the more powerful ones; but for all the effort, to date, in most places, one cannot find any tangible results. To my mind, it would be better to proclaim: 'Conquer the School!'

The well-known journalist S. J. Yatzkan went even further in writing pointedly: "That is why we want to conquer the communities, so that they will not be abandoned to coarse and aggressive men of means, so that the charitable institutions will not become seedbeds of deceit and flattery and the houses of prayer places for trafficking in honor and councils of ridicule." As he saw it there was no difference between Herzl's slogan and Ahad Ha'am's approach, and he employed a combination of Haskalah and Zionist rhetoric about the need "to prepare ourselves in the hallway before we will be privileged to enter the salon, so that we will be ready to live a life of culture, so that our sons will rise after us and be robust and healthy Jews in body and in spirit." Following this line, he arrived at much the same conclusion as Ahad Ha'am, namely, that it was necessary to establish modernized religious schools.[28]

The "conquest of the communities" formula was liable to spread a common ideological coating over a variety of ambitions that essentially traced to the desire to reform Jewish life in the diaspora. Thus we are entitled to question whether Ahad Ha'am was right in asserting in 1902 that the campaign to "conquer the communities" had still not yielded any tangible results. There is conflicting evidence on this matter. It is well known that at the turn of the century East

---

28 Léon Paperin, "La Conquête des Communautés," *l'Echo Sioniste* (June 5, 1900), p. 290; Levin, *Memoirs*, Vol. III, p. 168; Ahad Ha'am, "The Revival of the Spirit," *Hashiloah*, 10 (1902), p. 487 (Hebrew); Avi David (S. J. Yatzkan), "The Ragged Literature," *Sefer Hashanah*, 4 (1902/3), p. 275 (Hebrew).

European Zionists were engaged in vigorous efforts to persuade the community leadership to establish Zionist-oriented synagogues and educational institutions. On the other hand, at the 1902 Minsk Conference, Menahem Ussishkin tabled a series of organizational proposals to enhance the Zionist influence over ever-wider circles of the Jewish public, so as to "walk among the people and conquer the communities and public affairs in general," since Zionism had, for the most part, remained confined to "the Zionist societies."[29]

We learn of Herzl's direct involvement in the struggle to conquer the Western communities from his correspondence with Bodenheimer at the end of 1901, when he attempted to raise funds to support candidates in the election campaign in the Berlin Jewish community. Herzl explained that he was trying to place Zionists in positions of general importance, since the Berlin community was *ex officio* represented on the executive board of the Jewish Colonization Association.[30] To all intents and purposes, the Zionists deployed for a struggle with their opponents in Jewish public life and regarded themselves as an alternative to the incumbent leadership, without being fully cognizant of whether they wished to exploit their positions of power to win adherents to Zionism or to improve the quality of Jewish life in the diaspora.

The Source of Authority

As we have seen from Herzl's speech at the Second Zionist Congress, the "conquest of the communities" also answered the need to legitimize Zionism – to express the Zionist-oriented "people's will," as it were, and prove that the Zionists were not merely an isolated minority. Such legitimization had a practical purpose – a political show of strength toward the powers that be in Europe and public opinion at large, to demonstrate that the Zionists indeed spoke on behalf of the Jews – and a prescriptive aim – to establish Zionism as an author-

---

29 Mordechai Nurock, *The Minsk Conference of Russian Zionists* (Jerusalem, 1963), p. 80 (Hebrew); Ussishkin's address at the Minsk Conference, *Hatzfirah* (September 15, 1902), p. 1 (Hebrew).
30 Bodenheimer, *Im Anfang der zionistischen Bewegung*, pp. 211-212.

ized spokesman of the Jewish people. Herzl, who was educated in the law, believed it was vital to construct the future Jewish sovereignty on the philosophy of law. He devoted an entire chapter of *The Jewish State* to a concept borrowed from Roman personal law (*negotiorum gestio*) and tried to apply it to the state, in saying: "A state comes into being through a nation's struggle for existence. In such a struggle it is impossible to obtain the proper authority in any formal way." This was all the more true for "the Jewish people [which] is prevented by the Diaspora from conducting its own political affairs." Consequently, Herzl appointed a temporary trustee over the affairs of the Jewish people – the *Society of Jews* – which he equated with the leadership of the new movement.[31]

Presumably, then, the Zionist Congress was envisioned as the constitutional convention of the Jewish nation. Still, that did not obviate the need to obtain recurrent confirmation of the movement's representational status. This subject was broached at the congress by Max Bodenheimer, a lawyer by profession, who combined the legal theme with the populist strain in Zionism, by decrying the "existing assimilationist organizations" that failed to "provide expression for the Jewish people and its desire for power [*Machtwille*]," as they were merely "a small clique of moneyed, essentially cosmopolitan people." Zionism did not require an official mandate, he argued, for "the desire to aid their oppressed people burns in the breasts of hundreds of devoted people." Finally, Bodenheimer compared the convening of the congress in Basel to the oath taken by the patriots who pledged themselves to the liberation of Switzerland in the Middle Ages – a token of the spirit of Schiller's "Wilhelm Tell."[32] This formulation is close in spirit, though still not in letter, to the avant-gardist stance – meaning that although Zionism represented only a small minority of the Jews in strictly numerical terms, that minority was the truest expression of the Jewish nation. Hence the avant-garde argument posited that the Zionist movement was not just one

---

31 Herzl, *The Jewish State*, p. 93; Joseph Adler, *The Herzl Paradox* (New York, 1962), p. 75.

32 M. Bodenheimer, "Rede am 1ten Zionisten-Congress," *Die Welt* (September 10, 1897), pp. 6-9; cf. Hans Kohn, *The Idea of Nationalism* (Toronto, 1969), p. 16.

of many Jewish organizations and parties, but the *one and only* authorized representative of the Jews.[33]

The striving to be a genuine national movement and concomitant fear of remaining no more than a small party had been leitmotifs in Zionist writings prior to Herzl. But they became all the more prominent after the Zionist Congress because of its nature as a constitutional convention. Max Nordau's speech at the Second Zionist Congress was a classic expression of the disposition that attached to Zionism the biblical idea of the "remnant" (Isaiah 10:21), in the sense of the faithful minority, in contrast to the indifferent or alienated majority:

> When Ezra and Nehemia returned to Zion, the rich, the cultured, the Heine readers and Scholent lovers of that day remained in Babylon. Even in the present day it will not be different. Let it be so. It may be that the Zionists are yet a minority of the Jews. But because of them Jewry will be rejuvenated, through them it will obtain new life, and be rescued at a future time. On the other hand, the Jewish opponents of Zionism, be their number great or small, are destined to disappear from among the Jews. Perhaps this is the secret wish of their hearts. It will certainly be realized. On this account it is unbearable to hear them speak of a Zionist party in Jewry. We hurl back with contempt this distinction; the Zionists are no party, they are the Jewish body itself. Judaism is Zionism and Zionism is Judaism.[34]

This brings us back to the political Zionists' prediction about the future of the Jews who would remain in Europe and be assimilated into life there. Even though the matter at hand was not the actual exodus from the diaspora but merely the joining of the Zionist movement, we can assume that in 1898 the essential difference between holding membership in the Zionist Organization and the actual realization of Zionism was not yet manifest. Nordau's thinking was characteristic of many Zionists who looked to history as a

33 "We represent the whole national idea," T. Herzl, "A 'Solution of the Jewish Question,' " *The Jewish Chronicle* (January 17, 1896), p. 12.
34 Nordau, *Max Nordau to His People*, p. 90.

source of the authority denied to them by the contemporary Jewish public. As Fabius Schach – an East European Zionist journalist living in Germany – put it in attempting to justify the claim that Zionism was not a political party but the Jewish people itself: "Only they are the representatives of the nation – they who live their lives in the spirit of our history, who are loyal to its immanent nature and preserve its uniqueness." He too believed that their number was of no importance and went further in arguing that even if only twenty delegates had convened in Basel, they would still have been the legal representatives of Jewry as a whole. Schach also had a point to make about the other issue we have raised, namely, the difference between identifying with Zionism and actually leaving the diaspora. He echoed to the position taken by Rabbi Dr. Rülf (cited at the beginning of this chapter) in declaring, "We will not be full-fledged German citizens until we are once again full-fledged Jews."[35]

Invoking historical precedent to establish Zionism's avantgardism was promoted by the ongoing polemic with the movement's opponents. The same issue of the *Jüdischer Volkskalender* contained an article on "Zionism and the German Rabbis," in the wake of the convention of rabbis opposed to Zionism held in Berlin. The author of this piece followed Nordau's approach in referring to a parallel in Jewish history: "There were advocates of assimilation there too [in Babylonia]; the narrow-minded called for quiet and patience there too; they mocked the utopianism of the new enthusiasts there too; from the very start a national feeling welled up in a few there too, while the businessmen and millionaires, many rabbis and communal leaders kept their distance. But the youthful spirit and the truth prevailed over empty blather and senility."[36] And here again is Nordau, at the Third Zionist Congress: "How can we expect the world to accord us the rights and territory of a nation as long as it is not fully convinced that we really are a nation and wish to remain so. We Zionists know this, but the world does not have to believe us when both these points are viciously denied by a large number of savage

35 Fabius Schach, "Unser Programm," *Jüdischer Volkskalender* (1898/99), pp. 7-8.
36 H. Leumi (apparently Heinrich Loewe), "Der Zionismus und die deutschen Rabbiner," *Jüdischer Volkskalender* (1898/99), p. 140.

howls emanating from the ranks of Jewry." His obvious conclusion was to declare war on "*the enemies within*" so as to leave no doubt about "who is authorized to speak on behalf of the Jewish people." Nordau's address was punctuated by applause as he continued to develop the thesis he had introduced the year before: "In the Jewish heritage we repeatedly come upon the idea of a small minority being the vital, essential, and actually decisive part [of the Jewish people]." Nordau led his listeners through the ages, from Gideon's three hundred men to the legend of the thirty-six righteous men, and likened the Zionists to these paragons. Yet despite his audience's enthusiasm for this "proud nobility," Nordau confessed to the modern need to attain a majority and reckon with what he called the "brutality of the majority." He also warned the leaders of Orthodox Jewry that if they failed to lead the masses into accepting Zionism, they would have to account for their actions before "the people."[37] His address clearly expressed the dichotomy between the historical vindication of the elitist "remnant" and the pragmatic interest in generating mass support, especially for the conduct of diplomatic negotiations on behalf of the Jews. In placing the emphasis on the vanguard, he treated "the people" as an abstract concept and haughtily conceded the need to obtain its backing.

This dichotomy had already come out in Herzl's article scoring the so-called 'Protest Rabbis' (after having issued a manifesto against Zionism), in writing that, "Zionism is not a party. One can come to it from any party, for it encompasses all the parties in the nation's life. Zionism is the Jewish nation-in-the-making." So much for the pluralistic, all-national principle; then came the avant-garde sting: "But to belong to Jewry, to serve Judaism in a supposedly professional manner and simultaneously fight against it is an insult to any sense of justice."[38] Here Herzl made a semantic leap in gracing Zionism by implication with the epithet "Jewry," which could conceivably be justified by the stress on the national element in Zionism and its denial by the movement's opponents. But the term *Judentum*

37 M. Nordau, "Rede am 3ten Zionisten-Congress," *Die Welt* (August 25, 1899), p. 3.
38 H., "Protestrabbiner," *Die Welt* (July 16, 1897), p. 1; see also Ben Halpern, *The Idea of the Jewish State* (Cambridge, Mass., 1969), p. 86.

in German also implied *Judaism* in the spiritual sense, so that in fighting against Zionism the 'Protest Rabbis' were fighting against Judaism, as well. This article expressed the dynamic of a militant movement that could not accept the *status quo* but at the same time aspired to a broad, supra-party standing. Herzl's determination not to be confined to a small circle and to relate to the Jewish condition as a whole required the Zionist movement to safeguard its openness. Hence his critical attitude toward factionalism within the movement. Yet a broad-based Zionist Organization should obviously allocate a role to party activities; but it is also in the nature of ideological groups to try to influence the broader movement of which they are a part and at the same time to close themselves off. That was one aspect of Herzl's leadership that his critics ignored in assailing his one-man rule.[39]

Until now we have been examining the position taken by the political Zionists on Zionism's role vis-à-vis the Jews as a whole. This does not exhaust the subject, however, for in the meanwhile there was an upsurge of interest in these questions in Eastern Europe, where one of the venerated leaders of Russian Zionism, Dr. Max Mandelstamm, launched an attack on anti-Zionist activities by the Orthodox rabbis. When he published a letter in two Hebrew newspapers, *Hamelitz* and *Hatzfirah*, stating that "those Jews who are not Zionists, at least in thinking and conception, are not Jews, either," the piece sparked a bitter polemic, protests, and even a correction at the author's behest. Nevertheless, Mandelstamm reiterated in another article that, "Every Israelite is a Zionist or he is not a Jew."[40] One may well ask why Dr. Mandelstamm's statement created such an uproar while Nordau's elicited applause, for they appear to be similar if not actually identical. The answer is primarily that the circumstances differed. In the one case the Zionist Congress was being treated to a sonorous sermon by one of its leaders on Zionism's noble lineage – in contrast to the enemy within that wished to be rid of its Jewishness – whereas in the pages of the Hebrew press in

39 E.g. Bein, *Theodore Herzl*, p. 373.
40 Max Mandelstamm, "Open Letter," *Hamelitz* (March 24, 1899), p. 2 (Hebrew); M. Mandelstamm, "Why I Am a Zionist," *Hashiloah*, 6 (1899), p. 555 (Hebrew).

Russia, many of whose readers were Orthodox Jews, Zionism came across as repudiating Orthodox Jewry. Nordau portrayed Zionism as an alternative to assimilation, while Mandelstamm seemed to imply that it was an alternative to Orthodoxy.

This controversy was related to the continuous struggle in Eastern Europe between the "enlightened" Jews and their Orthodox counterparts. Mandelstamm's piece, like the rhetoric of so many other Zionists, was informed by concepts drawn from the Haskalah, so that even when he argued that Zionism did not detract from religion, he used language that grated on the Orthodox ear (e.g. "Every Jew will gain the Next World in his own way"). Defining Jewry on a national basis presumably did not preclude embracing all the Jewish variants within a common national framework, which is how Max Mandelstamm saw it. Yet all the same, his challenge illustrated that modern nationalism, not the traditional Jewish way of life, was to be the new substance of Judaism. This point was well expressed by Ahad Ha'am in a personal letter to a young relative, a scion of the Hassidic dynasty of Halberstamm, who asked him about the nature of Zionism. Ahad Ha'am replied:

> I could cite evidence from the Torah, as many rabbis and others have, that Zionism in no way contradicts faith and religion. . . . Scholars and writers have cited much evidence from the Talmud and later sages that there is no contradiction between faith and a liberal education . . . But experience shows that this is not so. And that is because there is sometimes a latent contradiction deep within the soul that ultimately leads a man to reject the demands of faith, though at first glance there is really no visible contradiction. The same is true of Zionism, when embracing all of Judaism as a complete system and not merely supporting the settlement of Palestine.[41]

Other participants in the Mandelstamm controversy were two Zionist writers who published their pieces in the Yiddish weekly *Der Yud*: Moshe Kleinmann, a political Zionist who supported the positions taken by Nordau and Mandelstamm; and the editor J. C. Ravnitski, Ahad Ha'am's friend, who rebutted them in an article

41 Ahad Ha'am, *Letters*, Vol. III (1924), p. 202.

entitled "Who Is a Jew." Kleinmann reasoned that "since many people do not believe in the messiah, for them Zionism remains the only hope of salvation from the diaspora. Thus the opponents of Zionism wish to deprive a large portion of the Jewish people of all its Jewishness." Ravnitski said that it was necessary to explain to the rabbis, gently, that "Judaism was declining, sinking, going astray; that the children of the most pious of Jews were straying far from the fold; that the situation was getting worse and worse" – and that Zionism meant to buttress Jewry. "It is a dangerous move to excommunicate anyone who does not think as I do," he argued, pointing out the potential for disaster if everyone thought that he alone or his party alone was Jewish and denied all the rest, for "that will be the end of 'All Jews are brothers,' the end of the Jewish people, and all will become chaos." In both these cases the Zionist rationale was based on the decline in the power of faith, but the conclusions were antithetical. A spiritual Zionist like David Neumark followed Ravnitski's approach in attacking Zionist elitism but admitted that his own view was unpopular: "If the Zionist movement fails to assemble the representatives of official Jewry [meaning the rabbis and communal leaders] under its banner, so that the congress will become the [equivalent of the] 'national council,' then it will be incapable of bringing about the redemption of Israel." As Neumark saw it, Zionism faced a choice: either to attract the "current official Jewry" – which for the present appeared to be impossible – "or to win the masses over to our idea, wherever they may be; to turn out the present leaders by force of a majority at election time, and to fill the communities with true Zionists."[42]

Actually, the elitist approach was fitting to spiritual Zionism, and Ahad Ha'am undoubtedly subscribed to it, from the time of the Bnei Moshe quasi-Masonic order (of which he said, "the *quality* of a moral society comes before its *quantity*"), through the expression of his personal mission. He regarded himself and a handful of associates as "the sole remnants" that "have kept faith with our nationality in its historical form" and pledged "to remain at my post to my

---

42 R., "Who Is a Jew?" *Der Yud*, 9 (1899), p. 2 (Yiddish); M. Kleinmann, "Zionism-Jewishness," *Der Yud*, 11 (1899), p. 1 (Yiddish); D. Neumark, "Zionism and the People," *Hashiloah*, 5 (1899), p. 98 (Hebrew).

dying day, even if I do so alone."[43] However, even Ahad Ha'am was not oblivious to the need for broad public support – at least not when he discussed the problem from an historical perspective. As evidence to this effect we can cite his piece on Pinsker, written on the tenth anniversary of the latter's death. In juxtaposing Pinsker and Herzl, he found a certain resemblance between the two figures, such as their attitude toward "the collective leader," for "without a 'national decision' stemming from a deep national feeling, without unity and a general organization that *will encompass all the people*, it is impossible to actuate his great idea."[44] All the same, Ahad Ha'am's way of thinking again led to the opposite conception, as we can see in the writings of a few of his young followers, especially Weizmann and Klausner.

During the Uganda crisis, Weizmann wrote something of an ideological manifesto for the Democratic Fraction, criticizing the Herzlian line and offering his own views instead: "We regard the concepts of Zionism and nationalism as identical and, therefore, the Zionist party as the only one capable and worthy of representing the entire people." This is a surprising statement, especially coming from Weizmann, who was in touch with reality, not some sort of idle dreamer. In this statement, however, not only was "the entire people" an abstract concept, "nationalism" (*Volkstum*, i.e. peoplehood, in the original) was likewise transformed and became the exclusive property of the "Zionist party." As we have noted, the circular was written in the context of the Uganda crisis, and in it Weizmann accused Herzl and his associates – who allegedly distinguished between the Zionist party and the people – of earmarking "Zion for the Zionists and Africa for the people." Another novel point is that up to now we have seen how the Zionists tried to portray their movement as not merely a party but as a popular movement – to the

43 Ahad Ha'am, *Collected Works*, p. 439; see also Bernfeld's letters of August 19, 1900, and January 22, 1901, in the Ahad Ha'am Archive, National and University Library, Jerusalem (II 175) and Ahad Ha'am's reply in Ahad Ha'am, *Letters*, Vol. II (1924), p. 196; Ahad Ha'am, "The Time Is Now," *Ha'omer* (January 30, 1907), p. 8 (Hebrew).
44 Ahad Ha'am, "The Doctrine and the Works," *Hashiloah*, 9 (1902), p. 14 (Hebrew).

extent of being "the Jewish people-in-the-making" – whereas Weiz-mann actually reverted to the term "party," but nonetheless claimed for it the exclusive right to represent the entire nation.

That was in 1903, a few months after the Bund (General Jewish Workers' League in Russia) had split away from the Russian Social-Democratic Party for being refused recognition as "the sole represent-ative of the Jewish proletariat." Unwittingly, perhaps, Weizmann availed himself of a formula similar to that of the Bund in regard to the representation of the Jewish people. The Zionist Socialist Nach-man Syrkin also resorted to almost the same language in his speech before the Uganda Congress: "We Zionists believe ourselves to be the sole representatives of the Jewish nation, and this we really are." But let us return to Weizmann's circular, which went on to state that: "We proceed on the principle that outside the Zionist Organization there are Jewish masses only, amorphous in form and still to be con-verted into a nation, that is, turned into Zionists. Another basic premise is that the Zionist vision is what has made us into the repre-sentatives of the people." The pronouncement about the conversion of the masses is related to "organic Zionism," which Weizmann advocated as a slow process of growth. What's more, his overall approach is redolent of the Marxist doctrine on the relationship between the avant-garde and the masses, the role of revolutionary theory and the consolidation of the working class.[45] Weizmann believed that (1) Zionism was the sole representative of the Jews as a people; (2) outside of Zionism there was only an amorphous entity; (3) the Zionists were acting on the basis of the Zionist theory or ideal; and (4) their role was to turn the masses into a people, that is, into Zionists. This resemblance does not imply that Weizmann had Marxist leanings or even that he had wittingly drawn upon the "Communist Manifesto." Like most of the Russian-Jewish intelli-gentsia, he held radical views and was involved in debates with the socialist émigrés in the West. The application of Marxist concepts

45 Typewritten circular dated October 26, 1903, in German, in the Ussishkin Archive of the Central Zionist Archives (A24/125/41), translation in Weiz-mann, *Letters*, Vol. III, p. 81; "Syrkin am 6ten Zionistenkongress," *Die Welt* (August 27, 1903), p. 9; cf. "Manifesto of the Communist Party" in Karl Marx, *The Portable Karl Marx*, ed. Eugene Kamenka (Harmondsworth, Mid-dlesex, 1983), p. 218.

to his Zionist theory was indicative of the generally revolutionary atmosphere in which he lived and worked during that period, yet it also suggests the profound influence that Socialism had on the Zionists of his generation, due to the extended ideological struggle between the two camps.

The most radical proponent of the avant-garde doctrine in Zionism was Ahad Ha'am's disciple Joseph Klausner, who was ostensibly acknowledging a fact when he wrote: "We Zionists are accustomed to regarding ourselves as if we were the entire people of Israel when we are actually only a relatively small party, only a part of the Jewish people." Yet he immediately qualified the statement by writing: "Our error is understandable: Since we, and we *alone*, have offered a basic solution to the question of the continuing existence of the Israelite nation, we are truly the lifeblood and powerhouse of this nation, and the historical-national process of Israel is transpiring in our camp alone." This article was written on the eve of the Seventh Zionist Congress – in anticipation of a decision in the struggle between the Zionists of Zion and the Ugandists – so that Klausner distinguished between the advocates of "rebellion against the diaspora," who aspired to a "complete revolution in Jewish life," and what he called the "hidden enemies," above all "the Ugandists or so-called political Zionists." He also took the opportunity to settle scores with other adversaries, such as the champions of practical work in the diaspora, the jargonists (Yiddishists) and the "revaluation of values movement" (this last reference being to the influence of Hebrew writers such as Micha Josef Berdyczewski and Saul Tchernichowski). "Assimilation is inherent" in those rival factions, he argued, "like a chick in an egg," since "wittingly or otherwise, *anyone* who destroys the historical foundation under the nation brings it closer to assimilation. Sooner or later, *dehistorization* must lead to denationalization, even if you do not wish it to." Klausner suggested to his fellow-militants that they completely dissociate themselves from the other factions, just as Jewry had once broken ranks with the Christians and the Karaites. One may thus conclude that just as Zionism spoke on behalf of the Jewish people even though it represented only a minority of the Jews, so a single faction within the Zionist movement could, in the last analysis, speak for the Jewish people as a whole. After the proposed purge, the "Zionist party" – this time Klausner's words – would gradually become "*the Israelite people incarnate!*" Such thinking was the climax of the process providing ideological justification for factional insularity, which was nowhere better exemplified than in the methods of Lenin.[46]

To suspect Klausner of Leninism is even more far-fetched than to ascribe Marxist leanings to Weizmann. For far from living among the revolutionaries in Geneva, Klausner confined himself to his study in Heidelberg. His focal interest was scholarly, and he was known for his devotion to spiritual Zionism. How, then, did he arrive at the doctrine of revolutionary avant-gardism? From Hegel's *Zeitgeist*? From the study of history, which had known many precedents of thinking along these lines – among the Jews and other peoples – well before the advent of Marxism-Leninism? Or from the internal dynamics of the elitist approach? The question remains open, yet it is precisely because of the differences between Zionism and Bolshevism – between Klausner and Lenin – that we should examine the reciprocal influences of these two very different movements, given the spiritual climate of the day.[47]

In summing up the discussion of avant-gardism, we should note that few voices were raised in favor of a pluralist approach and as a rule they belonged to the more conservative elements, which preferred a broad consensus based on national compromise over a revolutionary slant to Zionism. Consistent in this approach was the veteran leader of the Lovers of Zion, Lilienblum, who asked in his debate with the culturists: "Why should we introduce into Zionism, which must belong to all the people, special credos that are not subscribed to by all the people and thus upset the peace and unity without which Zionism itself cannot exist?" A similar view, albeit from a different standpoint, was expressed by Rabbi Samuel Jacob Rabinowitz in his attempt to persuade Orthodox Jews of the need to cooperate with their secular counterparts within the framework of

46 J. Klausner, "The Approaching Peril," *Hashiloah*, 15 (1905), pp. 419, 422, 424, 425, 428, 431 (Hebrew); cf. David McLellan, *Marxism After Marx* (Boston, 1979), p. 87.

47 See e.g. Eugen Weber, "Introduction" in Hans Rogger and Eugen Weber, eds., *The European Right* (Berkeley and Los Angeles, 1965), p. 2.

the Zionist endeavor: "We are unable to dissuade the secularists from adhering to the Zionist idea. Neither is the Zionist movement a talmudic or mishnaic society in which we can choose our associates according to our tastes and say: this member is to my liking and that one is not; so-and-so is deserving of a particular position and another is not. Zionism belongs to all the people." The Jerusalemite educator David Yellin used a similar argument against exclusivity in denying that "only the Zionists had the right to take an interest in the affairs concerning Palestine and its welfare." Yellin forwarded the argument that "no man can say to another: As long as you do not aim for what I do, you have no right to lay claim to Zion." Perhaps we should add to this category the positions taken by Bernard Lazare and Jacques Bahar – who explained their withdrawal from Zionist activity on the grounds of their democratic beliefs, which clashed with the "autocratic rule" of Herzl and his associates[48] – or that of Berthold Feiwel and the advocates of present-day work, who wished to overcome Zionism's inaccessibility to the masses. Both these groups spoke in the name of "the people," but it appears that rather than literally represent the people, their intent was to forge it.

The above exposition reflects Zionism's view of itself from the eve of the First Zionist Congress onward, as a minority with a sense of mission, that aspired to obtain authority from, and lead the Jewish public at large. When it failed to attain that goal, it reacted in a variety of ways, from mounting a campaign to "conquer the communities," through a willingness to compromise with the existing Jewish communal institutions, to the promotion of factional insularity. This variety of reactions was often a function of personality or temperament, though occasionally it reflected a specific ideological approach. The responses were not categorically divided according to faction, class, economic and social interests, or on the basis of East vs. West European Jewry. The only rule is that avant-gardism was characteristic of Zionism in its early years and endured thereafter,

---

48 M. L. Lilienblum, "To Those Who Seek Action," *Hamelitz* (March 9, 1900), p. 1 (Hebrew); Rabinowitz, *Religion and Nationalism*, p. 77; D. Yellin, *Works*, Vol. IV (Letters, 1878-1914) (Jerusalem, 1976), p. 125 (Hebrew); Jacques Bahar, "Explications," *Le Flambeau*, (April 1899), p. 5; B. Lazare, "Lettre à M. Herzl," *Le Flambeau* (April 1899), p. 3.

though it became less pronounced during the first years of the twentieth century, with the rising importance of present-day work. In essence, avant-gardism and practical work in the diaspora appeared to cancel each other out – though admittedly we can see this far more clearly in retrospect than was possible at the time.

The "conquest of the communities" was not a whimsical notion. It emerged in response to the vital need to attain influence within the Jewish world, to which hardly any Zionist faction was indifferent. Perhaps the only people who could fully identify with the avant-gardist (or "pioneering") approach, without fear that it would prejudice their standing, were the members of the *Second Aliyah* at the beginning of the century in Palestine. On the contrary, these young pioneers were driven by an elitist impulse, as attested, for example, by Joseph Vitkin's famed manifesto: "Brothers, our people has always paid homage to quality, not quantity. Our creed, too, exhorts us to expel from our midst anyone whose private life is suspected to be more important to him than our people, all the faint-hearted who in times of peril may cast down their standards and flee. Let us, too, follow this course." Vitkin called upon "the youth of Israel whose hearts go out to their people and to Zion" to fight not only "nature, disease, and hunger" but their friends and brothers, "enemies of Zion and Zionists," and he assured them that "your victory will be the victory of the people." Here Vitkin implied that Zionism in the diaspora was wholly at odds with the imperative to emigrate to Palestine, and he obviously held official Zionism in utter contempt.[49]

The Return to the Ghetto

For those Jews who had developed Zionist feelings, there appeared to be a contradiction between their newly discovered truth and the continuation of the diaspora. How did the Zionists differ from other Jews in their approach to life in the diaspora? And how was the Zionist outlook supposed to change diaspora life until the Jewish state was established? These questions were posed to the Zionists by

49 Joseph Vitkin, "Manifesto," March 1906, unpaginated; facsimile in Brakha Habas, ed., *The Second Aliyah Book* (Tel Aviv, 1947; Hebrew).

an incidental challenge from Max Nordau, and the ensuing controversy can help shed light on the Zionist approach to Judaism.

When various European intellectuals were interviewed in 1900
about granting emancipation to the Jews of Rumania, Nordau
responded in a way that left many Jews appalled – and hardly
delighted the Zionists, either. Extrapolating one step beyond what
was strictly required by the Zionist outlook, he called upon the Jews
to spurn the ambition to be accepted by non-Jewish society, and
remain within the bounds of the Jewish community – or, as his
opponents put it, to return to the ghetto. Here was Nordau, of all
people – the man renowned throughout Europe as a brilliant critic
and thinker – calling on the Jews to stop measuring their talents
according to the yardstick of "their success among the Christian public." As one who was somewhat removed from the daily rounds of
Zionist activity and the constraints imposed by public life, he
allowed himself to scorn the idea of emancipation, which was no less
welcome to Zionists than to other Jews. Actually he went one step
further, assailing emancipation as having failed in those places
where it had been achieved and disparaging the struggle for it in
those countries where it had not. He also lambasted the diaspora
mentality and its distorted hierarchy of values, based as it was on
the desire to become part of the surrounding society. As an alternative to this situation, Nordau proposed what he believed the policy
of diaspora Jewry should be: while fulfilling all their civil obligations
to the state, the Jews should "waive all political recompense for their
sacrifice and content themselves with the freedom to develop as
Jews." He further argued that, "We must wean ourselves of pleading
for jobs as judges, officers, and officials. Those desirous of a position
should request one in the Jewish communal organization . . . We
should also be wary of becoming those who shout the loudest in the
contest between the parties." The enormous energy he believed was
being wasted in irrelevant struggles, both within Western society and
in the form of revolutionary strivings in Eastern Europe, "brings
benefit to no one [and] causes the Jewish people very grave harm."
Instead, he projected the result, were these energies to be directed
toward the betterment of the Jews: "The communal organization will
be filled with vibrant life . . . It will be transformed from a community of ritual to a community of people. It will be a framework and

an impetus for fully actualizing all the powers within the Jewish people. The community will not have to be concerned solely with the synagogue and the cemetery; it will fulfill all the functions of a civilized commonwealth."[50]

Nordau appears to have been so absorbed in his diaspora policy that he lost sight of the primary objective of political Zionism, which favored the rapid departure of the "loyal Jews" upon whom his program was based. What he proposed was essentially no different from the program advanced by Ahad Ha'am: to establish for Jews elementary and high schools, and in the course of time perhaps also colleges and similar cultural enterprises, that would raise their self-esteem. Yet in the heat of scoring the negative role that the Jews played in Western society, Nordau transcended the bounds of political Zionism, straying beyond Ahad Ha'am's cultural work and perhaps beyond even the hopes of the cultural autonomists. His idea implied the creation of a Jewish community parallel to European society, into which the Jews had tried but failed to be accepted in the past. Unlike Ahad Ha'am and Dubnow, he did not address his program to East European Jewry – which was conceivably in a position to accommodate such a vision – but tried to impose his idea on a society that had made considerable headway toward assimilation. Dubnow wished to relate Jewish autonomy to a parallel process taking place among other European peoples, but Nordau proposed that the Jews unilaterally waive the right to be part of the surrounding society.[51]

This was not the first time that Nordau had deviated from the straight and narrow path of political Zionism. In an article published in Hebrew in the *Ahiasaf Calendar* for 1899 he wrote: "If we are about to return to Palestine as human dust and not as a living body united in its limbs and organs, then we have every reason to fear that the entire world will regard this 'return to Zion' as a harrowing

---

50 M. Nordau, "Die politische Gleichberechtigung der Juden," *Die Welt* (November 23, 1900), p. 7; (November 30, 1900), p. 5; (December 14, 1900), pp. 3-4. Nordau was probably influenced by Jacques Bahar's program, J. Bahar, "La Jeunesse juive et le Judaïsme," *Le Flambeau* (March 1899), pp. 11-12.

51 Ahad Ha'am, *Collected Works*, p. 153; Dubnow, *Nationalism and History*, p. 137.

display of rather pitiful anarchy." Nordau's conclusion was: "Every single Jew must first build Zion in his own heart so that Zion will be built in our holy land." Herzl feared that coming from his partner Nordau, such sentiments would be interpreted as a reproof of his own diplomatic efforts and the advocacy of gradually preparing the people for emigration, as opposed to an abrupt exit from the diaspora. Hence Ahad Ha'am had had good reason to believe that Nordau's thinking bore a certain affinity to his own ideas.[52]

However, Nordau was attacked not for the idea of maintaining a vigorous Jewish community in the diaspora but for its political implications. It was bad enough that he publicly told the Rumanians, when asked whether they should accord the Jews full equal rights, "No, I would not advise you to do so, at least not right now." Herzl personally informed Nordau that the Jews of Rumania were mortified by his reply, and Nordau was quick to promise, publicly, that he would soon publish a full explanation of his thinking and did not presume to speak on behalf of the Zionist movement. Yet the subsequent publication of his articles in *Die Welt* not only failed to assuage the uproar, it added fuel to the fire. For example, a Jewish weekly in Hamburg whose attitude toward Zionism was generally supportive, published an editorial on the "Nordau-Stöcker Alliance" (Stöcker being a famous antisemitic court preacher), noting, "We are not inclined to equate Mr. Nordau with Zionism, even though no disavowal has been evinced by the latter."

Max Bodenheimer wrote to Nordau challenging both his point of view and the wisdom of publishing it. He further pointed out that non-Jewish friends had been offended by it. In return, Nordau explained that, "All I asked was that we not demand any role in government." Whereupon Bodenheimer wrote to the Zionist Executive in Vienna suggesting that an official statement be issued on the subject. His status among the German Zionists notwithstanding, Bodenheimer evidently did not feel competent to take a public stand against a figure such as Nordau, so he published a response anonymously, in the same Hamburg weekly. Yet rather than take Nordau

---

52 Max Nordau, "The Aim of Zionism," *Ahiasaf Calendar* (1898), p. 168 (Hebrew); Herzl, *Diaries*, Vol. II, p. 779; Ahad Ha'am, *Letters*, Vol. I (1956), p. 254.

to task, he tried to smooth the matter over, arguing that: "If he blundered as a pragmatic statesman, we still haven't the right to cast aspersions on his intentions and brand him an ally of the antisemites." And further on in the article, Bodenheimer pledged that the Zionists of Germany would continue the struggle for the political rights of German Jewry. A similar approach appeared in the Paris *l'Echo Sioniste*, where A. Rokéach, one of the paper's editors, decried Nordau's "moral ghetto" but observed that "such pessimistic views have been voiced for quite a while by many Zionists, including the best of them, who are disappointed by the dubious advantages of European civilization." This appears to be an attempt to condone Nordau's position as an emotional outburst in response to the gathering wave of reaction and antisemitism.[53]

A far more penetrating polemic with Nordau went on for weeks in the pages of *Die Welt*. It was conducted by the editor of a Jewish newspaper in Holland, a Zionist by the name of Gerhard K. Polak who, in contrast to Nordau's arrogance and sharp wit, used patience and respect as his method of forcing his opponent to retreat step by step from his basic premises. Arguing from the standpoint of Dutch Jewry, whose experience belied the proposition that emancipation was bound up with humiliation, Polak forced Nordau to concede that his statements were not applicable to the Jews of either the United States or England, and perhaps not even of Italy and Switzerland either. However, Nordau remained staunch in his belief that the Jews should forgo participation in the politics of countries that had a strong antisemitic leaning. In conclusion, Polak noted the signs of Jewish activity in Austria and Germany aimed at achieving collec-

53 Shalom Schwartz, *Max Nordau Through His Letters* (Jerusalem, 1944), pp. 88-89 (Hebrew); M. Nordau, *Die Welt* (October 26, 1900), p. 3; "Die Alliance Nordau-Stöcker," *Israelitisches Familienblatt* (December 19, 1900), p. 2; the correspondence between Max Bodenheimer and Nordau in Central Zionist Archives (A-15/I/8b, December 27, 1900; A-15/III/4a, December 30, 1900); Bodenheimer, *Im Anfang der zionistischen Bewegung*, p. 98; Ein Zionist, "Für und Wider," *Israelitisches Familienblatt* (January 2, 1901), pp. 3-4; A. Rokéach, "Les Juifs et les droits politiques," *l'Echo Sioniste* (February 20, 1901), p. 97.

tive political representation for the Jews.[54] Throughout this debate, attention centered on the historical appraisal of the struggle for emancipation and on the distinction between civil rights and political rights. Yet there remained a substantive difference between Nordau's negative attitude toward the political involvement of the Jews as individuals and the notion of collective Jewish representation. While calling on the Jews to close themselves off within the Jewish community in the diaspora, he did not move in the direction of collective representation. Instead, his stand implied opposition to political activity of any form, and this attitude continued to inform the Zionist approach to practical work in the diaspora well after the controversy over a "return to the ghetto" had petered out.

Diaspora Politics

If Herzl's "conquest of the communities" had succeeded, the World Zionist Organization would have practically conducted the daily affairs of the Jewish communities in the diaspora. Had such an arrangement come to pass – assuming that the common framework could withstand the strain of the probable antagonism between the special interests of Zionists from different countries – the opponents of Zionism would have had all the more reason to accuse the movement of subverting the Jews' loyalty to their countries of residence, and the antisemites would have had all the more reason to make an issue of Zionism's international sway. Herzl was sensitive to this problem. In fact, he alluded to it as early as 1897 in a personal letter criticizing the Alliance Israélite Universelle. "Zionism can maintain its difficult venture without interference from the authorities," he wrote, "as long as it focuses its shared aspirations exclusively on the settlement of Palestine and not on the organization of the Jews in their present countries of residence." A month later he expressed this opinion in print as well – albeit in an unsigned article – again complaining that the Alliance had laid itself open to the charge of

---

54 Citations for the debate between Nordau and G. C. Polak: *Die Welt* (January 25, 1901), pp. 6-7; (February 1, 1901), pp. 1-2; (February 15, 1901), pp. 4-5; (February 22, 1901), pp. 1-3; (March 8, 1901), pp. 6-7.

being "a secret international conspiracy to achieve Jewish domination of the world." Contrasting this situation with the Zionist aim, he stated somewhat apologetically that "in order to solve the Jewish Question, we are interested not in an international organization but in an international debate; not intrigues, covert intervention, [and] evasive means but open-hearted discussion."[55]

But even for the international debate that Herzl had in mind, the proper channels would have to be found. A former parliamentary correspondent, Herzl imagined he could use the rostrums of Europe's parliaments for disseminating Zionist propaganda. In 1897, moreover, he corresponded with a number of leading Zionists in Galicia about the possibility of running a ballot of Zionist candidates in the Austro-Hungarian parliamentary elections. Estimates varied about the odds of getting a Zionist deputy elected, and at one point even Herzl himself was mooted as a possible candidate. What's more, Herzl asked David Wolffsohn (who would be his successor as president of the World Zionist Organization) whether he could raise funds in Germany for the election campaign – implying that the Zionist interest transcended national borders and that involvement in local politics should not be ruled out as long as it was for the sake of the Zionist cause. The idea of running a Zionist candidate in Austria-Hungary was not pursued, because of practical difficulties. We find no evidence of qualms that such a venture would rouse mistrust of the Jews – as Herzl had intimated about the 'Alliance' – or doubts that this strategy was less than fully consonant with Zionism's basic principles.[56]

Practical steps of this kind were in line with the ideological approach of an early Zionist Socialist, Saul Raphael Landau, who was then one of Herzl's closest aides. In 1897 Landau wrote (using arguments that would later reappear in the debates among Zionist Socialists on practical work in the diaspora): "Although there is also a trend among Zionists that objects to any local political appearance, it is unmindful of the consequence that, before they ever reach Palestine, the Jewish masses will be driven into the arms of the Social

---

55 Herzl, *Letters*, p. 324; "Leroy-Beaulieu über Antisemitismus," *Die Welt* (July 16, 1897), p. 3.
56 Herzl, *Letters*, pp. 199, 201-204, 206, 209.

Democrats – or into the jaws of starvation. The Zionist Organization must be to Zionists what the class struggle is to the Social Democrats: a means of achieving the ultimate goal more quickly and easily."

It soon became clear to the Zionists that they lacked the power to become an independent factor capable of representing the Jews in broader political arenas, so that any efforts in that direction would require them to collaborate with non-Zionists – or "assimilationists," in the language of the day. One early example of an attempt to strike such an alliance occurred in 1900, when Professor Martin Philippson called for a convention of German Jewry for the purpose of exercising its influence in national elections, much as the Catholics did. The chairman of the German Zionists, Max Bodenheimer, declared his support for Philippson's idea and, invoking the resolutions of the Zionist Congress, proclaimed, "We have set forth a program that is not just specifically Zionist." He further explained that Zionism addressed itself to all problems faced by the Jews that had some bearing on its aims. A key sentence in Bodenheimer's letter stated that: "In Germany we are therefore interested in stressing, above all, that we vigorously defend the patriotic rights of the Jews."[57]

Heinrich Loewe also backed Philippson's idea and published an enthusiastic article in *Die Welt*, praising first Philippson (who had been denied a professorship in Germany because he was a Jew and had been forced to resign his position in Brussels because he was a German) and then his program to organize the Jews of Germany. "Developing our Zionist program, expanding our point of view, [and] deepening our knowledge about the Jewish peoplehood speak strongly against fanaticism of any kind," he wrote, "*We wish to work not only for the sake of the future but also for the sake of the present.*" Toward that end, Loewe drew up an interim account of Zionism's accomplishments in Germany and explained: "While Zionism as *a closed party* has made headway among German Jewry but slowly from above, Zionism as an *idea*, a world view, the regeneration of the Jewish tribe, a sense of folk pride, and an assertion, has had a

---

57 S. R. Landau, "Die Lage der Juden in Westösterreich," *Zion* (May 31, 1897), p. 150; Bodenheimer, *Im Anfang der zionistischen Bewegung*, p. 187, n. 68.

marked effect." This conclusion led Loewe to some far-reaching concessions. For instance, he was prepared to abandon the struggle
against Zionism's opponents in the CV (Central Union of German
Citizens of the Jewish Faith), since their differences seemed to be
over semantics – religion or nationalism – rather than substance, if
only because "every union of organized Jews defending Jewish
honor, insisting upon Jewish self-esteem, embodies something of
Zionism."[58]

The Zionist Executive in Vienna applauded Philippson's initiative
and went out of its way to ensure that the Zionists would receive
appropriate representation at the convention of German Jewry.
Nevertheless, the venture failed. Bodenheimer charged that it had
been foiled by an aversion to Zionist participation. At a subsequent
public rally, he proclaimed outright that the *Judentag* – as the enterprise had been called – was a stage on the road to Zionism, for "If
rescue to the land of the Jews is not possible, flight from Judaism is
all that remains [as a remedy for] the distress of the Jews." His reasoning implied that there were actually three ways of solving the
Jewish problem in Germany:

* Emigration to the "Jewish state".
* Organizing the Jews in the diaspora.
* Assimilation.

Since the establishment of a Jewish state was not yet visible, Bodenheimer regarded the *Judentag* as the point of departure for a realistic
Jewish policy to block assimilation.[59]

Statements of this sort lead us to conclude that the Zionist did
not necessarily feel ill at ease in his diaspora environment and that
the leaders of the German Zionists tended to interpret the link
between Zionism and Judaism in a new way: Zionism was no longer
seen as an alternative to the existent Jewish community but as the

---

58 Eli Samgar (H. Loewe), "Ein Judentag," *Die Welt* (October 12, 1900), p. 2.
59 Bodenheimer, *Im Anfang der zionistischen Bewegung*, p. 203. The Zionists
   tended to assume that the total assimilation of the Jews in the diaspora was
   impossible. Max Bodenheimer was caught in the contradiction between the
   fear of assimilation and his memorandum commending assimilation as a
   desirable solution for the Jews who remained in Germany.

basis for a Jewish renewal in the diaspora. Even the followers of Herzl were caught up in the trend then evolving among the Jews in Central Europe, namely, to abandon the orientation toward the liberal parties and seek a way to activate the Jewish minority as an independent factor.

On the face of it, the Zionist position was not to intervene in matters of state, and leave the movement's members free to decide on such questions individually. This was likewise the official position of the Jewish establishment, though in the latter case it was a subtle expression of the long-standing collaboration with the liberals. At the close of the nineteenth century, the internal crisis in liberalism climaxed; antisemitism ceased to be a marginal phenomenon and began to make inroads on public opinion at large; and the Jews could no longer rely upon their traditional alliance with the liberals, which was predicated upon the ideology of the emancipation and the assimilation of the Jews into society. Thus it is understandable that the incumbent Jewish leadership had more difficulty than the Zionists in adjusting to the collapse of established conventions that had been rendered obsolete by the ongoing crisis in the liberal orientation. Moreover, the Zionists had always displayed a greater willingness to understand and even accept the mood of anti-liberal nationalism, while assuming a place for uniquely Jewish nationalism alongside it. This explains why Professor Philippson's challenge could overcome the Zionists' initial indifference to involvement in the political arena.[60]

The Shift in Outlook

This is the place to chart the change that occurred in the Zionist attitude toward practical work in the diaspora. At first the issue was a marginal one, often associated with philanthropic activity. As far back as the First Zionist Congress, for example, Bodenheimer had declared: "Nor is it enough for a poor man on the brink of starvation

---

60 See Uriel Tal, *Christians and Jews in Germany* (Ithaca & London, 1975), pp. 220-221; Ismar Schorsch, *Jewish Reactions to German Anti-Semitism, 1870-1914* (New York & London, 1972), p. 184.

due to anti-Jewish legislation to carry the hope of a better future; here the present urgently demands its due." Though Bodenheimer was a German Jew, his point was the need to improve the bitter lot of Galician Jewry, which had become a matter of concern for him out of a "sense of national solidarity." Similarly, at the London Zionist Congress, after being confronted with a display of poverty by the Jewish émigrés from Rumania, Nordau exhorted his fellow-delegates to donate to their welfare, elucidating that, "Even though the purpose of the congress is to deal with the *future* of the Jewish people, it cannot ignore the *present* and the demands it makes." The year was 1900, which can be regarded as a turning point in the Zionist thinking on practical work in the diaspora. It was the year of the controversy over the "return to the ghetto" and the attempt to organize the *Judentag* in Germany. The London Zionist Congress decided to charge its Economic Committee with deliberating suggestions "for improving the economic condition of the Jews" – such as cooperative enterprises, the extension of credit, professional training, and labor unions – "and formulating a precise economic program." This opened the way for a lively debate over all aspects of practical work in the diaspora.[61]

At the same time, a group of young people who had found a common framework in the Democratic Fraction began to organize for action, and it was they who provided the most consistent impetus toward practical work. Berthold Feiwel, one of the leading members of this group, wrote that: "This present-day work directly and indirectly serves the aim of national self-help. It embraces a variety of fruitful activities that are meant to aid the Zionists in leading the Jewish people back to its peoplehood [and] cultivating a physically stronger, spiritually loftier, economically healthier people than we have today." Feiwel compared this preparatory work to the forty years that the Children of Israel spent in the desert after leaving Egypt, but in a departure from Jewish tradition – he was not *critical*

---

61 M. Bodenheimer, "Rede am 1ten Zionisten-Congress," *Die Welt* (September 10, 1897), pp. 6-7; M. Nordau, "Debatte am 4ten Zionisten-Congress," *Die Welt* (August 31, 1900), p. 10; G. Herlitz and M. Gordon, eds., *Die Beschlüsse der Zionisten Kongresse I-XVIII, 1897-1933* (Jerusalem, 1933), (in typescript).

of this "lost generation." He went on to observe that even though the Zionist Congress had barely given its consent to engage in practical matters in the diaspora, lively activity had already developed in this sphere. His close friend Martin Buber went one step further in speaking of practical work as an "historical imperative" and according it distinctively moral significance, in writing: "On the other hand, we see the substance and soul of the movement in reshaping the folk life, in the education of a really *new* generation, in the transformation of the Jewish tribe into a strong, united, independent, healthy, and mature community." Another member of the Democratic Fraction, Alexander Hausmann, developed a program of practical work whose chief aim was to eradicate the ghetto heritage, so as to establish a "political commonwealth," create "a new type Jew" in Palestine, and fight against the economic ruin of the Jews in the diaspora. Yet he was careful to qualify that such action could not avert economic collapse, merely postpone it. Hence it would "never be able to supplant Zionism."[62]

These young people of the Democratic Fraction had come mostly from Austria-Hungary and were influenced by the local traditions of present-day work within the Zionist groups. Without doubt they were also keenly aware of the steady impoverishment of Galician Jewry, so that it was not merely by chance that Alexander Hausmann laid stress on the economic moment. Still, their affirmation of practical work derived from a complex of issues. In March 1901 the first conference of Austrian Zionists convened in Olmütz, Moravia, and ratified Feiwel's program to raise "the physical, economic, and spiritual level of the Jews in their present countries of residence." The champions of practical work took these resolutions to be a milestone in the history of Zionism in general, not merely in Austria.[63] For Feiwel and Buber, alternate editors of *Die Welt*, influenced the movement's ideological leanings; Feiwel also held a position in the Zionist Organization in Austria; and both of them had easy access

---

62 B. Feiwel, "Das Jahr 1900," *Die Welt* (January 18, 1901), pp. 1-2; M. Buber, "Gegenwartsarbeit," *Die Welt* (February 8, 1901), p. 4; A. Hausmann, "Gegenwartsaufgaben des Zionismus," *Die Welt* (April 12, 1901), pp. 7-8; (May 3, 1901), p. 6.
63 See the resolutions, *Die Welt* (March 29, 1901), pp. 2-3.

to its younger members. Despite their differences with Herzl over the issue of culture, they still enjoyed the confidence of the official leadership, which was also centered in Vienna. Most important of all, the new direction they represented – namely, that Zionism would branch out beyond diplomatic and organizational activities – reflected the desire of many Zionists throughout Europe.

Nahum Sokolow made this very point in *To Masters and Mentors*, his book on Zionist issues written in a pseudo-rabbinical style: "There are commandments that must be performed in the land [viz. Palestine] and commandments that are not dependent upon the land. Should we therefore do away with all the commandments here? . . . We must achieve at least *a touch* of perfection here. We *must* do this preparatory work for both 'here' and 'there.'" He was speaking not only of acquiring a grounding in "Hebrew culture" but of the occupational rehabilitation of the Jews, considering the drift of the economic boycott against them. It is not surprising that Sokolow was drawn to this position, since he had been committed to similar causes before joining the Zionist movement.[64]

The one figure who jealously guarded the purity of spiritual Zionism against the encroachments of practical work in the diaspora was Joseph Klausner, who regarded the Olmütz Conference as grossly overstepping the bounds of Zionism. Feiwel answered such criticism in kind, by arguing that even cultural work was effectively practical work, in that it bridged between the "Jewish past" and the "Palestinian future." On the face of it, the debate between Klausner and Feiwel (both of whom were soon to join the Democratic Fraction) traced to a common ideological basis. Feiwel contended that "he who truly aspires to the rebirth of the Jewish people and regards the body of the people as a living organism" would be loath to condemn any of the body's organs to paralysis, due to sheer stagnation, and would strive to destroy the wedge between the Zionists and the non-Zionists. Klausner, for his part, was alarmed by the erosion of the Zionist platform since the Fourth Congress – so much so that despite his negative attitude toward Yiddish, he published an article in that language taking to task a number of advocates of practical work: Sokolow (whom we have already mentioned here), Isidor

64 Sokolow, *To Masters and Mentors*, p. 106.

Marmorek (whose proposals were the basis for the economic resolutions of the London Congress), and Berthold Feiwel (the author of the Olmütz program).[65]

In December 1901 the Conference of Enlightened Zionist Youth convened in Basel and founded the Democratic Fraction on a platform that combined radicalism and populism, as reflected, for instance, in the debate between Klausner and Feiwel. As far as practical work in the diaspora was concerned, the conference dwelled at length on the economic issues – with an eye to the competition that Zionism could expect to meet from Social Democracy. Leib Jaffe, a friend of Klausner's from Heidelberg, argued against the majority: "If some [political] parties are engaged in economic activities, they are working according to their own systems, which presume the condition of the Jews in the diaspora to be a normal and permanent one. But we Zionists know that our people is sitting on a volcano." Similarly, the Socialist David Farbstein demanded that economic activity in the diaspora be excluded from the new faction's program. In an article published at about that time, he admitted that Zionism could well derive short-term benefits from efforts to allay the immediate distress, but he warned that "nothing will do any good. Any remedy will be but a placebo that will lead nowhere," for "planned emigration" was the only solution to the suffering. In the same article Farbstein spoke of non-proletarianization, which was to become an object of controversy within the Jewish labor movement. "It is impossible for a true industrial proletariat to emerge out of the Jewish masses in Eastern Europe," he wrote.[66] Farbstein was a well-known figure, and he commanded attention well beyond the circle of young Zionists. For example, Dr. Julius Moses, a physician from Mannheim who was chosen to speak on economic affairs at the Fifth Congress, laid aside the preparation of his lecture to persuade Farbstein that every effort should be made to rehabilitate the Jews

65 J. Klausner, "The Boundaries of Zionism," *Hashiloah*, 7 (1901), "Addendum" on pp. 424-425 (Hebrew); B. Feiwel, "Die Grenzen des Zionismus," *Die Welt* (October 4, 1901), p. 2; J. Klausner, "On Practical Work," *Yudisher Folks-Kalender* (1901/2), pp. 58-59 (Yiddish).

66 J. Klausner, "The Fifth Zionist Congress," *Hashiloah*, 9 (1902), p. 61 (Hebrew); D. Farbstein, "Die Wirtschaftlichen Fragen des 4 Zionisten-Congresses," *Die Welt* (October 11, 1901), p. 3.

in the diaspora as a stage on the path to the ultimate goal, "*For we must not only prepare the country for our people, we must also prepare the people for our country.*" In his address at the congress, Dr. Moses took up cudgels against "the doctrine of impoverishment," which he claimed was already in disfavor among the Socialists and the opponents of Zionism had tried to foist upon the Zionists, as though they took pleasure in exploiting the "agony in Jewish life."[67]

At that same congress Nordau spoke of the Jewish people as a *Luftvolk* ("people of air"), economically speaking, just as the individual Jew was known as a *Luftmensch*. He invoked this negative image of the Jew as a "man of air" not to support the standard Zionist argument, but to justify practical work in the diaspora. "We must begin by strengthening the Jewish people economically," he urged, "because only a people with some economic capability can follow the path to realizing the Zionist vision."[68] The consistency between his earlier, abortive attempt to "return to the ghetto" and his present effort to improve the economic condition of the Jews in the diaspora is patent enough. In the interim, moreover, the movement had come round to this way of thinking: practical work on the economic plane had found a place within Zionism in the Haskalah-inspired form – as the ideal of productivization – and in its socialist rendition – as the ideal of proletarianization – both being viewed merely as transitory stages en route to the future in the Jewish state.

We have already quoted Farbstein on the inability of the Jews to develop into a proletariat in the diaspora. His thinking on this point was followed by Dr. Chaim Dov Hurewitz, when he lectured on economic affairs at the conference of Russian Zionists held in Minsk in 1902. Hurewitz was considered the father of the doctrine of non-proletarianization, but although he shared Farbstein's assumptions, he came to radically different conclusions. For example, in an article published at about that time he portrayed the realization of Zionism as no better than a remote prospect; basing his prediction on the

---

67 J. Moses, "Die wirtschaftlichen Fragen des 5 Zionisten-Congresses," *Die Welt* (December 13, 1901), pp. 1-2; J. Moses, "Referat über die Fragen der wirtschaftlichen Hebung," 5 Zionisten-Congress, *Die Welt* (January 10, 1902), p. 6.

68 Nordau, *Max Nordau to His People*, p. 126.

"natural sense" of the masses and arguing that "the people had forced its deputies" to work toward the improvement of economic conditions for the Jews in their countries of residence. Implicit in this statement was an admission of the importance of practical work in the diaspora as an *end in itself*. Hurewitz reasoned that political Zionism did not preclude the possibility of improving the economic status of the Jews as a "temporary reform," and he added that without such an improvement "the realization of our idea is unlikely at any time." Not only did he regard practical work as a requisite stage, he believed "it should be considered an essential part of the redemption itself."

It is obvious that for those who approached the Jewish Question from the Marxist viewpoint, proletarianization was a decisive issue with direct bearing on the proposed rehabilitation of the Jews in the diaspora as well as on the Zionist solution, no less than on the shared interests of the Jewish workers and other strata of society. It became a focal issue for that generation, not least because of the emergence of a Jewish labor movement in Eastern Europe that had a growing influence on the Zionist movement and its thinking.[69] Moreover, the new trend toward shifting the application of present-day work from cultural to economic issues was soon to cross another thin line – that dividing economics from politics.

The Specter of Revolution

The delegates to the Minsk Conference feared that Dr. Hurewitz's words would be misconstrued as a call to "go to the people," in the style of the Russian revolutionaries. And indeed, the authorities expressed their dissatisfaction with the new turn being taken by Zionism. During one of their two meetings in August 1903, Russian Interior Minister Plehve told Herzl that he supported Zionism as long as it worked toward Jewish emigration from Russia. But in view

69 C. D. Hurewitz, "Theory and Action," *Ahiasaf Calendar* (1903), pp. 123-127 (Hebrew); C. D. Hurewitz, "The Economic Issue and Its Place in Our National Movement," *Hashiloah*, 10 (1902), pp. 329, 330-334 (Hebrew); cf. E. Kleiman, "An Early Modern Hebrew Textbook of Economics," *History of Political Economy*, 5/2 (Fall 1973), pp. 339-358.

of the Minsk Conference, he believed that a change for the worse had taken place: "There is less talk of Palestinian Zionism and more of culture, organization, and Jewish nationalism. That is not to our liking." The Polish nationalists likewise began to harbor suspicions that Zionism was bent not on building a Jewish state in Palestine but on creating a Jewish nation alongside the Poles and the Ukrainians, "on the banks of the Vistula."[70]

The political repercussions of practical work in the diaspora were therefore highly complex and included the identification of Zionism with the struggle of other nationalities against czarist rule, the fear that Zionism would compete with other national movements in the Russian empire, and above all the suspicion that there was a connection between Zionism and the revolutionary movement in Russia. Writing to Plehve a few months before his visit to Russia, Herzl boasted that in the past Zionism had offered the wretched masses a vision loftier than "revolutionary madness," but the Kishinev pogroms had left the people steeped in despair. Even Herzl ascribed the opposition within the Zionist movement to the revolutionary influence on the Jews, and he exhorted Plehve: "Help me to reach the land sooner, and the revolt will end. And so will the defection to the Socialists." In the course of a diplomatic conversation, which required sharp-wittedness and full attention to demands of protocol, Herzl took recourse to a number of points that had served him in the past. He had first proposed the Zionist solution as an alternative to revolution back in 1895, though at the time he was thinking not of the predicament of Russian Jewry but of the Jews of the West. Thereafter, in a conversation with the foreign minister of Germany in 1898, he remarked about having recently read that "Egypt was a socialist state in the pre-Mosaic period. With the aid of the Ten Commandments, Moses created an individualistic social order, and the Jews are [still] individualists." From time to time Herzl also returned to the theme of the Jews being "the proletariat within the proletariat," implying that they had despaired of society, which

---

70 Y. Gruenbaum, "From Warsaw to Helsingfors" in *Harvest: A Collection on the History of the Zionist Movement in Russia*, Vol. I (Tel Aviv, 1964), p. 31 (Hebrew); A. Raphaeli, "The Second Minsk Conference" in *Harvest*, Vol. I, p. 70; Theodor Herzl, *Tagebücher*, Vol. III (Berlin, 1923), p. 466.

regarded them as step-children, and supported the revolutionary parties – yet not as an oppressed class but as a people seeking redress for the injustice it had endured. As Disraeli had observed, "the Jew is, by nature, ultra-conservative," but "in his absolute lack of hope for improving his lot or simply for living, he became receptive to radical ideas."[71]

Thus in the last analysis, Herzl seemed to confirm the judgment that the Jews would join in the destruction of the social order, unless they received the aid to establish a Jewish state. He provided a similar response to Plehve's complaint against the Russian Zionists for turning their sights away from emigration in favor of practical work, thereby reinforcing the inferred connection between Zionism and revolutionary trends. Hence we should note the contribution that Zionism inadvertently made to corroborating the antisemitic claim that the Jews played a destructive role in society. It is in this context that we should also cite Nachman Syrkin's bitter attack on the attitude of the Jewish bourgeoisie toward the state. In his book on the socialist Jewish state, Syrkin charged that the Jewish bourgeoisie was masquerading as "friends of the government and as its closest allies," yet deep in their hearts they welcomed the advent of the "revolutionary parties." Although he explained this duplicity by asserting that they knew they could rely on these parties as Jews, he nevertheless denounced the hypocrisy of these "insidious subversives deep down in their avaricious souls." Bodenheimer's disapproving reference (in his memorandum to the German Foreign Ministry) to the Jewish youth in Germany who were attracted to Social Democracy, because they saw it as "the luring picture of a socialist society that predicates the equality of all races and nations" pales in comparison with Syrkin's outburst.[72]

The Zionist assurances to the authorities that it would be possible to shield the Jewish youth and intelligentsia from the influence of

---

71 Herzl, *Diaries*, Vol. I, pp. 180, 183; Vol. II, p. 667; Vol. IV, pp. 1493, 1526, 1554; T. Herzl, "Rede am 2ten Zionisten-Congress," *Die Welt* (September 2, 1898), p. 6; cf. Disraeli, *Lord George Bentinck*, pp. 498-499.

72 Ben-Eliezer (N. Syrkin), *Die Judenfrage und der Socialistische Judenstaat* (Bern, 1898), p. 49; Bodenheimer, *Im Anfang der zionistischen Bewegung*, p. 221.

Socialism bore little relation to reality. Much to the contrary, Jewish youngsters were galvanized into political activity, especially in czarist Russia, while the Zionist movement became bogged down in the Uganda crisis. As a result, the followers of Zionism in Russia were more and more attracted to the new vistas that seemed to open up before the czar's subjects and, by the same token, before the Jewish population as well.

Moreover, the struggle between rival Jewish movements was no longer over the dichotomy between nationalism and cosmopolitanism; it had become a disagreement over *which* national solution was best. In 1901 the Bund committed itself to Jewish national self-determination within an envisioned federation of Russian peoples, thus posing an ideological challenge to the Zionist labor movement. Shlomo Kaplansky, among the leading figures in the Poalei Zion movement in Austria, refuted the Bund's national approach by highlighting the two elements it lacked: historical continuity and any relationship to Jewry beyond the czar's realm. "History says: A people is born only *once*," Kaplansky wrote, "but not in the Russian Pale of Settlement; there we were only *on the way*." Further on he chided, "*National claims must have some relation to the history of a nation.*" Subsequently Kaplansky charged that the Bund's brand of national autonomy not only lacked roots in Jewish life, it was also opposed and ridiculed by Russian Social Democracy.

This argument was suitable for the members of Poalei Zion outside Russia, for they identified with the principle of Jewish solidarity – or at least the solidarity of Jewish workers everywhere. Meanwhile, the Poalei Zion within Russia were in the throes of a bitter internal struggle over their order of priorities: the realization of the remote Zionist ideal or immediate political action *here and now*. The history of this struggle was a highly involved affair, and to exemplify it we shall quote only one characteristic statement from the resolutions of the Poalei Zion Society of Dvinsk in 1904:

> Zionism is an historical ideal that will be realized through evolutionary development. But Zionism does not offer a solution to the state of lawlessness of the Jewish masses in the lands of the diaspora. We therefore see it as our obligation to wage a

war for the political and civil rights of the Jews in these countries. And since in Russia this war is bound up with autocracy, we include the domestic struggle in our program.[73]

Once again we have an expression of Zionism as a link between Jewish nationalism in the diaspora and the impending Russian Revolution. When we came across a similar combination earlier, the context was an assessment of the situation from without, or Herzl's diplomatic utilization thereof; yet here we have a specifically Zionist assertion of two domestic aims – securing rights for the Jews in the diaspora and a struggle against the regime – together with lip service to the Zionist idea as an "historical ideal." This position was not characteristic of all the Russian Zionists, nor even of all the Zionist Socialists in Russia. However, it did signal a growing impact of diaspora nationalism on the Zionist camp in Russia.

At much the same time, a parallel climate that could be called "compassionate Zionism" was developing outside Russia. While Max Bodenheimer continued his fight against the German Jewish establishment – comparing it to the leaders of the Israelites "who esteemed slavery in Egypt more than the liberty to which Moses strove to raise the people" – he simultaneously worked toward cooperation with non-Zionists who were motivated by "*Rachmoneszionismus*" (Zionism of pity) and, he believed, would eventually develop a national consciousness. At the 1904 conference of German Zionists, Bodenheimer justified this policy and refuted the charge that the local Zionist leadership had abandoned "*the Jewish national outlook as the basis of the Zionist idea*" – though he explained that the concept of "Jewish nationalism" was suspect, because it might cast doubt on the Zionists' patriotism as Germans.

It would appear that the failure of Herzl's diplomatic efforts had prompted a reversion to the viewpoint of the early Lovers of Zion. Yet in essence this was a new and more intricate approach to the concept of Jewish nationalism. As we saw in examining the early years of political Zionism, the Jewish national outlook comprised an

73 Elihu Ben Barachel (S. Kaplansky), "The National Consciousness and Russian Social Democracy," *Der Yudischer Arbeter* (February 1, 1904), p. 2 (Yiddish); Mendel Singer, *Early Zionist Socialism* (Haifa, 1958), p. 298 (Hebrew).

abstract sense of responsibility for the fate of the Jews together with a struggle against the incumbent Jewish establishment – and this was still true to some extent of Bodenheimer's approach. This initial stage was followed by years of activity in the same arena as other Jewish forces, and attempts to enter into cooperation with them, arising out of that same sense of responsibility. The period under examination here was marked by a growing willingness to play down the differences between Zionists and non-Zionists – or, put in more positive terms, to advance the interests of Jewry as a whole – and shy away from the concept of "Jewish nationalism." Within imperial Germany, it was impolitic to accentuate Jewish solidarity as a value that took precedence over loyalty to the fatherland, and Zionists like Bodenheimer felt a strong attachment to Germany, that was in no way mitigated by their Zionism. In any event, a greater propensity toward present-day work emerged here, too, and the accent shifted to concrete forms of Jewish nationalism, which by nature showed a preference for local affairs over the formerly all-embracing slant of Jewish nationalism. This trend, which tended to emphasize the uniqueness of each Jewish community, simultaneously gathered force in czarist Russia and Hapsburg Austria, as well as imperial Germany, and was fortified by mutual awareness of these parallel developments.[74]

Not only did the 1905 Revolution in Russia draw Zionism into the political arena, the movement seemed to be caught up in the wave of political fervor that swept through Russian Jewry – though it did its best to channel this energy into specifically national directions. For example, the young Yitzhak Gruenbaum was later to describe this period as one of cooperation with "national-oriented circles," in the framework of "the Union for the Attainment of Full Rights for the Jewish People in Russia," in the struggle for "the national demands" of Russian Jewry. Present-day work therefore became a platform shared by Zionists and non-Zionists and subse-

74 M. Bodenheimer, "Ansprache und Bericht des Vorsitzenden," *Jüdische Rundschau* (May 27, 1904), p. 222; Gelber, *A History of the Zionist Movement in Galicia*, Vol. II, pp. 486 ff.; J. Toury, "Plans for a Jewish Political Organization in Germany," *Zion, A Quarterly for Research in Jewish History*, 28/3-4 (1963), p. 180 (Hebrew).

quently led to ties even with anti-Zionists. As Joseph Klausner had warned, practical work in the diaspora was increasingly becoming an "end in itself," and he forecast that "dehistorization – the oblite-ration of historical hopes – would ultimately lead a large segment of the people to denationalization."[75]

Eventually the issues of Jewish solidarity and collaboration with non-Zionists became so important to the Zionist movement that its new leadership, headed by David Wolffsohn, convened an all-Jewish conference for Russian Jewry in Brussels in January 1906, following the wave of organized pogroms that had swept through Russia just weeks before. Few organizations responded to the initiative, and the conference ended in failure. Yet even so, some aspects of the con-clave had proved objectionable to sectors of the Zionist camp. Ahad Ha'am predicted the failure of the conference, if only because any Zionist initiative was, a priori, suspect in the eyes of the other Jewish organizations. On the other hand, he maintained that if "the meeting would indeed center solely on present-day work . . . it would not be of any real benefit." After the conference Chaim Weizmann wrote to Judah Leon Magnes, then secretary of the Zionist Organization in the United States, that: "The old delusion still persists that it is possible or desirable to cooperate with partly or wholly assimilated bodies. . . . Don't call me a fanatic, or a narrow-minded man. Zion-ism exercises its Maccabean force of attraction and its greatness as a freedom movement so long as it solves the Jewish question radi-cally, or strives to do so."[76]

In Austria the debate centered on two issues: the struggle between the supporters and opponents of present-day work; and the conflict over separate representation for Galician Jewry, versus a united front embracing *all* the Jews in the empire, with the Jewish National Party (founded on the initiative of the Zionists) trying to win the support of the non-Zionist organizations. The moving spirit of the pro-Zionist party, Dr. Marcus Braude, elucidated the latter issue in

75 Y. Gruenbaum, "From Warsaw to Helsingfors" in *Harvest*, Vol. I, p. 34; J. Klausner, "The Approaching Peril," *Hashiloah*, 15 (1905), p. 426 (Hebrew).
76 Ahad Ha'am, *Letters*, Vol. III (1924), p. 215; Weizmann, *Letters*, Vol. IV, p. 241 (original document in the Central Archives for the History of the Jewish People, Jerusalem, Magnes Collection P3/SP92).

his memoirs by describing his disagreement with his old friend Osias Thon. Thon feared that a united Jewish front would kindle the wrath of the Poles, because of its Viennese orientation, and place the Jews of Galicia in jeopardy. Braude retorted that "our approach to Austrian Jewry is a direct corollary of the national idea, which categorically rejects any distinction being made between the Jews of the same state." Pan-Jewish solidarity may have been a potent idea, but for political reasons it was confined to the borders of the Austrian state – just as the autonomy of the Bund was restricted, as a matter of principle, to the boundaries of czarist Russia. We must add to this another divisive factor of particular consequence to practical work in the diaspora: the Poalei Zion delegate at the conference of Austrian Zionists in Cracow made it painfully clear that his constituents were unable to support the Jewish National Party, because "in the diaspora they have special interests in their everyday lives." Hence the adhesive power of the Zionist idea was no match for the special needs of every Jewish community and each social group, when daily concerns were put first. This point was particularly salient in the search for direction going on in the Zionist labor movement, which aimed to achieve a synthesis between "the class program and the national program, their complete proletarian fusion, the closing of any gap between the burning problems of the day and the glorious aim of the distant future."[77]

Practical work of the political kind, especially in revolutionary Russia, led not only to a blurring of the lines between the Zionist and non-Zionist camps, but above all to an involvement in the country's political life. Inevitably, questions of a purely political nature invaded the pages of Jewish and Zionist publications, and one such issue – the choice of non-Jewish allies in the political sphere – drew Ahad Ha'am and his friend Dubnow into the debate. Ahad Ha'am, of course, denied the prospect of ever achieving "equal rights as a people to live a *national* life of our own" in the diaspora, but in his exchange with Dubnow he supported a policy of tactical flexibility,

77 Marcus Braude, *In Memoriam* (Jerusalem, 1960), p. 202 (Hebrew); Ben Barachel, "After the Conference," *Der Yudisher Arbeter* (August 1, 1905), p. 5; Ben Barachel, "At an Historic Moment," *Der Yudisher Arbeter* (December 15, 1905), p. 4; Manifesto in J. Peterseil, ed., *Anthology of Poalei Zion*, Vol. I (Tel Aviv, 1947), p. 22 (Hebrew).

as befits the latter's notion of Jewish national sovereignty. Contrary to Dubnow, who wanted nothing to do with the right-wing in the Russian Duma, Ahad Ha'am asked: "How will the 'sovereignty' of national politics look if this 'sovereign' is not entitled to protect his interests with the aid of parties that are somewhat less democratic?" When preparations for the Helsingfors Conference began, he wrote to Alter Druyanow, the secretary of the Executive Committee of the Russian Zionists, explaining his objections to the "national program" by saying: "If I thought there were room for the free development of our *national spirit* in the diaspora, I would not be a Zionist." And after the conference Ahad Ha'am grumbled that "whoever is not a Russian democrat according to the Helsingfors formula is ergo not a Zionist" and took solace in the stoic belief that this too would pass, as that "clever old woman . . . *history*" instructs us. Ahad Ha'am the skeptic would not toe Zionism's new line any more than he had toed its predecessor.[78]

The Helsingfors Conference had indeed utterly revolutionized (in the words of its chairman, Yehiel Tschlenow) the approach to practical work in the diaspora. In speaking of the ferment among the Russian peoples, Tschlenow prognosticated: "The hour draws near when the Jews of Russia will be freed of their shackles and will tend to their wounds by themselves." It was as if Helsingfors had signalled a return to the formulas born in Basel. Rallying cries like "We must take our fate in our hands!" were again being uttered, though this time the reference was not to leaving the diaspora but to fortifying it.

The outcome of the Helsingfors Conference was essentially a revision of political Zionism – to the point of creating a new doctrine. Yitzhak Gruenbaum, the young Zionist activist from Warsaw, saw a basic failing in the previous "*catastrophic* method for the fulfillment of Zionism," meaning the solution of the Jewish question at a single stroke. Daniel Pasmanik, a Zionist Socialist residing in Switzerland who took an active part in the deliberations, depicted Zionism as a cross between two opposing trends: "the purely territorialist," which only strove to establish a state in Palestine, and its opposite, which

---

78 Ahad Ha'am, "The Doctrine and the Works," *Hashiloah*, 9 (1902), p. 5, n. 1 (Hebrew); Ahad Ha'am, *Letters*, Vol. III (1924), pp. 242, 256; Ahad Ha'am, "Things That Are Forgotten," *Hashiloah*, 16 (1907), p. 380 (Hebrew).

regarded Zionism as an "evolution of Judaism." Once again, as during the conference of Austrian Zionists, the question of an independent Zionist posture or a "common Jewish front" was discussed at length. The position that ultimately prevailed was that of Vladimir Jabotinsky – whose star had recently begun to rise in the Russian-Zionist firmament – emphasizing the differences between Zionists and other Jewish nationalists. But these differences notwithstanding, what emerged from Helsingfors was a broad consensus on a number of points that could be taken as a comprehensive system of ideas. They included a heightened awareness that the Jews were fated to live in the diaspora for many years to come, so that Zionism would have to purge itself of the "symptoms of utopianism" and overcome its dependence on diplomacy to obtain a charter for Palestine. Instead, the movement would have to adopt the "principle of development," meaning both "to cater to the masses" and return to pragmatic work in Palestine.

This return to a pragmatic program in Palestine was not an original proposal of the Helsingfors Conference but the adoption of resolutions that had been passed the previous year at the Seventh Zionist Congress. Still, the idea was consonant with the new direction that Zionism had taken. Instead of trying to realize the Zionist idea all at once, there was now talk of an evolutionary approach that entailed day-to-day activity both in Palestine and the diaspora. The Helsingfors Program fulfilled the twofold task of according practical work in the diaspora a hearty stamp of approval while distinguishing Zionism from autonomist trends by reinforcing the accent on Palestine. It is hardly surprising that the convention delegates wildly applauded Daniel Pasmanik when he quoted the saying (attributed to the Socialist Revisionist Eduard Bernstein): "The final goal is naught; the movement is all!"[79]

79 *The Third Zionist Conference in Helsingfors* (Vilna, 1906), pp. 6, 9, 10, 19, 25 (Yiddish); Dr. Tschlenow's speech, "Spezialbericht über die III Allrussische Zionistenkonferenz," *Die Welt* (December 14, 1906), p. 9; Dr. Pasmanik's contribution, *Die Welt* (December 14, 1906), p. 12 (December 21, 1906), p. 5; J. Grünbaum, "Spezialbericht (Schluss)," *Die Welt* (December 28, 1906), p. 5; Schabotinsky, "Frage der nächsten Tätigkeit," *Die Welt* (December 28, 1906), p. 7.

The Movement Is All!

We have already come across this motif in the writings of Marcus Ehrenpreis, and its presence was felt in the Zionist movement throughout the period under review – either as a colorful symbol denoting practical work or as consolation for the absence of tangible achievements. Even people outside the Zionist camp acknowledged Zionism's innovative effect upon Jewish life by forging a new self-image, revising the relationship with the non-Jewish environment, prompting a revival of interest in Jewish issues, and fostering Jewish creativity. All this implied that even if the Zionist goal were not attained, the movement would have nonetheless made its mark on the here and now. It is difficult to determine whether these achievements can be credited directly to the organized Zionist movement or whether some, at least, resulted from the conditions in which Zionism operated. However, there was no disputing the phenomenon itself. Benzion Dinur, an historian of unquestionably Zionist persuasion, asserted that "Zionism reorganized the people anew," yet even Salo Baron, a renowned historian of rather different leanings, wrote that "Jewish nationalism and, especially, Zionism have profoundly transformed the spiritual and material physiognomy of the Jewish people."[80]

In tracing the early steps of political Zionism, we occasionally saw signs of Zionism's modernizing role in Jewish life. Nordau touched upon this subject in replying to the charge that Jews would succumb to despair once they were disabused of the illusion of political Zionism. "And what if Zionism leads nowhere?" he asked rhetorically. His reply was to cite a parable about a yeshiva student who was ordered to wash himself, so that he could be presentable before his prospective bride and fretted that if the match were to fall through, he would have bathed for naught. Returning to the issue at hand, Nordau answered his question caustically: "So a few Jews will have cleansed themselves of their filth and healed themselves of their leprosy." Sometime thereafter Moshe Kleinmann, a political Zionist

---

80 Benzion Dinur, "Zionism" in Benzion Dinur et al., eds. *The Jews* (Jerusalem, 1954), p. 546 (Hebrew); Salo W. Baron, *Modern Nationalism and Religion* (New York, 1960), p. 247.

from Eastern Europe, found that even the "most ardent political Zionist" was capable of understanding that "for the time being, organizing into Zionist societies is in itself a step toward creating [the future] Jewish society." Kleinmann welcomed the fact that the Zionists "were growing closer to the people" and concluded that Zionism "*in itself* leads . . . to the advancement of national and social life." And at the Fifth Zionist Congress, Herzl spoke of the "vitality that Jewry unexpectedly acquired through our [Zionist] societies." Not even its opponents could deny Zionism's spiritual and moral contribution, or so Herzl believed, and he ascribed to it a "pleiad of writers, artists, and learned men inspired by our vision." As was his wont, Herzl made a point of stating that, surprising as it may seem, he was speaking not only of Jews, and *that alone* was proof that Zionism held a message for all mankind.[81]

If the political Zionists were speaking this way, how much more so were the spiritual Zionists and others with Haskalah leanings. The writer Israel Chaim Tawiow forecast the "rebirth of Judaism through spiritual Zionism," in contrast to the disruptive influences on the urban Jewish population in Russia. He pronounced in no uncertain terms that "the movement in itself (even beyond its 'economic' purpose) is boon to the perpetuation of Judaism, to the revival of Jewry beyond the walls of the ghetto." During that period Nachum Sokolow wrote: "And even if Zionism could quickly advance from theory to practice, its *potential* prior to going into action, the conceptual [stage] that precedes the concrete, even the reality we imagine to ourselves, our deepest yearnings are enough to move us toward some beneficial change and proper measure, without which no people can exist." Ahad Ha'am phrased the same sentiment more succinctly when, after the Kishinev pogroms, he called for raising "the banner of *inner* liberty" and defined "our own mission" as "above all to educate the people in a new way *by means of* Zionism." A similar approach can be found in the plaint of the Mizrahi people

81 M. Nordau, "On Zionism" (Letter to the Editor), *Hashiloah*, 4 (1898), p. 556 (Hebrew); M. Kleinmann, "The Meaning of the Words," *Hashiloah*, 5 (1899), p. 3325 (Hebrew); T. Herzl, "Eröffnungsrede, 5 Zionisten-Congress," *Die Welt* (December 27, 1901), p. 3.

against the ultra-Orthodox camp. In his mock-literary polemic reflecting the opposing positions in the religious community, Meshulam Nathan Brozer, a craftsman and scholar, said of Zionism: "How can we not feel drawn to and identify with such a fine and sacred movement with the power to return to us the cherished sons of Zion even before it restores Zion to us?"[82]

By the same token, we are sometimes able to discern a benevolent attitude toward Zionism even among its adversaries, due to the positive effect it was thought to have upon Jewish life. Following Herzl's visit to Jerusalem in 1898, the representative of the Alliance Israélite Universelle in Palestine, Nissim Béhar, reported to the Paris office on the diplomatic errors that had been committed by Herzl and his associates, but he nonetheless spoke of Zionism as "one of the greatest movements in our history" because it was responsible for "touching our co-religionists with joy and hope." Furthermore, he forecast that the impression made by Zionism would endure as a bright spot in Jewish literature.

In so writing, Béhar focused on the emotional aspect of Zionism, implying that eventually all that would remain of the movement was its literary imprint. A few years later Hippolyte Prague, the editor of the Paris Jewish weekly *Archives Israélites*, who was associated with the 'Alliance', asked rhetorically whether Zionism was destined to pass from the world without leaving a trace. He too conceded that Zionism was not a wholly negative phenomenon, for it could be credited with "an awakening of Jewish consciousness" within a broader climate of indifference. Among the movement's other merits, he cited a revival of Jewish solidarity and the intellectual florescence of Jewish topics. But even though this judgment was written prior to the Uganda crisis, Prague was quick to eulogize Zionism as though it were already a thing of the past. Hence there seems to have been little difference whether Zionism was embraced or rejected as a political movement; the rule that emerges from these citations is

---

82 I. C. Tawiow, "The Duties of Spiritual Zionism," *Hamelitz*, 166 (1900), p. 1 (Hebrew); Sokolow, *To Masters and Mentors*, p. 32; Ahad Ha'am, *Letters*, Vol. III (1957), p. 252; Brozer, *The Righteousness of Zion*, p. 88 (Hebrew).

that its essential virtue was perceived as having a stimulating effect upon the Jewish people.[83]

Conclusions

In the decade that transpired between Herzl's publication of *The Jewish State* and the Helsingfors Conference, Zionism established itself as a force of consequence in Jewish life. Yet the price of this process of entrenchment was the loss of the movement's early revolutionary character. If we return now to the questions raised at the beginning of the chapter, viewing them in light of the Cracow and Helsingfors conferences, we can see that a decade after Herzl's appearance:

* Zionism no longer anticipated the imminent departure of the Jews from the diaspora.
* It conceded that there was considerable room for improving the condition of the Jews in their countries of residence.
* Zionists were working toward cooperation with non-Zionists, without in any way obscuring their own distinctiveness.
* Zionists were actively involved in the political life of their countries of residence and yet kept in close contact with fellow-Zionists in other countries.

One could therefore equate the Zionism of 1906 with Nathan Birnbaum's approach of 1892, in lauding the establishment of a Jewish national party in Galicia while exhorting it to remain faithful to the Zionist credo. Despite the many changes that had occurred in the interim, Zionism was still seeking a synthesis between the same two elements, with the local one constantly developing and the vision of Palestine serving mainly as an inspiration. During the period under review the Second Aliyah to Palestine was also in progress; yet it was taking place on an entirely different level and was all but

---

83 André Chouraqui, *l'Alliance Israélite Universelle et la renaissance juive contemporaine* (Paris, 1965), p. 60; H. Prague, "Le Sionisme, Visées et résultats," *Archives Israélites* (January 30, 1902), p. 34.

ignored by the Zionist establishment. In effect, all the factions of the Zionist movement acknowledged the coexistence of the Palestinian vision and practical work in the diaspora – even though the new line did not yet receive the official sanction of the World Zionist Organization. Zionism continued to exist as a worldwide movement despite internal conflicts between elitist ideologies, class interests, and local concerns. Theoretically speaking, if the cohesive forces prevailed over the disjunctive ones, it may have been because the common framework became little more than a symbolic outer shell, while attention really focused on the clash between the movement's rival tendencies. Besides, not every disagreement is bound to climax in a split in the ranks, and during the period under review even eminent Zionist figures were showing signs of gradually growing away from the movement.

Yet even without presenting detailed proof of Zionism's fundamental unity, we can appreciate the internal logic of its existence. Had the Zionist Organization never been founded, the impulse toward practical work in the diaspora would probably have existed anyway, for it was shared by the Zionists and other Jewish groups. The ideological enhancement it received from Zionism had two aspects to it: (1) the qualification that practical work in the diaspora was merely a temporary course that did not preclude working toward a more fundamental solution in the future; and (2) a link with the Jewish past and with the contemporary Jewish world (which was true, to one degree or another, of other Jewish movements as well). One can say with confidence that this dual motif played a unique role by furnishing Zionism with a dimension of historical continuity, similar to that of non-Jewish national movements. As a rule, such movements tended to draw their hopes for the future from the evidence of their nations' glorious past – real or imagined. The Jews had, by all accounts, an inordinately rich history, yet their golden age belonged not only to the remote past but to a remote place. In some cases, the Jews had actually preceded the arrival of various European peoples in their countries of residence. But that did not change the substantive difference between the national movements of these territorially defined peoples and that of the Jews – if only because the Jews perpetuated an ancient chain of history that was formed in one country and continued in dispersion throughout many others.

Zionism's frame of reference was a chain of continuity that extended from the ancient past in Palestine through practical work in the diaspora toward the renewal of independence in Palestine in the future. It provided Jewish nationalism with an acceptable substitute for the standard properties of nationalism. Even though there was a seeming contradiction between the Zionist goal and practical work in the diaspora, the imaginary leap to ancient Palestine furnished the movement with a symbolic territorial attribute that was missing in the Jewish diaspora nationalism. This was Zionism's advantage over the Bund – which had tried unsuccessfully to model itself on the national movements rooted in Russia – and over autonomism – which, though tracing its lineage to the classical past, had difficulty in claiming the legitimacy of a Jewish national entity in Europe. Zionism also used the historical tie to explain the synchronic bond between Jewish communities throughout the world, which was not quite compatible with genuine autonimism. For this reason, Zionism's historical chain of continuity was integral to the development of practical work and may explain the change that occurred in Zionism after Herzl's death, but had begun to take shape even before his appearance on the scene.

Finally, practical work in the diaspora often had a certain political and social character because it was generally associated with the trend toward social change. In czarist Russia it was generally aligned with the forces fighting absolutism, whereas in Central Europe it was associated with the dissolution of the alliance between the Jews and the old liberal camp. Practical work in the diaspora was also a manifestation of the growing strength of the Socialists and their allies in the Zionist movement. As a rule we can say that in its early stages, Zionism was characterized by avant-gardism, on the one hand, and a conservative political orientation, on the other. In the course of time, present-day work – which incorporated both populism and a progressive social outlook – became an increasingly established trend. This development can generally be described as *Zionist radicalism* giving way to locally oriented *socio-political radicalism*. In retrospect, it appears that Zionism was affected by the social ferment then spreading through the Jewish public, especially in the Pale of Settlement, and supplied a legitimate outlet for it within its own framework. In the process, however, Zionism itself was gradually altered.

CHAPTER FOUR

THE UGANDA CRISIS

Antecedents

The gravest crisis that Zionism had faced since its inception, broke out in 1903 at the Sixth Zionist Congress in Basel and continued until the Seventh Congress in 1905, when the territorialists broke away from the Zionist movement. The object of contention was Herzl's proposal to have the Zionist Organization look into the British plan for Jewish settlement in East Africa. The scheme had been officially broached by Britain a week before the Congress, but it is pertinent to note that the East Africa plan (or the "Uganda scheme," as it was erroneously dubbed) was not an entirely novel idea for the Zionist movement. This may have been the first time the Zionist Organization was called upon to take an official stand on such a proposal, but plans to settle Jews in places other than Palestine had long been mooted in the annals of Zionism.

Ever since the emergence of the Lovers of Zion societies in the 1880s, a parallel national current had been espousing organized Jewish settlement overseas in countries other than Palestine – mostly in the United States and Argentina. Moreover, the line dividing the Palestinian-oriented camp from the so-called territorialists was not always distinct.[1] The territorialist current had developed against the background of the latest surge of European colonial expansion from the 1870s onward. In his pamphlet *Autoemancipation*, for example, Leon Pinsker spoke of finding a territory suitable for Jewish settlement either in North America or in Asia Minor and mentioned Palestine only incidentally. His approach toward Palestine was essentially pragmatic and could be characterized as positive – as Ahad

---

1 Jonathan Frankel, *Prophecy and Politics* (Cambridge, 1981), pp. 87-88.

Ha'am noted – only insofar as he "did not single Palestine out from the rest of the countries in *negative* terms."[2]

In this same context, Ahad Ha'am also claimed that the chief opponents to Palestine were "our brothers in the West." However, reservations about the country had also come from enlightened-national quarters in Eastern Europe. It is sufficient to cite the open letter from the Hebrew writer Judah Leib Levin to the editor of *Hamagid* in 1881 expressing the fear that "in the course of returning to the Holy Land, they will lose everything they have acquired from the European Enlightenment." Further on in the letter, Levin denounced those who hoped to renew the ritual sacrifices once practiced in the Temple, and ultimately he arrived at the conclusion that settlement in America was preferable. In 1883 the Hebrew writer Eliahu Wolf Rabinowitz wrote to Levin expressing his own misgivings about "the idea of settlement in Palestine" by asking: "Would you like me to describe to you the effect of a theocracy on real life were we to become a nation tomorrow?"[3] Thus, ironically, the anti-clerical argument was used in fact against secular Jewish nationalism, directing the thrust of the complaint at the national renaissance in Palestine. It is worth noting that this motif would come up again during the Uganda conflict.

In 1892 Leo Motzkin wrote to the editor of *Selbst-Emancipation* denying the rumor that the Young Israel Society in Berlin was a territorialist group and that "the national idea had nothing to do with Palestine." He also refuted the allegation that the society's main purpose was to support the settlement of Russian Jews in Argentina and North America.[4] The journal's editor, Nathan Birnbaum, also came out against Jewish settlement in Argentina, though he supported settlement in "the Orient" – meaning Asia Minor, Cyprus, and perhaps even Egypt – "in close proximity to the national homeland." In a piece written in 1894, Birnbaum warned of the danger entailed in moving masses of Jews far from the contemporary centers of Jewish

---

2   Ahad Ha'am, *Collected Works*, p. 44; Pinsker, "Autoemancipation," p. 194.
3   Letter to the publisher from Judah Leib Levin, *Hamagid* (October 6, 1881), p. 322; A. Druyanow, ed., *Documents on the History of Hibbat Zion and the Settlement of Eretz Israel*, Vol. III, pp. 556-557.
4   Leo Mozkin, *Selbst-Emancipation* (July 18, 1892), p. 149.

life – by which he meant emigration to countries in the Western hemisphere and elsewhere overseas – for he believed that distances would determine the future of the "spiritual tie." He preferred Palestine to anywhere else but acknowledged the difficulties involved in settlement there and held that the next best choice was to settle nearby. Two years hence, in commenting on the wave of protest against any attempt "to find a *new* country," Birnbaum defended the exclusivity of "the ancient Holy Land of the Jews." And in addressing the First Zionist Congress in the following year, he remarked: "The choice of Palestine, far from being an arbitrary one, strengthens the guarantee that the possession of the land [*Landnahme*] by Israel is in the spirit of history."[5] A similar sentiment had earlier been expressed by the German Zionist Heinrich Loewe in an article published in 1895 stating: "In settling in the land of our forefathers, we are drawing a conclusion from our history."[6]

In an earlier chapter, we explored how history was employed to prove the legitimacy of the Zionist idea. Here we find it being used to justify the choice of Palestine, even though the country was not equipped to absorb masses of Jewish immigrants. In the course of the debate over Palestine, another consideration would emerge, namely, the need to base the Jews' right to Palestine on historical evidence. In any event, it is clear that in the period prior to Herzl's appearance, the territorialist approach was in no way at odds with the national idea. Much to the contrary, the presumption of Palestine's priority was forced to compete with territorialism under circumstances that appeared to favor settlement elsewhere, for the Palestinian enterprise was in the throes of a crisis.

Herzl and Palestine

Herzl's attitude toward Palestine had been ambivalent from his earliest days as a Zionist. It went through various phases, with a prefer-

---

5 B., "So lange es Zeit ist!" *Jüdische Volkszeitung* (April 3, 1894), p. 260; N. Birnbaum, "Das jüdische Nationalleben" in *Protokoll des 1ten Zionisten-kongresses in Basel*, p. 108.

6 Heinrich Loewe, "Der Nationalismus," *Zion* (March 15, 1895), p. 41.

ence for Palestine sometimes dominating and at others succumbing to a territorialist bent. Still, it does not appear that Herzl ever felt a deep personal attachment to Palestine. In diary entries for 1895, he wrote: "For a time I had Palestine in mind. This would have in its favor the facts that it is the unforgotten ancestral seat of our people, that its very name would constitute a program, and that it would powerfully attract the lower masses." But ultimately Herzl explained that he had abandoned the idea of settling in Palestine because "most of the Jews are no longer oriental, have grown accustomed to completely different regions, and it will be difficult to apply my system of transplantation there."

The Jewish State contains but a brief paragraph on the choice of a territory – "Palestine or Argentina" – and its approach is wholly pragmatic. Speaking of the society to be created so as to implement his program, Herzl ventured that it "will take whatever it is given and whatever is favored by the public opinion of the Jewish people." He then proceeded to explain the advantages offered by Argentina – considering its natural resources, climate, and the like – and weighed the odds of persuading the Argentinian authorities to accept the Jews. The rest of the paragraph was devoted to Palestine and essentially reiterated what Herzl had earlier expressed in his diary, in writing: "Palestine is our unforgettable historic homeland." In projecting the prospects of obtaining a charter for Palestine, he enumerated the benefits that would accrue to the sultan's treasury in return for according Palestine to the Jews but immediately added an important ideological clarification: "For Europe we could constitute part of the wall of defense against Asia; we could serve as an outpost of civilization against barbarism."[7] He further pledged that the Jewish state would remain neutral in the struggles between the European Powers and would grant extra-territorial status to the Christian holy places. The paragraph ends on this note, with the issue of whether the future Jewish state would be constituted in Palestine or Argentina remaining open.

Michael Berkowitz, the translator of the Hebrew edition of *The*

7   Herzl, *Diaries*, Vol. I, p. 133, Vol. II, p. 550; Herzl, *The Jewish State*, p. 52; cf. Geoffrey Barraclough, *An Introduction to Contemporary History* (Harmondsworth, Middlesex, 1976), p. 81.

Jewish State, which appeared in the same year, appended an explanation on the author's behalf. First he corrected the impression that Herzl harbored a negative attitude toward the Hebrew language; then he turned to the matter of Palestine, explicating:

> As to the *location* of the settlement, after his inquiry and thorough investigation of what the people desired and their sense of national mission, the author understood that our holy land is the country that all the Jews look to, and that there alone are embedded all the precious virtues through which our people will be reborn. He subsequently recanted the view he had expressed in the chapter 'Palestine or Argentina.'

Indeed, the claim that Herzl had renounced the neutral position on Palestine expressed in the book is not without foundation, especially as he became increasingly aware that his supporters regarded this country as the natural place to implement his program. Berkowitz based this assertion on one of Herzl's letters and on the case that Herzl made before "various philanthropists in London," when – as Berkowitz informs us – "he no longer made mention of Argentina and addressed himself solely to the land of our forefathers, for which our souls yearn." It is true that Herzl spoke in this spirit during a visit to London, but he did so not in elegant drawing rooms but before a mass rally in the East End and may simply have yielded to the pressures exerted on him on that occasion.[8]

Herzl's accommodation to the idea of Palestine was influenced by the mood of the Jewish public at large, which became increasingly important to him as he resolved to establish a mass movement, rather than entrust the Zionist program to the goodwill of prominent personalities. However, he wished to keep other options open as bargaining cards in his negotiations to obtain Palestine for the Jews. Thus in a conversation with Ottoman officials during a trip to Constantinople in 1896, Herzl was careful not to betray any eagerness for Palestine: "I had declared that we wished to acquire Palestine as a completely independent country, and if we could not get it as such, we would go to Argentina." Similarly, Herzl's agent in Constantino-

---

8 Theodor Herzl, *The Jewish State*, trans. Michael Berkowitz (Warsaw, 1896), p. iv (Hebrew); Hertzberg, ed., *The Zionist Idea*, p. 231.

ple, Count Newlinski, told the sultan (as Herzl subsequently recorded in his diary): "If the Jews cannot have Palestine, they will simply have to go to Argentina."

Clearly, at this stage Palestine was still the preferred destination, and the mention of Argentina was merely of tactical value. Indeed, at the beginning of 1897 the periodical *Zion* published Herzl's address to a "Zionist club in London" commending a "return to Palestine." On that occasion he spoke of the country as a future crossroads of international transport (in light of the plan to extend the railway network from Europe to Asia), adding:

> I cannot imagine which masses, if not the Jews, should go to Palestine. For anyone else it is no more than a precarious patch of wilderness that certainly does not encourage settlement. Why, it would be possible to obtain far more fruitful regions far more easily. But the land of our forefathers, as our historic homeland, has never lost its attraction for our masses, as we have seen for centuries and as has been proved by the recent attempts at settlement.

On the theoretical plane, Herzl based his plans on the vistas opened by modern technology – projecting Palestine's future as an international crossroads requiring modern settlers – while actually arguing that the country was not fit for anyone except the Jews, who were drawn to it for historic or sentimental reasons. But though the logic of this speech leaves something to be desired, it attested to Herzl's growing appreciation of Palestine's importance to the Jews.

A few months later Herzl wrote a letter to the English journalist and adventurer Sidney Whitman in Constantinople, to be used to further the Zionist cause in contacts with Ottoman court circles. In it Herzl submitted that his book *The Jewish State* was more a rough idea than a fully formulated program. In justifying this statement, he wrote: "The best proof of this is that I suggested we settle [*nous établir*] either in *Argentina* or in *Palestine*. But since that publication, the neo-Jewish movement has taken on an entirely different complexion, and it has become practical and practicable. We take circumstances into consideration; we want to conduct ourselves well politically, sincerely and effectively." Whitman was asked to make it clear to the sultan's aides that various options remained open, though the Jews would prefer Palestine. And while Herzl indicated that a change had taken place in Zionism – in favor of Palestine – since he had written his book, he intimated that the alternative of Argentina was still operative. His formulation stressing the movement's pragmatism may also have implied that it would be flexible regarding the choice of a territory.[9]

Naturally, this instrumental approach to Palestine was not to the satisfaction of the Lovers of Zion and like-minded members of the Zionist Organization. It had been the object of controversy since the inception of political Zionism, with Max Nordau treating the subject of Palestine in the Herzlian spirit. In 1897 Nordau published an article in *Die Welt* castigating the chief rabbi of Vienna, Moritz Güdemann, for having written a pamphlet denouncing Zionism. Yet in so writing he conceded: "And if it should turn out that the attainment of Palestine for the Jews is quite impossible and that it is far easier to find another country of sufficient size with the suitable properties of soil and climate, then certainly most, if not all, of the Zionists would be prepared to settle that country without hesitation." After the publication of the article, I. E. Lubetzki, a young artist from Russia who resided alternately in Paris and Vienna, wrote Nordau an open letter stating: "There is a rumor about you and your friends that if you fail to obtain Zion, you will go off looking for another country. My heart will not allow me to believe that. And at any rate, the people will not pay you any heed." The quick-tempered Nordau responded to this letter sharply but refrained from addressing himself to Lubetzki's complaint regarding Palestine and certainly did not reiterate his territorialist thesis.[10]

In 1898 the historian S. P. Rabinowitz, a veteran Lover of Zion who had served as secretary to Rabbi Shmuel Mohilever (the founder of the early Mizrahi), published a book on Zionism entitled *On Zion and Its Scriptures*. The work not only assailed political Zionism for ignoring the existent Jewish community in Palestine, it

9   Herzl, *Diaries*, Vol. I, pp. 367, 395; T. Herzl, "Die Rückkehr nach Palästina," *Zion* (February 1, 1897), p. 37.
10 Max Nordau, "Ein Tempelstreit," *Die Welt* (June 11, 1897), p. 2; I. E. Lubetzki, "Zionism and Its Opponents (An Open Letter to Max Nordau)," *Hashiloah*, 4 (1898), p. 379 (Hebrew); Max Nordau, "As to Zionism (Letter to the Editor)," *Hashiloah*, 4 (1898), pp. 555-556 (Hebrew).

decried the new trend as *"idolatrous fire, the product of imitation in order to be like all the nations that have a 'state.'"* There were a number of aspects to Rabinowitz's attack on political Zionism. One was his opposition to making settlement in Palestine contingent upon the attainment of a charter. Another was his opposition – characteristic of the spiritual Zionists – to the conception of Zionism in political terms. In the book Rabinowitz also addressed himself to the issue under discussion here – the place held by Palestine – in writing: "A community of that kind can be established only in the Land of Israel, the place of the nation's growth and its historical center, for only there will the nation's past and present converge and join in unity."[11]

Ahad Ha'am had been a foe of political Zionism from its inception, one of his main targets being its stand on Palestine, or, as he put it, "its negative attitude toward settling the country." Throughout Herzl's Zionist career, Ahad Ha'am relentlessly subjected him to barbed criticism that was fuelled by his doubts about the Zionists' loyalty to Palestine. When the Jewish Colonial Trust was registered in London in 1899, Ahad Ha'am bombarded his associates in the Zionist leadership with sharply worded letters inspired by the phrasing of the bank's statutes. He sent Bernstein-Cohen an enraged missive for allowing the statutes "to extend the bank's colonization work 'throughout the world.'" In that particular letter Ahad Ha'am, who was usually fastidious in his choice of language, even permitted himself to snarl: "No, my dear doctor! This will not pass without a fight. We will rouse all of Israel to rebel against you and not allow you to behave so crudely toward the national ideal and the national money." As far as Ahad Ha'am was concerned, there was no better proof of the Zionist leadership's adverse attitude toward Palestine than the blatant contrast between its opposition to practical work there and its pointed mandate to the Jewish Colonial Trust to foster Jewish settlement the world over.[12]

To return to Herzl, it is worthwhile comparing his stand on Pales-

11 S. P. Rabinowitz, *On Zion and Its Scriptures* (Warsaw, 1898), pp. 23, 28 (Hebrew).
12 Ahad Ha'am, *Collected Works*, p. 289; Ahad Ha'am, *Letters*, Vol. II (1924), p. 46.

tine with his attitude toward the idea of a state. For the founder of political Zionism, the choice of a territory was secondary to the abstract idea of a political entity. In the famous entry written in his diary after the First Zionist Congress – "In Basel I founded the Jewish State" – he also remarked: "The foundation of the States lies in the will of the people for a State. . . . Territory is only the material basis. The State, even when it possesses territory, is always something abstract." Thus it would appear that in this instance, at least, Herzl viewed the future in terms similar to that of his adversary Ahad Ha'am. The latter regarded the "redemption of the *spiritual Israel*" as the heart of the matter, and Herzl conceived the state as primarily an idea, "the will of the people for a State." Actually there was a substantial difference in the way they perceived the *substance* of the Zionist idea. Spiritual Zionism disdained the notion of a state but held fast to Palestine as "the place where the national ideal was forged," whereas Herzl valued the idea of political sovereignty and was less interested in its concrete particulars.[13]

After 1897, although the Zionist Congress had accepted the Basel Program – which spoke only of Palestine – Herzl continued to seek alternative countries for Jewish settlement. On July 1, 1898, he wrote in his diary: "I am thinking of giving the movement a closer territorial goal, preserving Zion as the final goal." It was a statement prompted by his desire to circumvent the machinations of Turkish politics, but it also referred to the dire condition of the Jewish masses. So he mooted interim solutions that would hold until the eventual dissolution of the Ottoman Empire: Cyprus, South Africa, and America. These proposals were recorded as no more than random thoughts that deserved further attention and should be discussed with Nordau before the next congress. His diary entry for October 30, 1899, for example, contained a comment praising the plan for settlement in Cyprus forwarded by Davis Trietsch, the author of a number of ambitious settlement schemes. Yet Herzl drew a clear distinction between Trietsch's position and his own in musing: "Trietsch is spreading successful propaganda in Rumania for the Cyprus project, which I consider very sensible, although out of consideration for the *Hovevei Zion* I must not come out in favor of it."

13 Ahad Ha'am, *Collected Works*, p. 7; Herzl, *Diaries*, Vol. II, p. 581.

About a week later Herzl sent a letter to a highly placed Ottoman official designed to help him obtain an audience with the sultan. Referring to Cyprus, he noted: "Seeing that the Turkish government does not appear disposed to come to an understanding with us, they [the Zionist rank and file] want to turn toward the island which is controlled by England and is always accessible to us." He also described the prospect of the Jews achieving autonomy in Cyprus within a number of years and intimated that if Turkey did not respond to him quickly, he would be unable to avert the triumph of the pro-Cyprus camp within the Zionist movement. Three more years were to pass before Herzl would have the opportunity to discuss the possibility of settlement in Cyprus with a British minister – and then the British reply would be negative. It is quite clear that his assertion that Cyprus would always be at the disposal of the Jews was actually a diplomatic feint to improve his bargaining position in negotiating for Palestine.[14]

Herzl's meeting with Colonial Secretary Chamberlain took place in the midst of a new phase of Zionist diplomacy that ultimately led to the proposal of the East Africa plan. Just prior to the breakdown of Herzl's negotiations in Constantinople in 1902, contacts were initiated with Britain over the idea of permitting Jewish settlement in the vicinity of Palestine. Herzl never abandoned the hope of obtaining Palestine, but he ventured – as he wrote to Lord Rothschild – that "a great Jewish settlement east of the Mediterranean will strengthen our prospects for Palestine." When he visited Constantinople for the last time, in July 1902, he tried to exploit the British card, telling the grand vizier of the request to permit colonization in Africa and the favorable terms being offered by Britain while avowing that "we would prefer the expensive little area of Palestine" if only because "our people's spirit depends upon it." The suffering of the Jews in Eastern Europe received repeated mention in Herzl's diary, but the remedy for it seemed to change from day to day. On August 2, 1902, he wrote of the British proposals to establish a Jewish colony in Africa, and two days later he entertained the hope that the sultan would grant him the district of Beirut as a stepping stone

---

14 Alexander Bein, *A Biography of Herzl* (Jerusalem, 1977), pp. 339-340 (Hebrew); Herzl, *Diaries*, Vol. II, p. 664, Vol. III, pp. 882, 883.

toward obtaining Palestine. And so it went until the Sixth Zionist Congress, in August 1903, when he unexpectedly raised the East Africa plan for public discussion.[15]

Historic Rights

Let us now make a brief detour and turn to a less focal problem that was intimately related to Palestine, namely, the Jews' historic right in that country. If we were to try to isolate an issue that was common to all the sectors of the Jewish national movement, it would undoubtedly be the demand for recognition of the Jews' right to self-determination. Applying this right to the Jews was a logical corollary of emancipation, although the proponents of emancipation certainly had not had it in mind. What's more, even those who spurned Jewish nationalism manifested their right to self-determination in their own way.[16]

Yet in the course of a discussion on Jewish settlement in Palestine, we come across a Zionist line of argument that drew its inspiration from a completely different source. Its point of departure was not the right to self-determination for the Jews but the right to their historical homeland. This claim resembled the platform of the Czech national movement – to cite but one example – which based itself on the historical legacy of the ancient kingdom of Bohemia-Moravia, rather than any presumed right of self-determination for the modern Czech nation. Thus the source of the historical right was territorial and did not reside in the inhabitant population – which had profound implications for the relations between the various nationalities living within the same territory. One consequence of invoking the historical claim was that the Czechs dismissed the idea of a nation-state – which was the model adopted by many other national movements – in favor of a regime that would allow for the free devel-

---

15 (No headline or signature), *Die Welt* (August 8, 1902), p. 1; Herzl, *Diaries*, Vol. IV, pp. 1302, 1330, 1337, 1344.

16 E.g. Reinhard Rürup, "European Revolutions and Emancipation" in Werner E. Mosse et al., eds., *Revolution and Evolution* (Tübingen, 1981), pp. 31, 49-50; Wormser, *Français Israélites*, pp. 26-28.

opment of various national groups within the same political framework.[17] This is not the place to evaluate the success of Czech nationalism during the life of the Austro-Hungarian Empire or after the establishment of the Czechoslovak republic. However, we should note the profound difference between Czech nationalism, representing a constituency that resided in its historical homeland, and Zionism, which presumed to speak for a dispersed national entity that could point to only a tiny minority living in its national homeland, Palestine. This major difference relegated the claim based on historic rights to a secondary place in the Zionist argument, and here the issue of historic right was perceived primarily as an indication of the Jews' attachment to Palestine.[18]

The invocation of the historic right goes back to the earliest days of Zionism. In an article entitled "On the Rebirth of Israel on the Soil of Its Homeland," published in 1882, Moses Leib Lilienblum claimed: "We have an historic right to [Palestine] that did not end and was not lost when we lost our rule, just as the right of the Balkan peoples to their land did not end when they lost their rule." In addressing a Lovers of Zion society in London's East End in 1897, Dr. Moses Gaster, the spiritual leader of the city's Sephardi Jewish community, declared: "Palestine belongs to us. Nations speak of an historic right, and no people has more of an historic right to Palestine than we do. We fought for it, our martyrs gave their lives for it, and we are duty bound to retrieve it." In a radically different style, Adolphe Raskine, a French Zionist of progressive leanings, wrote of the same subject in the same year: "When we demand a corner [of the earth] to create a center [for the Jewish people], we are standing on our inalienable historic rights." Raskine stressed that he was speaking of a country devoid of population that belonged to no one. Since he invoked the principles of the French Revolution and spoke of nationalism as a "progressive movement," he undoubtedly saw a

17 Thomas Garrique Masaryk, "The Case for the Successor States" in Ivo J. Lederer, ed., *The Versailles Settlement* (Boston, 1965), p. 102.
18 Y. Arieli, "Historical Attachment and Historical Right," *Forum*, 28-29 (Winter 1978), p. 92.

connection between the alleged vacancy of Palestine and the invocation of the historic right to it.[19]

Now let us again return to Herzl, whose approach was not
anchored in the historic right. That argument was eminently suitable
to men like Lilienblum, who advocated gradual settlement in Palestine; but a man of Herzl's leanings was more disposed to believe that
the power to dispense rights to a country was invested in its legal
sovereign. His objection to the method of "infiltration" and his
insistence upon obtaining a charter reflected not only purely political considerations; they were functions of his adherence to the principle of sovereignty. Hence in *The Jewish State* he categorically
demanded, "We must be accorded sovereignty" – though his solution to the problem of Jerusalem and the holy places indicated a
willingness to compromise on this principle. In *The Jewish State* he
spoke of a formula for granting extraterritorial status to the sites
sacred to Christianity; and in May 1896, after being informed that
the sultan would refuse to yield Jerusalem, Herzl theorized: "We
shall extraterritorialize Jerusalem, which will then belong to nobody
and yet to everybody . . ."

Herzl was to reiterate that position repeatedly, the speech he prepared for his meeting with the kaiser in Jerusalem being but one
instance: "And thus the actual city of Jerusalem, with its fateful
walls, has long since become a symbolic city sacred to all civilized
men." Another was in a letter written in 1903 to a prominent figure
in the czar's court: "This is perhaps proved by my plan to
exterritorialize the holy places, to make them *res sacrae extra
commercium gentium* [holy places above the trafficking of the
nations]." Finally, of his audience with the pope in 1904, Herzl
wrote: "I recited my little piece about the extraterritorialization."[20]
Actually, Herzl proposed extraterritorial status for the holy places
without making a clear distinction between these sites and the city
of Jerusalem itself, for he envisioned the involvement of several par-

19 Moses Leib Lilienblum, *Selected Writings* (Jerusalem, 1957), p. 37 (Hebrew);
   Rev. Dr. Gaster, "Nationale Bewegung," *Zion* (March 1, 1897), p. 90;
   Adolphe Raskine, "Ce que nous demandons," *Zion* (October 1897, French
   section), pp. 78, 80.
20 Herzl, *The Jewish State*, p. 93; Herzl, *Diaries*, Vol. I, pp. 345-346, Vol. II,
   p. 741, Vol. IV, pp. 1556, 1603.

ties by virtue of the moral rights they enjoyed in Jerusalem. Herzl was very particular about the concepts he was using, as if he were composing a legal document, yet his formula should not be taken as a constitutional definition. In saying that Jerusalem would belong to no one and yet to everyone, he was denying the validity of all claims to sovereignty over it. This was presumably the magic formula that would enable the Jews to have a hold on Jerusalem without arousing Moslem and Christian opposition.

Against this background we should pay note to an address in which Herzl came very close to wielding the argument of historic rights. In his speech at the Second Zionist Congress in 1898, Herzl already had his sight on the kaiser's forthcoming visit to Palestine when he pledged, in effect, that "the Jews are not, and will nevermore become, a political power." In a poetic vein, he spoke of the ravished land that so many nations had coveted and that had produced values for all mankind. Switching then to analysis, he declared that this was precisely the reason "nobody can deny that there is a deathless relation between our people and that land. If there is such a thing as a legitimate claim to a portion of the earth's surface, all peoples who believe in the Bible must recognize the rights of the Jews." Even though Herzl did not invoke the Jews' historic right by name, it seems obvious that he was referring to it here – in the absence of a recognized political status for the Jews in Palestine. Thus Herzl, the champion of sovereignty, fell back on the claim of historic right in order to play down the importance of political might. Not only did historic right and political power operate on two separate planes, the very appeal to the kaiser's conscience testified to Zionism's political weakness.[21]

Historic right did not take pride of place in the debates over the Uganda affair, however, for the crux then was to prove that Palestine was preferable to any other country, not to establish the Jews' right to it. Nonetheless, a similar line of argument was followed by the supporters of practical work within the Zionists of Zion, that is, the opposition to Uganda. Lilienblum, the veteran Lover of Zion, now returned to the question of historical rights, handling it somewhat differently than he had before. In a debate with the radical territori-

21 Herzl, *The Congress Addresses of Theodor Herzl*, p. 13.

alist Hillel Zeitlin, he characterized the Jewish people's right to Palestine as an eternal legacy that the present generation was not entitled to relinquish at the expense of future generations. As Lilienblum was usually far from being an elitist, he had to rally covert allies yet unborn to vindicate the minority claim, at a time when the majority was turning its back on Palestine. "The *Jewish people* is not only the present generation," he argued, "but even more so our children and our children's children and the generations that will follow them. This Jewish people, in line with the generations to come, will not relinquish its right to the land of its forefathers, just as all the generations of our people stretching back to the time of the destruction [of the Temple] have not relinquished that right." Perhaps it was not just coincidence that this statement was made in the context of Lilienblum's objection to Herzl's idea of obtaining a charter. There is no doubt an immanent connection between invoking eternal and inalienable historic rights and disregard for the rights that derive from international law.

The leader of the Zionists of Zion, Menahem Ussishkin, who also advocated practical work in Palestine, seemed to echo Lilienblum's argument: "The Arabs live in peace and brotherhood with the Jews. *They acknowledge the Children of Israel's historic right to the country.*" But Ussishkin's interpretation of historic right was viewed rather skeptically by Micha Josef Berdyczewski, who asserted in rebuttal: "Neither, for the most part, were our ancestors natives of the land; they were *conquerors* of the land, and the right we acquired thereby was also acquired by those who subsequently conquered it from us." Hence the historic claim could be a double-edged sword, for it was essentially the right of the conqueror. In Ussishkin's reading, the historic right that Lilienblum had depicted as an intrinsically Jewish affair became a source of authority that rested on none other than its recognition by the Arabs of Palestine. In the same pamphlet Ussishkin warned against leaving the labor in the colonies to Arabs, expressing the fear that in time the fellah "would shake off the dust of his lowliness" and demand his share, "for *it was by his hand* that the Jews had prospered so." This specter was undoubtedly influenced by a tradition popular among the peasant class in Russia, namely that the land belonged to those who worked it. In any event, Ussishkin took a strange tack in attempting to reconcile this double paradox: he claimed that the Jews had an historic right to the land but simultaneously tried to base this right on the Arabs, who were not even sovereign in the country and, worse yet, might someday rebel against the Jews. Thus it appears that he was basing the historic right upon sand – and indeed, Ussishkin's main purpose was to encourage practical work in Palestine, rather than to establish theoretical principles.[22]

It is important to appreciate the difference in mentality represented by figures such as Lilienblum and Ussishkin, on the one hand, and Herzl and his colleagues, on the other; those who invoked historic rights but were really talking about practical work in Palestine, and those who made the realization of Zionism conditional upon first achieving a recognized legal standing in the country. This fundamental discrepancy influenced the course of the Uganda affair and would continue to leave its mark on the movement for years to come in the clashes between the so-called political and practical Zionists. Here and there the concept of "historic rights" found its way into the heated exchanges of the Uganda affair, such as the speech of the Zionist Socialist Shlomo Kaplansky, who interpreted it positively, and the rejoinders of the Socialist Territorialists, who adamantly dissociated themselves from it. It is not surprising, however, that Berthold Feiwel, who hailed from Moravia and was doubtless familiar with the claims of the Czech national movement, employed the concept in a positive sense in the debate with the political Zionists. At any rate, it is clear that what these speakers usually meant was historic rights in the sense of historic *attachment*, not any strict right of possession over Palestine.[23] And as a rule, the whole question of rights remained marginal throughout the period under discussion.

---

22 Lilienblum, *Selected Writings*, p. 209; M. M. Ussishkin, *Our Zionist Program* (Warsaw, 1905), pp. 17, 33 (Hebrew); Berdyczewski, *Complete Works*, Articles Volume, p. 81; cf. Richard Pipes, *Russia Under the Old Regime* (Harmondsworth, Middlesex, 1979), p. 153.

23 Ben Barachel (Kaplansky), "An Interpretation of Zionism," *Der Yudisher Arbeter* (February 10, 1905), p. 3 (Yiddish); *Socialist Territorialism* (Paris, 1934), p. 144 (Yiddish); B. Feiwel, "Zur Situation im Zionismus," *Jüdische Rundschau* (February 17, 1905), p. 73.

The Outbreak of the Crisis

The year of the Sixth Zionist Congress (the Uganda congress) opened with negotiations over the possibility of settling Jews in the vicinity of El Arish and elsewhere in Sinai. Yet by the time Herzl met with the British foreign secretary, Lord Lansdowne, on April 23, 1903, the prospects of such a venture were already looking bleak. The next day Herzl wrote of the talks in his diary:

> "During my journey I saw a land for you," said the great Chamberlain, and he meant Uganda. . . . "I said to myself: This will be the country for Dr. Herzl. But he wants only Palestine or its surroundings." "Yes, I must," I replied. "Our basis must be in Palestine or its vicinity. Afterwards we can settle Uganda as well, for we have masses of people who are prepared to emigrate. But we are obligated to build on the national basis, so we need the political attractiveness of El Arish."

The Sinai plan came to naught, however, and in the meanwhile the Kishinev pogroms had broken out, leaving Herzl desperately clutching at any prospect that came along. On June 4 he proposed to the Sublime Porte "an arrangement for settlement either in Mesopotamia or in the Acre district" while simultaneously trying to institute contacts with Portugal on Mozambique ("so as to demand Palestine all the more emphatically"). And all the while the talks with Britain over a Jewish colony in East Africa continued.[24]

Herzl wrote Nordau about the East Africa plan at the beginning of July, and on the 4th of that month, speaking before an assembly in Paris, Nordau exhorted his audience: "Do not place the accent on the word Zion." Yet on the 17th he wrote to Herzl disqualifying the plan on the grounds that Uganda was unsuited to Jewish settlement for practical reasons. He also reminded Herzl that the Jewish public had not accepted the original formula laid down by Herzl in *The Jewish State*, so that the Basel Program established Palestine as the movement's objective. Nordau viewed the Uganda scheme as a panicked response to the Kishinev pogroms and Herzl's failure to make progress on the diplomatic plane. At the same time he developed an

24 Herzl, *Tagebücher*, Vol. III, pp. 412, 442, 444.

idea that to some degree merged two motifs of his earlier Zionist thinking. "In being a Zionist, the Jew has a thread that connects him to Judaism," he wrote to Herzl, "[a thread that] snakes its way everywhere, flexibly, without being torn, that follows him everywhere and preserves the bond between him and the community." In a sense, this was the theme of the Zionist's superiority over the assimilated Jew, as Nordau had conceived it at the beginning of his Zionist career when he argued that whoever was not a Zionist could not be a Jew. Here it was joined by a second motif, almost a paraphrase of the return-to-the-ghetto theme or the imperative that the Jewish community in the diaspora isolate itself from public life. The conclusion was that one must not latch onto hasty solutions, for the Zionist idea still had the power to sustain the Jews, even without any change in their objective situation. Nordau had come to see Zionism as essentially a subjective posture that had the power to protect the Jewish collective in the diaspora from internal disintegration. Thus he called upon Herzl to be patient and hold fast to the goals of Zionism, for it would teach the Jewish people "to feel itself and impress others as being a nation." Nordau's objection to Jewish settlement in Africa was sincere, but his loyalty to the Basel Program was mere lip service. He preferred the formula accepted by the First Zionist Congress to the original territorialist approach not because Palestine was dear to him but because it was generally popular among the Zionists. Anyone who submits Nordau's reasons for opposing the Uganda scheme to a close reading will not be surprised to learn that a month later he came out roundly in Herzl's defense and championed the idea of a *Nachtasyl* ("shelter for the night") in Uganda.[25]

While Nordau was able to solve a problem by proffering a new formula (the *Nachtasyl*), for Herzl the Sixth Zionist Congress was a grave test that exposed the inherent contradiction in his attitude toward Palestine. When he realized that the opposing positions on the East Africa scheme were beyond reconciliation, Herzl told his associates: "Although I was originally only a Jewish State man, *n'importe où*, later I lifted up the flag of Zion and became myself a

25 M. Nordau, "Discours sur l'éducation du peuple juif en vue de ses destinées futures," *l'Echo Sioniste* (July 15, 1903), p. 128; Michael Heymann, ed., *The Uganda Controversy*, Vol. II (Jerusalem, 1977), pp. 121-123.

Lover of Zion." By that point he was talking of resigning his leader-ship and establishing two executive bodies, one for East Africa and the other for Palestine, in the hope that such a move would heal the rift within the Zionist movement. After the congress he again tried to use the Uganda scheme as a springboard for renewing negotia-tions on Palestine. Immediately after the conclave had ended, Herzl called upon his benefactor, the archduke of Baden, and subsequently recorded in his diary that the old man seemed moved when "I told him that we would gladly renounce the good land in East Africa for the poor land in Palestine. I would particularly regard it as a vindica-tion for us avaricious Jews if we gave up a rich country for the sake of a poor one." Their talk was meant to signal that Germany could still play an active role in the Zionist arena if it would at last exercise its influence with Turkey. Yet we should also note Herzl's way of por-traying Zionist politics almost as a morality play, in which the righte-ous protagonist overcomes every temptation to sin, set against the backdrop of the usual prejudices about the Jews.

In a letter to the Russian minister of the interior, Plehve, penned a week later, Herzl raised the matter of Russian Jewry's adverse atti-tude toward settlement in East Africa. "I have had the opportunity to hear the views on this subject of a number of Russian Jewish revo-lutionaries living abroad," he wrote. "It seems to me that they are opposed to Africa and in favor of Palestine." The remark strongly intimated that the problem troubling the authorities in czarist Rus-sia – revolutionary ferment among the Jews – would not be solved by founding a colony in Uganda. Consequently, he was soliciting the aid of the Russian government in prevailing upon the sultan to change his mind. Still, the comment about the "Russian Jewish revo-lutionaries" is rather surprising, for Herzl seemed to apply the test to people who had little use for Zionism anyway.[26]

Britain's willingness to grant the Zionist Organization a franchise for a settlement project to be carried out under its aegis might well have served Herzl as the opening for a maneuver to play the Powers off against each other and establish the conditions for alternative negotiations. This had been his approach as far back as his earliest feelers in Constantinople in 1896, and he continued to steer the

26 Herzl, *Diaries*, Vol. IV, pp. 1547-1548, 1549, 1552.

Zionist strategy along these lines throughout his diplomatic activities. Even at the height of the Uganda crisis, Herzl stuck to the political strategy he had pursued from the start. His outlook on Palestine had been and remained an instrumental one; yet he ascribed ever greater importance to Palestine as time wore on and he became increasingly involved with the Jewish public. Ironically enough, when he was attacked for his hostility toward Palestine during the Uganda crisis, his attitude toward the country was actually more positive than it had been in his early years as a Zionist, when few doubted his allegiance to it.

The one man who had always doubted Herzl's loyalties and had protested his policy from the start was Ahad Ha'am. And when the Uganda crisis came to a head, events seemed to vindicate the suspicions he had harbored throughout the years. As far as he could see, there was nothing surprising about the fact that Herzl and his followers were able to "substitute Africa for Zion without the least remorse," for "they had never seen in Palestine a moral national ideal." Above all, however, Ahad Ha'am was incensed by the fact that East European Zionists had initially aligned themselves with political Zionism and were still trying to reach a compromise with the supporters of the Uganda plan. In a letter sent to a Russian Zionist immediately after the Sixth Congress, he predicted both the failure of the Uganda scheme and the complete collapse of the Zionist movement: "It will not return to Zion again, for in matters such as these regret is of little avail, and the work will come to a halt until a new generation will start it all over again." Neither was Ahad Ha'am above scolding: "As far as I can see, what you have done in Basel is tantamount to *apostatizing in public*." In an article entitled "The Weepers," he published a claim formerly expressed only in private and castigated the half-hearted opponents of Uganda – who "in the meanwhile have become slaves of the West" – for their readiness to compromise on "the articles of faith." He also offered a sociological reason for rejecting Uganda, positing that the Jews were no longer capable of "creating a new culture" in any country of immigration; hence they were trying to assimilate into developed countries, where "they can only *perpetuate* the life they have been living until now." The one exception to this rule, "by virtue of the historic feeling," was Palestine, which Ahad Ha'am referred to as "a national venture that means completely changing the people's frame of mind and way of life." It follows that he rejected Uganda because it would not lead to any change in the Jewish way of life, whereas the historic tie would make it possible for a total revolution to occur in Palestine and for the Jews "to create a new culture" there. Here Ahad Ha'am appears to have reached the height of the dialectic between the two concepts that regularly informed his writing: the historic feeling and innovative creativity.[27]

Elsewhere in the same article, Ahad Ha'am lauded Franz Oppenheimer's speech at the Sixth Zionist Congress, though he had difficulty explaining how Oppenheimer had been permitted "to speak from the Basel political rostrum about the *spiritual* foundations without which the *Yishuv* [in Palestine] cannot be constituted!" Ahad Ha'am's doubts about Herzl and his followers were compounded by his sense of alienation from the Western-type Jew. Admittedly, he was disappointed in the Russian Zionists who had been captivated by Herzl, but then again he had expected them to display greater perspicacity from the start, whereas he had had rather dim expectations of German Jews such as Oppenheimer. Hence his great surprise over Oppenheimer's address. What's more, despite his ties and points of contact with the Zionist Organization, Ahad Ha'am evidently did not have a very accurate picture of the relations that obtained at the top. Just as he had earlier held Herzl responsible for Nathan Birnbaum's remarks at the First Congress, so he now searched for Herzl's hidden hand behind Oppenheimer's address at the Sixth Congress. Needless to say, Herzl did not control every word that was uttered from the congress rostrum, and the barrier that Ahad Ha'am imagined to exist between the Jews of the East and the West was similarly artificial and exaggerated.

Franz Oppenheimer was already known as a man with his own approach to social and economic affairs, when Herzl invited him to address the Sixth Zionist Congress on the subject of settlement. His address made a particularly strong impression due to the sharp clash over the East Africa issue. Oppenheimer used the concept "imponderabilia" to denote the human factor in the settlement process, and

27 Ahad Ha'am, *Letters*, Vol. III (1924), pp. 136-138; Ahad Ha'am, "The Weepers," *Hashiloah*, 12 (1903), pp. 149-150 (Hebrew).

it was to echo throughout the subsequent debates on Uganda. Among his "imponderables" was "the indomitable power of the soul," which would sustain the settlers when physical power failed them, and the "longing of these exiles of two thousand years for the land of their forefathers." His words assumed a particularly topical relevance when he added that "allocating them the most magnificent expanses of farm land in Canada or Argentina will not enhance the strength of the wandering Jew as much as settling on the lowly plain through which the Jordan flows and upon which the Lebanon looks out."[28]

We shall quote two examples of how Ahad Ha'am's followers availed themselves of Oppenheimer's address. Relating to Oppenheimer's concept of imponderabilia, Joseph Klausner wrote:

> These "imponderables" are: the sense of lordship and longings for the homeland. The sense of lordship that the Jews never lost, even at their nadir, is the direct result of the inner genius that is borne by the great awareness – that the Jews alone have had a unique past and they alone have known a history that is rich in joyous events and uplifting even in its saddening events. This awareness has planted in the Jewish heart the strong hope that the Jewish people will become a great people again, its own master in its own land and the master of others in spirit.

Klausner's "sense of lordship" and his hope that the Jews would become "the master of others in spirit" went much further than anything suggested by Oppenheimer, who later broke with Zionism because he proclaimed an aversion to chauvinism. Marcus Ehrenpreis, on the other hand, interpreted Oppenheimer's concept – in line with Ahad Ha'am's approach – as proof of the original sin, as it were, of political Zionism. He held that "the Uganda proposal was the inevitable result of the fundamental beliefs held by the congress president" and offered as his evidence the reasoning that "it could have been born only in the mind of a politician who does not

---

28 Ahad Ha'am, "The Weepers," *Hashiloah*, 12 (1903), pp. 150-151 (Hebrew); Franz Oppenheimer, "Referat über Ansiedlung," *Die Welt* (August 26, 1903), separate edition, pp. 11; and see G. Kressel, *Franz Oppenheimer* (Tel Aviv, 1972), pp. 38-39 (Hebrew).

deal in historic 'imponderables,' whose Zionism is an artificial national construction *divorced from and devoid of historic life.*" Ehrenpreis also pointed out the inherent connection between the opposing positions on cultural work and allegiance to Palestine, and he concluded that "*the national culture* was buried at the Sixth Congress." This reaction was typical of many of the people who viewed cultural work as a prime *raison d'être* of the Zionist movement.[29]

The sudden proposal of the East Africa scheme at the Sixth Zionist Congress caused widespread chagrin and brought out feelings and views that had remained dormant during less turbulent times. The spiritual Zionists of Ahad Ha'am's school rediscovered their opposition to political Zionism and vice versa. Particularly interesting in this light was the position assumed by the socialist Nachman Syrkin, who had been in opposition to Herzl from the start but now suddenly found himself defending the policy of the Zionist leadership. While conceding that "romanticism is planted deep in the heart of every Zionist" – which was evidently an allusion to the attachment to Palestine – Syrkin insisted that the Uganda proposal was engendered not by "disloyalty to Zion" but by "a need that has ripened among the Jewish masses, the need to regulate emigration." The views held by Syrkin and Ehrenpreis, respectively, were characteristic of the disputes that now divided the Zionist camp. Syrkin did not underestimate the importance of Palestine, just as Ehrenpreis did not dismiss the suffering of the Jews. Both men spoke of a decision born of necessity, under the pressure of unfolding events, when it appeared that there was no longer any room for compromise between the historic ideal and the needs of the present. This sense of an inevitable decision was shared by many Zionists on both sides of the line dividing the warring camps.[30]

When the Sixth Congress came to a close, the two sides began to organize for the decisive struggle between them. In the course of that struggle, the clash between the self-styled Zionists of Zion and the so-called Ugandists grew increasingly bitter. The pitched battle over

29 J. Klausner, "An Accepted Lie," *Ahiasaf Calendar* (1903/4), p. 69 (Hebrew); M. Ehrenpreis, "From Uganda to Kharkov," *Hashiloah*, 13 (1904), p. 176 (Hebrew).

30 Dr. Syrkin, "In der Uganda-Debatte," *Die Welt* (August 27, 1903), p. 9.

the future direction of Zionism was to rage on relentlessly for the next two years.

Two Years of Struggle

Much has been written about the struggle that rent the Zionist movement from the Sixth Zionist Congress until its successor, convened two years later. A considerable amount of material has survived on the organization of the Zionists of Zion and the discussions held in the Zionist Organization's official bodies. In part this material has been systematically processed and explicated by historical scholarship.[31] Hence we do not intend to describe these events in detail. Instead, our interest is in focussing on those aspects of the dispute that are germane to our subject, namely, the attitude toward the past as it was expressed in connection with Palestine. The Uganda affair was a major convulsion that put all the tenets of Zionism to the test. It was of course a crucible of the Zionists' attitudes toward the heritage of their historic homeland, but it also raised many other issues, such as religion, modernization, the nature of Jewish culture, and so forth. In the course of our discussion, we have seen that there was no dividing line between the champions of historical continuity and the proponents of modernization. The dialectical approach adopted toward these issues by various circles within the Zionist movement continued to hold true during the Uganda affair. Yet here a new factor came into play: the constraints of real-life politics. The discord deprived the Zionists of the luxury of entertaining and cultivating fairly abstract propositions and obliged everyone to define himself as one thing or another. In the course of the struggle, these sympathies crystallized into more or less rigid positions representing defined political camps. As a result, loose ideological proclivities were superseded by strict political loyalties, tactical considerations, and occasionally something approaching combat discipline – all of which added up to a kind of revolutionary solidarity. In discussing

---

31 It is worth noting the two volumes based on the protocols of the Zionist Executive edited by Michael Heymann, and see Robert G. Weisbord's monograph on the subject, *African Zion* (Philadelphia, 1968).

the course of the Uganda crisis, we must therefore remain alert to the submergence of the ideological moment into the dynamic of internal politics.[32]

The man who conducted negotiations with the British government on Herzl's behalf was a Zionist journalist by the name of Leopold Greenberg. After the Sixth Zionist Congress, he appeared at an assembly in Liverpool and explained why he was in favor of Uganda. Contrary to what might be expected, Greenberg did not lay stress on the sufferings of the Jews – which was the usual line commending Uganda – but justified the East Africa scheme by wielding an argument that was typical of his opponents. "We do it because we feel a pride in our race," he said, "because we feel a pride in our history, and above all we do it because we feel that we have a mission to perform here upon earth." Thus autonomy in Africa became an alternative to Palestine not just in the practical sense but also as an expression of the spiritual aspect that accompanied the Zionist idea. If a colony were to be founded in Africa, Greenberg prophesied, it would draw all the Jews by virtue of the "Jewish rules" that would obtain therein and because the Jews would be offered a better opportunity "to exercise the tenets of their faith" in Uganda than anywhere else on earth. This was not a declaration of religious import, as might be inferred from the wording, but an expression of the national approach, as we can see from the broader context: "They will know that their lives and the lives of their children will be developed upon Jewish lines, with Jewish ideas and Jewish thought."

A different attitude was taken by Greenberg's partner to this phase of the struggle, Israel Zangwill, who was soon to become the leader of the new territorialist movement. Zangwill repudiated both a devotion to Palestine and the religious tradition that had sanctified the country. In one instance he compared Dr. Moses Gaster, the head of the Sephardi community and leader of the Zionists of Zion in England, to the czarist minister of interior in saying: "De Plehve and his satellites wished to see a Holy Russia" (using Plehve as a symbol of the dominance of religion in Russia), "and Dr. Gaster desired a Holy Palestine." This analogy, drawn half in jest, was based on a presumed resemblance between Jewish and Russian "Orthodoxy" and

---

32 E.g. Mannheim, *Ideology and Utopia*, p. 170.

wholly ignored the fact that Gaster was a modern rabbi who did not represent typical Orthodox positions. As far as Zangwill was concerned, his campaign against Gaster helped to elucidate the relationship between Palestine and religion, which was to become a prominent motif in the territorialist argument.[33]

Indeed, Gaster's style, born of years of preaching from the pulpit, could be misleading. Both in public addresses and in private letters, he indulged in a penchant for rhetorical flourish – often at the price of conveying his message clearly. In November 1903 Gaster responded to a call, signed by Weizmann and Buber, to publish a new periodical that would fight for the ideals of the "Jewish renaissance movement." The circular explained that the journal would treat Judaism not as something "aged and sealed" or "molded by rigid formulas" but as "the living organism of the nation." It also pledged to level "healthy criticism" at all that was "diseased and corruptive" and give expression to the "movement for Jewish renaissance" – all in the spirit of the "synthetic-historic outlook" propounded by Buber and his associates. Gaster responded positively and commented to Buber: "The 'modern,' as such, will be fully meaningful only, as I have learned from your letter, if based upon the past." Though he took pains to stress attachment to the past in this quote, he was fundamentally in agreement with Buber's outlook.[34]

Yet Gaster's piece on Uganda and Palestine, published during the same period, was informed by a different spirit. "For us Zionism means the thrust toward the East (*Drang nach Osten*) but to a particular East, to the ancient homeland in the East, to the Holy Land, so as to rebind the old ties, revive Jewish national and religious life, realize the old hopes and strivings" – as if Gaster's sole desire were to turn back the clock. In the English version of his article, he ridiculed the Herzlian school of Zionism and the "fantastic idea of a

---

33 "Zionism & East Africa, Mass Meeting at Liverpool," *The Jewish World* (October 23, 1903), pp. 76-77 (Greenberg's speech); "Zionism & East Africa, Meeting at St. James's Hall," *The Jewish World* (November 20, 1903), p. 158 (Zangwill's speech); see also Moses Gaster, *Gaster Centenary Publication* (London, 1958), p. 20.

34 Hans Kohn, *Martin Buber* (Hellerau, 1930), pp. 296-300; Buber, *Briefwechsel*, p. 221.

Jewish State." He also accused Herzl of practicing a brand of philanthropy designed to help needy Jews from the East escape persecution and solve the economic problem, criticizing: "It is neither bound up with the old tradition nor is it limited to place or country." Gaster mocked political Zionism for striving for "free political and economic development," even though his reply to Buber reflected his own desire for such development "so that we will no longer be forced to deny our faith and have our political existence depend upon the goodwill and tolerance of others." While Gaster spoke of "a fundamental political-national and religious redemption," it appears that in terms of his political views he was not as removed from Herzlian Zionism as he seems to have imagined. There is reason to assume that the Uganda affair gave him the opportunity to shift his personal antipathy for Herzl onto ideological lines and then explicate the crisis as a symptom of a far more profound conflict.[35]

After Herzl's death Gaster reiterated his call to abandon the idea of settlement in Uganda, adding: "We must remember that in Zionism we are not dealing solely with the physical liberation of the masses but first and foremost with spiritual liberation from the pressures of centuries and from the ghetto spirit, which is not above even trafficking in ideals." In this case the "ghetto spirit" symbolized the willingness of Gaster's adversaries to renounce their vision and trade Palestine for East Africa. According to Gaster, the opposing positions within the Zionist movement did not represent legitimate differences of opinion; they exceeded even a fundamental difference in principle between two systems of thought, as Ahad Ha'am held. Instead, the struggle at hand was between those faithful to the liberation movement and those who had betrayed it by succumbing to the "ghetto spirit." Although at first glance it may appear that Gaster would advocate a conservative position, his statement about "spiritual liberation from the pressures of centuries" and the like placed him firmly in the camp advocating a "Jewish renaissance." As we saw earlier, decrying the "ghetto spirit" was usually an expression of the dialectic approach that viewed the diaspora as the antithesis of

---

35 M. Gaster, "Zionismus und Neu-Zionismus," *Ost und West* (October 1903), p. 671; Moses Gaster, "Zionism and New Zionism," *The Jewish World* (October 23, 1903), p. 72.

the ancient past. On the whole, Gaster espoused not strict historical continuity but a modernist revival of Judaism that drew on the distant past and rejected the recent one. It was this outlook – and not Orthodox motives, as Zangwill imagined – that made for his uncompromising stand in favor of Palestine.[36]

Their differences notwithstanding, it is interesting to note the resemblance between Zangwill and Gaster when it came to their historical outlook on Jewish nationalism. Zangwill hoped that "our oppressed Masses shall draw free breath" in East Africa (which he then regarded as a "provisional Palestine"), "soul and body shall grow straight again where the Marrano Judaism shall give place to the Maccabean Judaism." "Marrano Judaism" was essentially another way of saying assimilation, while "Maccabean Judaism" was its proud and militant opposite. Zangwill invoked the image of Jewry from the Second Temple period as his paradigm for the future, in contrast to the posture and lifestyle characteristic of the more recent past.

This statement dates to the middle of 1905, when Zangwill still regarded Africa as no more than a surrogate; by the end of that year, however, Weizmann reported that Zangwill was opposed to settling Palestine as a matter of principle. On October 20, 1903, Weizmann wrote to Ussishkin: "Zangwill is the true ideologist of East Africa; he went much further than Herzl would approve. He is in fact an opponent of Palestine, because, in his view, the old Jewish tradition, with its sacrifices and prayers, would have to be re-established and would exclude the building of a secular state there." In a similar letter written to Gaster, he carefully left out the term "secular state" and described Zangwill's chief complaint about Palestine as the assumption that it would be impossible to "lead a modern life there." Weizmann evidently felt that Gaster would be offended by the notion of a secular state, whereas his point was to establish the absurdity of Zangwill's premise in equating Palestine with a theocracy. In effect, Weizmann ascribed to Zangwill an approach that had appeared in the early 1880s in the writings of Judah Leib Levin and Eliahu Wolf Rabinowitz, Hebrew writers who had difficulty choosing between Love of Zion and Jewish settlement in America.

36 M. Gaster, "Herzl und weiter," *Ost und West* (August-September 1904), p. 527.

Weizmann's major criticism of the supporters of Uganda was rooted in another matter, however. Like Ahad Ha'am, he regarded "Ugandism" as a function of the estrangement from Jewish life of the "Westerners," and like Ehrenpreis he associated it with their opposition to "cultural work." In a circular dated October 26, 1903, issued on behalf of the Democratic Fraction, Weizmann wrote: "The wretched cultural issue, prowling unsolved like a ghost from one Congress to the next, was in essence the psychological evidence of what has now, of course, emerged into the open more drastically through the Africa issue. It is definitely no coincidence that the most embittered opponents of Zionist cultural activities were the strongest adherents of the Africa project." He then went on to propound a theory about the basic difference between Herzlian Zionism and "organic Zionism," holding – like Gaster – that political Zionism was fundamentally philanthropic and intended "Zion for the Zionists and Africa for the people."[37]

However, it was Moshe Smilansky who did the most to develop the notion of the philanthropic nature of Herzlian Zionism. Smilansky had spent part of his youth in the colonies in Palestine and was able to relate the Uganda affair to the history of the Yishuv. He traced the antagonism between the two types of Zionism – philanthropic and national – to differences that had pertained between the radical group of early settlers, called the Bilu, and the other Lovers of Zion. "The members of the Bilu were pure nationalists, of course, not philanthropic nationalists," he wrote in an article published at the end of 1903. "After them 'bourgeois' Jews entered the nascent nationalist movement and comprised an alien element therein – an offshoot of philanthropy." Their parole was, according to Smilansky, "Zion in theory for us; Zion in practice for our paupers." Smilansky then traced the development of the two opposing systems from the Love of Zion movement through the heyday of political Zionism and pronounced: "That same philanthropic impulse within Zionism is what led the Zionists as far as Uganda." We should note that like Gaster, Smilansky spoke derisively of political Zionism for setting its sights on a "Jewish state that would come

---

37 Zangwill, *Speeches, Articles and Letters*, p. 226; Weizmann, *Letters*, Vol. III, pp. 62-63, 81; Central Zionist Archives (Ussishkin Archive) , A24/125/41.

into being instantly, magically." This demonstrates how the Uganda affair put to the test not only the Jewish attachment to Palestine but the tenets of Zionism as they had been fashioned since the First Zionist Congress.[38]

The genealogy of the Zionists of Zion, as traced by Smilansky, was but one thread in the welter of historic claims cited by the debaters on both sides of the issue. Weizmann, for example, seized upon the support that his camp received from an explorer of Africa, Sir Harry Johnston, who had been the British commissioner in both South Central Africa and Uganda. Johnston had told him that the white settlers in Uganda were opposed to Jewish immigration, though he had been careful to couch this revelation in terms that were flattering to the Jews. Indeed, Sir Harry was applauded at a Zionist rally in London when he told his audience, "If I were a Jew, I should be proud of belonging to a people with such a magnificent history; but my very attachment to Jewish history would make me devote money and life to the re-establishment of the Jewish State in Palestine and Southern Syria." Apparently the respected expert spoke to the hearts of his Jewish listeners, and none more than the leader of the Sephardi community, Dr. Moses Gaster, who presided over the meeting.[39]

One of the spiritual Zionists closest to Ahad Ha'am, David Neumark – who was later to become a professor of Jewish philosophy in the United States – tackled the Uganda issue from the vantage of the Jews' historic attachment to Palestine and categorically pronounced that: "*The Holy Spirit, our national Divine Presence, will dwell within us only in the Land of Israel.*" He then attempted to resolve the contradiction between Ahad Ha'am's approach – which played down the importance of political success – and the attachment to Palestine that was highlighted, in effect, by Jewish sovereignty. Neumark claimed that throughout Jewish history cultural florescence had always gone hand in hand with political weakness. He noted, for example, that "the greater Prophets came forth and were

38 Moshe Smilansky, "A Forgotten Legacy," *Hazman*, 6 (1904), p. 2 (Hebrew).
39 Sir Harry Johnston, "East Africa or Palestine," *The Jewish Chronicle* (December 25, 1903), p. 13; Chaim Weizmann, *Trial and Error* (New York, 1969), pp. 89-90.

active during times of political decline or even the destruction of the political entity." This train of thought might lead to the conclusion that if spiritual values were the antithesis of political might, they were bound to reach their acme when and where the Jews were at their political nadir. Indeed, Neumark quickly moved on to the subject of exile and discussed the applicability of his rule to Babylonia. Having argued that the Divine Presence dwelled solely in Palestine, he was now forced to concede that "to some degree the national Divine Presence was to be found in *Babylonia* as well." Neumark regarded this exception as a result of the situation then prevailing in Palestine and explained that since the death of Rabbi Yohanan Ben-Zakkai, when Palestine's sway declined sharply, "every spiritual creation has smacked of the *diaspora*."[40]

It is hardly surprising that Ahad Ha'am let it be known the article was not to his liking, for Neumark had inadvertently exposed the flaw in spiritual Zionism's argument. It seemed to have become tangled in an inherent contradiction while trying to follow to their logical conclusions two given premises: one associating Judaism with the negation of political power, the other linking the thriving of Jewry to Palestine. Logic dictates that either Palestine should be established as the basis of Judaism, in which case the importance of the political framework in the First and Second Temple periods deserves to be acknowledged; or the political aspect of Jewish existence should be discounted, in which case equal or even greater credit must be ascribed to the role of the diaspora in fashioning Judaism. Furthermore, no one affirmed the multiformity of Jewish creativity throughout the ages more than Ahad Ha'am and his followers. So how could they, of all people, focus solely on the Palestinian period of Jewish history and ignore later products of Jewish experience? Ahad Ha'am himself was later to comment on this illusion in no uncertain terms in writing: "It is impossible to pass over thousands of years of history and educate 'primeval Jews' now as if they lived in Isaiah's time."

Although Ahad Ha'am envisioned a spiritual center arising in Palestine, his system had much in common with Dubnow's doctrine of

---

40 David Neumark, "A Plethora of Troops," *Ahiasaf Calendar* (1904), pp. 30-33 (Hebrew).

Jewry's shifting centers, in both its acceptance of the past and its prognosis for the future.[41] Thus one of the ironies of the Uganda affair was that Ahad Ha'am's disciples were among the first to attack those unfaithful to the Land of Israel, without sensing the need to set their own house in order. Perhaps the reason for this paradox lay in the symbolic-historic function that Palestine played in Ahad Ha'am's system. Spiritual Zionism had never subscribed to the notion of solving the Jewish problem, for it had consistently distinguished between the Jews (or Jewry) and Judaism. Consequently, neither diplomatic achievements nor political setbacks could detract from the power of the symbol. On the other hand, the symbol as such was irreplaceable, so that it had to be preserved in its purity. This is why identification with the symbolical Land of Israel was able to coexist with skepticism about the prospects of Palestine as a Jewish country. A similar paradox was even more flagrant in the writings of S. J. Ish-Horowitz, who shocked the Hebrew-reading public with his heretical pronouncement about the future of Jewish nationalism. At the end of the article in which he expressed his maverick views, Ish-Horowitz aimed his sarcastic barbs at the supporters of Uganda and accused them of "soul burning," by which he meant that "they believe it possible for the Jewish people to divorce itself from its entire past, forget all the hopes that it has always borne, and establish in Uganda a new Israelite kingdom with a new future and new hopes."[42]

In the context of the struggle being waged by the young Zionist intelligentsia against the views of the territorialists, Joseph Klausner warned against harboring the illusion that Zionism had the power to "put an end to the material hardship of the Jews." He contrasted the "spiritual Zionists or culturists," who built their case on an "historical basis," with the political Zionists, who were bound to degenerate into a "philanthropic movement." Klausner also used this opportunity to criticize the Zionist approach that had been taken in the past, by claiming a necessary contradiction between "*a*

---

41 Ahad Ha'am, *Letters*, Vol. III (1957); see also Ahad Ha'am, *Collected Works*, p. 420; cf. Dubnow, *Nationalism and History*, pp. 48-49.

42 S. J. Ish-Horowitz, "The Question of the Existence of Judaism," *Hashiloah*, 13 (1904), p. 293 (note; Hebrew).

movement for rescue" and *"a movement of renaissance."* From there he proceeded to analyze two categories – one representing a devotion to history, the other a striving for change – which on the face of it appeared to be mutually exclusive. Appearances notwithstanding, however, Klausner held that there was no substantive antagonism between the old and the new. On the one hand, "a renaissance is always the restoration of what is good in the old." Yet "even though it means to refashion something, rather than create something *ex nihilo,* Zionism is a highly radical Jewish movement, for it aspires to a total revolution in Jewish life: *to a revolt against the diaspora.*" The political conclusion that followed from this statement was that there was no room for compromise with his adversaries in the Zionist movement.

A similar tactical position was taken by Jan Kirschrot, a member of the Democratic Fraction from Warsaw who espoused the dialectical synthesis between history and revolution. Kirschrot believed that the strength of the anti-Uganda minority at the Sixth Zionist Congress resided in its desire "to connect the present moment in the life of our people with its history." For him Zionism was "a movement whose source lay in earlier generations and whose end is a complete revolution in our national life." In this same context he spoke of "the messianic idea and its actual embodiment – the Land of Israel," and finally reached the practical conclusion that it was necessary "to make open war on the majority, drive out the decadent elements."[43] In the case of both Kirschrot and Klausner, espousal of a revolutionary theory clearly implied the adoption of a radical stand in the internal struggle, as well.

Territorialism as an Ideal

In Hillel Zeitlin the Ugandist camp found a trenchant Hebrew polemicist who could hold his own against the intellectuals support-

---

43 Joseph Klausner, "The Economic Side of Zionism," *Ahiasaf Calendar* (1905), pp. 149-150 (Hebrew); Joseph Klausner, "The Approaching Peril," *Hashiloah,* 15 (1905), pp. 419, 421, 425 (Hebrew); J. Kirschrot, "The Sixth Zionist Congress – Reflections and Thoughts," *Hashiloah,* 12 (1903), pp. 187, 189, 191 (Hebrew).

ing the Zionists of Zion. One of the more interesting debates of the period was conducted by Zeitlin and Vladimir Jabotinsky, who had published a theoretical article in Russian on "Zionism and Palestine." Jabotinsky tried to defend the minority position on Uganda by contending that the "will of the people" should not be measured by a majority vote. Instead, he developed the argument of authenticity, predicating that "every new trend in the life of the nation must follow directly from its entire past." Zeitlin replied by charging:

> Mr. Jabotinsky forgets that this is precisely what all the reactionaries and obscurants say when they are confronted with the *natural and actual* needs of the people: you see only the external surface; you are concerned only about material needs; and you do not see the needs of the spirit. And in the name of those spiritual needs the people is being misled and imbued with a sense of lethargy, dreariness, and darkness; in the name of that same spirit it is being oppressed unto dust.

Once again we have before us the motifs of avant-gardism and plain democracy. Though Jabotinsky belonged to a more moderate wing of the Zionists of Zion than Klausner and Kirschrot, he was a party to their basic outlook. Thus where Klausner declared, "For truly we are the lifeblood and powerhouse of this nation," Jabotinsky added, "The true expression of the people's will is not to be found in what the people shout." Zeitlin, however, rebutted by referring to the situation at hand and contended that "the people are not at all moved or taken by such lofty words." As if mocking the avant-gardist and progressive pretensions of his adversaries, he chose to highlight the resemblance between their position and the classic stance of the ultra-conservative.[44]

Another side of Zeitlin's thinking came out in his criticism of Lilienblum, who remained one of the leading champions of Palestine. Until then Zeitlin had spoken as a realist who intended to expose his adversaries' reactionary character cloaked under the guise of spiritualism. But the Zeitlin who took on Lilienblum came across

44 Vladimir Zeev Jabotinsky, *Early Zionist Writings* (Jerusalem, 1958), pp. 112, 113 (Hebrew); Hillel Zeitlin, "Things as They Stand," *Hador* (July 12, 1904), pp. 2-3 (Hebrew).

as an idealist with nothing but contempt for the narrow horizons of the old Lovers of Zion. He dismissed Lilienblum with the cavalier remark, "He measures everything by the yardstick of a merchant," and jeered in reply to his own rhetorical question, "And what is Lilienblum's ideal now?": "A donation of three rubles to buy a goat for a colonist." For all its sting, this attack on Lilienblum's goat – which has long become a byword among Zionists – was no more virulent than the usual criticism voiced against practical Zionism. However, we should have a look at the difficult pass in which Lilienblum nevertheless found himself as a result of the Uganda affair.

Lilienblum's Zionism was built upon national compromise and finding the common denominator of all strata of society. This principle had informed his thinking as far back as the 1880s, when he rejected Eliezer Ben-Yehuda's claim that "whoever has despaired of the hope of redemption has ceased to be a Jew." It had been articulated primarily during the controversy over cultural work, when Lilienblum called for reaching an understanding with the Orthodox groups so as to preserve "the peace and unity without which Zionism itself cannot exist." Yet now Lilienblum was forced to choose between defending the minority position of fidelity to Palestine or following the majority – in which case he would find himself in the company of "the faint-hearted," as he put it, who "have blamed the people's faults on the country and have begun to look for other lands." Lilienblum's solution was to extend the electorate, in a manner of speaking, by bringing the question before not just the present generation but the generations to come. Thus he juxtaposed the "right" of all this progeny with "the matter of the livelihood of one or two generations," which enabled him to reconcile the two positions without relinquishing his fundamental approach. It is interesting to note the parallel between the tangible ideal symbolized by the goat, attributed to Lilienblum, and his dismissal of Uganda as no more than a source of livelihood for a generation or two.[45]

45 Hillel Zeitlin, "Conversations," *Hador* (March 29, 1904), p. 15 (Hebrew); Lilienblum, *Selected Writings*, p. 209; on Lilienblum and Ben-Yehuda see Ben-Yehuda, *Israel to Its Land and Language*, p. 223.

We were in the midst of discussing Zeitlin, who had gone as far as supporting territorialism as a matter of principle. Zeitlin was later to be remembered for his conspicuous return to religion. During this period, however, he was known for his association with the territorialist camp. He had praised Herzl's *Altneuland*, for example, but found that the novel had one major failing: that its author applied his plan to Palestine. Like others before him, Zeitlin feared that a return to Palestine would result in the creation of a "theocracy." "It is *impossible* to create a modern society in Palestine," he pronounced, explaining that "the rabbis' control of the masses will not falter there, as the free-thinking Zionists hope. On the contrary, it will grow stronger and stronger and spread further and further." Zeitlin surpassed even Zangwill in his objections to Palestine and added: "If we revert to Judaism's public ideal, meaning theocracy, we are better off remaining in the diaspora and enduring what we suffer hundreds of times over. The most important thing is man's absolute and total liberty." To avoid any misunderstanding on this point, we should note that Zeitlin merely made use of such rhetoric to illustrate the extent of his objection to religion. Essentially he shifted to a new country the goals that had long been associated with Ahad Ha'am's followers (who were themselves faithful to Palestine). For example, he praised those who aspired "to abandon petty trade and beggary," as an expression of their complete dissociation from the old way of life, and intended "to revise their mode of living from start to finish." In speaking of the need to bring territorialism to fruition, Zeitlin cried: "We cannot bear the eternal diaspora and the eternal ghetto."

Zeitlin's crusade against religion was not an expression of his alienation from Judaism; rather it was an attempt to develop a new attitude toward it. "The moral ideal of Judaism is infinitely lofty and sublime" he wrote, but the same could not be said of the "public order" that followed therefrom. Consequently it should be "purged and refined by the new European aspirations." No less interesting was Zeitlin's ambivalent attitude toward nature. On the one hand, he expressed a sense of alienation from it in asking, "What do all these things have to do with a Jew, with a man who recognizes that all this is for others and for us there is only Galuth and more Galuth." Only in the future would the Jew be permitted to derive enjoyment from nature, "When I see that Israel is again becoming the Chosen People, when I see the redemption and its glow, when I see our ideal beginning to become reality." Considering Zeitlin's opposition to Palestine, there was a special resonance to his adherence to both traditional conceptual forms and the Haskalah-Zionist outlook. Most, if not all, of the proponents of the latter view were opposed to Uganda, and we have already attempted to relate this phenomenon to the symbolic-historical part that Palestine bore in Ahad Ha'am's doctrine. How, then, can one explain Zeitlin's departure from this norm?

First we should examine a piece in which Zeitlin formulated his view on Palestine's role in Jewish history. Contrary to David Neumark's contention about Palestine's centrality over the ages, Zeitlin wrote:

> Throughout the history of the Sons of Israel, there is not a single moment in which the *specifically Palestinian* character stands out and is recognizable. All those longings for the ingathering of the exiles and all the messianic movements and messianic legends are essentially expressions of the people's desire to live a natural, healthy, and normal life again and of universally religious messianic longings that have found the best and strongest expression in the saying: "The Land of Israel is destined to extend throughout all lands."

In effect, what Zeitlin did here was turn an idea found in Jewish lore on its head. On the face of it, he subscribed to the Zionist interpretation that drew upon messianism; but he differed on the conclusion that the messianic idea would be realized in Palestine. What we have here actually signifies a substantive clash between the Jewish heritage and the trend toward normalization. In contrast to the striving for synthesis so popular among the adherents of the Haskalah-Zionist school, Zeitlin propounded antinomy. It appears that the still-secular Zeitlin was beginning to show signs of his future turnabout in the direction of Hasidism and mysticism. He rejected Palestine because it was associated with religion but affirmed a mes-

sianism of a universal-mystical nature that was soon to lead him out
of the national movement altogether.[46]

One of the most respected supporters of the Uganda scheme was,
ironically, Eliezer Ben-Yehuda, who in 1879 had called for "the
rebirth of Israel in its homeland" and had himself settled in Palestine two years later. For all that, however, in 1905 he published a
pamphlet entitled *The Jewish State* presenting his views in support
of settlement in East Africa. In his youth Ben-Yehuda had expressed
his belief in a redemption in Palestine, yet now he accused the Zionists of Zion of being "*oriented toward the country,* while we are *oriented toward the people,*" meaning that "For us *the people* is the
important thing . . . and to you, gentlemen, the land is the main
thing." One might have assumed that in the intervening years, his
vision of redemption would have been subordinated to the concrete
needs of the Jewish masses. Yet Ben-Yehuda was taken by the
Uganda Scheme less because it was an answer to actual needs than
because of its implicit promise of redemption. He believed that the
main benefit of Jewish settlement in East Africa was the political
status it would accord the Jews. "*The moment* it is written and
signed by both sides," he wrote of the envisioned agreement on Jewish settlement in East Africa, "*at that very instant we will officially
have a Jewish state.*" Yet in addition to regarding the establishment
of the state as a foregone conclusion, he believed the act itself would
have far-reaching implications for the status of the Jews the world
over. If only a "few hundred" Jews settled in the East African state,
he predicted, "our entire moral status in the world will change,
immediately; at that moment we will have ceased to be gypsies, people without a country."

Like Klausner, Ben-Yehuda based himself on the "sense of lordship," but whereas Klausner regarded it as an immanent component
of historic consciousness, Ben-Yehuda expected it to develop among
the Jews as a result of their new status. This inordinate stress on
political status was a function of his lack of confidence in the Jews'
ability to act on their own, articulated in his complaint that "our

46 Hillel Zeitlin, "Things as They Stand," *Hador* (July 12, 1904), pp. 7, 9
(Hebrew); Hillel Zeitlin, "The Crisis – A Territorialist's Notes," *Hazman*, 3
(1905), pp. 283, 295 (Hebrew).

national substance has *become flimsy and thin.*" We should note parenthetically that Zeitlin too expressed doubts about the Jews' ability to change, when he remarked, "I have misgivings about the material from which the great structure must be built. It is too battered and shaken." One could take this mood of discouragement as a reaction to the nadir that Zionism had reached after repeated failures on the diplomatic plane. Yet it probably had deeper roots that traced to either Jewish feelings of inferiority or the flagrant gap between expectations and reality.

This type of criticism came up repeatedly in Ben-Yehuda's writings from his youth onward. In his 1905 piece he interpreted the laxity of the national will and deterioration of the national feeling among the Jews much as Berdyczewski had before him. "Had it not been for that," Ben-Yehuda wrote, "we would not have been exiled from our country, *by our own will*; and would not have been driven off our land, *by our own will*; and would not have *willingly* abandoned our language, which has no parallel in history; and would not have sat idly by for eighteen hundred years in humiliation, in such awful exile." He added a topical dimension to this complaint, in arguing that had it not been for the fact that the national feeling had dimmed, "we would *already* have returned to Palestine – after the expulsion from Spain, for example – or would have sought and found a place to settle as proprietors in one of the corners of the earth that had been empty till then, in America or Australia or Africa." His heavy accent on the Jews' readiness to go into exile raises the distinction between an active desire to leave the country and abandon the language and what Ahad Ha'am called the "atrophy . . . of the national feeling." Although the result in both cases may have been similar, there is a great difference between succumbing to the debilitation of the national will and acting willfully. Ben-Yehuda was inclined to blame the Jews for their exile, and he noted that they preferred to wait for "an *unnatural*, miraculous redemption."

In Ben-Yehuda's conception of history, the choice of locale for the political framework had not been of importance in the past, either. Since he did not regard its territory as an immutable component of nationhood, he was able to ask: "Did not and do not most of the peoples that have been on earth since time immemorial live in *for-*

eign places? And our own people, does it not live in a foreign place? Was Israel a *native* of the Land of Israel?" This argument is reminiscent of Berdyczewski's remark that the Jews' right to Palestine was the right of conquerors. Ben-Yehuda's justification of the territorialist idea went almost as far as the creation of an entirely new national entity, though he never crossed that threshold. He wanted to draw an analogy about the Jews from the founding of new states in Australia and Canada. Though they were "of English stock," the inhabitants of these countries had ceased to be Englishmen and had become "peoples in their own right." Hence he reasoned that the Jews need not necessarily be subject to the ruling culture of Uganda, and "if they so wish they can become *a separate people*, a people distinguished for its character and sense of self."

Here Ben-Yehuda confronted the need to prove that the Jews would indeed be able to withstand the competition from English culture. Had he taken his analogy to its logical conclusion, he would have deduced that the Jews in Uganda were likewise destined to become a new people. Furthermore, if the "unique selfhood" of the Australians and the Canadians (being, as he said, of English origin) was becoming increasingly manifest, this would be all the more true of the selfhood of the Jews, who were not comparably attached to English culture. Yet quite surprisingly, at that point Ben-Yehuda brought in the historic heritage of the Jews – "for they have another life thousands of years old, with other memories, another mind, another way of thinking, another literature and, *if* they wish to, they will speak another language" – implying that the new national entity to be forged in Uganda was nevertheless a continuation of historic Jewry.[47]

The national outlook sketched out in broad lines by Ben-Yehuda may not have been adequately developed but it did point to a territorialist trend with an ideology all its own. We have already referred to the similarity between Ben-Yehuda's and Berdyczewski's criticism of the Jews for choosing exile of their own volition. Actually, criticism like theirs could be applied to territorialism, as well. However, if Berdyczewski disparaged the prospects of settlement in East

47 Eliezer Ben-Yehuda, *The Jewish State: Articles on the East Africa Proposal* (Warsaw, 1905), pp. 9, 23, 33, 37, 38 (Hebrew).

Africa, it was not because he subscribed to the exclusivity of Palestine but for purely pragmatic reasons. As far as he was concerned, the search for a new country was in itself a positive phenomenon. Just as Ben-Yehuda believed that the political act would revive the atrophied national feeling, so Berdyczewski believed that "through this will something new is born in us that we lacked in diaspora life, namely, a collective national feeling." Berdyczewski attacked the direction being taken by Jewish emigration in observing: "We have learned to go to only those places where others have already gone." Therefore, he praised the willingness to begin everything anew: "And if the nation has realized that the departure and the journey must assume a new form, and that we are better off having people who live independently and make their way in a virgin land than having thousands upon thousands move together to a place already well trodden and settled by others, this is indeed a sign of life . . ." Berdyczewski's objection to the East African program, for practical reasons, attested all the more to the benefit he saw in the conquest of a "virgin land." There, in the wilds of his imagination, the principle of innovation would reign in all its purity and the diaspora tendency "to be tied to their mother's apron strings, like little children, without trying to stand on their own feet," would melt away.

Berdyczewski was not alarmed by the specter decried by the Zionists of Zion in accusing the territorialists of a desire to "tear the Jewish people away from its past . . . and make it into a different nation." On the contrary, as far as he was concerned both camps were bound to be torn away from the Jewish past. As he commented with unabashed satisfaction: "As if they themselves, if they truly adhere to the idea of rebirth to the end, would not undergo a complete revaluation of values, of everything that is treasured in the diaspora and of everything that made them exiles in the first place." In a similar vein Ben-Yehuda wrote: "And *we all, all of us, have turned our backs* on the past, and that is greatly to our credit."[48] Territorialism was of value to Berdyczewski only as a means for expressing his attitude toward diaspora Judaism. His rejection of the diaspora characteristics led him to support the creation of a new nation,

48 Berdyczewski, *Complete Works*, Articles Volume, pp. 81-83; "Echo from the Newspapers," *Hahashkafah*, 48 (1905), p. 4 (Hebrew).

just as it had led Ben-Yehuda to embrace the Australian and Canadian models. This was a noteworthy development, for it implied not only the extrapolation of ideas embodied in Zionist ideology but a qualitative innovation, as well. There was a definite correlation between the notion of creating a new people and the search for a new country far from the "Galuth" of Europe and from the religious yearning for Palestine. By choosing such a country, the Jews would be able to join in the process of colonization that had led emigrants from Europe overseas to create new states and even new peoples. We can see a resemblance here to the paradigm of the American people, whose forefathers came from Europe, cast off their past and, rather than build upon a common national origin or religion, chose to create an entirely new people and place the accent on the future.[49]

It would thus appear that East Africa was a fitting solution for those who wished to divorce themselves from religion and from the past. Yet here we come to the great paradox of the Uganda affair: Mizrahi's support for the plan to settle in East Africa. Rabbi Isaac Jacob Reines, the leader of the religious wing of the Zionist movement, expressed complete faith in Herzl's leadership, to the point where he referred to Herzl as a "big brother" upon whom "the lives of all the House of Israel" depended. Reines accepted with regret but understanding Herzl's appraisal that the odds of obtaining a charter for Palestine were dim. In a vein similar to the distinction that Ben-Yehuda was to draw between the good of the people and the good of the country, Reines explained: "We have agreed to the African proposal because . . . the needs of the people are dearer to us than the country." For Mizrahi, then, the people took priority over the Land of Israel.

To achieve a better understanding of Reines's thinking, we should dwell on the approach of the religious circles to Zionism. Mizrahi drew a distinction between the element of nationalism, which was the province of the Zionist movement as a whole, and the religious outlook that was particular to Mizrahi as one wing of that movement. (The integral philosophy of religious Zionism that would be developed in the works of Rabbi Kook had not yet taken shape.) For

49 Kohn, *The Idea of Nationalism*, p. 276; Hans Kohn, *Nationalism: Its Meaning and History* (Princeton, 1965), p. 19.

a man like Rabbi Reines, the longing for Zion would always prevail and would never be prejudiced by the needs of the hour. As he declared in a letter to Herzl written in 1903: "As long as Israel continues to exist, the hope for Zion will not be lost." Moreover, this "hope for Zion" had nothing to do with diplomatic achievements; it was an inalienable part of the religious Jew's world view. On the other hand, Rabbi Reines did express certain misgivings about the chances of bringing political Zionism to fruition – doubts that seem to have existed well before the outbreak of the Uganda crisis. Such sentiments were implicit in the praise that he now bestowed upon those "who had kept their distance from Zionism because they did not believe in its ability to act and actually do anything" but who would evidently support the Zionist proposal to settle in Uganda. His implication was that Uganda had opened the way for Zionism to succeed, making it possible "to save a substantial portion of our people and render it whole in body and spirit."

Rabbi Reines drew a logical conclusion from the division that placed Zionist affairs in Herzl's hands and reserved matters of religion as Mizrahi's exclusive province. In contrast to the bleak prospects of realizing the Zionist idea in Palestine, the Uganda scheme appeared to be a viable enterprise, and it seemed only right to aid the Zionist leadership in implementing it. Moreover, there was no reason, in principle, to withhold support from a workable program like the Uganda scheme for the sake of the rather dubious idea of obtaining a charter for Palestine. After all, the articles of the Jewish faith would remain no less valid for having supported Jewish settlement in a place other than Palestine. As Rabbi Reines summed up his approach in writing to Herzl: "If there is no Israel . . . there is no Zion," meaning that Uganda would both save the Jews and, incidentally, perpetuate the traditional faith in the return to Zion. We can conclude from this statement that Rabbi Reines's conception of "Zion" was basically identical to the anticipation of redemption that informed the ultra-Orthodox world view. Thus religious faith could exist side by side with political activity but have no direct bearing upon worldly decisions. The Uganda issue was not a matter for theological debate; it was a question of *Realpolitik*.

We find an illustration of this position in a reference to Rabbi Reines's work on behalf of the Uganda scheme within the Mizrahi movement itself. Rabbi Meir Berlin (Bar-Ilan) related in his memoirs that Reines had portrayed the minority in Mizrahi, who were opposed to Uganda, as "young, impractical people; hence they fail to appreciate the practical value of settling Uganda, which will help if not all the Jews, at least hundreds of thousands of them." Bar-Ilan, who was himself opposed to settlement in Uganda, observed of this assessment: "It is not surprising that Rabbi Reines spoke of Uganda in this way, for even people who were more worldly-wise than he, regarded Uganda as a very 'practical' and workable venture."[50]

Rabbi Abraham Isaac Kook, then the chief of the Rabbinical Court of Jaffa and the surrounding Jewish colonies, took a generally neutral stand on Uganda – though he was disposed to honor Mizrahi's position despite the fact that he did not belong to that movement. In 1905 he wrote an "open letter to our young brothers living on the holy soil" in which he disputed the views of the "editor of *Hahashkafah*," Eliezer Ben-Yehuda. Ben-Yehuda had used his paper to answer the charge, of the Zionists of Zion, that "the Ugandists were turning their backs on our entire past." "What hypocrisy!" Ben-Yehuda fumed. "People who have themselves *turned their backs on our past* accusing others of doing the same! For we must not deceive ourselves. Only the members of the committee for the 'Search for Sin' (meaning religious bigots) have not turned against our past." And then came the startling sentence: "And *we all, all of us, have turned our backs* on the past, and that is greatly to our credit." Further on Ben-Yehuda quoted at length from Tawiow's piece favoring the rejection of the past and exclaimed: "Words of truth!"

Sharply denouncing Ben-Yehuda's stance, Rabbi Kook argued that there were "honest folk who truly love their people" among the supporters of Uganda, just as there were among the Zionists of Zion. What's more, such people could likewise be found "among those who oppose the precept of the Zionist movement altogether." After calling for tolerance, he denied that the advocates of Uganda

---

50 Letter from Reines to Herzl in Heymann, ed., *The Uganda Controversy*, Vol. II, p. 180; Meir Berlin, *From Volozhin to Jerusalem*, Vol II. (Tel Aviv, 1940), p. 4 (Hebrew); Abraham Isaac Kook, *The Lights of Penitence* (New York, 1978), p. xiii.

renounced the past and cited as his evidence "the members of Miz-rahi, whom no one can suspect of turning their backs on all of the past, and yet they are Ugandists."[51] For the most part, the ideological disparity between the parties supporting Uganda for different reasons reached its height in this exchange. When the Zionists of Zion accused the Ugandists of negating the past, Ben-Yehuda charged them with hypocrisy, for he believed that all were partners to the negation of the past – with the exception of a handful of fanatic ultra-Orthodox Jews. Rabbi Kook, on the other hand, attributed the negation of the past to a marginal group comprising "the editor of *Hahashkafah* and those who imbibe his brew."

We must bear in mind that Rabbi Kook probably took the catch phrase "negation of the past" to mean the renunciation of religion, whereas Ben-Yehuda – like Berdyczewski and Tawiow – extended the concept to embrace criticism of Jewish history and particularly of diaspora Jewry. One may conclude that the territorialist ideology was a radicalized form of the negation of the past, which had at any rate been one thread in the fabric of Zionism throughout its history. The members of Mizrahi remained on the sidelines of the ideological struggle during the Uganda crisis, just as they had remained aloof from the ideas contested in the debate over cultural work. Their position was unique because of the dichotomy which then obtained between religious faith and their participation in Zionist activities. Hence contrary to Rabbi Kook's premise, they could serve as neither a standard for the conduct of other circles in the Zionist movement nor as proof of the Ugandists' devotion to the past.

Another group that was put to a severe ideological test by the Uganda controversy was the Zionist Socialists. We have already referred to Nachman Syrkin's support for Herzl's proposal at the Sixth Congress. Presumably, settlement in Uganda was a logical corollary of the socialist world view, oriented as it was toward solving the pressing problems of the masses. Yet Syrkin's support for Uganda was just the opening stage of Zionist Socialism's internal strife and search for a consistent policy. At the outbreak of the Uganda crisis, the Zionist Socialists were not yet an organized party

---

51 Abraham Isaac Hacohen Kook, *Letters* of Evidence (Jerusalem, 1962), pp. 16-17 (Hebrew); "Echo from the Newspapers," *Hahashkafah*, 48 (1905), p. 4.

and were best described as a conglomeration of cells with varying ideological orientations. This is not the place to enter upon a description of these orientations. Suffice it to say that the Zionist Socialists were divided not only on questions related strictly to Zionism but over their approach to Socialism, as well.[52] We shall confine ourselves to dividing the Zionist Socialists into three principle categories, based on their attitude toward Palestine – and even here the division will necessarily be schematic. The three general approaches were:

* The advocacy of territorialism as a matter of principle.
* A conditional commitment to Palestine.
* A categorical commitment to Palestine.

Those who supported territorialism as a matter of principle espoused the idea of "the economic-political freedom of the broad Jewish masses." They decried the "romantic blindness" of those who aspired to revive "traditions that have survived in the popular psyche as pale, imaginary forms from the past." The manifesto of the Zionist Socialist Workers Party, framed in anticipation of the Seventh Zionist Congress, warned against the attempt to turn Zionism into "a cultural-educational movement in which the broad Jewish masses will be charged with working to fulfill the spiritual-traditional needs of the small minority in Palestine." The issue of "historic rights" was also discredited in this context, even though here it signified a mere attachment to Palestine, not a claim to ownership or sovereignty.

In defending territorialism, the theoretician Daniel Pasmanik argued that its chief motive was "to make the immediate emigration of the masses possible" and that the negative attitude toward Palestine had been exacerbated by the struggle against the Zionists of Zion and the need to repress the "instinctive love" for the country. Nachman Syrkin's declaration when the Zionist movement split at the Seventh Congress, after the opponents of territorialism had carried the day, was made up of two elements. First he expressed his opposition to reducing the scope of Zionist activity to Palestine,

---

52 Jacob Kenner, *A Cross-Cut* (New York, 1947), pp. 82-83 (Yiddish); and Singer, *Early Zionist Socialism*, pp. 294, 313.

which, he complained, was "unable to offer the minimum conditions necessary to realize our ideal." In essence, he contrasted the needs of the "broad masses of the Jewish proletariat" with what he termed the "petty colonization" in Palestine. This was the practical basis of his position; it was followed by an ideological motive. For Syrkin spoke of Palestine as "a dying tradition of the goal-unconscious and uncultured part of the Jewish masses." His delivery was interrupted by both outraged objections and enthusiastic applause as he branded his adversaries as pursuers of the "reactionary-nationalist" ideal.[53]

Even if the opposition to Palestine was designed to repress the instinctive support for it, as Pasmanik claimed, this in no way detracted from the vehemence of the argument that was aired in public. Territorialism regarded Palestine as the symbol of reaction and romantic longings for the past (in contrast to its self-image of being anchored in reality and boasting a progressive social character). It is in this light that one may appreciate the position of the faction that was prepared to support Palestine conditionally, that is, if it proved to be a practical solution to the Jewish problem. In 1904, for example, the members of Poalei Zion in Minsk adopted a resolution whose negative wording smacked of territorialist influence: "The fact that we are bound to Palestine by historic memories is of importance only insofar as we choose it over every other country when the possibility of realizing [Zionism] in Palestine becomes manifest. But we do not regard historic memories from so long ago as an historic factor of such great import that it precludes the rebirth of the Jewish people occurring elsewhere." The concept "historic," used repeatedly in this passage, has a different meaning each time. The expression "historic memories," for example, related solely to the past and had no active effect on the present, whereas the "historic factor" was a force that made history and therefore had a bearing upon the present and the future.

To examine the crystallization of the position that actively affirmed Palestine, we must first trace the rather tortuous development of Zionist-Socialist thinking. At the start of 1905 Shlomo

---

53 *Socialist Territorialism*, p. 144; Daniel Pasmanik, "Zeit und Streitfragen im Zionismus," *Die Welt* (March 3, 1905), p. 3; Dr. Syrkin in *Verhandlungen des VII Zionisten-Kongresses* (Berlin, 1905), p. 135.

Kaplansky, among the leading figures of the Zionist-Socialist movement, set forth his thinking on Palestine's standing in the Poalei Zion doctrine. In terms of the past, it was "the land in which we lived the greatest and proudest part of our history." In terms of the present, he distinguished between "the scientific content of the Jewish idea of liberty" – which was an abstract striving for territory – and the "shell around our core, which is called Zion." Kaplansky synthesized this abstract content with "its historical form" – namely Palestine – by availing himself of "the will of the people." That brings us to the argument – which had already been aired in the debate between Zeitlin and Jabotinsky – over the nature of the "people's will," or to the strategy of invoking the will of the generations to come, as Lilienblum did. Kaplansky believed that territorialism followed an abstract-intellectual approach, whereas the "will of the people" was "something complex and involved: it is not intellect, not feeling, not pain, and not longing, but all of them combined." And when he wrote these words, it was clear to Kaplansky that the amorphous thing he called the "will of the people" could not prevail without the tangible goal of Palestine.

It is also worthwhile dwelling on the resemblance that Kaplansky saw between Zionism and two other national movements. The first was the Italian Risorgimento – an observation that, in itself, was little more than the reiteration of a common simile. Then, however, he made reference to "the establishment of the Negro republic of Liberia," and that was a completely original insight, not only because he was speaking of blacks but because the case of Liberia was unique. As an attempt to resettle freed slaves from the United States in Africa, it differed radically from the paradigm of national movements in Europe, which strove to liberate their countries from foreign subjugation. In addition to being an instance of founding a new country based on immigrants from overseas, the Liberian model featured the theme of the return to Africa, the continent in which the forefathers of these immigrants had originated. Thus it bore a striking resemblance to both the territorialist idea of finding a new country for the Jews and to the Return to Zion (Psalms 126:1), or the restoration of the Jews to their original homeland. Kaplansky's conclusion was that while Zionism should focus on Palestine, there was also room for forces outside the Zionist Organization to try to secure Uganda.[54]

This thinking was also typical of the more moderate Zionists of Zion, who wished to retain the option of settlement in East Africa without conclusively committing the Zionist movement to the venture. It was also the view taken by Hillel Zlatopolsky in 1903, when he served as an acting member of the Zionist Executive, representing the Zionists of Russia, and suggested: "If the expedition finds the country [Uganda] to be pleasing, let us turn the matter over to various societies, such as ICA, the Alliance Israélite Universelle, and B'nai B'rith; they should deal with the matter." At the same time, Zlatopolsky warned against the phenomenon of territorialism gone overboard and complained of those "who had begun to chant Psalms and would demand Uganda as an absolute necessity." Similarly, Rabbi Meir Berlin (Bar-Ilan) complained of his colleagues who were so enchanted by the idea of Uganda that "they had concocted a theory that Mizrahi and Ugandism were one and the same."[55]

Let us come back to Zionist Socialism, however. From Kaplansky's moderately pro-Palestine stance, the path led on to the militantly pro-Palestinian views of Ber Borochov. In a series of articles on "The Question of Zion and Territory", published in 1905, Borochov identified himself as an historical materialist. He set down three distinct objectives and ranked them in order of priority: the liberation of the people, the return to the ancient homeland, and the revival of Hebrew culture. For Borochov it was beyond question that "the most important and decisive of them all is the rescue and liberation of the people," though fidelity to Zion was to remain in effect "until it is proved that Palestine is locked before the Jewish people." Borochov objected to the "spiritual-national" line of argument on the grounds that "not *all of the past* determines the future," though he conceded that "there can be no nationalism without a past." In

---

54 Singer, *Early Zionist Socialism*, p. 304; Ben Barachel, "An Interpretation of Zionism," *Der Yudisher Arbeter* (February 10, 1905), p. 2, (March 1, 1905), p. 5 (Yiddish) and cf. Theodore Draper, *The Rediscovery of Black Nationalism* (New York, 1970), pp. 8-9.

55 Hillel Zlatopolski, "Uganda at Basel," *Hatzfirah* (October 15, 1903), p. 1 (Hebrew); Berlin, *From Volozhin to Jerusalem*, Vol. II, p. 4.

the final analysis Borochov believed not only that Palestine offered the most desirable solution but that it did so "due to historic necessity."

Borochov's chief contribution to the struggle for Palestine was in fighting Socialist Territorialism with its own weapons. He portrayed the Palestinian objective not as a spiritual or romantic goal but as "the recognition of the law of development of Jewish life" (Shazar). In other words, through his analysis Borochov arrived at what he called "synthetic Zionism" by merging the past and the present. The past was no longer a dead era; instead it served the same dialectic function that the Marxist doctrine ascribed to history, so that progress was conceived as an organic development tracing to the past.[56]

To sum up, the point that was common to all the Zionist Socialists was the stress they placed on the actual needs of the Jewish masses. Historical attachment – to the degree that it played a role in their thinking, as in the works of Kaplansky and Borochov – took second place. Thus the Zionist-Socialist attitude was closer to Herzl's concern over the "predicament of the Jews" than to Ahad Ha'am's approach. It was their position on fulfilling the needs of the masses that drove the Zionist Socialists to seek out comprehensive, quick solutions, like the order of magnitude proposed by political Zionism. Hence they were far removed from the modest Palestinian-settlement program that had been the darling of the practical Zionists since the days of the Love of Zion. Add to this their disdain for the "dying tradition" and the romanticism of the past and you have the reasons why many of the Zionist Socialists supported first Uganda and then territorialism.

A Complete Realignment

As long as Herzl was alive, there was no doubt – notwithstanding the rival camps within the movement – of the dominant direction of Zionism. Political Zionism set the tone, and Herzl enjoyed both

56 Matityahu Mintz, *Ber Borokhov* (Tel Aviv, 1976), p. 10 (Hebrew); Borochov, *Selected Works*, Vol. I (Tel Aviv, 1944), pp. xxxix, 20, 21, 23, 33, 56, 57, 66, 89, 146.

the movement's confidence and an aura of prestige that may have
been tarnished to some extent but was certainly not destroyed by
the Uganda crisis. After his untimely death, however, the Zionist
movement was racked not only by a leadership crisis but by a complete realignment of forces. The clash between the Zionists of Zion
and the supporters of Uganda gave rise to doubts about the cardinal
precepts of the Basel Program – meaning both the viability of Palestine as the objective of Zionism and political activity as the means
of obtaining it. Just as territorialism had arisen as a categorical
opposition to Palestine, so practical Zionism now offered itself as an
alternative to the Herzlian approach. What's more, there was a certain overlap between the practical Zionists and the Zionists of Zion,
on the one hand, and the political Zionists and the territorialists, on
the other – leading to confusion in the ranks and an atmosphere of
turmoil on the leadership level.[57]

Considering this state of affairs, Theodor Zlocisti's fear that
Ussishkin's followers might lead the movement to deemphasize its
"political character" is understandable. Zlocisti was one of the political Zionists who had remained faithful to Palestine. Hence there is
a certain irony in the fact that in an article published in February
1905, he used an argument that Ahad Ha'am's disciples had usually
wielded against Herzl. Zlocisti feared that Zionism would deterio-
rate into a philanthropic society for Palestine appealing to the
"historical attachment to the old homeland" and came out sharply
against this prospect in proclaiming, "For us the national idea is not
historic-romantic drivel." The author of a biography of Moses Hess,
Zlocisti had earlier devoted himself to cultivating the historical
approach. Yet here he was speaking in strongly anti-historical terms.
It seems that Zlocisti had his sight trained on two trends that nour-
ished the coalition of the Zionists of Zion: the tradition of philanthropic settlement dating to the days of the First Aliyah, and the
Ahad Ha'amist approach that aspired to establish in Palestine a
"spiritual-national center." Moreover, he assailed this coalition as a
mixture of philanthropic activity and historic romanticism, as if to

57 Mordechai Eliav, *David Wolffsohn* (Jerusalem, 1977), pp. 18-20, 27-30
    (Hebrew).

say that Ahad Ha'am's doctrine was merely an intellectual cover for settlement in the style of the Lovers of Zion.[58]

Berthold Feiwel of the Democratic Fraction challenged Zlocisti by advancing the diametrically opposite view in praising the "historic-romantic" element in Zionism and dismissing the prospect of mass emigration. In Feiwel's scheme of things, there was little point in generating sympathy for Zionism among the Powers, if it were built upon "*the predicament of the Jews* and upon *egoism.*" Much to the contrary, the basis of Zionism had to be positive and moral. Here Feiwel proposed a rather vague formula, based upon "historic, cultural, and liberationist claims and rights," as a means of generating sympathy for the renaissance of the Jewish people – much as enthusiasm had been roused by the Greek war of independence in its time. We may well wonder why Feiwel believed his formula was more moral, positive, and likely to be acceptable to the Powers than the brief presented by political Zionism. In essence he did not dispute political Zionism's premise that the support of the Powers must be sought. But in contrast to Herzl – who pandered to the interests of the Powers – Feiwel wanted to acquire their support on moral grounds. And rather than endorse the contrariety of prophets and diplomats (as posited by Ahad Ha'am), he seemed to be trying to enlist prophecy in the service of diplomacy.

Feiwel's criticism of Herzlian Zionism was also directed at the illusion that it ensured swift solutions. He argued that "only those who believed that Zionism was meant to cast masses of people into Palestine tomorrow or the day after will be impatient and back out. Only those for whom Zionism is an 'historic-romantic' affair of the heart, hard work from one obstacle to the next, will be persistent and grow ever stronger." This combination of a new political orientation and a call for patience indicates that Feiwel was aiming not for a spiritual center but for the realization of Zionism in a gradual manner. One of the architects of practical work, he symbolized the mood that would ultimately lead to the domination of the evolution-

---

58 Theodor Zlocisti, "Zur Situation im Zionismus," *Jüdische Rundschau* (February 10, 1905), p. 60.

ary approach and the renewal of practical work in both Palestine and the diaspora.[59]

This mood also found expression in a series of articles written by Daniel Pasmanik, analyzing the situation from the Zionist-Socialist viewpoint. Pasmanik insisted upon preserving the popular nature of Zionism as a movement that had arisen to meet the real needs of the Jewish masses. He advocated both mass settlement in Palestine and the surrounding countries and practical work in the diaspora. He also attacked Feiwel as the representative of the "cultural Zionists" who determined that "mass settlement is impossible" – or so Pasmanik interpreted his stance – and therefore elevated practical work to an aim in its own right. But he then warned against Ussishkin's brand of practical Zionism, for fear that it might lead back to small-scale settlement in the spirit of the Lovers of Zion. Incidentally, Pasmanik confessed that for a time he had supported the Uganda scheme in the belief that the Jewish people was strong enough to fight "on two fronts," but he withdrew his support when the territorialists began to "preach against Palestine." Like Kaplansky and Zlatopolsky, he wanted to turn the settlement in East Africa over to non-Zionist bodies. He remained a political Zionist in his striving for broad and swift solutions and continued to believe that mass settlement would be possible within the Ottoman Empire, since "the Jews do not aspire to have an army of their own and ambassadors of their own." Pasmanik was convinced that eventually the Turks would recognize the benefit they stood to gain from Jewish settlement and the Zionists' loyalty to their regime.

On the face of it, there was little substantive difference between Pasmanik and Feiwel: both supported practical work, in Palestine as well as in the diaspora. Where they differed was in their perception of the quantitative element and the time factor, which were vital considerations for Pasmanik and of little consequence to Feiwel.[60] Once again one can see that these two factors – time and scope –

59 Berthold Feiwel, "Zur Situation im Zionismus," *Jüdische Rundschau* (February 17, 1905), pp. 73-74.

60 D. Pasmanik, "Zeit und Streitfragen im Zionismus," *Die Welt* (March 3, 1905), pp. 3, 4; (March 17, 1905), p. 3; (April 7, 1905), p. 4; Berthold Feiwel, "Zum Artikel: Zeitund Streitfragen im Zionismus," *Die Welt* (March 17, 1905), p. 4.

were of crucial importance to the Zionist Socialists. Pasmanik wished to resolve the seeming contradiction between the broad vision of Zionism and the small scale of settlement by expanding the scope of the settlement enterprise in Palestine and its vicinity. This solution was envisioned as an alternative to both territorialism and practical Zionism. Another attempt to resolve the same contradiction was that of the young Zionist-Socialist leader Ber Borochov.

Borochov's article "On Questions of Zionist Theory" opens with the words "We must not wait," while another article (assailing territorialism) written in that same year was already referring to Zionism as an "historical process." A year earlier Borochov had written to his parents, "It is possible that the Jewish people will return to Palestine *quickly, in our own day*"; yet now he was arguing that "We cannot agree to the need to make haste." This turnabout in valuing the time factor had implications for both defining the social agent of Zionism and establishing the means to attain its goal. While deploring haste, Borochov nevertheless determined the need for concrete action. At that time, his followers were deliberating "the gradual and inexorable growth of the Jewish positions in Palestine." This formulation indicates a shift away from the Zionist-Socialist tenet of a quick, mass solution toward an evolutionary approach; and together with this shift, Borochov's thinking began to show signs of avant-garde leanings. For viewing the realization of Zionism as a gradual process precluded the activation of the masses – at least for the time being – and implied an "*avant-garde* [pioneering] *enterprise*" by groups of idealists, instead. Only later, as the young Borochov saw it, would this venture turn into "*a popular enterprise,*" bringing the Jewish masses into the movement.[61]

This meant that Borochov's activities in the framework of the Zionists of Zion entailed identifying with the idea of pioneering work in Palestine, and, indeed, he found an acceptable Zionist parallel to the avant-garde socialist doctrine. It was fine for its day, though later Borochov was to underscore the "stychic process" involved in the realization of Zionism. Here, however, we shall limit ourselves

---

61 Borochov, *Selected Works*, pp. xxxviii, 52, 105-106; Mintz, *Ber Borokhov*, pp. 92-99, 243.

to the stage at which Borochov began to perceive Zionism as a gradual process and arrived at pioneering as an operative conclusion. In terms of these two points, there was a certain similarity between Borochov's thinking and views that had already taken root within Zionism, particularly in the Democratic Fraction. Suffice it to recall the avant-gardism of Weizmann and Klausner and the evolutionary approach found in Feiwel's writings – which soon became the dominant view within Zionism – to say nothing of the influence wielded by Menahem Ussishkin, practical Zionism's Man of Iron.

Hence the struggle against territorialism gave rise to certain shared modes of thinking among the Zionists of Zion, despite the obvious differences between the practical Zionists, spiritual Zionists, and certain Zionist Socialists collected under that heading. The common front that emerged in the struggle for Palestine also led to internal changes that, in turn, spawned similar approaches on other issues as well. Political Zionism, in contrast, found its most cogent expression among the territorialists, who – like Ben-Yehuda – expected an immediate change to follow from the revision of the Jews' political status – or, as anticipated by the Zionist Socialist Territorialist Party, a quick solution for the broad masses. In effect, those who remained in the Zionist movement after the departure of the territorialists diluted the wine of political Zionism with the water of the other currents that had been latent, marginal, or oppositional until then.

To describe the state of the Zionist movement following the Seventh Congress, we shall cite the testimony of the political Zionist Moshe Kleinmann. Like Zlocisti before him, Kleinmann had warned that the victory of the Zionists of Zion would turn into a triumph for small-scale settlement. He was the first to appreciate the dynamic of the struggle between the two opposing trends within Zionism. Kleinmann discerned the tension that had existed between political and practical Zionism as far back as the First Zionist Congress and remarked on the "psychological wont" that had developed out of it. He observed that each of these two trends was subject to "the moral supervision" of the other, explaining that this resulted in a situation whereby "Zionism tried to please the Lovers of Zion and vice versa, even though they were simultaneously fighting each other." The focal issue of the struggle between them was, in Kleinmann's rendering, "deeds." He indicated that the political

Zionists were far more sensitive to the moral pressure of the practical Zionists than vice versa. Kleinmann even hypothesized that "this psychology may have been what *drove* Herzl and his supporters to clutch at Uganda as the first thing of real substance." In portraying this clash between the two trends as a constant theme within the history of Zionism, Kleinmann gave added weight to Ahad Ha'am's premise that it was not by chance that political Zionism found its way to Uganda, for its very nature bore signs of where it would lead. As it happened, Kleinmann himself favored Palestine (though he was opposed to the "dogmatism of the Holy Land"), but in retrospect he conceded that political Zionism and Uganda were "psychologically intertwined."

Kleinmann's piece reflected the defensive posture of the political Zionists after the territorialists had broken with the Zionist Organization. It also bespoke a need to repair the ideological breaches that the Uganda crisis and the split in the movement had wrought in political Zionism. The sense of inadequacy – alluded to by Kleinmann – in face of the practical Zionists' demand for concrete action was of special import. (Kleinmann's style in describing the conflict over "action" brings to mind the theological debate over man's works versus God's grace.[62]) Furthermore, the existence of the territorialist movement as an independent entity outside the Zionist fold created a new political reality and forced those who hesitated, or preferred sitting on the proverbial fence, to define themselves one way or the other. Up to the point of the actual split, Zionism had been in the throes of a struggle between rival schools and factions. But the internal debates, bitter as they may have been, could hardly be compared to a clash between two competing movements – especially when both had derived from the same source but differed on the authoritative interpretation of the original doctrine and the rightful legacy of the mother movement. After the split each of the movements took measures to unite its ranks and deploy for war against the other. And it was in the course of that development that a process of rethinking took place. Thus the clash between Zionism

---

62 Moshe Kleinmann, "The Seventh Congress," *Yudisher Folkskalender* (1905/-1906), pp. 126, 131, 132, 133 (Yiddish). cf. A.C. Bouquet, *Comparative Religion* (Harmondsworth, 1954), p. 204.

and territorialism was no longer over the question of Palestine alone, but over the basic precepts of the national movement.[63]

To illustrate the change in the Zionists' attitude toward the territorialists, we shall follow Nahum Sokolow, the Zionist *arbiter elegantiarum*. Sokolow had abstained in the vote on East Africa at the Sixth Zionist Congress but subsequently defended the supporters of Uganda in writing, "It is not true that they have trampled upon any principle!" Yet by 1905 he was already remarking derisively on the philanthropic trend taking shape within the territorialist movement. Commenting on Zangwill's efforts to raise support among the leaders of German Jewry, Sokolow wrote: "Mr. Zangwill has not come on behalf of some Zion – Turkey – Asia Minor, but on behalf of England, colonization. This is a sweet, soft, youthful tune. It rings almost like good tidings. And when the Russian Jews are concentrated in Surinam, how will the assimilation of the Jews in Germany be the worse for it?"

Of course Sokolow's barbs were directed primarily against the search for a country other than Palestine. Yet he also implied that it was more convenient for the assimilationists to support territorialism than Zionism. Later in the same paragraph he stated: "If, for instance, a Jewish center were established in Palestine – even if only by the Russian Jews, or the Rumanians, or whom you will – this center would necessarily have an influence over the Jews even [as far away as] Australia because of the power of an historic center. But in Uganda, or in Manchuria, does it make much of a difference whether the Russian Jews are scattered or gathered together?" Note the implicit allusion to the motive of prestige that emerges from the ironic juxtaposition of "England, colonization" with "some Zion – Turkey – Asia Minor" – almost a reverse analogy to what he had written in praise of Palestine and against "some China, some Patagonia." It appears that Sokolow failed to sense the contradiction between the earlier and later parts of the paragraph quoted here. On the one hand he charged the assimilationists with harboring a measure of contempt for Palestine ("Asia Minor"), but at the same time he established that it was precisely the centrality of Palestine that

63 David Isaac Marmor, "The Diplomatic Negotiations of the I.T.O. and Reasons for Its Failure," *Zion*, 11 (1946), p. 110 (Hebrew).

was a thorn in their sides. Perhaps this paradox reflected the ambivalence that Sokolow himself felt toward Palestine as the "historic
center" but nonetheless part of the decaying Ottoman Empire. In
any event, Sokolow portrayed territorialism as being designed to
relieve Western Jews of the threat that Jewish immigrants from Russia
and Rumania would stand in the way of their own assimilation.[64]

This depiction was indeed vindicated by events once the Jewish
Territorial Organization (I.T.O.) began to function as an independent
entity. The most conspicuous indication to that effect came when
the prominent journalist and leader Lucien Wolf joined Zangwill's
movement. In 1896 Wolf and Zangwill had been members of the
Maccabean Society in London, when Herzl repeatedly approached
it with his idea for a Jewish state. Zangwill, who was to become a
Zionist, actually responded more negatively than his colleague Wolf,
whose name would in the course of time become synonymous with
anti-Zionism. Now that Zangwill had left the Zionist movement and
founded the territorialist organization, the two men entered into
talks on the terms under which Wolf would join the new movement.
Wolf, who at first opposed the plan for Jewish settlement in East
Africa, was now persuaded that since it had been divorced from
Zionism, the project was deserving of his support. Once the two men
reached an understanding, they published an exchange of letters that
was effectively a programmatic agreement on cooperation between
assimilationists and nationalists to assuage the suffering of Russian
Jewry. Lucien Wolf's letter of September 1, 1905, stated that he was
prepared to join the I.T.O. so as not to miss "the historic chance"
offered by the British government in allowing the Jews to found a
"Self-governing Colony" in one of the uninhabited areas of the
empire. At the opening of his letter, Wolf stressed that he had not
changed his position on Zionism in the least, "We Jews have out-
grown the uninational stage of our history, and we have far larger
destinies to fulfil in our Dispersion." This was not abstract theory,
for further on in the letter Wolf asserted that the solution for the

---

64 N. S. (Sokolow), "The Foundations of the Renaissance (3): Where Did the
Many Go Wrong?" *Hatzfirah* (December 7, 1903), p. 1 (Hebrew); N. S., "Mr.
Zangwill's Travels and the Hearts He Won," *Hatzfirah* (September 14, 1905),
p. 2 (Hebrew).

Jews of Russia lay in a struggle "for the liberation of the whole Russian people," not in emigration.

How did Wolf nevertheless justify his support for a Jewish colony? He drew a distinction between the political issue – which affected the Jews as well as the rest of the Russian population – and the social deprivation that was driving many Jews to leave Russia in any case. Considering these circumstances, Jewish emigration might as well be channelled to a British colony where the Jews would constitute a majority. However, Wolf was careful to qualify that a Jewish majority was in no way destined "to make a sort of Ghetto or 'native reservation' out of the proposed colony." He made it sound as if the Zionists had made their acceptance of the British proposal conditional upon "reviving an obsolete polity and . . . crystallising so-called national customs and modes of life which are not essentially Jewish." Wolf expressed his readiness to join the I.T.O. at that point because, in his words, it no longer intended "to perpetuate the alien condition of the colonists in the land of their adoption." Further on he made reference to the separation of church and state and the reign of British law in the Jewish colony, as in the other colonies of the empire. The only statement suggesting any national aspect was Wolf's hope that the settlement would be "a source of happiness to many thousands of Jews and of pride to our entire people."

When Zangwill confirmed receipt of the letter about a week later, he was full of enthusiasm, in contrast to Wolf's skepticism and reserve. He argued that British law left room for domestic legislation to answer the needs of the population in the colonies and reasoned that "the spiritual genius of our race, which once found expression in Mosaic legislation and prophetic aspiration, will again be inspired to contribute to civilisation sociological improvements suited to these latter days." At the same time he complained that the territory in East Africa that had been offered to the Zionists was neither large enough nor fertile enough, and argued for a place with brighter economic prospects. Neither did he discount the idea of abandoning the British orientation altogether and entering into negotiations with other Powers.

Wolf and Zangwill evidently differed on the issue of whether the Jews should emigrate from Russia or participate in the struggle against the czarist regime with the aim of achieving emancipation.

At this stage Zangwill still followed Herzl's formulation in declaring that territorialism was meant for "those Jews who cannot, or will not, remain in the lands in which they at present live." As for the role that religion would play in the future colony, he agreed with the principle of separation of church and state but believed that the official day of rest should be Saturday. The conclusion that followed from the exchange of letters was that the two had arrived at "the grounds . . . on which to cooperate," namely, a compromise between Zangwill's nationalist outlook and Wolf's old-school diplomacy. The letters would subsequently be regarded as a seminal document of the new organization, and the compromise reached therein would play a pivotal role in shaping its character and future course. To fully understand this compromise, we must first appreciate the gap that existed between these two men. Wolf was prepared to support a program that had earlier been far too Zionist for his taste, just so that the British offer would not be spurned. Zangwill subscribed to the Zionists' criticism of the proposed territory and forgot that the proposal to settle in East Africa had been the cause of the crisis over which he had split with Zionism. The British orientation was thus a vital requisite for Wolf and a political expedient for Zangwill. Yet we should note that the selection of a territory, which was a matter of principle for the Zionists, was merely a tactical question for them both. Thus they were able to join forces in support of a common platform that embodied constructive aid for emigration from Russia and a concerted struggle against Zionism.[65]

All this considered, there was little sense to Leopold Greenberg's interpretation of this alliance as a promise of future cooperation between Zionism and territorialism. Greenberg, always the political Zionist, claimed that the merit Wolf now saw in the Uganda scheme had actually been there from the start and that the Zionists had supported the same principles that Wolf now espoused. He construed Wolf's move as a sign that he was veering toward Jewish nationalism, though still "hesitant about taking the full course." What's more, Greenberg was prepared to welcome the new territorialist program and rest content with this limited version of Jewish autonomy,

---

65 Jewish Territorial Organisation, "Correspondence Between Mr. Lucien Wolf and Mr. Israel Zangwill," *The Jewish Chronicle* (September 15, 1905), p. 16.

relinquishing the hopes he had expressed in 1903 about the definitively Jewish character of Uganda. Yet his words rang like a lone cry
in the wilderness, since the two movements had in the meantime
grown ever farther apart and continued to move in diametrically
opposite directions.[66]

Some three months later the I.T.O. published a manifesto in reply
to the attack – by the leaders of the British Jewish community – on
its proposed solution to the problem of Russian Jewry. The document quoted the exchange of letters between Wolf and Zangwill as
proof that the organization did not intend to establish a "Ghetto
State." It spoke sympathetically of Russian Jews and denied that
they were merely "emigrant beggars," as they appeared to the Jewish
philanthropists in England. Among the things singled out for praise
in the document was the Bund's struggle for liberty in Russia, in the
spirit of what Wolf had written to Zangwill upon joining the movement. Yet the manifesto also reflected Zangwill's nationalist leanings, for it stated that the establishment of a "model British Colony
with a Jewish majority in the population will be the best answer to
anti-Semitism everywhere." Yet alongside this confident pronouncement is the confession that "our colony can be of little immediate
help." One might have thought that the territorialists would subscribe to Ben-Yehuda's thesis that the very founding of a Jewish colony would immediately improve the Jews' status in the world. But
that was not the case. In fact, the manifesto was pessimistic about
the prospects for Russian Jewry even were it to obtain "complete
civic rights."

The operative part of the document was a proposal for cooperation between the leaders of British Jewry and the I.T.O. It asserted
that there was no difference between the customary assistance to
Jewish migrants and the establishment of a Jewish colony. Moreover,
it reasoned that while Jewish immigrants would be eagerly received
by the members of their families in the colony, there was reason to
fear that the governments of other countries would be strongly
opposed to Jewish immigration. Signed by nineteen members of the
I.T.O. council, the manifesto was couched in terms that reflected
their various outlooks, while offering a conciliatory hand to Lord

66 Greenberg's letter in *The Jewish Chronicle* (September 15, 1905), p. 16.

Rothschild and his associates, who had earlier attacked territorialism. It contained a mixture of national and philanthropic ingredients, but there was no doubt about its ultimate point, which was attested by a number of features. The most important was the absence of any mention of a Jewish problem outside of Russia. Another was its specific citation of the Bund for its "brave deeds" as a symbol of the uncompromising struggle against czarism. A third was its reference to British statesmen who had backed the idea of a Jewish colony, as a source of benefit to the empire, while no other Power was mentioned by name. Finally there was the denial that the I.T.O. aspired to create a "Ghetto State," which was an unmistakable allusion to Zionism and Jewish nationalism. All in all, the manifesto was an important step toward establishing the I.T.O.'s credentials in the Anglo-Jewish community as an organization capable of advancing the cause of emigration from Russia without departing from the consensus that united British Jewry.[67]

As the Jewish Territorialist Organization is not the subject of this work, this is not the place to trace its development after parting ways with Zionism. One may arrive at various assessments of the extent to which its character was already embodied in the Uganda scheme or was even latent in political Zionism, as Ahad Ha'am and his disciples argued. However, it is beyond question that from the time of the break with the Zionist Organization, the current running counter to Zionism grew steadily stronger in the I.T.O., regarding both the choice of a territory and the tenets of Jewish nationalism. To some degree the thinking introduced in the 1880s by Judah Leib Levin and Uri Wolf Rabinowitz – who had cast aspersions on the Zionist idea out of opposition to the historical associations with the Holy Land – had now come full circle. It would be worthwhile to compare the direction taken by the I.T.O. to that of the Socialist-Territorialist movement in Russia, which was clearly involved with grass-roots politics. Such a comparison would help elucidate whether the philanthropic direction taken by the I.T.O. stemmed from a waning of public interest and the need to court new political supporters or from the inner logic of the territorial idea when dissociated from any concrete setting. And, of course, in the case of both the I.T.O. and the

67 "The Russo-Jewish Committee's Letter," *The Jewish Chronicle* (December 15, 1905), p. 23.

Russian territorialists, one must take into account the dynamic of the competition with Zionism, which dictated political strategy while influencing ideological content.

For the sake of comparison, if we now examine the Zionist response to territorialism, we will find – in addition to motifs dating back to the period of the Uganda crisis – numerous references to the territorialists' secession. Elias Auerbach, one of the early German immigrants to Palestine, wrote of that dramatic event at the Seventh Zionist Congress: "We have divested ourselves of some scrap metal. They were alien material." To his way of thinking, those who had broken with Zionism "had never been Zionists" in the first place. Further on Auerbach explained the difference between Zionism and territorialism in writing: "*Zionism accentuated and affirmed the historical and the national, as opposed to the economic.*" He believed that the Seventh Congress had endorsed this choice and was therefore the most important of the Zionist congresses since 1897. Osias Thon referred to this same matter a year later, by which time territorialism was already competing with Zionism, in postulating: "The only fundamental difference between these two organizations is that Zionism is based upon an existing empirical feeling – love, the Jews' adoring romantic love for Palestine – whereas territorialism disdains romanticism of any kind and wants to solve the nation's problem drily, like an arithmetical exercise." Further on he asserted that history shows "the imponderabilia of the nation's soul" to be the basic element in the building of a people and a state. Here Thon reiterated the familiar slogan, dating back to Zionism's earliest days, that the Jewish people was about to "take its fate in its own hands."[68] Invoking the historical and national themes (or romanticism and love) as foils of cold economic calculation was not a new tack for the proponents of Palestine. They had always regarded their adversaries as people who had lost touch with the deeper reaches of national feeling, as if renouncing Palestine had sentenced the Jew to sterile materialism. However, this criticism may best apply to the mature phase of territorialism, when it was steadily outgrowing the specific circumstances of the Uganda crisis and coming to symbolize the unsuccessful search for a territory anywhere at all.

68 Elias Auerbach, "Nach dem 7 Kongress," *Jüdische Rundschau* (August 28, 1905), p. 423; Thon, *Essays zur zionistischen Ideologie*, pp. 121-122.

Conclusions

The Uganda controversy has been described in this chapter as the most bitter internal struggle that Zionism had known since its inception. It was the test that harsh reality placed before the potpourri of ideas and balance of forces that had been in conflict within the Zionist movement since its beginnings. The affair was touched off by the challenge to the exclusive status of Palestine, but before it was over it had revived the debate over the cardinal principles of Zionism. The question facing the Zionist movement in 1903 was whether Palestine was the only territory suitable for the fruition of Zionism. Once this question had been posed to it from the outside, the Zionist Organization was obliged to take an unequivocal and official stand on the matter. For although the Basel Program of 1897 spoke explicitly of Palestine, this was neither Herzl's position in *The Jewish State* nor Pinsker's presentation of the matter in his *Autoemancipation*. In the course of his Zionist activity, Herzl became more amenable to the choice of Palestine, having come to appreciate its importance to the Jewish public at large. Nevertheless, from time to time he attempted to negotiate the acquisition of an alternative territory. He also assumed that negotiations over an alternative territory would give him a tactical advantage in treating with the sultan over Palestine. However, in 1902, when he realized that his efforts in Constantinople had failed irreparably, he concentrated increasingly on contacts with the British – initially to institute Jewish settlement in the territories under British control to the south of Palestine and from 1903 onward with the aim of establishing a Jewish colony in East Africa (mistakenly referred to as Uganda).

It is in this context that we have discussed a special subject in this chapter: the Jews' historic right to the Land of Israel. We inquired into two types of claims made by different national movements: one based on the right to self-determination by a group of people who regard themselves as a national entity; the other based on the hereditary or historic right to a specific country. Herzl and his associates geared their programs toward obtaining a recognized legal status from a sovereign Power; hence they did not base their claim on historic rights. Lilienblum and Ussishkin, on the other hand, were inclined to base their claim on the Jews' right to Palestine since antiquity – a right they believed was more pertinent and bore more weight than diplomatic efforts to obtain a charter. Herein lay one of the major differences between political and practical Zionism, and it found its most striking expression in Ussishkin's relentless fight for the exclusivity of Palestine.

The spiritual Zionists regarded the Uganda crisis as proof that Herzlian Zionism was inherently bound to deny Zion – because it was divorced from the historical basis of Judaism – and would inevitably develop into a philanthropic movement. Ahad Ha'am did not predicate the solution of the Jewish problem on a return to Palestine, for he regarded it as the *spiritual* center of Judaism, yet he and his followers felt obliged to defend the purity of the Zionist ideal against the heresy of Ugandism, because they wanted to fortify the symbol of Palestine. Moreover, the Uganda controversy clearly demonstrated the polar opposition between the future territorialists and the spiritual Zionists, for the territorialists were to reject Palestine as the factor binding Zionism to antiquated traditions, while the spiritual Zionists held that only in Palestine would the Jews be able to reestablish contact with their ancient past and effect a complete national revolution.

The religious Zionists supported Herzl's policy on Uganda even though their spiritual devotion to Palestine was beyond question. The explanation for this seeming paradox evidently lies in the conceptual distinction, then prevailing in Mizrahi, between national activity and religious faith. The traditional bond with the Holy Land would exist regardless of the concrete political circumstances, so that there was nothing to prevent Mizrahi from supporting an alternative solution to Palestine, should that prove necessary.

The struggle over the Uganda scheme was the matrix of the territorialist ideology, whose hallmarks were:

* Liberation from the binds of religion and history.
* Skepticism about the ability of the Jews to maintain themselves as a group.
* The anticipation that the condition of the Jews would change as a result of their newly acquired political status.
* Concern for the immediate needs and democratic representation of the masses.

We have paid special note to Eliezer Ben-Yehuda's outlook, which concurred with Berdyczewski's. Their approach tended to negate the Jewish past and linked the search for a new country with the creation of a new people – fashioned after the overseas colonies established by other European immigrants.

In this same context we surveyed the opposing theories on Palestine's role in Jewish history as formulated by David Neumark and Hillel Zeitlin. Both touched upon the historical debate over the Jews' voluntary departure into exile during the Second Temple period, as well as the so-called legacy of Jabneh, that is, the spiritual versus the political tendencies in Jewish history.

Thereafter we delved into the impact of the Uganda controversy on Zionist Socialism, which had a strong bias toward immediate, mass solutions and was therefore drawn to territorialism. Many members of the Zionist Socialist camp regarded the Zionists of Zion as devotees of the romanticism of the past who displayed petty-bourgeois and reactionary inclinations. In contrast, Borochov arrived at his determination of Palestine's role in the national scheme by means of his Marxist analysis. Instead of predicating a swift, mass solution, he arrived at the evolutionary process of realizing Zionism via the avant-garde approach. We have also noted the similarity between this system and the outlooks that developed in other quarters of the Zionist movement – particularly the Democratic Fraction – following the Uganda crisis. The Seventh Zionist Congress climaxed with the territorialists seceding from the Zionist movement, thereby heightening the impetus toward change within both Zionism and the territorialist organization. After this split Zionism was no longer identified exclusively as political Zionism – as it had been in Herzl's day – and integrated the attitudes of the other currents, such as spiritual and practical Zionism.

The territorialist impulse led to the rise of Zangwill's I.T.O., which soon developed into a philanthropic organization for Jewish emigrants from Russia. The Zionist Socialist groups espousing territorialism without a territory remained active in Russia for the time being. But they were necessarily forced to abandon the hope that had drawn them to territorialism in the first place, namely, the prospect of an immediate solution through mass emigration. This process ran parallel to a similar development within the Zionist movement, which had essentially despaired of finding swift mass solutions.

EPILOGUE

Our inquiry into the attitudes toward the Jewish historical past during Zionism's early years has demonstrated how much this particular moment influenced the life and ideas of the nascent movement. Consciousness of the past played a number of distinct roles, though occasionally they were found working in concert. One was the invocation of the past as a means of restoring Jewish dignity. Thereafter Zionist thinking cited the past to support its argument positing the existence of a Jewish nation as a bulwark against the present dispersion and disintegration. These two themes initially played a role of the first order, but their importance waned as Zionism steadily consolidated into a proper movement. The third theme – that of utilizing the heritage of the past as the raw material for building a new national Judaism – remained a vital one. These three ways of treating the past were not confined to Zionism alone. For example, the glorious past had been invoked long before the emergence of Zionism, both as an argument for improving the social status of Jews and as a means of fostering their self-esteem. Neither did the conception of Jewish history as the common fate of the Jews, past and present, necessarily lead to the profession of Zionism, for to some degree it was common to all the schools of Jewish national thinking. And certainly the struggle against antiquated traditions was not a Zionist innovation, for it had appeared as a leitmotif in the works of various thinkers and currents in modern Judaism. Because its adherents were divided on this matter, one might be led to conclude that Zionism lacked a distinctive attitude toward the past and that everything we have said of Zionism was likewise true of other movements. But that was emphatically not so. Not only did these three motifs appear in concert more frequently in Zionism than elsewhere, the Zionist movement was keenly aware of the immanent connection between them. In other words, Zionist thinking was essentially based upon the link between the affirmation of Jewish identity, recognition of the common fate of the Jews, and the revitalization of their historical legacy.

What set Zionism apart from other currents in Jewish nationalism was its vital connection between the past and the future. Zionism regarded the annals of the Jews from antiquity onward as an unbroken progression of national history, contradictory trends notwithstanding. Moreover, it wanted to translate latent manifestations of Jewish nationalism into a so-called normal national life, along the lines of the distant past. A movement that aspires to restore the past must first establish how faithful it intends to be to the hallmarks of the past. For Zionism this meant confronting such questions as whether the Zionist idea could be realized outside of Palestine, or whether the movement's aim was unquestionably to establish a sovereign state and what the social order and spiritual contours of that new political framework would be. At the same time, Zionism had to bridge the gap between vision and reality, which required it to create the means for implementing its program and define its attitude toward the contemporary condition of the Jews. Hence the attitude toward the past was rather like a crucible in which positions on both the elemental issues and daily affairs of Zionism were refined. The bond between the past and the present determined the general direction in which Zionism developed, but it left room for varying interpretations of the extent to which the future should be a reflection of the past. Thus some believed that Zionism aimed almost to reproduce the past, while others treated the past as merely a foothold or basis from which to effect far-reaching innovations. These interpretations operated simultaneously on two levels: the theoretical plane – in the form of determinism versus voluntarism, historical continuity versus avant-gardism, and the like; and the operative plane – where the issues were Palestine versus territorialism, Hebrew culture versus European culture, and so on. The interesting thing is that these planes never fully overlapped and that there was a dynamic development within the bounds of each. Suffice to cite the avant-gardism of the Democratic Fraction alongside its support for historical continuity and against Uganda; or precisely the opposite in religious Zionism, which actually supported a break with the past in the Uganda proposal. Another type of example was the similarity between the arch-rivals Herzl and Ahad Ha'am in their contempt for Jewish philanthropy, opposition to present-day work in Palestine, and particularly their presumption of Zionism's universal significance.

Throughout most of the period surveyed in this work, the Zionist movement was engaged in a debate over two issues that, reduced to their simplest form, can be characterized as fidelity to Palestine and the negation of the diaspora, Herzl was trying to obtain a charter for Palestine but continued to maintain alternative diplomatic contacts. The Uganda affair was essentially the culmination of the territorialist trend, which had been one aspect of Zionism from its inception. Zionism also comprised an autonomist undercurrent that expressed itself in practical work in the diaspora. Like territorialism, it predated Herzl and would grow stronger after his death. Hence autonomism and territorialism were both integral to and rivals of Zionism.

The character of the Zionist movement evolved out of the struggle between three archetypes of the national solution: settlement in a completely new territory; autonomy in the countries of residence; and the return to Zion. These three approaches were able to coexist within the movement until an external challenge required that a definitive choice be made. For years these ideas hovered over Zionism without ever crystallizing into clear-cut positions, let alone organized factions. A Zionist could have supported settlement both in Palestine and elsewhere without being accused of duplicity. At the same time, many Zionists held that practical work in the diaspora in no way contravened the idea of the return to Zion. One could even say that the idea of the return to Zion commended practical work in the diaspora, as an interim measure toward the ultimate goal. Similarly, territorialist solutions were perceived by their supporters as necessary evils; it was only after the eruption of the Uganda controversy that the cry of those who negated the return to Zion as a matter of principle rose to a clamor.

Even the Palestinian solution, which appeared to be a classic expression of identification with the past, embraced a number of conflicting views. For Ahad Ha'am Palestine was a symbol whose purity was sacrosanct, whereas the Jewish question would probably be solved elsewhere. For the members of Mizrahi, support for Jewish settlement in Uganda in no way detracted from the everlasting attraction of Palestine. Thus it appears that a spiritual attachment to Palestine did not necessarily imply the realization of Zionism there (this was best exemplified by the outlook of the ultra-Orthodox community). The point here is not to criticize the discrepancy between theory and practice, but to show that despite the importance of historical attachment, Zionism was not based on this element alone. Moreover, historical attachment was in itself a highly complex matter that comprised a paradox. No Zionist – not even radical critics of Jewish history like Zeitlin, Berdyczewski, or Ben-Yehuda – would deny the past altogether. Yet it is pertinent to ask what the historical attachment of these critics had in common with the allegiances of men like Ahad Ha'am and Buber; or with the devotion of the religious Zionists, or for that matter with the so-called neo-Orthodox school founded by Rabbi Samson Raphael Hirsch, which likewise professed an historical attachment. Clearly this term did not mean the same thing to all these figures and groups. The concept of "history" entailed both continuity and change, but while some underscored the theme of continuity, others placed the accent on its opposite.

This wide disparity in the conception of historical attachment was reflected in the various attempts to define the relationship between Zionism and Judaism. To sum them up in brief:

* Herzl held that Zionism was a return to Judaism.
* Ahad Ha'am regarded it as a means to revitalize Judaism.
* Nordau and Mandelstamm contended that Zionism was requisite to Judaism.
* Ehrenpreis contended that Judaism was requisite to Zionism.
* The Mizrahi saw Zionism as a means to reinforce Judaism.
* Berdyczewski saw it as the diametrical opposite of Judaism.

We can classify these statements into categories; for example, that Zionism and Judaism are congruent, complementary, or contradictory. Clearly, most of the Zionists believed there was a positive connection between Zionism and the legacy of the Jewish past, and only a few radicals claimed the opposite. However, one must distinguish between the movement's religious constituents, who regarded Zionism as a direct continuation of Jewish tradition, and those Zionists whose identification with Judaism was consciously selective. The range of views from Herzl and Nordau, through Ahad Ha'am and Ehrenpreis was similarly marked by a certain ambivalence about the import of historic continuity. Berdyczewski's rebellion against Jewish history and Ben-Yehuda's thoughts on the creation of an entirely new nation were radical – and sometimes paradoxical – expressions of the prevailing mood. The reigning approach was notable for its negative attitude toward the recent past combined with hopes for a modern renaissance, that would draw its inspiration from both the ancient Jewish past and contemporary European culture. In short, between the two poles of continuity and rejection, Zionism established itself on a broad common base best described as dialectical continuity with the past.

The need to define the relationship between Judaism and Zionism stemmed from the young movement's claim to speak on behalf of all the Jews or in the name of Judaism. This pretension was anchored in Zionism's creative ambition – to build a nation and create a culture – and was meant to compensate for its lack of established authority to represent the Jews. Here we come upon a highly important theme in the fluctuation of Zionist thinking between elitism and pluralist nationalism. Elitism was consonant with Zionism's promise of innovation. It refused to bow to the existing situation and ignored the short-range interests of the masses. On a deeper level, elitism was nurtured by the voluntarism and the rebellion against history, which it challenged as a petrified tradition. Yet Zionism also had a pluralist bent that predicated the legitimacy of class and ideological differences; respect for the interests of specific Jewish communities; and national compromise rather than revolution. This leaning affirmed the integrity of Jewish history and believed in historic continuity and the solidarity of Jews everywhere.

Theoretically it should have been possible to divide these approaches into two distinct systems, each offering a different set of solutions to the questions confronting Zionism. But in actuality things were not quite so clear-cut. These trends and biases not only

clashed but also mixed and merged with one another, so that ultimately they defied classification into definitive "schools." Moreover, though some of these motifs were at odds with one another,
Zionism managed to integrate them all, making it a pluralistic movement that took part in local Jewish affairs, while espousing a basic
change in the Jewish way of life through territorial concentration –
all under the rubric of the return to Zion. Indeed, Zionism was a
conglomeration of different, sometimes antagonistic elements – but
that was only fitting for a living movement. In fact, variety may well
have been the secret of its appeal as a movement that tempered ide-
alism with a sense of realism. And the coexistence of these disparate
components may have enabled Zionism to adjust to new situations
as they arose, without losing its basic sense of direction.

BIBLIOGRAPHY

Books in English and other Languages

Achad Haam. *Ten Essays on Zionism and Judaism.* Translated by Leon Simon. London, 1922.

Acher, Matthias (N. Birnbaum). *Die jüdische Moderne.* Leipzig, 1896.

Adler, Joseph. *The Herzl Paradox.* New York, 1962.

Ahad Ha'am. *Nationalism and the Jewish Ethic.* Edited by Hans Kohn. New York, 1962.

Aron, Raymond. *Dimensions de la conscience historique.* Paris, 1961.

Bainton, Roland H. *The Reformation of the Sixteenth Century.* Boston, 1952.

Baron, Salo W. *Modern Nationalism and Religion.* New York, 1960.

Barraclough, Geoffrey. *An Introduction to Contemporary History.* Harmondsworth, Middlesex, 1976.

Barrès, Maurice. *Barrès par lui-même.* Edited by Jean-Marie Domenach. Paris, 1954.

Barzun, Jacques. *Race: A Study in Superstition.* New York, 1965.

Bein, Alex. *Theodore Herzl: A Biography of the Founder of Zionism.* Translated by Maurice Samuel. Philadelphia, 1962.

Ben-Eliezer (pseud. N. Syrkin). *Die Judenfrage und der Socialistische Judenstaat.* Bern, 1898.

Berlin, Isaiah. *Vico and Herder: Two Studies in the History of Ideas.* London, 1976.

Biddis, Michael D. *The Age of the Masses.* Harmondsworth, Middlesex, 1977.

Bodenheimer, Max. *Im Anfang der Zionistischen Bewegung.* Edited by Henriette Hanna Bodenheimer. Frankfurt on Main, 1965.

Borochov, Ber. *Class Struggle and the Jewish Nation.* Edited by Mitchell Cohen. New Brunswick and London, 1984.

Bossuet, Jacques-Bénigne. *Discours sur l'Histoire Universelle.* Edited by Jacques Truchet. Paris, 1966.

Bouquet, A.C. *Comparative Religion*, Harmondsworth, Middlesex, 1954.

Buber, Martin. *Briefwechsel aus sieben Jahrzehnten.* Edited by Grete Schaeder. Vol. I. Heidelberg, 1972.

―――. *Der Jude und sein Judentum.* Cologne, 1963.

Cassirer, Ernst. *The Myth of the State.* Garden City, N.Y., 1955.

Chouraqui, André. *l'Alliance Israélite Universelle et la renaissance juive contemporaine.* Paris, 1965.

Cohen, Gustav G. *Die Judenfrage und die Zukunft.* Hamburg, 1896. (Published anonymously with an appendix dated 1891; most of the book was written in 1881.)

Disraeli, Benjamin. *Lord George Bentinck: A Political Biography.* London, 1851.

Draper, Theodore. *The Rediscovery of Black Nationalism.* New York, 1970.

Dubnow, Simon. *Nationalism and History.* Edited by Koppel S. Pinson. New York, 1970.

Frankel, Jonathan. *Prophecy and Politics: Socialism, Nationalism, and the Russian Jews, 1862-1917.* Cambridge, 1981.

Freidenberg, Abraham Jacob, *The Memoirs of a Zionist Soldier.* Brussels, 1938 (Yiddish).

Gaster, Moses. *Gaster Centenary Publication.* Edited by Bruno Schindler. London, 1958.

Güdemann, Moritz. *Nationaljudentum.* Leipzig, 1897.

Halpern, Ben. *The Idea of the Jewish State.* Cambridge, Mass., 1969.

Hegel, G. F. W. *The Philosophy of History.* Translated by J. Sibree. New York, 1956.

Heine, Heinrich. *Jüdisches Manifest.* Edited by Hugo Bieber. New York, 1946.

Herzl, Theodor. *Altneuland.* Leipzig, 1902.

―――― *The Complete Diaries of Theodor Herzl.* Edited by Raphael Patai. Translated by Harry Zohn. Vols. I-V. New York and London, 1960.

―――― *The Congress Addresses of Theodor Herzl.* Translated by Nellie Straus. New York, 1917

―――. *The Jewish State.* Translated by Harry Zohn. New York, 1970.

―――. *Old-Newland.* Translated by Paula Arnold. Haifa, 1960.

―――. *Tagebücher.* Vol. III. Berlin, 1923.

Hirsch, Mendel. *Der Zionismus.* Mainz, 1898.

Jászi, Oscar. *The Dissolution of the Habsburg Monarchy.* Chicago, 1964.

Katz, Jacob. *Out of the Ghetto.* New York, 1978.

Kaufmann, Walter. *Nietzsche.* Cleveland, 1962.

Kedourie, Elie. *Nationalism.* London, 1978.

Kenner, Jacob, *A Cross-Cut (1897-1947).* New York, 1947 (Yiddish).

Kohn, Hans. *Martin Buber.* Hellerau, 1930.

―――. *Nationalism: Its Meaning and History.* Princeton, N.J., 1965.

―――. *The Idea of Nationalism.* Toronto, 1969.

―――. *Pan-Slavism, Its History and Ideology.* Notre Dame, Ind., 1953.

Kook, Abraham Isaac. *The Lights of Penitence.* Translated by Ben Zion Bokser. Preface by Jacob Agus and Rivka Schatz. New York, 1978.

Kraus, Karl. *Eine Krone für Zion.* Vienna, 1898.

Landau, Saul Raphael. *Sturm und Drang im Zionismus.* Vienna, 1937.

Laqueur, Walter. *A History of Zionism.* New York, 1976.

Lazarus, Moritz. *Wass heisst national?* Berlin, 1880.

Lessing, Theodor. *Der jüdische Selbsthass.* Berlin, 1930.

Levin, Nora. *While Messiah Tarried, Jewish Socialist Movements 1871-1917.* New York, 1977.

Lewis, Bernard. *History – Remembered, Recovered, Invented.* Princeton, N.J., 1975.

Lichtheim, Richard. *Die Geschichte des deutschen Zionismus.* Jerusalem, 1954.

Mannheim, Karl. *Ideology and Utopia.* New York, no date.

Marmor, Kalman. *My Autobiography.* Vol. II. New York, 1959 (Yiddish).

Marx, Karl. *The Portable Marx.* Edited by Eugene Kamenka. Harmondsworth, Middlesex, 1983.

McLellan, David. *Marxism After Marx.* Boston, 1979.

Michelet, Jules. *Le peuple.* Introduction by Robert Casanova. Paris, 1965.

Mosse, George L. *The Crisis of German Ideology.* New York, 1964.

———. *Germans and Jews.* New York, 1970.

———. *Towards the Final Solution: A History of European Racism.* London, 1978.

Neusner, Jacob. *Development of a Legend: Studies on the Traditions Concerning Yohanan Ben Zakkai.* Leiden, 1970.

Nordau, Max. *The Interpretation of History.* Translated by M. A. Hamilton. New York, 1910.

———. *Max Nordau to His People.* Edited by B. Netanyahu. New York, 1941.

Nussenblatt, Tulo. *Ein Volk Unterwegs zum Frieden.* Vienna, 1933.

Oppenheimer, Franz. *Erlebtes, Erstrebtes, Erreichtes – Lebenserinnerungen.* Düsseldorf, 1964.

Pinsker, Leon. "Autoemancipation." In *The Zionist Idea.* Edited by Arthur Hertzberg. New York, 1981.

———. *Road to Freedom: Writings and Addresses.* Edited by B. Netanyahu. Translated by David Blondheim. New York, 1944.

Pipes, Richard. *Russia Under the Old Regime.* Harmondsworth, Middlesex, 1979.

Poliakov, Léon. *Histoire de l'Antisémitisme: de Voltaire à Wagner.* Vol. III. Paris, 1968.

———. *Le mythe arien.* Paris, 1971.

Popper, K. R. *The Open Society and Its Enemies.* London, 1966.

Pulzer, Peter G. J. *The Rise of Political Anti-Semitism in Germany and Austria.* New York, 1964.

Renan, Ernest. *Histoire d'Israël.* Vol. III. Paris, 1891.

Roazen, Paul. *Freud and His Followers.* Harmondsworth, Middlesex, 1979.

Rosenzweig, Franz. *Kleinere Schriften.* Berlin, 1937.

Rülf, Isaak. *Aruchas Bas Ami,* Frankfurt/M, 1883.

Runes, Dagobert D., et al. *Dictionary of Philosophy: Ancient – Medieval – Modern.* Ames, Iowa, 1955.

Salvador, Joseph. *Histoire des Institutions de Moïse et du Peuple Hébreu.* Paris, 1862.

Schach, Fabius. *Über die Zukunft Israels.* Berlin, 1904.

Schauer, Josua. *Briefe eines polnischen Juden.* Prague, 1897.

Scholem, Gershom. *The Messianic Idea in Judaism & Other Essays on Jewish Spirituality.* New York, 1971.

Schorsch, Ismar. *Jewish Reactions to German Anti-Semitism, 1870-1914.* New York and London, 1972.

Socialist Territorialist Memoirs and Material on the History of the S.S., JS and "Fareinkte" Parties. Paris, 1934 (Yiddish).

Stern, Fritz. *The Politics of Cultural Despair.* New York, 1961.

Tal, Uriel. *Christians and Jews in Germany: Religion, Politics and Ideology in the Second Reich, 1870-1914.* Ithaca and London, 1975.

Tennenbaum, Joseph. *Galicia - My Old Home.* Buenos Aires, 1952 (Yiddish).

Thon, Osias. *Essays zur zionistischen Ideologie.* Berlin, 1930.

Toury, Jacob. *Die politischen Orientierungen der Juden in Deutschland.* Tübingen, 1966.

Trachtenberg, Joshua. *The Devil and the Jews.* New York, 1966.

Tuchman, Barbara W. *The Proud Tower: A Portrait of the World Before the War, 1890-1914.* New York, 1967.

Vital, David. *The Origins of Zionism.* Oxford, 1980.

_____. *Zionism, The Formative Years.* Oxford, 1982.

Weininger, Otto. *Geschlecht und Charakter.* Vienna, 1921.

Weisbord, Robert G. *African Zion.* Philadelphia, 1968.

Weizmann, Chaim. *The Letters and Papers of Chaim Weizmann.* Vol. I. Edited by Leonard Stein and Gedalia Yogev. London, 1968. Vol. II. Edited by Meyer W. Weisgal. London, 1972. Vol. IV. Edited by Camillo Dresner and Barnet Litvinoff. Jerusalem, 1973.

_____. *Trial and Error.* New York, 1969.

Wohlgelernter, Maurice. *Israel Zangwill: A Study.* New York and London, 1964.

Wormser, Georges. *Français Israélites.* Paris, 1963. (Private edition of some 600 copies.)

Zangwill, Israel. *Speeches, Articles, and Letters.* Edited by Maurice Simon. London, 1937.

Anthologies

Ben Sasson, H. H. and S. Ettinger, eds. *Jewish Society Through the Ages.* New York, 1973.

Birke, Ernst and Eugen Lemberg, eds. *Geschichtsbewusstsein in Ostmitteleuropa.* Magdeburg-Lahn, 1961.

Feiwel, Berthold, ed. *Jüdischer Almanach, 5663.* Berlin, 1902. Herlitz, G. and

M. Gordon, eds. *Die Beschlüsse der Zionisten Kongresse I-XVIII, 1897-1933.*
Jerusalem, 1933. (Typescript, Central Zionist Archives, 638/28 244 G.)

Hertzberg, Arthur, ed. *The Zionist Idea.* New York, 1981.

Heymann, Michael, ed. *The Uganda Controversy: Minutes of the Zionist General
Council.* Vol. I. Jerusalem, 1970. Vol. II. Jerusalem, 1977.

Jüdisches Lexikon. Vol. III. Berlin, 1929.

Kamenka, Eugene, ed. *Nationalism: The Nature and Evolution of an Idea.* London, 1976.

Lederer, Ivo J., ed. *The Versailles Settlement.* Boston, 1965.

Mosse, Werner E. et al., eds. *Revolution and Evolution: 1848 in German-Jewish
History.* Tübingen, 1981.

Nussenblatt, Tulo, ed. *Theodor Herzl Jahrbuch.* Vienna, 1937.

Protokoll des 1ten Zionistenkongresses in Basel, 1897. Prague, 1911.

Protokoll V Zionistencongress, Basel 1901. Vienna, 1901.

Rogger, Hans, and Eugen Weber, eds. *The European Right: A Historical Profile.*
Berkeley and Los Angeles, 1965.

Schön, Lazar, ed. *Die Stimme der Wahrheit.* Würzburg, 1905.

The Third Zionist Conference in Helsingfors. Vilna, 1906 (Yiddish).

Tramer, Hans, ed. *In Zwei Welten.* Tel Aviv, 1962.

Verhandlungen des VII Zionisten-Kongresses. Berlin, 1905.

Zucker, Nehemia, ed. *The Galician Register.* Buenos Aires, 1945 (Yiddish).

Books in Hebrew

Ahad Ha'am. *Collected Works.* Tel Aviv-Jerusalem, 1961.

———. *Letters.* Edited by Ahad Ha'am. Vol. I, Jerusalem-Berlin, 1923. Vols II,
III. Jerusalem-Berlin, 1924.

———. *Letters.* Revised and Expanded Edition. Edited by Aryeh Simon. Vols.
I-IV. Tel Aviv, 1956-1958.

Bein, Alexander. *A. Biography of Herzl.* Revised and Emended Edition. Jerusalem, 1977.

Ben-Yehuda, Eliezer. *Complete Works.* Vol. I. Jerusalem, 1941.

———. *Israel to Its Land and Its Language.* Edited by Itamar Ben Avi. Vol. I.
Jerusalem, 1929.

———. *The Jewish State: Articles on the East Africa Proposal.* Warsaw, 1905.

Berdyczewski, Micha Josef. *Complete Works.* Articles Volume. Tel Aviv, 1960.

———. *On the Agenda.* Warsaw, 1900.

———. *Epigones.* Warsaw, 1900.

Berlin (Bar-Ilan), Meir. *From Volozhin to Jerusalem: Memoirs.* Vol. II. Tel Aviv,
1940.

Bernfeld, Simon. *An Account of Our Literature.* Warsaw, 1899. Bernstein-Cohen,
Jacob. *The Bernstein-Cohen Book.* Edited by Miriam Bernstein-Cohen and
Isaac Korn. Tel Aviv, 1946.

Borochov, Ber. *Selected Works*. Edited by Zalman Rubashov (Shazar). Vol. I. Tel Aviv, 1944.

Braude, Marcus. *In Memoriam*. Edited by Dov Sadan and Chaim Ormian. Jerusalem, 1960.

Brozer, Meshulam Nathan. *The Righteousness of Zion*. Berdichev, 1903.

Canaani, David. *The Socialist Second Aliyah and Its Attitude Toward Religion and Tradition*. Tel Aviv, 1976.

Dinaburg (Dinur), Benzion. *Israel in the Diaspora*. Jerusalem, 1926.

Dinur, Benzion. *Historical Writings*. Jerusalem, 1955.

——. *A World in Decline – An Autobiography*. Jerusalem, 1958.

Ehrenpreis, Marcus. *Thoughts on the Second Zionist Congress*. Berlin, 1898.

Eisenstadt, Shmuel. *Chapters on the History of the Jewish Labor Movement*. Vols. I-II. Tel Aviv, 1970.

Eliav, Mordechai. *David Wolffsohn: The Man and His Times*. Jerusalem, 1977.

Gelber, Nathan Michael. *A History of the Zionist Movement in Galicia*. Vols. I, II. Jerusalem, 1958.

Gordon, Judah Leib. *Poems*. Edited by Moshe Mahler and David Neiger. Jerusalem-Tel Aviv, 1952.

Gronemann, Sammy. *The Memoirs of a Jekke*. Translated from a manuscript by Dov Stock (Sadan). Tel Aviv, 1946.

Hacohen, Mordechai Ben Hillel. *The Book of Names*. Jerusalem, 1938.

Herzl, Theodor. *The Jewish State*. Translated by Michael Berkowitz. Warsaw, 1896.

——. *Letters*. Edited by A. Bein. Translated by D. Sadan. Jerusalem, 1958.

Jabotinsky, Vladimir Zeev. *Early Zionist Writings*. Jerusalem, 1958.

Katznelson, Berl. *The First in Battle: Introduction to the Writings of Nahman Syrkin*. Tel Aviv, 1939. Separate Edition.

——. *Writings*. Vol. I. Tel Aviv, 1947.

Kaufmann, Yehezkel. *Diaspora and Exile*. Vol. I. Tel Aviv, 1929. Vol. II. Tel Aviv, 1930.

Keshet, Yeshurun. *M. Y. Berdyczewski (Bin Gurion): His Life and Works*. Jerusalem, 1958.

Klausner, Yisrael. *Opposition to Herzl*. Jerusalem, 1960.

Klausner-Eshkol, Alizah. *The Influence of Nietzsche and Schopenhauer on M. Y. Bin-Gurion (Berdyczewski)*. Tel Aviv, 1954.

Kook, Abraham Isaac Hacohen. *Letters of Evidence*. Jerusalem, 1962.

Kressel, Getzl. *Franz Oppenheimer*. Tel Aviv, 1972.

Kurzweil, Baruch. *Our New Literature: Continuation or Revolution?* Jerusalem-Tel Aviv, 1971.

Levin, Mordechai. *Social and Economic Values in the Ideology of the Enlightenment Period*. Jerusalem, 1975.

Levin, Shmarya. *Memoirs*. Translated by Zvi Wislawski. Vol. III. Tel Aviv, 1939.

Lilienblum, Moses Leib. *Selected Writings*. Edited by S. Breiman. Jerusalem, 1957.

Mintz, Matityahu. *Ber Borokhov: One Circle, 1900-1906.* Tel Aviv, 1976.

Motzkin, Leo. *The Motzkin Book.* Edited by A. Bein. Jerusalem, 1939.

Nir, Nahum. *Chapters of a Life.* Tel Aviv, 1958.

Nordau, Max. *Max Nordau in His Letters.* Edition by Shalom Schwartz. Jerusalem, 1944.

Nurock, Mordechai. *The Minsk Conference of Russian Zionists.* Introduction by Yisrael Klausner. Jerusalem, 1963.

Oren, Elhannan. *Hibbat Zion in Britain, 1878-1898.* Tel Aviv, 1974.

Rabinowitz, Elijah Akiva. *Justice Shall Redeem Zion: A Rabbinical View of Zionism.* Warsaw, 1899.

Rabinowitz, Shaul Pinkhas. *On Zion and on Its Scriptures.* Warsaw, 1898.

Rabinowitz, Samuel Jacob. *Religion and Nationalism.* Warsaw, 1900.

Scholem, Gershom. *Explications and Implications: Writings on Jewish Heritage and Renaissance.* Tel Aviv, 1975.

Salmon, Yosef. *The Attitude of the Ultra-Orthodox to the Early Zionist Movement: Russia-Poland (1882-1900).* Jerusalem, May 1974. Doctoral dissertation, Hebrew University

Simon, Aryeh and Joseph Heller. *Ahad Ha'am: The Man, His Works, and His Doctrine.* Jerusalem, 1956.

Singer, Mendel. *Early Zionist Socialism: History and Personalities.* Haifa, 1958.

Smolenskin, Perez. *Articles.* Vol. I. Jerusalem, 1925.

Sokolow, Nahum. *To Masters and Mentors.* Warsaw, 1901.

Syrkin, Nahman. *Works.* Vol. I. Collected and Arranged by B. Katznelson and Yehuda Kaufmann. Tel Aviv, 1939. (Katznelson's Introduction was also issued separately.)

Tabenkin, Yitzhak. *The Jewish State and the Road to It.* Ein Harod, 1944.

Talmon, Jacob. *Unity and Uniqueness.* Jerusalem-Tel Aviv, 1968.

Tcherikover, Eliyahu. *Jews in Revolutionary Times.* Tel Aviv, 1957.

Turtel, Max. *Nationalism in Ahad Ha'am's Writings.* Jerusalem, 1942.

Ussishkin, Menahem. *Our Zionist Program.* Warsaw, 1905.

Vardi, Aaron. *My King in Zion.* Tel Aviv, 1931.

Yaron, Zvi. *Rabbi Kook's Philosophy.* Jerusalem, 1974.

Yellin, David. *Works.* Vol. IV (Letters, 1878-1914). Edited by Yisrael Klausner. Jerusalem, 1976.

Anthologies in Hebrew

An Awareness of the Past in the Consciousness of the Jews and Other Peoples: Lectures from the Thirteenth Historical Congress. Tel Aviv, 1969.

Cohen, Yisrael and Dov Sadan, eds. *Chapters from Galicia.* Tel Aviv, 1957.

Dinaburg-Dinur, Benzion, ed. *The Book of Zionism.* Vol. I, Book 1. Tel Aviv, 1939.

Dinur, Benzion, et al., eds. *The Jews: Chapters on the Sociology of the Jewish People*. Jerusalem, 1954.

Druyanow, Alter, ed. *Documents on the History of Hibbat Zion and the Settlement of Eretz Israel*. Vol. III. Tel Aviv, 1932.

Habas, Bracha, ed. *The Second Aliyah Book*. Tel Aviv, 1947.

Harvest: An Anthology on the History of the Zionist Movement in Russia. Vol. I. Tel Aviv, 1964.

Historians and Schools of History: Lectures from the Seventh Historical Congress. Jerusalem, 1963.

Klausner, Yisrael, trans. *The Minsk Conference of Russian Zionists*. Jerusalem, 1963.

Mishkinsky, Moshe, ed. *Gal-Ed: An Anthology on the History of Polish Jewry*. Vol. II. Tel Aviv, 1975.

Peterseil, Jacob, ed. *Anthology of Poalei Zion*. Vol. I. *The First and Second Revolutions in Russia (1905-1917)*. Tel Aviv, 1974.

Yaffe, Leib, ed. *The Congress Book*. Jerusalem, 1950.

INDEX

compiled by Moshe Shalvi

319